1997
S.A.

Jaque,
Birthday Wishes to you.
Lots of love.
Mark x

Colonel Robert Jacob Gordon (1743-1795) in the uniform of commander of the garrison at the Cape.

ROBERT JACOB GORDON
1743–1795

The Man and his Travels at the Cape

PATRICK CULLINAN

STRUIK
WINCHESTER

Sponsors

Generous financial assistance in the production of this book was provided by the following sponsors, who, in particular, made possible the reproduction of a comprehensive selection of illustrations from the Gordon Atlas, housed in the Rijksprentenkabinet at the Rijks Museum, Amsterdam.

The Anglo American and De Beers Chairman's Fund

The Cape Tercentenary Foundation

The Centre for Science Development

The Lorenzo and Stella Chiappini Charitable and Cultural Trust

The Mauerberger Foundation Fund

Mr Gavin Relly

The Van Ewijk-Stigting

Vereeniging Z.A.S.M.

Contents

List of Illustrations   *page 6*

Acknowledgements   *page 8*

Preface   *page 9*

The Gordon Manuscripts and Atlas   *page 11*

The Translation of Gordon's Papers   *page 16*

Chapter One
The Early Years: More than a Military Man
(1743–1777)
page 19

Chapter Two
The Second Journey: To the 'Great River'
(October–December 1777)
page 27

Chapter Three
The Second Journey: The Eastern Cape Explored
(December 1777–March 1778)
page 47

Chapter Four
The Third Journey: An Ambitious Plan Thwarted
(August 1778–January 1779)
page 59

Chapter Five
The Fourth Journey: To the Mouth of the
Orange River (June–August 1779)
page 71

Chapter Six
The Fourth Journey: The Land of the
Camelopards (August–October 1779)
page 91

Chapter Seven
The Fourth Journey: A Triumphant Return
(October 1779–January 1780)
page 111

Chapter Eight
Command of the Garrison
(1780–1785)
page 131

Chapter Nine
The Fifth Journey: Familiar Places and Forgotten
Monuments (November 1785–April 1786)
page 139

Chapter Ten
The Turbulent Years
(1786–1795)
page 159

Chapter Eleven
Betrayal and Suicide
(June–October 1795)
page 175

Epilogue
Gordon's Descendants
page 191

Notes to the Text   *page 193*

Bibliography   *page 202*

Index   *page 205*

List of Subscribers   *page 212*

List of Illustrations

Abbreviations:

RM   Gordon Atlas, Rijksprentenkabinet, Rijks Museum, Amsterdam.
Note: the numbers quoted are Gordon Atlas reference numbers.

BP   From Paterson albums, reproduced in Peter E. Raper and Maurice Boucher [eds], *Robert Jacob Gordon: Cape Travels, 1777 to 1786,* 2 vols, Johannesburg, © The Brenthurst Press, 1988.
Note: the plate numbers quoted are those appearing in the 1988 Brenthurst Press publication.

Frontispiece:
Colonel Robert Jacob Gordon (1743-1795) in the uniform of commander of the garrison at the Cape. (The William Fehr Collection, the Castle, Cape Town.)

1. The opening page of Gordon's journal for the second journey. (R.J. Gordon, Papers, MS. 107, The Brenthurst Library, Johannesburg, © 1992.) *10*
2. *Homoglossum watsonium.* (RM 47) *13*
3. Probably Cape dwarf chameleons (*Bradypodion pumilium*). (RM 100) *15*
4. One of the six notebooks in which Gordon recorded his remarkable travels. (R.J. Gordon, Papers, MS. 107, Johannesburg, The Brenthurst Library, © 1992.) *17*
5. *Aloe dichotoma*, often referred to as the 'quiver tree'. (BP Pl. 6) *18*
6. Soldiers of the Scots Brigade in uniforms of the 1770s. (J. Ferguson [ed.], *The Scots Brigade in the Service of the United Netherlands, 1572-1782*, Edinburgh, The Scottish History Society, 1901.) *21*
7. The title page of the *Supplément* to Buffon's encyclopaedia of natural history, *Histoire Naturelle*. *22*
8. Male springbok. (BP Pl. 89) *23*
9. Denis Diderot. *24*
10. François le Vaillant's drawing of the much disputed 'Hottentot apron'. (F. le Vaillant, *Voyage de F. le Vaillant dans l'Intérieur de l'Afrique*, vol. 2, Paris, Chez Desray, 1796.) *25*
11. A 'Hottentot' mother and child. (RM 84) *26*
12. A view of Swellendam. (RM 44) *30-31*
13. William Paterson as lieutenant-governor of New South Wales. (Oil by William Owen, the Mitchell Library, State Library of New South Wales.) *32*
14. The black wildebeest or gnu. (RM 182) *35*
15. Gordon's drawing of selected 'Bushman' paintings. (RM 195) *36*

16. A female and male hippopotamus from *Histoire Naturelle*. *37*
17. Chief Coba and his wives. (RM 73) *38-9*
18. Chief Coba wearing a grenadier's cap. (RM 75) *42*
19. The confluence of the Orange and Caledon rivers. (RM 60) *43*
20. What appears to be a Cape wagtail perches on a branch of *Acacia karroo*. (RM 9) *46*
21. A 'Hottentot' man in traditional dress. (RM 85) *51*
22. *Phoenicopterus ruber*: the greater flamingo. (BP Pl. 28) *55*
23. *Lachenalia bulbifera*. (RM 36) *58*
24. The governor's hippopotamus hunt. (RM 66) *62*
25. The *Histoire Naturelle* black rhinoceros. *64*
26. Gordon at the 'Bushman' kraal of Chiefs Gronjam and Doerop. (RM 32) *66-7*
27. The Heerenlogement as depicted by Le Vaillant. (F. le Vaillant, *Travels into the Interior Parts of Africa*, London, G.G. & J. Robinson, 1796.) *69*
28. Male ostrich, *Struthio camelus*. (RM 306) *70*
29. 'Meerhof's Casteel', where Simon van der Stel chiselled his initials on a rock. (RM 47) *74*
30. Ellenboogfontein. (RM 31) *75*
31. Tribespeople of Namaqualand. (RM 3) *76*
32. *Carpobrotus sauerae* (also known as 'Hottentot fig'). (BP Pl. 49) *78*
33. *Sarcocaulon l'heritieri* (often referred to as 'Bushman's candles'). (BP Pl. 54) *79*
34. A pack-ox laden for a journey. (Watercolour by F. le Vaillant, Library of Parliament, Cape Town.) *80*
35. The 'moggel' or mud mullet (*Labeo umbratus*). (BP Pl. 51) *82*
36. *Equus zebra* (mountain zebra). (BP Pl. 70) *83*
37. 'Bushman' and 'Hottentot' weapons. (Watercolour by F. le Vaillant, Library of Parliament, Cape Town.) *84*
38. The 'so-called Strandlopers'. (RM 91) *86-7*
39. *Giraffa camelopardalis*. (RM 148) *90*
40. A 'Hottentot' dance. (RM 89) *94-5*
41. The spiny, or wild, cucumber. (Watercolour by F. le Vaillant, Library of Parliament, Cape Town.) *97*
42. A male 'Hottentot' lies ready to be buried. (RM 86) *99*
43. A giraffe hunt. (RM 64) *102-3*
44. The giraffe skeleton sent to Willem V. (RM 153) *104*
45. The Augrabies Falls. (RM 20) *106-7*
46. A 'Hottentot' chief's grave. (RM 93) *108*
47. *Pachypodium namaquanarum* (a member of the Num-Num family). (RM 26) *110*
48. The *Histoire Naturelle* hartebeest. *113*
49. 'Moetjoaanaas Huishouding'. An artist's impression of a Batswana kraal, taken from Gordon's 'great map'. (RM 3) *114*
50. A Namaqua bull. (RM 183) *115*
51. Two 'Moncaboo' tribesmen reminded Gordon of this Gibbon ape ('Jokko') in Buffon's *Histoire Naturelle*. *116*

52. The *Histoire Naturelle* aardvaark.   *117*
53. A detail from Gordon's 'great map', showing a 'Bushman' settlement. (RM 3)   *118*
54. A young quagga. (RM 190)   *119*
55. 'Another sketch of a Bushman household. They are sitting next to a pot eating soup with a brush, their customary spoon.' (RM 90)   *121*
56. The gifboom or 'poison tree' (*Euphorbia virosa*). (BP Pl. 72)   *122*
57. Great Namaqua and Strandloper kraals – a detail from the 'great map'. (RM 3)   *123*
58. *Pterocles namaqua* – Gordon's 'Namaqua partridge'. (BP Pl. 62)   *126*
59. *Asclepias fruticosa*. (RM 16)   *127*
60. A second drawing of the giraffe skeleton sent to Willem V. (RM 151)   *128*
61. Susanna Nicolet. (The William Fehr Collection, the Castle, Cape Town.)   *130*
62. A groundplan of the Castle as it was in the late eighteenth century. (From a thesis on the Castle by F.W. Mullins, published in the 'South African Architectural Record', September 1927.)   *132*
63. Doughty Le Vaillant, on a remarkable craft, undergoes a 'dangerous crossing of the Olifants River'. (Watercolour by F. le Vaillant, Library of Parliament, Cape Town.)   *135*
64. The corner of Strand and Burg streets, Cape Town, in 1790. ('Home of the Fiscal Beelaerts van Blokland', watercolour by Samuel Davis, 1790, the William Fehr Collection, Rust-en-Vreugd, Cape Town.)   *136*
65. Gordon's 'Caapse Baviaan' is the chacma baboon, or *Papio ursina*. (RM 124)   *138*
66. Roodezand, or Tulbagh as it is known today. (RM 41)   *142-3*
67. An example of the double column format used for the journal of the fifth journey. (R.J. Gordon, Papers, MS.107, The Brenthurst Library, Johannesburg, © 1992.)   *145*
68. Female painted snipe (*Rostratula benghalensis*). (BP Pl. 85)   *146*
69. Queek Valey (present-day Prince Albert). (RM 65)   *150*
70. Rough going over rocks and mountains in the Southern Cape. ('Journey into Kaffraria', watercolour by F. le Vaillant, Library of Parliament, Cape Town.)   *153*
71. A view of 'Plettenbergs Bay or the Keurboom River mouth'. (RM 38)   *154-5*
72. *Gethyllis ciliaris*. (RM 40)   *158*
73. A view of Cape Town from Signal Hill by Johannes Schoemaker. (Copper engraving by I.H. Schneider, Amsterdam, 1778 [reproduced by C. Struik (Pty) Ltd, 1973], from a watercolour by Johannes Schumacher [a variant spelling of 'Schoemaker', the artist who accompanied Gordon on his travels]. The original watercolour hangs in the Swellengrebel Archives, Breda, Netherlands.)   *161*

74. *Rothmannia capensis*: a forest flower from the Eastern Cape. (RM 8)   *163*
75. *Massonia depressa* – found in the Karoo. (RM 30)   *166*
76. Governor Cornelis Jacob van de Graaff. (AG 7359, State Archives, Cape Town.)   *168*
77. The brass plates from Gordon's portable barometer. (The South African Cultural History Museum, Cape Town.)   *171*
78. *Hoodia gordonii*. (RM 91)   *174*
79. Admiral Sir George Keith Elphinstone at the Battle of Muizenberg. (Source unknown.)   *176*
80. The south-western Cape: a detail from Gordon's 'great map'. (RM 3)   *178*
81. A view of Table Bay. (RM 21)   *179*
82. The Battle of Muizenberg. (Watercolour by J.C. Frederici, the Mendelssohn Collection, Library of Parliament, Cape Town.)   *180-81*
83. Willem V, Prince of Orange (1748-1806). (Oil, attributed to Z.G. Ziesenis, part of the House of Orange-Nassau Historic Collections Trust, The Hague.)   *183*
84. A view of the Hottentots Holland Mountains, showing today's Sir Lowry's Pass and a part of the coast now known as Gordon's Bay. (RM 36)   *186-7*
85. *Cyrtanthus obliquus*: a rare amaryllid. (RM 79)   *190*
86. A decorative motif from Gordon's 'great map'. (RM 3)   *191*

LIST OF MAPS

Map 1. Gordon's second journey: to the eastern frontier and the Great River, returning via the east coast.   *28-9*
Map 2. The expanding frontiers of white colonists at the time of Gordon's second journey.   *49*
Map 3. Gordon's third journey: first to the Zeekoei River with Governor Van Plettenberg and thereafter with his own party to the west coast.   *60-61*
Map 4. Gordon's fourth journey: to the mouth of the Orange River and east along its course towards present-day Prieska.   *72*
Map 5. A section of Wikar's map, copied from the original. (E.E. Mossop [ed.], *Journals of Wikar, Coetsé and Van Reenen*, Cape Town, the Van Riebeeck Society, 1935.)   *89*
Map 6. A redrawn section of Gordon's 'great map', showing where he crossed to the north bank of the Orange River and his later turning point. (V.S. Forbes, *Pioneer Travellers in South Africa*, Cape Town, A.A. Balkema, 1965.)   *112*.
Map 7. The unexplored section of the Orange River, from a redrawing of Gordon's 'great map'. (V.S. Forbes, *Pioneer Travellers in South Africa*, Cape Town, A.A. Balkema, 1965.)   *120*
Map 8. Gordon's fifth journey: up the west coast and then to the Bushman's River in the east.   *140-41*

ACKNOWLEDGEMENTS

While working on the transcription and translation of Gordon's journals, and later while engaged in research for this book, I sought the help of many experts in various fields of knowledge. I would like here to thank every one of those who helped me, but the following names must be singled out for special mention.

First and foremost I owe a deep debt of gratitude to Professor Vernon Forbes. It was he who encouraged me to start this enterprise and then to persist with it. He has given me access to his research on Gordon and other eighteenth-century travellers and personages; he has withstood further enquiries, made continuously, with endless patience and goodwill; in addition, anyone who knows his published work will realise how much I have relied on it to supplement my own meagre learning. In general, his meticulous scholarship and historical acumen have served to both inspire and sustain me in this task.

The passages dealing with Gordon's sheep-breeding activities and his military career rely heavily on Mr C.J. Barnard's thesis 'Robert Jacob Gordon se loopbaan aan die Kaap'. No original research was undertaken by me in these areas since the main emphasis of my biography is on the travel journals, Gordon's European contacts and other related material. I therefore owe much to Mr Barnard whose work has complemented my own lack of expertise.

I am also much indebted to Dr L.C. Rookmaaker for his interest in this work and for allowing me to see and use the fruits of his research, which are contained in his doctoral thesis on the zoology of R.J. Gordon. He has helped greatly by examining my translations relating to this part of Gordon's activities, as well as in many other ways.

I must also thank, most warmly, Mr Ernst Kotze, formerly of the University of the Witwatersrand, for his help with the translation of the journals, especially in the early stages of this work when my knowledge of Dutch was somewhat scant.

A special word of thanks must go to Miss Mary Gunn of Pretoria who provided me with a wealth of material on the lineage, life and progeny of Gordon.

Among others who have given me valuable assistance and comment are: Mr Alex R. Willcox, Professor Eric Axelson, Dr John Rourke, Mrs Enid du Plessis, the Reverend and Mrs John Burgess, Dr Frank Bradlow, Mrs Margaret Cairns, Mr Robin Fryde, Mr Ian Goldin, Mr Murry Michel, Mr Julian Rollnick, Mrs Wenda Melck, Mr Roy Macnab, Mr Stephen Watson, Mr Michael King, Mr Douglas Reid Skinner, Dr Cyril Hromnic, Mr Nigel Penn, Miss Inge Breevoort, Mrs Diane Schneier, Mrs Betty O'Grady, Mrs H.M. van der Spuy, Professor Andy Smith and Mr Mike Wilson.

I have also received much help from the South African Library, the Cape Archives and the Pretoria Archives.

My thanks, too, go to Mr H.F. Oppenheimer who allowed me to view the original Gordon papers; also to Mrs Cynthia Kemp of the Brenthurst Press who helped me to clarify obscurities in the photocopies.

I am indebted to Mr A.A. Balkema for the use of his photocopies of the original manuscripts.

I would like, most earnestly, to thank my former secretary and dear friend, Mrs Mags Robertson, who typed the many drafts of the translation of the journals with such fortitude and good humour.

I would also like to pay tribute to Mr Doug van der Horst, publishing director of Struik Winchester, for his expert overview of the editing needs of this book, and to Mr Abdul Amien for the refinement and elegance of his graphic design.

My final accolade goes to Valerie Streak, also of Struik Winchester, for the many improvements she has brought to my work. Her sensitive editing has combined good sense, precision and creativity – no writer could ask more.

 PUBLISHER'S ACKNOWLEDGEMENTS

We wish to thank the many individuals who so willingly assisted us in finding and gaining access to illustrative material for this work, and we gratefully acknowledge the following institutions for their permission to reproduce the selected material: The Brenthurst Library, Johannesburg; The Brenthurst Press, Johannesburg; the Cape Archives, Cape Town; the trustees of the Mendelssohn Library, Library of Parliament, Cape Town; the Mitchell Library, State Library of New South Wales, Sydney; the Rijksprentenkabinet, Rijks Museum, Amsterdam; the Royal Archives at The Hague; the South African Cultural History Museum, Cape Town; The South African Library, Cape Town; and the William Fehr Collection, Cape Town. Our thanks, too, to Professor V.S. Forbes for giving us permission to reproduce sections of maps 15 and 21 from his book *Pioneer Travellers in South Africa*.

A special word of gratitude is due to Mrs Cynthia Kemp of The Brenthurst Press, whose help and advice in various matters relating to this book have been invaluable.

We also acknowledge with thanks the work of photographers James de Villiers (cover photograph, frontispiece and illustrations 7, 16, 25, 31, 37, 41, 48, 52, 61, 63, 64, 70, 73 and 81) and Alan van Rooyen (illustrations 1, 4, 5, 8, 22, 33, 34, 35, 36, 56, 58, 67 and 68).

Finally, we express a deep debt of gratitude to the sponsors listed on page 4 for their generous financial assistance.

Preface

In his own day Robert Jacob Gordon was considered an original spirit – a remarkable being – even by his detractors. His actions and personality compelled interest and conjecture from all who met or corresponded with him – a response which, briefly, was heightened after his death by suicide in 1795. For the greater part of the nineteenth and early twentieth centuries, however, his name and fame slipped into obscurity, while his unique collection of drawings and maps, known as the Gordon Atlas, and his remarkable manuscripts lay forgotten in the library of an English nobleman.[1]

In 1914 the Rijks Museum, Amsterdam, acquired the Atlas – though not the manuscripts and journals, which were to remain unknown for a further fifty years – and a slow revival of interest in Gordon followed. This led to the publication of certain Gordon-related material by Professor E. C. Godée Molsbergen in 1916. Then, from the 1940s onwards, a few specialist articles began to appear on subjects such as Gordon's botanical studies. But the first modern work to discuss Gordon in any depth or breadth was an article by Professor V. S. Forbes, published in 1949 and later to be incorporated into his seminal book *Pioneer Travellers in South Africa* (1965). A noteworthy addition to Forbes's article followed in 1950 with the publication of C. J. Barnard's thesis on Gordon, particularly impressive for its analysis of his military career.

The journals and miscellaneous manuscripts were eventually 'discovered' in 1964 and subsequently were bought by Mr H. Oppenheimer in 1979. Translated by P. E. Raper and M. Boucher, the publication of the journals in 1988 gave another strong impetus to Gordon studies. Television and radio interviews followed, arousing further interest and comment in the Press, while public lectures given by me in Cape Town were also well attended, testifying to the growing interest in Gordon. It seemed appropriate, therefore, that a full-scale biography of Gordon should appear.

In setting myself the task, I have studied all the Gordon papers and virtually all the secondary sources available. I have made my own translations of the travel journals and have incorporated significant and interesting passages into my discussion of the journeys – a major theme of the book.

This, then, is the first comprehensive biography of Gordon in any language. It covers what is known of his early life, examines in detail four of his journeys into the interior, relates his correspondence with the learned men of Europe and, finally, tells the story of his last tragic days when the Cape fell to the British. But my main quest has been to find Gordon the man. Despite many difficulties, it has been an absorbing task, in the course of which I have been led to confront a diverse and complex personality: simultaneously pragmatic and urbane; genial, though testy at times. Gordon was hardy, reticent and proud, but, above all, he was a humane and civilized man, a paragon of the Age of Enlightenment.

Maandag den 6 october 1777

om 9 uren vertrokken van de Kaap met de heer Paterson en myn schilder.

gisteren avondt omtrent 5 uren spoelde er een grote menigte tonynen op die zeequst waaren naar gedagten, in een gewigt zy waaren 6 en 7 voet lank.

myn portative barometer lekte, dus zond hem na de kaap om verholpen te worden. bleven onse coers langs de tafelbergen voortzetten, arriveerden omtrent twe uren aan 't goed geloof een wyn plaats behoorende, aan eenen becker, waar wy aten, en na rond gewandelt te hebben om 5 uuren naar de plaats van Pieter eckSteen, genaamt bergvliet reden, waar wy vernagten, leesden daar dat indien men as van hout in een kokende ketel water doet men er eyeren in kan koken zonder dat ze te hard worden.

den 7 omtrent tien uuren wilden vervolgden wy onse reis langs het binnenste strandt van baay fals. vervolgens na dat de wind ging leggen begon het met buien sterk te regenen. zo dat wy besloten nog deese dag te bergvliet te blyven. gingen in de agtermiddag naar de Constantias en quamen op bergvliet in de avond terug, en vonden de proef van de asch faliquant.

den 8 vervolgden onse voorgenomen coers oost aan, nadat wy langs de zandvaley daar wele Slaanckbos in waaren, naar muisenburg door gereden waaren. deze zand valey ontfangt zyn water door overstrooming van baay fals, en het water dat van de bergen, in den omtrent van Constantia, komt, is dus zeer brak, zy is een uur gaans in den omtrek en ondiep. uitgenomen in swaare regens en zee overstroomingen die hier in de kwade moussons voorvallen. de mond die een fyftig roeden van muisenburg is was door het zeer zand toegespoeld. als men deze plaats doorwaad moet men digt aan zee uit hoofde van het welzand zulks doen, de ordinaire passagie der wagens is als men van muisenburg noord oost op het ende der hooge duinen, aanrydt kunnende men verder het wagenspoor zien.

het water nog vloeiende hadden onse paarden een swaare marsch het strand is vlak en zandig, dog agter het eiland, dat redelyk hoog is beginnen eenige lage klippen. zulks continueert by tussen posingen, tot agter de zogenaamde swarte klip alwaar men, uitgenomen in heel laag water een halfuur om de duinen moet draagen liggende deselve steil by de zee, waarna het strand weer vlak word. hier by ligt een visschers hut waar in twe europeanen laagen die ons een stuk brood gaaven, het eiland legt anderhalf uur van strand, dit helle strand brande geweldig wel een quartier ver in zee, en doet zulks by de muissonwind hebbende het gegroeven is geswaar

The Gordon Manuscripts and Atlas

In June 1964, after having been lost for over 150 years, the journals and papers of Colonel Robert Jacob Gordon were rediscovered in the county archives of Staffordshire, England. How they arrived there is a fascinating, though poignant, story.

Building and expanding on earlier research by writers such as Forbes and Barnard, the Dutch scholar L. C. Rookmaaker has added substantially to our knowledge of the history of the Gordon Collection (meaning the drawings and maps, as well as the manuscripts) through his uncovering of Mrs Gordon's correspondence with one John Pinkerton. These papers which, as Rookmaaker modestly puts it, had been 'overlooked' until now,[1] have provided the crucial key to understanding how documents of such significance in their day could have failed to find recognition for so long.

The following pages trace first the historical progress of the complete collection, and thereafter the separate histories of the Atlas (meaning the drawings, maps and charts) and the manuscripts.

In 1797 Gordon's widow sailed from the Cape to England on her way back to her native Switzerland. In London she was delayed by customs formalities and enlisted the help of a certain Captain Philip Gidley King (later, governor of New South Wales) whom she had known at the Cape.[2] King, in turn, wrote two letters to Sir Joseph Banks, president of the Royal Society, asking for further assistance. They are both dated 27 May 1797 and contain some interesting information:

The number of the charts is *Ninety Five*, & upwards of *600 Drawings* of Natural History, & Views in Caffraria & other parts of Africa. It is Mrs Gordon's wish to withdraw these two boxes from the Custom house to her Lodging: her words are these – 'The Charts, Manuscripts & Drawings are arranged in some measure by the deceased for publication. He had during his life been solicited on the part of the Emperor & Stadtholder, as well as many other men of Science, to publish them during his life, this he declined, & has left them for the advantage of his family. – Had circumstances allowed of her presenting them to the Stadtholder in *Holland*, that was her intention, but as she observes, the Cape now being in the possession of the English, & as the charts convey the greatest information, which as she says are by no means known, she has thought it her duty to admit them to your inspection; and will be extremely thankful, if it is not intruding too much on your goodness, to procure her an order for their delivery from the Custom house . . . .

In the second letter further intriguing details emerge. There is, King writes,

a manuscript wrote in Dutch. There are also a few bundles of family papers. The second box contains a very full & large Book, in which are arranged upwards of 400 drawings of Natural History, appropriated to the Charts and Views. The Charts and Natural History Mrs Gordon informs me were all designed by her own husband, who drew every outline, and had them finished under his own eye.

It seems certain that the collection remained in England when Mrs Gordon returned to Switzerland. From a third letter written by King to Sir Joseph Banks, dated 7 October 1797, it is clear that guardianship of the collection had passed to Captain Edward Riou, a notable sea captain, who had met Gordon at the Cape in 1789-90.[3] In this letter reference is made to a meeting with the secretary of the Treasury, George Rose, who represented the British Government in the matter of the proposed purchase of the collection. The letter states that 'after much conversation [with George Rose], the result was that Riou was to write to Mrs G as from himself, and to ask her what she valued the Charts &c. at, and that if the sum was anyways reasonable, Government would make the purchase'.

It appears that nothing came of this potential transaction, and when Riou died in 1801 it seems that the collection went back to Mrs Gordon.

The next mention of the collection comes in a letter from Mrs Gordon to the John Pinkerton mentioned earlier. Pinkerton was born in Edinburgh in 1758 and was well known as a writer, editor and belletrist of the period. His most celebrated work was probably the 'eccentric but very clever' *Letters on Literature*, published under the pseudonym of Robert Heron. This earned the praise of Horace Walpole, but it is worth recording that Edward Gibbon and Bishop Percy also thought highly of Pinkerton. Nevertheless, he appears to have been the archetypical eighteenth-century hack, putting out book after book on subjects as diverse as ancient Scottish poetry (some of which he composed himself), medals, rocks and, in particular, a compilation in seventeen volumes known as the *General Collection of Voyages and Travels* (1807 to 1814). This interest in travel may explain why he wrote to Mrs Gordon on 25 May 1803.[4] We do not have a copy of his letter but we know of its existence from Mrs Gordon's reply to Pinkerton on 3 June 1803. From her letter, translated here from the French sometime before 1830 and contained in the book *The Literary Correspondence of John Pinkerton Esq.*, one can infer that Pinkerton had shown interest in the publication of the Gordon Collection. It is an interesting document, calling for comment – and for more than one reason. Here it is in full:

MRS. GORDON TO MR. PINKERTON.
Province of Leman, at Sarras in Switzerland,
June 3rd, 1803.

Your letter of the 25th May claims my confidence, which I am still more willing to give to a gentleman who is a native of Scotland: it was to that country that my late husband belonged; and to the last hour of his life he always cherished feelings of warm attachment towards it. I may still further add that our best friends are in England, and that I have always entertained a hope that I might eventually have to treat with an Englishman for a work which is deserving the attention and support of the nation.

My husband, Colonel Gordon, was a man who was generally known, and had an extensive correspondence with literary men in all countries: I am aware that appearances are against what I have the honor to state to you, but the fact itself is unquestionable; and if I should ever have the good fortune to make your personal acquaintance, I will explain to you the circumstances that have caused me to adopt my present line of conduct.

If you will give yourself the trouble again to read my prospectus, you will see that the journals are written in Dutch; and it is my opinion that they would not fill more than a single quarto volume. The bulk, I am aware, promises much more; but it is swelled by numerous maps and the explanation of them, as well as by a great variety of drawings, some of them representing the interior of the country, others of plants and animals of all kinds. No statement which I could make would enable you to form an idea of the extent of the labor: to judge of it adequately, you must see it with your own eyes. I should be delighted to have the honor of receiving you in Switzerland; but, if it should suit you better to look over my collections at Paris, I would willingly make the journey, and bring with me all my papers, provided you feel there is a reasonable expectation of our coming to terms. In this important respect I am willing to place the most entire confidence in your character. Should your answer be favourable, I may arrive at Paris before the end of the present month.[5]

Mrs Gordon's letter does more than merely respond to Pinkerton's enquiry. It also confirms much of what we know about her husband's ambiguous loyalties. She affirms in the first paragraph that he 'belonged' to Scotland and she emphasizes that 'our best friends are in England'. Of course, this is by way of flattering Pinkerton, since we can be sure that she was still eager to see the collection published. But the second paragraph is also interesting. Does it allude to the disgrace of Gordon's suicide, or is it merely to assure Pinkerton that the collection is important and well known? Either or both interpretations could be placed on this passage.

It is clear from the concluding paragraph that Mrs Gordon had some kind of 'prospectus' in circulation which, presumably, Pinkerton had read. This could indicate that some editing had been done on the collection though, if this is so, it is not evident from the present state of the manuscripts.

It seems likely that Pinkerton and Mrs Gordon did meet in Paris — on 28 August 1803. Certainly, according to the editor of *The Literary Correspondence of John Pinkerton Esq.*, Pinkerton 'was zealous in his endeavours to serve Mrs Gordon'. On 20 April 1804, writing from a Paris address, Pinkerton drafted a letter to an unspecified English publisher, giving details of the collection consistent with those given above. It is also stated, by this same editor, that several leading English publishers had declined to take the collection because 'Mr Barrow's excellent work on the same subject had just made its appearance so that Colonel Gordon's was in a great degree superseded; and it was feared the publication would be of too expensive a nature to afford much chance of remuneration; nor were the times favourable for large speculations'.[6]

However, Pinkerton's draft also hints at a 'French bookseller' involved in a 'translation'. But this arrangement can, it seems, be dropped, for as the letter concludes:

... in case you purchase the work, you may arrange matters with her for the French translation. In all respects she is a religious and most respectable character, and too wealthy to stoop to any duplicity: so you may rest assured that if you purchase this work no other edition will be thought of, and even the French translation left to your discretion.

I suppose £600 for one, or £1 200 for two volumes, would be a fair price. Less than £600 for one would not be accepted, as the booksellers here offer a corresponding value, and with less trouble.

I beg your answer as soon as possible.[7]

The next letter from Mrs Gordon on 27 April 1804 says nothing of a possible English publisher but refers directly to a French 'bookseller' — presumably the one cited in the draft letter. The import is that negotiations are at a fairly advanced stage.

Mrs Gordon starts the letter by declaring her great diffidence 'in speaking of matters outside my sphere'.[8] She emphasizes her confidence in Pinkerton, explicitly granting him '*carte blanche*'. However, she then proceeds to make detailed objections to the terms that, presumably, he has submitted for her approval.

Firstly, the 'bookseller' wants to print too many copies of the book: 'three thousand in octavo, and three hundred in quarto'. She fears it will take too much time to sell all these copies 'so that it will be long before we can look for a second edition'. Secondly, she objects to the deferred terms of payment the bookseller wants, as well as the 'small sums into which it is intended to divide' the payments. Shrewdly, she states that she cannot see how 'money coming in such a manner should be laid out to advantage'. She is also fearful that Pinkerton may have left Paris when the time comes for a new edition, thus depriving her of 'anyone to look to my interest, and to see that the bookseller does what he ought'. But that is not all: she does not want twenty free copies of the book, only ten in quarto, so that the amount of the rest should be added to the first payment. And why, she demands, will she only receive 'an allowance' for a translation into English? She feels she should 'claim the same privilege ... in German or any other language'. She then adds: 'I am persuaded you will see it appear very soon in German; for I know that many inquiries have been made after it beyond the Rhine, and particularly at Berlin.' Her final quibble on this matter is the difficulty of selling 'the manuscript and drawings'. They will have lost their value once publication has taken place, since every one will be able to 'satisfy their curiosity at a small cost' simply by reading the book.

There is not much that Mrs Gordon has overlooked. Indeed, she seems quite convinced that the transaction will go ahead, notwithstanding her objections. There is a sad irony in her confidence when she speaks of her delight that Pinkerton has arranged to have the book published in Paris: '. . . for you will have the opportunity of superintending every thing personally'. As we shall see later, the agreement was not concluded due, possibly, to her inflexibility at this point.

Two more matters conclude the letter. The first concerns the portrait of her husband, which she is sending to have copied in Paris because she cannot find a painter to do this in Switzerland. Her anxiety is almost obsessive, movingly so:

But, my dear Sir, I cannot trust to you this, my greatest treasure in the world, without intreating you to take care that it comes to no harm in your possession, and without earnestly begging that you will never allow it to go out of your house, and will cause the artist whom you employ to work upon it in your presence. You will receive it by the Geneva diligence; and as soon as you do so, I hope you will favor me with the news of its safe arrival. No pains have been spared on my part to pack it carefully. When copied, I will beg the favor of you to replace it in the box in which it travels to Paris, and to allow it to remain under your roof till I meet with some friend who will bring it back with him to Switzerland.

The last matter of any importance in the letter concerns the fact that 'There is now at Paris a German gentleman, Mr Frederick Schlegel, eminently versed in the literature of that country, to which he devotes his time, who would probably be glad to be employed in translating the work into German'.

Mrs Gordon was evidently well informed. This 'German gentleman' was undoubtedly Friederich von Schlegel (1772-1829), the eminent writer and critic, 'the originator of many of the philosophical ideas that inspired the early German Romantic movement'. He was in Paris at this time, studying Sanskrit for his work on comparative Indo-Germanic linguistics. The fact that he never did make this translation must be added to the list of misfortunes which have steadily dogged the Gordon Collection.[9]

It appears, anyway, that this whole transaction came to nought, though how and why this happened is not on record.

The next move in the saga of the collection is provided by the editor of *The Literary Correspondence of John Pinkerton Esq.*:

At the close of 1804, the manuscripts were offered to the French Government, with whom Madame Gordon endeavoured to stipulate that one of her sons, then an ensign in the army, should be made a lieutenant-colonel, and the other, who was serving in the navy as a lieutenant, should be promoted to the rank of post-captain. But Bonaparte's officers were not so formed. Denon took a kind interest in the affair: there is a letter of his, stating that he had recommended the purchase to the emperor, but without success: and that he advised Mr. Pinkerton to lay them before the minister of war, to the papers of whose office, in the geographical department, they would form an important accession.[10]

No one can fault John Pinkerton for his assiduity, or, indeed, his ingenuity in trying to help Mrs Gordon. The fact that he could enlist the aid of Denon, Napoleon's art advisor and director-general of museums, also indicates how influential he was. There is evidence too that she appreciated his zeal. On 26 March 1805 she signed a document giving him a power of attorney to

negotiate with London booksellers for the publication of journeys made in Africa by her husband Colonel Gordon . . . and to sell, for the highest price he could obtain, the maps, drawings and papers of which she has a catalogue received from his hand . . . and which she shall keep for him according to the agreement executed in Paris on 28 August 1803.[11]

The last letter from Mrs Gordon contained in *The Literary Correspondence of John Pinkerton Esq.* is dated 19 April 1806. She begins by regretting the fact that Pinkerton had 'not even yet been able to do anything with the papers; and it grieves me that I did not conclude the treaty which you had set on foot with the Parisian bookseller before you left that city'.

Responding to a suggestion, apparently made by Pinkerton, that she wait another year, her tone becomes more than a little brusque:

The booksellers, you tell me, already throw cold water upon my work; and surely I cannot with any reason expect that the allowing of it to add twelve months to its age will obtain it any accession of favor in their eyes. It were indeed strange if either with them or the public it acquired a value then which it has not now . . . . I therefore intreat you, my dear Sir, to use your utmost endeavours to bring these matters to a conclusion as speedily as possible.

Evidently, Pinkerton had also suggested the possibility of putting the 'papers' up to auction. She presumes, however, that this would not take place until the work was published 'when their value would be materially increased'. This contradicts her opinion, mentioned earlier, that their value would be diminished if they were published first. But she now makes an interesting statement which is also somewhat baffling: 'I have still to learn from you what progress is made in the printing, or even if it is yet begun; and this is a point on which I am very anxious to be informed.'

We have, of course, no means of knowing to what this mention of printing refers. However, it is likely that at this point there was a plan to print some part of the collection, probably the travel journals. How this would tie in with the presumably different subject of 'publication' is a further matter on which we can only speculate today. Another possibility is that the 'printing' was to form part of Pinkerton's *General Collection of Voyages and Travels* which he was busy with at the time, the first volumes of which began to appear in 1807.

Concluding her letter, Mrs Gordon returns to the subject of auctioning the papers:

I feel, indeed, an almost unconquerable repugnance to the idea of bringing these valuable memorials of my husband's labors and abilities to auction; but I will, nevertheless, not withhold my consent, if you find that nothing better can be done . . . we shall thus, at least, settle the matter speedily, which will necessarily be to the advantage of us both. Indeed, there is nothing I so much deprecate as delay.[12]

This letter inspired Pinkerton to once again approach the British government by responding to a letter from William ('Weathercock') Windham, who was at the time secretary of state for war and the colonies.[13] In this capacity he was responsible for the Cape, which the British had just reoccupied. It is clear, though, that it was Pinkerton who had initiated the correspondence with a 'little memoir' which he refers to in his letter. (This is possibly the 'prospectus' mentioned earlier by Mrs Gordon.) Pinkerton's letter, in full, follows:

Clement's Inn, no 7, May 14, 1806. Sir – I was duly honoured with your letter of the 27th March with regard to the papers, maps, and drawings of Colonel Gordon, formerly commandant of the Cape of Good Hope, in which you are so good as to say you shall at a future opportunity take the opinion of competent judges how far they might be proper objects to be purchased at the national expense. I am well aware, with the public at large, of the multitude of your avocations, and have not therefore wished to press the matter; but having just received an earnest letter from Mrs Gordon in Switzerland accusing me of unnecessary delay, I hope you will pardon me taking this liberty. I have myself some skill in geography, and if I had not thought these papers of great importance to this commercial country, and the interest of its oriental colonies, I should not have taken charge of them. I suppose that Mr Faden or Mr Arrowsmith the geographers would readily inspect them, and give a just and candid report. I have no doubt that the acquisition would be of lasting advantage, and be esteemed honorable to an enlightened administration who should order it to be made. But on this subject I must refer to the little memoir which I had the honour to send you and remain with the greatest respect &c. signed John Pinkerton.[14]

But despite this plea, nothing came of this eloquent attempt to sell the collection. No more letters from Mrs Gordon are preserved in *The Literary Correspondence of John Pinkerton Esq.*; however, the eventual sale is recorded, some four years later, in the same work. In a letter from the Marchioness of Stafford, dated 30 March 1810, we read:

I beg to express my thanks to you for the offer of the Gordon collection of drawings, &c. &c. Though I do not particularly collect drawings of that kind, yet the moderate sum you mention, of one hundred guineas, induces me to avail myself of this, provided you continue disposed to part with it; and I shall be glad if you will have the goodness to direct Mr. Christie to let it be sent here; as I shall be glad to look at it, and will willingly give that money.[15]

The marchioness was Elizabeth Leveson Gower, wife of the 2nd Marquis of Stafford. It is said that around the year 1803 the marquis, 'a leviathan of wealth', began to devote himself 'to the patronage of art, probably under the influence of his wife, herself an artist in water colours of considerable skill'. She was also 'Countess of Sutherland in her own right and proprietress of the greatest part of Sutherland'. In 1833 her husband was 'raised to the Dukedom . . . and selected the title Duke of Sutherland'.[16]

It is, I believe, reasonable to assume that what the marchioness bought was the entire Gordon Collection: the manuscripts as well as the 'drawings, &c. &c.'. There is,

2. Homoglossum watsonium

3. *Probably Cape dwarf chameleons* (Bradypodion pumilium)

however, no record that anyone took an interest in either the maps and drawings or the papers during the next one hundred years. Perhaps that is an exaggeration. Someone did write in one of the bound volumes of bird drawings the following observation: 'A collection made by Colonel Gordon of Scotch family settled at the Cape & highly esteemed by the Dutch Government. It was intended to be sold at a public auction but was bought by the Marquis of Stafford about 1802.'[17] As we now know, the information is wrong in at least two respects, so it can be assumed that it was added some time after the collection was bought, when the actual dates and facts were not accurately known.

It was only in 1913, when the library of Stafford House was put up for auction, that the collection re-emerged. The Sotheby's catalogue for the sale on 30 October 1913 reads: '[Lot] Nr. 445. A collection of 387 very clear original coloured drawings of the Quadrupeds . . . mounted and bound, in 4 vol. half red morocco.'[18] From the number and description given here, it is evident that the maps, charts and landscape drawings were not included in the sale. The London booksellers, Maggs Bros, were the buyers, paying £690 for the four volumes. However, they must have been told of the missing items because when the collection was put up for sale in 1914, there were six not four volumes, the additional two being the maps and other drawings.

The price, for what was then known as the Gordon Atlas, was £1 250 and was paid by a Dutch bookseller, Martinus Nijhof of The Hague. Subsequently, the Dutch Government and a group of citizens, under the chairmanship of Professor Godée Molsbergen, took over the purchase and presented the collection to the print section of the Rijks Museum, where it rests today, duly honoured and preserved.[19]

The Gordon papers (the manuscripts of his travel journals, correspondence and related material) were not even mentioned as being part of the Stafford House library. That such papers had once existed seems to have been forgotten. However, it may be that when the sale of the library took place, some home had to be found for them. Whether they were lent to the county archives in Stafford at this time is not known, but that is where the papers were discovered in 1964 by the chief archivist, Pretoria, Dr A.J. Kieser, who was in Britain on 'a busman's holiday'. While visiting the Stafford Archives, as a 'purely routine enquiry, Dr Kieser asked whether there were any old Dutch manuscripts in the archives. "Yes," said the Stafford archivist, "there are, but they have never been translated as no one here knows High Dutch." To Dr Kieser's amazement he was handed Robert Gordon's original journals – written during his travels into the interior . . . .'[20]

In April 1979, under the title 'Valuable autographs and manuscripts, the property of the Duchess of Sutherland's settlements', the papers were put on sale by Christie's of London. They were bought by Mr H.F. Oppenheimer for his Brenthurst Library in Johannesburg and that is where they are now lodged.

In conclusion, one can only speculate how our perception of southern Africa in the eighteenth century would have been affected had Gordon's journals been published in Paris during 1804-5. Indeed, it is not just a view of history that is in question. Gordon's observations of the interior tribes, the fauna and flora, the topography of the country, as well as his charts and maps, would all have had far-reaching effects on the ideas and knowledge of succeeding generations. Gordon's name would have stood at the front of all the travellers and writers of the period, because his journeys were, undoubtedly, the most remarkable and well documented of the time. There is one final irony: had Friederich von Schlegel then brought out a German edition, Gordon's accomplishments would have been spread even more widely and even more decisively.

The Translation of Gordon's Papers

Incorporated in this biography are translations which I have made from Gordon's four travel journals and other miscellaneous papers. Apart from a photocopy of the journals, which was lent to me, I also consulted photocopies of the Gordon papers in the Pretoria and Cape Archives. In addition, I was given access to the original manuscripts in the Brenthurst Library, Johannesburg, which enabled me to decipher some passages that were faint or illegible in the copies.

Whenever I have needed to quote from Gordon's original Dutch, French or English, I have aimed to transcribe his words exactly, however eccentric the spelling, however haphazard the punctuation. Indeed, his style is steadfastly erratic. He seldom bothered to use capital letters, either at the start of a sentence or for place or personal names. Indeed, often the spelling of a name, let alone an ordinary word, will differ when used twice in the same sentence. My transcriptions endeavour to reproduce these variants exactly.

Concerning the translations in general, however, I have felt that some uniformity would be desirable, since I would not be quoting the original text. Thus, in order to have a reference that was, to some extent, constant for place names, I have generally adopted the spelling used in Gordon's 'great map' (Map 3 of the Gordon Atlas in the Rijks Museum).

The names of people have presented a separate problem. In most instances the first version given by Gordon has been used, but where a name recurs frequently the commonest version has been adopted. Complete uniformity, however, is almost impossible, so I beg the reader's indulgence in this matter, pleading, at the very least, that some flavour of the original is retained when variant spellings occur.

Nevertheless, though Gordon's handwriting was not neat or handsome, though he wrote all over the margins and jumped pages in continuing a sentence, it is astonishing how little of what he wrote is illegible. His handwriting remained as clear, decisive and vigorous as the man himself.

A vexing issue in translating a work of this nature is the question of anachronisms. Words like *veld*, *outspan*, *inspan*, *vlei* or *krantz* were not in use in English at the time Gordon wrote. On the whole, therefore I have tried to follow the terms used by Paterson, Gordon's contemporary, in translating words such as these. Consistency here is again difficult since each journal varies, if only slightly, in style and approach. The aim to ensure consistency was there, however. In turns of phrase I have tried to use locutions that are neither aggressively modern nor whimsically archaic.

It will be noted that in the translations the word 'Caffer' is used instead of 'Kaffir'. To have abandoned this word entirely would have been historically inaccurate. Today, however, the term 'Kaffir' is offensive. It seemed, therefore, a happy compromise to use the spelling Gordon himself used in the Dutch, i.e. Caffer, thus preserving the historical nomenclature but creating a distance from the modern form of the word. Similarly, in translating 'wilden' it may seem more correct to use the word 'savages' rather than my choice of 'wild people', but since 'wilden' is almost always applied to the 'Bushmen', and because Gordon manifestly had a real sympathy for these people, I have chosen to use the latter term, keeping in this way an etymological link between the Dutch and English.

Again, the decision to use 'Bushmen' and 'Hottentot', with or without inverted commas, was also a difficult one. My reason for retaining these terms was that, in the first place, they were the words Gordon used in Dutch, i.e. 'Bosjesmans' and 'Hottentotten', and secondly, having reviewed the current controversy surrounding the words San and Khoi, it seemed better to keep the historical link with Gordon's terms than to use the words most commonly employed today. Indeed, Gordon was well aware of what these people called themselves. In a draft letter of 1779, addressed to his friend and mentor in the Netherlands, the Greffier Hendrik Fagel, Gordon wrote: '. . . as far as I know Hottentots call themselves Quoi Queuna. However, in dialect . . . some say Queina or Eina for Queuna. Literally, this means person people; Queuna being the plural of Quoi-person.' A few lines later he cites the word 'Saaneina' for 'Bushmen'.[1]

Perhaps the last word on this subject of nomenclature should be left to M.L. Wilson of the South African Museum. Concluding a trenchant and comprehensive article, he writes:

. . . the choice of terms such as 'Hottentot' or 'Khoikhoi' or 'Bushman' or 'San' should be dictated by the context or individual preference. To those who see derogatory, racist or sexist connotations in the use of any of the names (although 'San' definitely does seem to be derogatory), the words of the motto of the British Order of the Garter apply: *Honi soit qui mal y pense*, shamed be he who evil thinks.[2]

Gordon's own manner of expression in the journals is rough, even clumsy in places, and often monotonous with its meteorological and cartographical repetitions. No attempt has been made to render the style more elegant. The journals, in particular, were kept for information and primarily must be seen and read as such. (One

16

can imagine, for example, Gordon turning to them when he advised Le Vaillant how to proceed with his travels.) However, they would have emerged in a very different form had Gordon gone on to write a book from them – which was almost certainly his intention. Indeed, several of Gordon's contemporaries refer to the fact that he intended 'to give to the world, from his own hand, a history of his travels'. In particular, it is sadly ironic to read the words of the Dutch naval officer, Rear-Admiral Stavorinus, who had met Gordon in 1778:

It is to be hoped that the death of colonel Gordon will not deprive the world of the invaluable results of his researches; and that, in whatever hands his papers may be, they will not be consigned to oblivion, or withheld from the public, who might justly form great expectations from his long residence at the Cape, his frequent journies up the country, and his well-known zeal for the promotion of knowledge.[3]

Finally, in considering the nature of the texts, and therefore the nature of the translations, it must be remembered that Gordon was writing his journals in the veld, under harsh conditions and whenever the occasion presented itself – which most probably was at night with poor illumination. This alone – the physical act of writing – was a remarkable feat considering the distances he covered, the people and places he had to see, the often strenuous demands of mapping, as well as the need to hunt game for food and to reconnoitre a path for the wagon. He was, of course, aided in these tasks by his servants and companions. Nevertheless, it is clear from the narrative that he never shirked these duties and responsibilities. His pragmatic zeal, his daily regimen of writing in the field and his dedication to accuracy can only be admired by posterity.

4. One of the six notebooks in which Gordon recorded his remarkable travels.

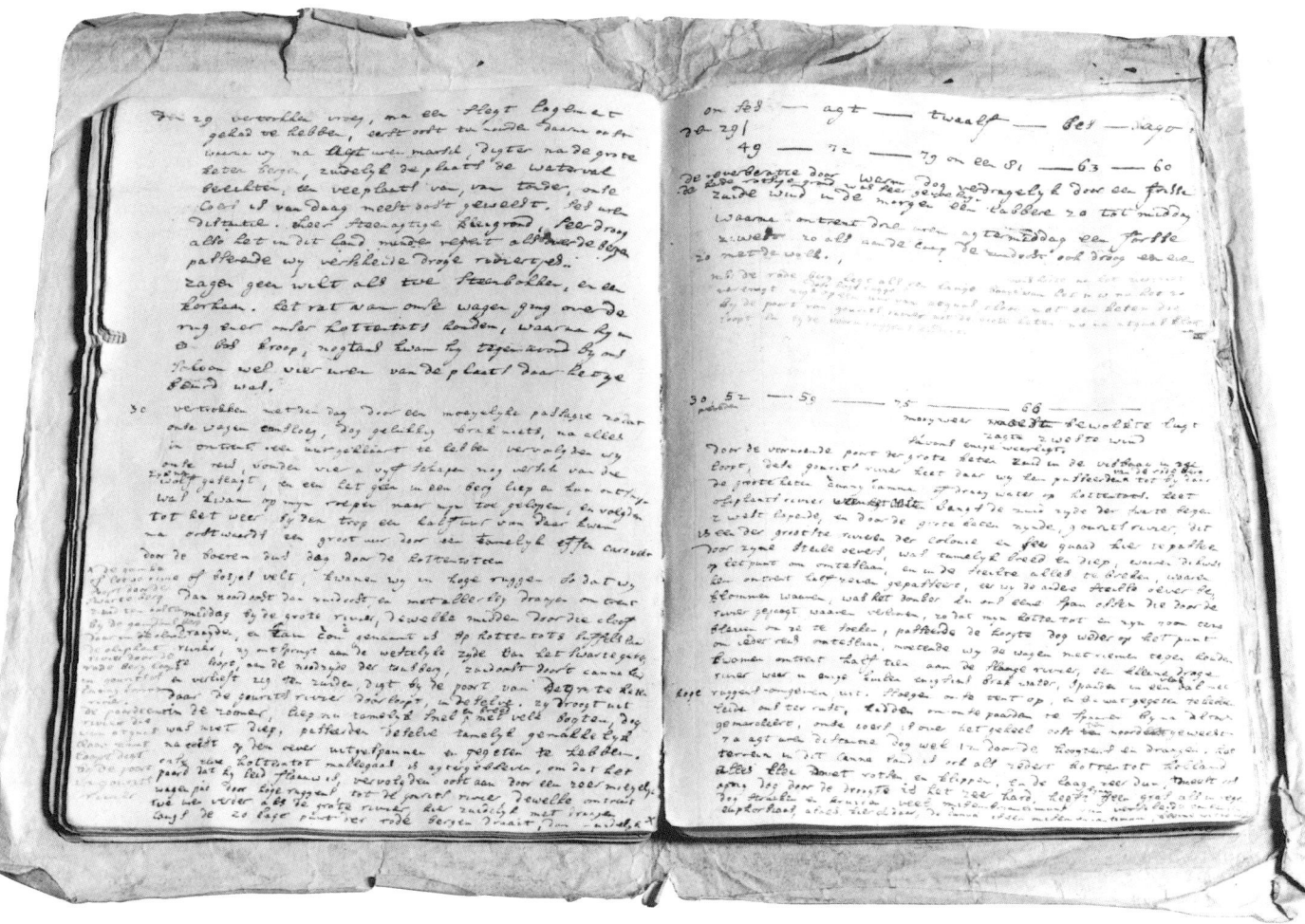

5. Aloe dichotoma, *often referred to as the 'quiver tree'.*

CHAPTER ONE

THE EARLY YEARS: MORE THAN A MILITARY MAN

(1743-1777)

The Gordon family in the Netherlands; early career of Robert Jacob Gordon; first visit to the Cape and first journey (1773-1774); return to the Netherlands; meetings with Diderot, Allamand and other prominent figures; posting to the Cape garrison and return to the Cape, June 1777

When Robert Jacob Gordon shot himself in October 1795, life ended for a man who had been both widely praised and vilely execrated.

His was a career of singular achievement. He had penetrated the interior of southern Africa further than any other eighteenth-century explorer who recorded his travels. He was acclaimed for his studies in zoology, botany, meteorology and geology. He had made close contact with the tribes of the land and spoke both Hottentot and Xhosa. He had corresponded with the great men of Europe – savants, scientists and statesmen. He had produced the finest maps of the country and had brought in new methods of gunnery to his garrison. By introducing merino sheep at the Cape Colony he was to profoundly influence the direction of farming in southern Africa. He was an urbane and genial companion whose hospitality was renowned, yet he died with the abuse of his fellow-countrymen shrill in his ears. He was, they said, a traitor, a coward and a turncoat.

Gordon's life, in its accomplishment and tragedy, was a drama of loyalty, or rather of loyalties, embodying the kinds of dilemma that have always confronted honourable men in times of rapid change or revolution. The history of South Africa is especially fecund in these conflicts and ambiguities of allegiance. Gordon's life, and particularly his death, epitomize the nature of these predicaments.

Through his journals and papers we can see what interested Gordon; through the accounts of companions, travellers, officials and enemies, we can see how he appeared to others; through historical documents we can trace his career; but of the man himself – how he felt, how he perceived himself – very little evidence remains. He left almost no records of his personal life; there are no letters extant between himself and his family; he was taciturn about his political beliefs and only one letter, written a few months before his death, makes these clear.

To understand Gordon the man, therefore, we must work largely from the outside, using the events of his life as signposts to his inner workings, inferring from his background why he acted as he did. As a result, conclusions about his personal motives can only be tentative, arrived at by accumulating evidence over the whole extent of his life and by viewing that life in its contemporary context. To understand why he committed suicide in 1795 we must understand the background against which he grew up and the vital role that his ancestry played throughout his life.

Though descended from a Scotsman, Gordon's family was thoroughly Dutch and had been for over a hundred years. The first Gordon of this line had come to the Netherlands in the early part of the seventeenth century as a naval cadet.[1] It appears that the family prospered modestly but it is clear that a tradition of service to the new country had started with the first Gordon. This is convincingly borne out by the career of Gordon's father, who was known by the single name of Jacob. It is worth taking a brief look at his life for the light it casts on his son's early years and upbringing.

Jacob Gordon senior was born in 1701 and entered the Dutch Dragoon Guards at an early age, but soon transferred to the Scots Brigade, taking command of a company in 1724.[2] It is said that the influence of his father, a burgomaster, as well as his Scots name, helped him to make this move. This may well be so, for it is recorded that the Scottish officers of the Brigade resented him, considering him a Dutchman in all but name. This is significant, for it illustrates that the father experienced something of the same dilemma, the same resentment and the same conflict of loyalties that were to beset the son.

Jacob Gordon had joined a famous body of men. For two centuries the Scots Brigade had formed part of the permanent military establishment of the Dutch Republic. During this period officers and men were recruited almost solely from Scotland. At times the lower ranks were bolstered by other nationalities, but the officers were exclusively Scotsmen, apart from rare exceptions like Jacob Gordon. A chaplain to one of the battalions wrote:

The officers entered into the service very early; they were trained up under their fathers and grandfathers who had grown old in the service; they expected a slow, certain and unpurchased promotion, but almost always in the same corps, and before they attained to command they were qualified for it. Though they served a foreign state, yet not in a distant country, they were still under the eye of their own, and considered themselves as the depositaries of her military fame. Hence their remarkable attachment to one another, and to the country whose name they bore and from whence they came; hence that high degree of ambition for supporting the name of Scotland and the glory of the Scots Brigade.

We can imagine, therefore, how difficult it must have been for Jacob Gordon, the young Dutchman from Schiedam, to become part of this establishment. It is recorded that even the word of command was given in the 'Scotch Language'. It was a clannish body of men, to say the least.

Nevertheless, no matter how deep and extensive his difficulties in adapting to this new ambience, Jacob Gordon proved to be a brave and successful soldier both in the service of the Brigade and in the defence of his fatherland. He was present at the siege of Bergen-op-Zoom in 1747 where the Scots Brigade stationed there lost two-thirds of their number against the French. He was captured in this engagement; yet even this event failed to influence his military career which, as was customary, continued to be marked by 'slow, certain and unpurchased promotion'. By the age of forty-seven he had attained the rank of lieutenant-colonel; ten years later, in 1758, he was made a full colonel; and in 1767 he became major-general.

There is one further point about the Scots Brigade that should be made. For seventy years, from the Peace of Utrecht until 1783, it had been the chief duty of the Brigade to garrison the cordon of fortresses in Flanders and the Walloon provinces known as the 'Barrier of the Dutch'. During this period the fortunes of the Brigade were always closely associated with those of the House of Orange. In 1755 the Brigade was not recalled to fight for Britain against France because 'the Princess Dowager of Orange had requested the late King, her father, to leave these regiments in Holland as a sure support to the interest of her infant son against the French faction'.[3] This close link between the Scots Brigade and the House of Orange, this particular loyalty, is one of the factors that will have to be taken into account when considering the Gordon family background.

Apart from the sparse details of Jacob Gordon's career there is one further incident in the Brigade records that is worth noting, for it illustrates that he was a proud and stubborn man. It concerns a clash with his brother officers over church matters, specifically the election of elders and some trial of 'the new way of singing'. He writes to a Major Buchanan: 'I desire that you will order the minister, the elders and deacons [all of them officers] to your house and order them in my name to undoo these things immediately.' Meeting with resistance Gordon threatens that if they disobey 'he knew what to doo'. 'For the sake of peace' the officers agreed 'for the time to lay it aside'. Not satisfied with this, Gordon ordered the minister's stipend to be stopped and demanded the Session register. The minister was hesitant, but on the intervention of the Duke of Brunswick Gordon got his way.

We can deduce from this episode that Jacob Gordon was a stern man, conscious of his rights, somewhat moralistic and authoritarian, but a successful soldier nonetheless. He was married to a Dame Johanna Mariah Hydenryk, about whom nothing further is known. He had seven children by her. Robert Jacob, the subject of this study, was the fifth son and sixth child.[4]

By taking a brief look at the careers of Robert's brothers, we can appreciate something of the background and ambitions of this family. Menso, the eldest, became an advocate and Adam Bernard, the second son, became a minister of religion. Joan (Johan) Gordon, the next in line, was the burgomaster of Wageningen and later held the important post of 'Receiver of Convoys'. The fourth son, Otto Dirk, followed a military career, possibly also in the Scots Brigade, and later ardently enlisted in the Patriot Party — that is to say, the faction opposed to the House of Orange — an interesting deviation that will be considered later.

Certainly this was a family of some eminence and, with the possible exception of Otto Dirk, respectable and successful in the bourgeois careers pursued by its members, for the daughters too made 'good' marriages. It is also clear that, however strong were its ties to the Scots Brigade — the two eldest children were actually baptized by the regimental chaplain — this was a very Dutch family. The roots and bonds of these Gordons were firmly interwoven with the fabric of eighteenth-century Holland.

*I*nto this well-established family, at Doesburg in Guelderland, Robert Jacob Gordon was born in September 1743. It is possible that the Gordons had a permanent house here, for Robert's eldest brother was born in the same town some twenty-one years before, as were two of his other kin, according to the available records. Robert's father would, of course, have been with his regiment.

No record of Robert Jacob's earliest years has been found, but we do know that he enlisted in the Scots Brigade when he was only ten years old. We have noted too how it had become a tradition for officers to enter the service 'very early', to be 'trained up under their fathers and grandfathers'. It would appear that Robert was merely following this tradition. Nevertheless, it is interesting to see that three of his four brothers did not follow their father into military service.

Robert was to remain a soldier all his life. It is feasible, then, to presume that he joined the Brigade because he wanted to make his career as a soldier — not as a duty but voluntarily — even though at the age of ten his judgement would have been swayed by the glory and prowess of the regiment and by the example of his father.

It was a time of comparative peace. The regiment moved from one garrison town to another: it was stationed in Ypres in 1754, just after Robert had enlisted as a cadet, and in Namur from 1759-62. In 1756, an event of particular

6. *Soldiers of the Scots Brigade in uniforms of the 1770s.*

import to the Gordons – Jacob and Robert – took place. By an act of the English Parliament, the officers of the Scots Brigade were required to take the oath of allegiance to the King of Great Britain. Now whether these two Gordons, serving with the regiment but subjects of the Dutch Republic, took this oath, has not been established. However, one can speculate as to the attitude of their brother officers had they not sworn allegiance. The sneers about being 'Dutch but in name' would have gained fresh currency. In this closely knit group of men, the odium they would have incurred by refusing can easily be imagined. But nothing like this is recorded. Indeed, Jacob Gordon gained further promotion two years later and continued in the service until his death in 1776.

Just by joining the Scots Brigade dual loyalty was immediately implied. Was this double allegiance now reinforced? The question will recur when we consider the suicide that ended Robert Gordon's life.

Whatever the truth of this matter, young Robert's duties with the Brigade could not have been very exacting, for in September 1759 he entered Harderwijk University.[5] He was sixteen at the time. It was said that he excelled in 'Nature Studies' and this may have been one of the attractions of Harderwijk, as it was at this institution that the great naturalist Linnaeus received his degree. We also know that the young Gordon showed an aptitude for languages. Under his father, one writer observes, 'he was brought up to arms and acquire the English and Gaelic languages',[6] both of which would have been essential in the Scots Brigade. In addition, in the latter half of the eighteenth century no European gentleman or man of learning could afford not to speak French, the *lingua franca* of the courts and scholars.

Certainly Gordon would have needed French in order to read contemporary scientists, naturalists and *philosophes* like Buffon. It was the Age of Enlightenment, when men of learning believed that reason, rightly conducted, could find both truth and knowledge and thus bring happiness to mankind. Since Gordon was very much a part of this movement, it can be assumed that he had acquired the language of this new knowledge by the time he entered Harderwijk. Indeed, in time, he would himself contribute to Buffon's great encyclopaedia, *Histoire Naturelle*, and it is likely that his passion for natural history was in fact awakened by reading these volumes as they appeared (the first fifteen tomes were published between 1749 and 1767).

In the meantime, Gordon's military career continued. In 1761 he became an ensign in the regiment, and by 1765, at the age of twenty-two, he had become a lieutenant. However, according to one source, 'the stationary life of a soldier in peace serving the garrisons of the United Provinces, ill accorded with the activity of a mind thirsting for a variety of knowledge'.[7] The young man therefore 'visited such parts of Europe as his leisure would admit'. Although there is no explicit record of where he went, in the journal of his second journey of exploration at the Cape there is some inferential evidence that he had visited Ireland, as he refers to the Giant's Causeway in County Antrim, likening it to the cliffs of the Sneeuberg (as seen from present-day Aberdeen). It would be unlike Gordon to compare one geographical feature with another which he had not seen, and his notes of the Sneeuberg are quite specific, stating that 'there is no basalt and not the slightest trace of volcanic material' – an unlikely observation unless he knew that the Causeway was formed of lava and basaltic pillars. Another clue to his travels is found in a letter dated 8 April 1789 which suggests that at some time he had been to Lake Geneva.[8] It is possible that he met his future wife on that visit, for she came from Lausanne.

*F*ortunately, as Gordon's career advanced, more facts were recorded and there is less and less need to speculate or deduce.

In 1773, at the age of thirty, Gordon made his first visit to the Cape, arriving in the ship *Holland* in January of that year.[9] We know for certain that he made one long journey on this occasion but where exactly he went is a matter of conjecture. It seems likely that he travelled as far as Plettenberg Bay, or even further east to the mouth of the Fish River, but there is no doubt that he went to the Berg River on the west coast and spent some time there observing hippopotamus. He also spent time exploring the Cape Peninsula in the company of the Swedish naturalist, Thunberg. For six days during May 1773 they walked from Table Mountain to False Bay and Simon's Bay, botanizing and examining all manner of natural phenomena.[10]

The main achievement of this first visit was undoubtedly the long journey along the coast of the Colony, referred to above. On this expedition Gordon's physical vigour and active mind would have been put to good use. Even if we cannot be sure of his exact route, both Allamand (the professor of natural history at Leyden) and Paterson (who was later to travel with Gordon to the Orange River mouth) record that on this first visit he penetrated deep into the interior 'with only a single Hottentot to accompany him'. Paterson claims he went 1 500 miles into the country while Allamand more reasonably estimates 200 leagues − approximately 600 miles or 1 000 kilometres.

Being Gordon, his time was not spent in idle wandering. Before he returned to Holland in May 1774 he had made studies of many animals, all of which he took back to Allamand to examine and write up.[11] The result of this collaboration was the series of articles that appeared in *Histoire Naturelle* under Professor J. N. S. Allamand's name but acknowledging Gordon as the source. Among others, studies of the gnu and hippopotamus date from this period. Also during this visit Gordon had learned 'Hottentot' − an accomplishment that was to serve him well in the future.

Gordon left the Cape on 1 May 1774 on the ship *Azia* together with a certain Van de Copello, who had accompanied him on the outward voyage. Twelve springbok were taken on board but only one survived the sea journey. On 30 July this remaining animal was presented to the zoological garden of Willem V, Prince of Orange.

Whether Gordon now rejoined the Scots Brigade as an active officer is not established. We know that during his visit to the Cape he had been promoted to captain;[12] but then, later in 1774, he is listed as being 'à la suite' − in other words, not in active service. We know too that he paid a visit to Aernout Vosmaer who was the director of Willem V's menagerie at The Hague, on which occasion they discussed the characteristics of African animals and the difficulties of the 'Hottentot' language, in particular its frequent clicks of the tongue.

Perhaps more important, however, was his visit to Professor Allamand at this time. In a letter written about January 1788, which is discussed in some detail on pages 161-2, Gordon claimed he had known Allamand since the age of seventeen (when he was at Harderwijk University). It seems likely, then, that it was his profound interest in natural history that recommended him to the professor at Leyden at this early age. Whatever the case, it was in this period, between 1774 and Gordon's return to the Cape in 1777, that the foundation for their collaboration was laid. On this occasion they discussed the many curiosities and discoveries of his African journey and, in particular, the animals. Gordon also gave him a skin from the head of a gnu − or wildebeest, as it is now known. It is evident that Allamand had great respect for the younger man's enterprise and knowledge. He described him as a 'true naturalist' when relating the exploits of his first visit to the Cape. Indeed, it is perfectly possible that the professor himself had inspired this first visit, knowing Gordon's zeal and capabilities as a naturalist. He would reiterate his admiration in the years to follow.

There is one further episode which occurred during Gordon's return to Holland that must be recorded. The famous, radical and brilliant *philosophe*, Denis Diderot, returning from the court of Catherine II at St Petersburg, broke his journey in the Netherlands, staying there from May to October 1774.[13] This celebrated editor of the *Encyclopédie* subsequently wrote a long essay describing his visit, entitled *Voyage de Hollande*.

While at The Hague he writes of meeting 'a young Englishman called Gordon, who was returning from the Cape of Good Hope, where he had spent several years'.[14] This traveller was undoubtedly Robert Jacob Gordon. That Diderot took him for an Englishman need not surprise us. Almost certainly Gordon would have been wearing the uniform of the Scots Brigade and may even have used English in discourse with Diderot, since the philosopher knew the language well. Furthermore, given what we shall later learn of Gordon's anglophile feelings, it is altogether possible that he may have been happy to let the Frenchman assume that he was English. However, it is the actual content of the discussion that leads us overwhelmingly to the conclusion that this was indeed Captain Robert Jacob Gordon, newly returned from the Cape.

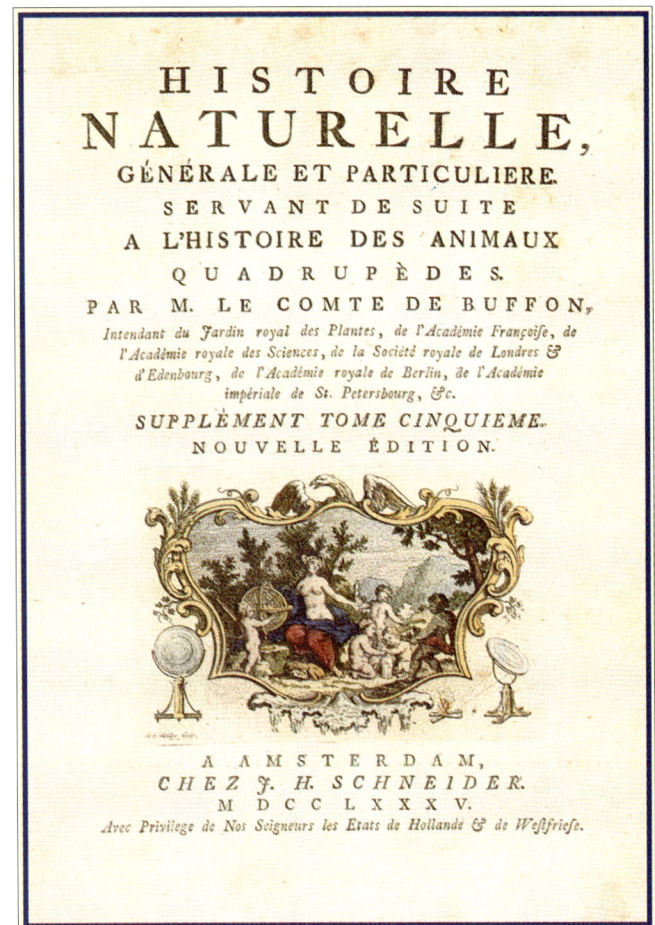

7. *The title page of the* Supplément *to Buffon's encyclopaedia of natural history,* Histoire Naturelle.

8. *Male springbok.*

The whole passage concerning Gordon is worth quoting.[15] As will be seen, a third character — a certain 'Doctor Robert' — is also present. Diderot uses him as a foil to Gordon, and makes him an example of petty bigotry and prejudice.

At The Hague I saw a young Englishman called Gordon, who was returning from the Cape of Good Hope, where he had spent several years.[16] I questioned him on the Hottentots. He assured me that they were not at all stupid as was believed, that it was extremely difficult to verify the fact of the alleged 'apron' for women because they rejected this kind of curiosity, that for a long time he had looked out for such an opportunity without finding any; that finally he did see one and that the apron did not hang from the stomach, but from the upper part of the natural parts; that it would be easy to take it for an exorbitant clitoris, although it certainly was not; that they were nothing but much extended labia minora which hung down like a wattle of a turkey-cock and that this excrescence showed no erection whatsoever.[17]

According to this witness the singing of the males would sound like unmodulated shouting, whereas that of the women could be written down in our musical notation.

Here is a translation of two Hottentot songs that he made for us:

'Run to me, my women; sing, I return from far away. Your song will delight me.'

Here is their war chant: 'To war, to war; to arms, to arms; let us go, let us go to war. Courage, my friends, if we have courage we shall defeat our enemies.'

The kind of click sound made by our coachmen to encourage their horses is one of the sounds in their language and singing.

While Mr Gordon was speaking, Doctor Robert, who was sitting beside me, said to me very softly: 'Don't believe a word that this man tells you about the Hottentots and their apron. I have lived at the Cape for a long time and I have also seen the Hottentot apron. These women are utter tarts whom their husbands prostitute for a pinch of tobacco. I would think that their apron was the result of pregnancy since there were no traces of them on the men. It is the skin of their stomach which hangs over their pubis.'

Which of the two, Mr Gordon or the Doctor, was telling the truth?

At this point Diderot breaks the narrative in order to relate a totally different, seemingly unrelated, anecdote about Doctor Robert. The effect of this diversion, however, is to call in question the Doctor's good sense. In this way Diderot answers his own question about who was telling the truth: it is obvious that it is Gordon he believes. The philosopher then resumes his original theme without further ado, abruptly, thus totally dismissing Robert. Once more he takes up Gordon's conversation, quoting him with respect; almost, it would seem, quoting him word for word.

The Hottentots rub themselves with the fat of animals: cattle, sheep, buffaloes, snakes. By doing this their limbs become more supple, they sweat less abundantly, their bodies are less exposed to insects, their bare feet are less sensitive to hard stones, they walk longer and are less exhausted from it. But they do exhale a stench that reaches for fifty paces around them. They also rub themselves with the fat left over from their meals.

If a Hottentot and a European are attacked by a lion, the animal would rather pursue the Hottentot, swayed, it would seem, by the emanations from the fat which strike its sense of smell.

Mr Gordon said that Kolb, upon whom Monsieur de Buffon relied, knew nothing and was a liar, but he praised the truthfulness and accuracy of Monsieur l'Abbé de Lacaille, who he added was not often mistaken. He was accorded great respect by the Dutch of the country who could not understand how a man could have come from so far, encountering a thousand different dangers, just for the advancement of astronomy and without any design of ambition and wealth.[18]

There can be absolutely no doubt that this is the Gordon who had penetrated deep into the interior of southern Africa, observed the tribes and the animals and who had learned 'Hottentot'. Who else, called Gordon, could have discoursed with such persuasive, scientific authority about the indigenous people, could have had first-hand knowledge of the so-called 'Hottentot apron', could have translated their songs, and could, above all, have spoken so convincingly and positively of their language, nature and customs?

Perhaps the most striking aspect of this meeting is the evident, though tacit, sympathy between the two men on the subject of the 'Hottentots'. The current stereotype of these people, as portrayed even in Buffon, was far different:

The head covered with bristling hair or a curly wool ... the eyes round like those of animals; the lips thick and protruding, the nose flattened; the gaze stupid and timid, the ears, body and members matted with hair; the skin hard like black or tanned leather; the nails long, thick and hooked; the sole of the foot calloused in the form of a corn; and as for sexual attributes, the breasts long and soft, the skin of the abdomen hanging as low as the knee, the children wallowing in muck and crawling on all fours, the mother and father seated on their heels, all of them hideous, covered with a pestilent scum. And this sketch, drawn from observations of the Hottentot savage, is a flattering portrait. For it is farther from man in a natural state to the Hottentot than from the Hottentot to ourselves.[19]

Gordon's rejection of current prejudice, such as Buffon's crude caricature of the 'Hottentot', must have delighted Diderot. Furthermore, the young traveller's logical explanation for the use of fat on their bodies, in the best traditions of enlightened enquiry and reason, could only have gained the approval of the philosopher. Diderot, after all, was convinced that 'savages', such as the Tahitians, had much to teach the so-called civilized nations.[20] He believed, furthermore, that these simple races were more virtuous and happy than the Europeans who had intervened so viciously in their way of life.

This meeting with Gordon had no further direct influence on Diderot's writing. But the subject of 'Hottentots' does arise in a work by the Abbé Raynal known, in translation, as *A Philosophical and Political History of the Settlements and Trade of the Europeans in the East and West Indies*.[21] This was first published in 1770 but went through further editions until it was re-issued in 1780 'with changes of an audacious nature'.[22] It is this last edition that will interest us, for it is well attested that Diderot was one of the major collaborators in this work and that he was writing for the Abbé Raynal during the winter of 1766 – in other words, barely two years after the meeting with Gordon.[23]

In Book II of the work there is a section devoted to the Dutch settlement of the Cape and there can be little doubt that this is Diderot speaking. There is a direct reference once more to the 'Hottentot apron', confirming Gordon's observation that

The fabulous accounts, which say that women of this nation have a fleshy apron, falling down from the middle of the belly, over the parts of generation, are at length discredited. It has been certified that these women are formed nearly in the same manner as [are] ... many others in hot climates, where the external organs, both upwards and all round, acquire a longer size and more extended shape than in temperate climates.[24]

Diderot – or, to be pedantic, the writer of this passage[25] – then goes on to praise the 'Hottentots' who dwell in 'the happiness, innocence, and tranquillity of a patriarchal life'. This account need not detain us here, but it should be mentioned that the passage does contain a vivid and passionately partisan view of these 'noble savages', followed by an eloquent denunciation of the Dutch settlers,

9. Denis Diderot.

an oration on what would today be described as the evils of colonialism.

One can only speculate on whether Gordon was, in any way, influenced by this meeting with one of the most famous savants in Europe. All we know is that, in his extant writings, there is no mention of Diderot. Although there was much that Gordon could respond to in the philosopher's character and spirit of enquiry, there was also a great deal that could have divided them conceptually. Certainly, as we shall see later, Gordon would not have shared Diderot's anti-royalist and egalitarian sentiments. In fact, at the end of his life Gordon scornfully referred to these as 'French principles', principles which, he emphasized, he 'abhored'.

It would seem that Gordon's many talents had been given direction and purpose by his first stay at the Cape. To a vigorous and enquiring young man, garrison duty in the Low Countries could have held little attraction. Africa, on the other hand, had much to offer. It was a world rich in unknown or scarcely known fauna, flora and peoples, about which the learned men of Europe were eager for information, and which Gordon was so well equipped – both mentally and physically – to explore, chart and describe. In addition, service in the Cape was certain to provide Gordon with greater opportunity to further his military career than would remaining in Holland.

Why, then, did he delay three years before returning to the Cape? First of all, there would have been the matter of transferring from the Scots Brigade to the service of the Dutch East India Company. Secondly, Gordon's father, Jacob, may have been ill during this period and the son may have thought it his duty to be with him — a reasonable assumption since we know that the major-general died in February 1776. It is also highly probable that during this period he was courting his future wife. But whatever the reasons for the delay, Gordon received his commission in the service of the Dutch East India Company in the November of 1776.[26] It was further understood that when the commanding officer at the Cape, Lieutenant-Colonel Prehn, retired in 1780, the young captain would assume his duties.

Another reason for Gordon's departure for Africa is hinted at by Professor Allamand in 1778: 'The Dutch East India Company have entrusted Gordon with a confidential mission,' he writes, 'which could not be better accomplished than by him. It will not however prevent him from prosecuting his investigations as a naturalist.'[27] Whatever the nature of this mission was, it is not known today. Possibly his knowledge of 'Hottentot' had not gone unnoticed and the directors of the Company felt that Gordon would be able to treat with the tribes in the interior with more ability than someone who did not have this qualification. For certainly this did seem to be part of his duties, if not the main aim of the journeys he was to make. So it was then, at the age of thirty-three, on 1 June 1777, that Gordon landed once more on the shores of the Cape.

It is entirely characteristic of Gordon that he began to 'prosecute his investigations as a naturalist' almost at once. We have drawings of wild animals dated July 1777, indicating that his military duties at the Castle could not have been very onerous. We are also given a fascinating glimpse of Gordon's life and leisure at this period. In this same July, a certain William Hickey — an English traveller on his way to India — called at the Cape. He recounts how Gordon showed 'us everything that was worth seeing'.[28]

This 'very accomplished man', Gordon, proposed that they make up a party to climb Table Mountain — a proposal that was agreed to enthusiastically. Altogether there were nine in the party which, interestingly, included an 'ingenious young man, Mr Paterson, a great botanist'. An early start had apparently been insisted upon by Gordon, for Hickey says that they left their lodgings at four o'clock in the morning — three hours before sunrise.

At first they found their path 'dreadfully steep and rugged' but by eight o'clock they had reached a cave 'forming a spacious apartment and were agreeably surprised at seeing a table spread with tea, coffee, cold ham, fowls, with other articles of food, all of the best kind. With keen appetites we fell to . . . .'

The view was magnificent, the weather 'mild and pleasant'. And then: 'I thought we were suddenly got into enchanted ground, such celestial sounds burst upon our ears. It seemed to come from the air above us.' The music came from two of Gordon's servants playing upon flutes, but the sound had a 'peculiar sweetness and melody' because 'the spot where they had performed . . . . was surrounded by echoes innumerable . . . . It was,' says Hickey, 'the pleasantest breakfast I ever made.'

The going continued to be rough but Gordon urged them on while showing them 'every object deserving attention . . . a variety of beautiful wild flowers and plants'. At the summit another feast was awaiting them 'with large draughts of delicious cool wine'. They next explored the top of the mountain, admiring the view over "Paradise", where grew the only grape from which the proper Constantia was made'. One of the party nearly got bitten by a dangerous snake but they 'put it into a bottle with gin' and 'returned to the tent at two o'clock and sat down to a capital dinner'. They started the descent at half past four, suffering great pain in their legs, and only got back to their lodgings at eleven thirty that night. Hickey says it took him five days to recover!

What is interesting here is that Gordon could mount such an expedition, sparing neither expense nor ingenuity in entertaining his visitors, a bare month after his own arrival in the country. This is the first account of Gordon's hospitality. It would be followed by many more in the coming years.

10. *François le Vaillant's drawing of the much disputed 'Hottentot apron'.*

11. *A 'Hottentot' mother and child. The beadwork worn by the woman is made from ostrich eggshell; her 'brush' could be used as a spoon or a handkerchief.*

CHAPTER TWO

THE SECOND JOURNEY: TO THE 'GREAT RIVER'

(OCTOBER – DECEMBER 1777)

To Swellendam and Beervlei in the company of Paterson; the Sneeuberg; evidence of the 'Bushmen'; hippopotamus on the Zeekoei River; return to Bruintjieshoogte; extensive contact with the Xhosa; across the Great Fish River; journey to the 'Great River'; the river renamed

On 6 October 1777, barely four months after landing at the Cape, Gordon set off into the interior. It is the first of four journeys of which we have a record. Gordon, however, called it his 'second' journey; no doubt regarding his expedition of 1773-4 as his first. Much later he was to refer to six journeys 'in different directions . . . the least of which was about six months'.[1] Unfortunately there is no record of this sixth journey, nor do we know when it took place.

One purpose of this second journey was to try to put an end to the conflict between the colonists and the tribes he referred to as 'Bosjemans', though it can be questioned whether these 'wild people' were true 'Bushmen' or San. It was his aim to see, as he himself says, 'if this savage war cannot be brought to an end'.[2] As Paterson records, he also intended to make contact with the Xhosa chiefs near today's Somerset East and with the tribe then known as the Gonaqua.[3]

Throughout the five months he was away (he returned to Cape Town on 8 March 1778) Gordon was accompanied by his artist, Johannes Schoemaker, who had already travelled much of the same country with Swellengrebel (the son of a former governor) a year earlier. Schoemaker was to accompany Gordon on all of his long journeys into the interior, yet it is a curious fact that Gordon seldom referred to him by name in his journals; when he mentioned him at all it was usually as 'the artist'. Whether this was because he considered him beneath his notice, or because he simply took him for granted, is not clear. However, a quantity of fine drawings did spring from this collaboration, although there is controversy as to which drawings are Gordon's and which are Schoemaker's.

At the outset of the journey Gordon was accompanied by the young Scot, William Paterson, mentioned earlier. He was later to publish an account of his own journeys in southern Africa, some of them made with Gordon, whom he admired greatly.[4] As we shall see, he was a genial companion, if somewhat maladroit.

From time to time Gordon was joined by other travellers or guides – frontier farmers as well as 'Hottentot' and Xhosa individuals. He had one wagon, but it seems he seldom, if ever, travelled in this himself. He and his 'Hottentot' servants ranged the veld on horseback, hunting game, exploring and observing the countryside.

Temperatures were taken daily; the direction of the wind and the state of the weather were noted frequently. Gordon used a barometer to record altitude and a compass to take bearings. The hours travelled and directions were also meticulously recorded. Although these make tedious reading today, they were essential information for guiding other travellers of the period. Altogether Gordon was an assiduous gatherer of facts, many of which he incorporated later into a treatise on meteorology; others were used in the compiling of his 'great map', as well as other lesser ones.

The greater part of this journey was travelled over well-established routes. He did break new ground, however, when he reached the Orange River close to where Bethulie is today. Broadly stated, his journey took him from Cape Town to Swellendam via Cape Hangklip. From Swellendam he went through the Plattekloof to Beervlei and then on to present-day Aberdeen. He then continued north over the Sneeuberg to a point on the Zeekoei River approximately fifteen kilometres west of Colesberg.

Returning by roughly the same route, he then headed for the vicinity of Cookhouse. From there he made various short sallies to meet Xhosa chiefs, going as far east as the Koonap River. His next major objective was the 'Great River' to the north (the Orange) which he reached by travelling up the Great Fish, Tarka and Vlekpoort rivers, and continuing past the site of modern Steynsburg to the confluence of the Orange and the Caledon.

His return journey to the vicinity of Cookhouse followed much the same route as his outward journey. Then, making his way south past the spot where Alicedale stands today, he continued south-east to the mouth of the Bushman's River. From there he turned west, passing the

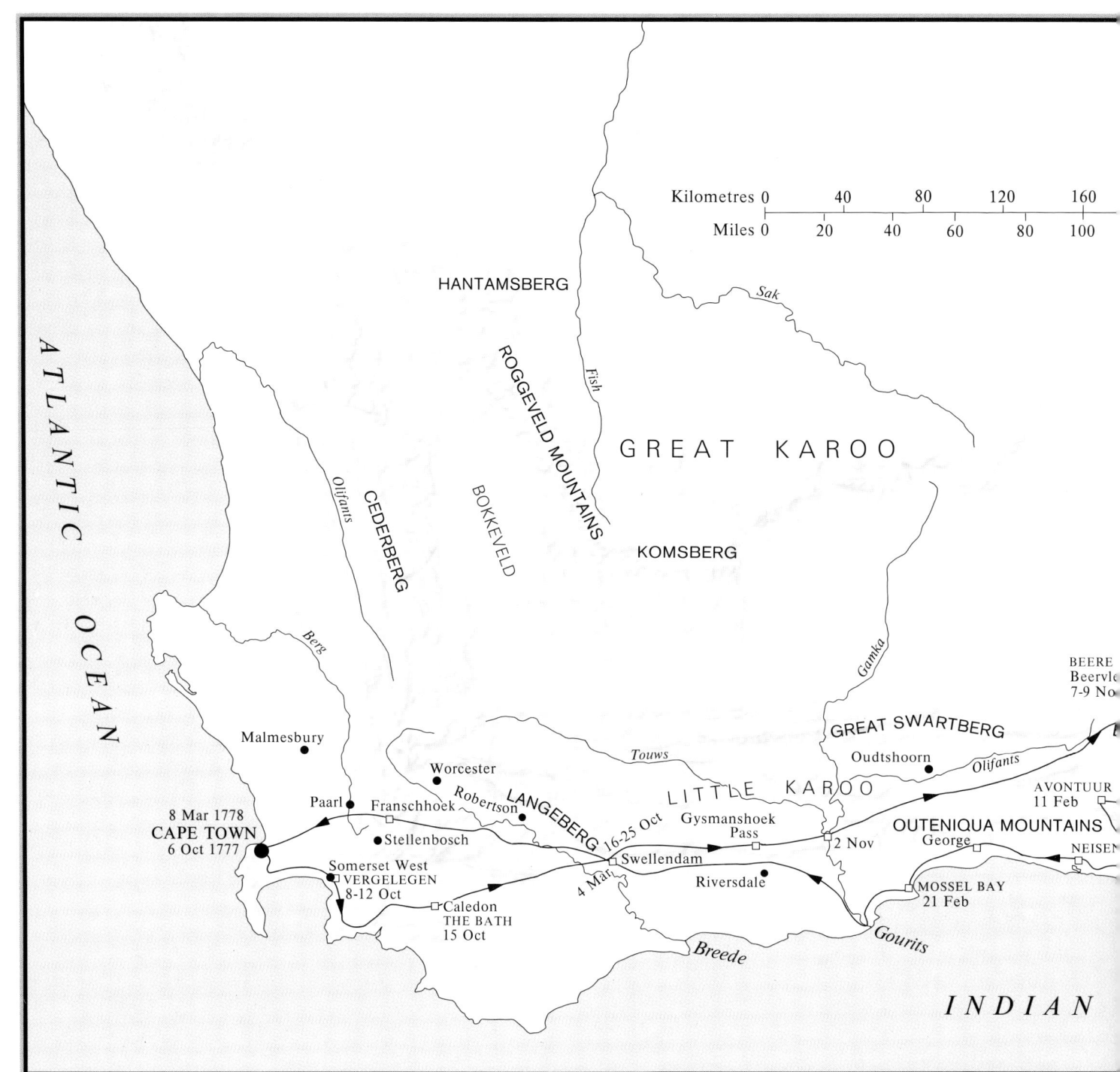

Map 1. *Gordon's second journey: to the eastern frontier and the 'Great River', returning via the east coast.*

environs of present-day Port Elizabeth and travelling through the Langkloof to Avontuur, from where he descended to the coast and Plettenberg Bay. At this point he renewed his westward direction, going past Knysna and Mossel Bay to Swellendam. Then, for some unknown reason, instead of taking the easiest route back to Cape Town, he made a brief excursion to Franschhoek on horseback. Only then did he return home. He had been away just over five months.

Reading the journals – particularly for the first time – one is struck by Gordon's laconic, often clumsy, style of writing. It is formalized rather than formal, as though modelled on a military report where the facts matter and not the expression. The journals contain no rhetorical flights and few personal sentiments or opinions. Nor are there any spasms of disingenuous sensibility such as those that inflate Le Vaillant's prose. Instead, we need to make extensive use of our imagination to paint on the mind's eye what, for example, it must have been like to see the 'Great River' for the first time. Gordon merely tells us 'all of a sudden we came upon the steep bank of a great river'. Thereafter, we are given bare facts: its direction and width, the rate of flow, the type of surrounding vegetation

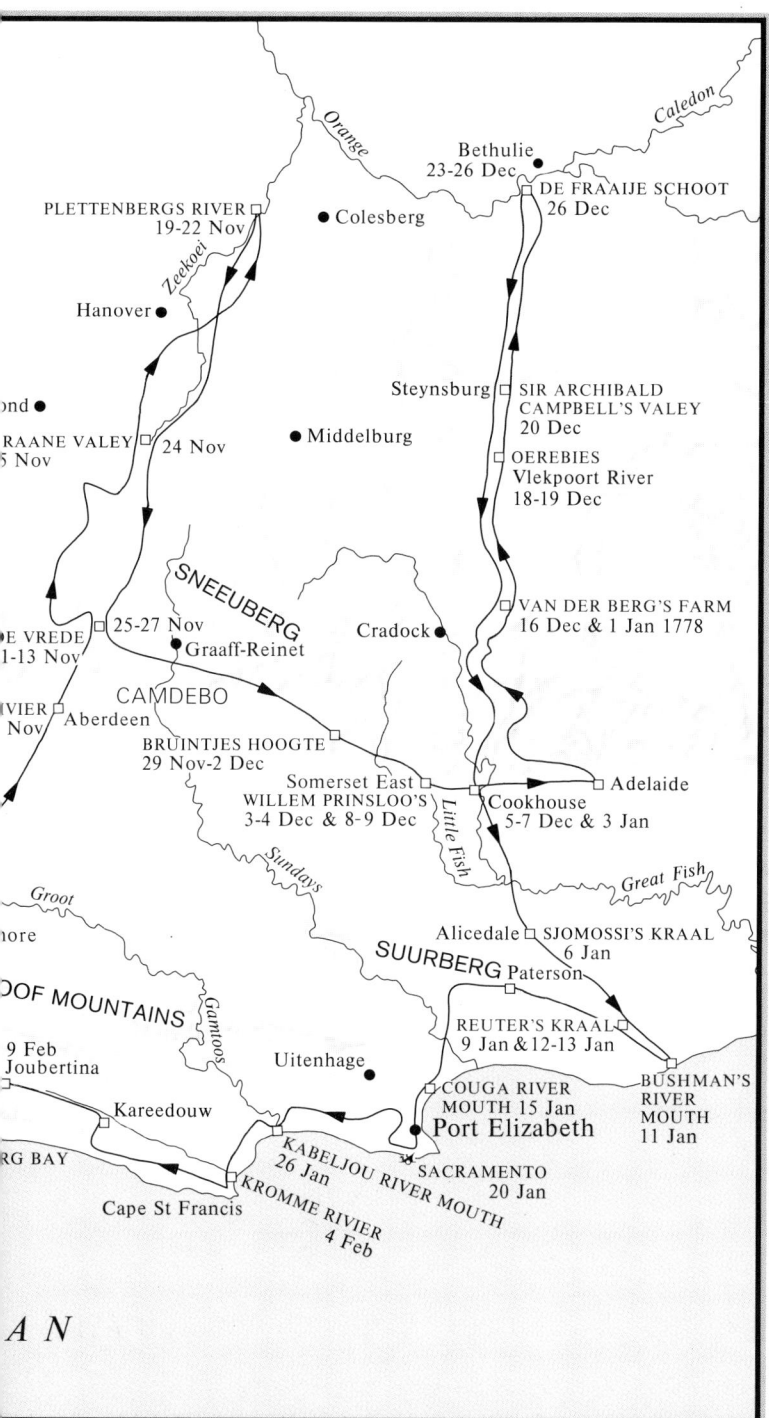

confirms this almost obsessional characteristic as he notes what he regards as a curious phenomenon: 'Yesterday evening about 5 o'clock there was washed up a large quantity of porpoises. They had been injured, most probably in a fight. They were six and seven feet long.' Again, when Gordon and his party reach their evening destination ('the farm of Pieter Eksteen called Bergvliet'), there is no description of the house and its inhabitants, but there is an account of an absurdly trivial 'scientific' experiment: a proposition that 'by putting wood-ash in a kettle of boiling water one cooks eggs without them becoming too hard'. Whether Gordon took this seriously or not is open to doubt. All we have is his possibly sardonic utterance that the 'experiment' proved 'fallacious'. Nevertheless, these two observations demonstrate from the start that Gordon was interested in facts – not sentiments, not speculation, and certainly not trivial gossip about the people he travelled with or met on his journey.[6]

They next made their way to the farm Vergelegen, which is close to the present-day town of Somerset West, but instead of taking the more direct route inland they followed the seashore. It is virtually certain that Gordon chose this way in order to assess whether a seaborne invasion of the Colony from the False Bay side of the Peninsula was feasible. Hence, when he remarks that 'it is impossible to land troops here' (meaning somewhere near present-day Swartklip), it is not idle speculation. Further observations along these lines were later made at Mossel Bay and at Knysna.

What is already emerging from the journal is Gordon's resolute activity and busyness. The days spent at Vergelegen were occupied in exploring the surrounding countryside, in botanizing and recording what was farmed and produced in the area. Even a tame bontebok which came 'sniffling' about his papers was useful to Gordon and he seized the opportunity to take its measurements. In the course of the journals we shall encounter many more of these measurements, some of which were to find their way, via Professor Allamand, into *Histoire Naturelle*.

Another preoccupation common to all the journals is also beginning to emerge, namely the meticulous recording of such topographical information as the lie of mountain ranges, the source and direction of rivers, as well as details of other geographical facts and features. As stated earlier, this was undoubtedly intended to aid him in his mapping, as were his painstaking descriptions of bays and inlets.

It is interesting to note here that the area he describes on the coast and refers to as De Combuis, is one of the few places that today bears his name – Gordon's Bay. And, as we shall learn, how characteristic it is of Gordon to record that he has 'observed everything accurately'.

On 12 October 1777 the party set out to round Cape Hangklip. It took them three days to the 'Bath at Dirk Gildenhuisen's' – or what is now Caledon. It was an uncomfortable, even dangerous, journey that he recorded as they made their way along the cliffs and through swollen rivers. Paterson seems to have been a remarkably clumsy young man and sustained two falls from his horse,

and soil, and so forth. It is certain there will be no rapturous exclamations from Captain Gordon. Even so, the excitement is there if we are sensitive enough to feel it in the dry soldierly phrases – and if we use our imagination.

The journal opens abruptly:[5] 'Monday 6th October 1777. Departed from the Cape at nine o'clock with Mr Paterson and my artist.' This dry statement sets the tone of the journal from the outset. There is no intimation of mood – whether they are apprehensive or confident, subdued or excited by the prospect of travelling great distances into the interior. Facts and matters of scientific import only are what interest this writer. The very next sentence

12. *A view of Swellendam showing the drostdy (centre right) where Gordon and his party stayed.*

one nearly fatal. Gordon was kind enough to blame the horse, but surely there is a degree of humour displayed in his wry comment that 'Mr Paterson, who was looking elsewhere, rode into a large leucadendron'?

In this day's entry we encounter Gordon's interest in geology for the first time when he states that 'the strata of the rocks, though parallel to each other, stand aslant and even vertical'. This interest was undoubtedly influenced by Buffon's theories on the formation of the earth, which were so lucidly expounded in a section of *Histoire Naturelle*. Elsewhere Gordon even uses Buffon's French terms, inserting them into the Dutch text of his journal.

Having arrived at night at what is now Caledon, they passed the next morning examining the 'Bath'. Gordon's account of the temperature, his careful descriptions of the soil and the taste of the water are characteristically detailed. That is what interested him, who the Bath attendants were did not.

Other details occupied him in Swellendam, where the party stayed with the landdrost, Daniel van Ryneveld. Here Gordon is busy taking a form of census, noting the number and composition of the inhabitants of the district. These notes would be used later in a long letter to his patron, the Greffier Fagel,[7] describing the Colony.

It is evident that he was also there at that specific time to observe the military exercises that took place every year in October. As he says, he 'examined everything', and this information was no doubt transmitted to the governor.

Either at Rietvaley, their next stop, or at a kraal where Paterson says they halted, they observed what Gordon calls 'Hottentot cards'. It is fascinating how, even at this early stage of the journals, Gordon's appreciation of the tribespeople can be sensed. However, being Gordon, the technical aspects of the game are not neglected; the steps are complicated and Gordon painstakingly notes them, as this extract from the passage demonstrates:

They start by singing, first blowing and then droning through their lips thus: 'Vie, brr, ho camei!' which has no meaning other than as an encouragement, so far as I could establish. (Some of them who had seen Hollanders playing cards said it meant the same as 'trumps' meant.) The whole idea of the game is that the challengers must each deceive the other group as to where the sticks are by making many twists of the body and hand. Each holds his hands closely together, then the challenger separates his hands and his opponent must also do likewise. He then shows which hand his stick is in, between one or the other finger . . . . Most of the time they do not play for any prize – buzzing, singing, twisting, jumping . . . .

The whole tone of the passage is one of amused absorption. Gordon had a keen interest in these people who were, as he notes towards the conclusion of this episode, 'sometimes serious, sometimes jolly, all at the same time'.

It is sad that there is not more of this involved comment in the journals. Here and there a sardonic geniality seems

to be lurking — a comic sarcasm which only emerges occasionally in the writing. One often wishes there were more details, further explanation. What, for instance, is to be made of the following episode, which forms one day's entry and is recounted here in its entirety?

22nd October 1777.
Went to Swellendam to buy some drink for our journey and to settle a case about my Hottentot's son with the Landdrost. Returned to Rietvaley in the evening, having settled the case to the great satisfaction of my Hottentot. He displayed much parental love and 'point d'honneur' in this case.

Such passing comments are provocatively inadequate.

Again, who were the friends that Gordon says 'had arrived in Swellendam from Cape Town' and who wrote him a letter, persuading him, it seems, to return to the village to watch further drilling and to join the 'celebrations' in the evening? As no mention of this diversion appears in Paterson's account either, it is unlikely that we shall ever know. The omissions do not distort our view of history but to have known a little more may have enhanced our knowledge of Gordon. They may also have contributed to the interest of his journal. But we must remember that what we are reading is exactly that — a journal. Had Gordon gone on to incorporate these daily notes into a book, these tantalizing fragments would have been either expanded or perhaps dropped entirely.

The party left Rietvaley on 25 October and rode to the farm of Jacob van Reenen. This was the same Van Reenen who was to accompany Paterson to the mouth of the Orange in 1779, there to witness Gordon celebrate the renaming of the Gariep, or 'Great River'.[8]

The next day they came to Grootvadersbos. This was a noted landmark and is described by many of the travellers of this era. Here Gordon records that he examined the extended vaginal labia of a 'Hottentot' woman on this day. As we have seen from the Diderot episode, this 'Hottentot apron' was a matter of intense speculation in the eighteenth century. There is a drawing of some notoriety in certain editions of Le Vaillant's *Travels*, and Sparrman also comments upon this curiosity. But Gordon, as we can see from this short entry dated 25 October, treats the matter with clinical objectivity, both here and in the drawing which can be found in his papers:[9] 'Heavy rain, fresh N.W. wind. Cool weather. Examined a Hottentot woman. Found that the labia of the vagina were long, in two flaps of a triangular shape and two inches long. The opening of the vagina slightly concealed: had no hair whatsoever.'

Passing up the Plattekloof, now Gysmanshoekpas, a fine panorama of Cannaland was drawn. It was sketched from a point somewhat east of the summit. Some idea of the pains taken by Gordon to record places of interest can be deduced when the length of the drawing produced on that day is known: it is 2,4 metres long.[10]

On this occasion Paterson distinguished himself by losing the thermometer, so the whole party had to re-climb the mountain to search for it. Yet there is no note of irritation in Gordon's account — further evidence, one must assume, of his tolerance and of his affection for the young man.

The next few days were hard going as they travelled to the Gouritz River. They had to walk to spare their horses and the wagon overturned for the first time. This Gordon records as a minor mishap, but the crossing of the Gouritz was a perilous undertaking. However, a near disaster lay ahead of them when, after crossing the river, the wagon overturned for the second time. This took place on 2 November 1777:

At about half past nine, in fine starlight, we reached a hill beside a small stream. We intended to travel down the hill to a farmer, Roelof Kamfer, who lives on the other side. In spite of my taking every precaution, since it had become dark, and walking in front of the wagon in order to point out the holes, it nevertheless did pitch over. It fell on to its side and then completely over, landing in the hollow with a crash so that we thought it had all been smashed to powder. I thought that my artist, who against every warning always remained in the wagon, was lost. Reaching the wagon however we at first heard nothing, then after a while, a wretched moaning. When we had pulled him out it seemed that he had broken everything but after examining him and giving him some wine, found that he had only bumped the side of his cheek and had a light bruise on one hand. The man who made this road ought to be punished before more wagons overturn here. We went to the house where we found the owner absent and, after knocking for a long time, were allowed to enter. Spent the night here. This place is called Rietfontein.

Here again we find Schoemaker referred to merely as 'my artist'. He does not receive the respect of a name as does Paterson, and a real irritation can be detected in Gordon's tone, particularly in his reference to the man's 'wretched moaning'. From this account it might be tempting to assume a hint of harshness in Gordon's character, but it is more likely to be the exasperation expressed by someone who does not readily tolerate fools or whiners. As a later incident on this journey indicates, Schoemaker was apt to grumble and lose hope all too easily — hardly the sort of character to appeal to Gordon.

But who was this Johannes Schoemaker, or Schumacher as his name is sometimes spelled? And why did Gordon refer to him in such a seemingly disparaging way? Information is scant but we know that he was born in Germany and came to the Cape in 1770 as a soldier in the company under the command of Major Hendrik Prehn, who Gordon was to replace as commandant. We know, too, that in 1776 he accompanied Hendrik Swellengrebel, the son of the governor, on a journey to the Eastern Cape, on which occasion, according to Professor Forbes, he was merely listed as 'een tekenaar (an artist), ranked between two wagon-drivers and above the cook'. The writer, A. R. Willcox, states that Schoemaker became Gordon's batman in 1777 ('with the added usefulness of being a competent artist'), and the muster rolls for 1778-81 confirm that he was indeed in Gordon's company at that time.[11]

Bearing in mind, then, the amount of travelling that Gordon intended to do, and the need for every traveller to record pictorially the findings of his explorations, selecting an artist who could double as a batman, or vice versa, would have made sound sense to a man as practical as Gordon. After all, a servant was supposed to be useful, not companionable; and it would seem from his ranking in the Swellengrebel party that in those days it was perfectly normal for a common soldier to be regarded as just that — a useful servant.

Schoemaker accompanied Gordon on all four of the journeys recorded in the journals, but very little more is know about his life except that his official designation from 1782 to 1789 was 'assistant in the armoury' at the Castle. He could also have been the person mentioned by the English traveller, George Thompson, who wrote in July 1823 that he had spent 'nearly seven hours in surveying the [Cango] caverns and in sketching with the aid of an old German draughtsman who resided in the vicinity'.

To return to the incident of the overturned wagon: fortunately the damage was not great and the party could continue on its way to Beervlei.

By 5 November Gordon had reached the mineral springs that lie about four kilometres east of the southern entrance to the Towerwaterpoort. Again he is busy measuring and recording his observations — including the effect of a snake-bite — before passing on his way.

Approaching Beervlei Gordon nearly shot a calf in the dark, believing it to be a lion. (This incident was also noted by Paterson.) It is more than just an amusing traveller's tale and the party was clearly most apprehensive. Gordon, however, does not admit to these fears and is dis-

13. *William Paterson as lieutenant-governor of New South Wales, a post he held from 1794 to 1795.*

missive of his servants' justifiable alarm. There were, in fact, plenty of lions around, as they discovered the next day when they came across a lioness caught in a trap – 'six feet from snout to tail' – and learned of a further four killed the previous month.

On this same evening Gordon tells us that he

saw some Hottentots singing and dancing. The women sang, clapping their hands and one struck upon a pot that had a wet skin stretched across it. Their songs were: the song of the lion, of the wolf, of the eland and so on with other animals, singing the characteristics of each. Each song had a somewhat different melody. I noticed that they all took a turn in it together but it was all very wild and disorderly.

This little vignette is undoubtedly interesting, but it should be noted that Gordon was not wholly enchanted by the festivities. However sympathetic he might have been towards these people, he also found it necessary to record that they lacked order.

At Beervlei Paterson fell ill, complaining of a pain in the chest, and sensibly he decided to return to the Cape. It is evident that the two men had become close friends, for Gordon talks of the young Scot's 'fine character' and the 'great companionship' between them, while Paterson records his regret at leaving his 'good friend'. Presumably they had a lot in common besides a natural liking for one another. Above all, they would have had a shared fascination with the plant life of the Colony as both were keen botanists. This bond of friendship and scientific enquiry would draw them together again in the future.

It is worth noting that in the manuscript version of his narrative Paterson wrote that Gordon thereafter 'proceeded to the Kaffirs'.[12] From this it can be deduced that Gordon had already made plans to meet the Xhosa on this journey, a fact he does not mention himself in his journal.

Despite his regret at losing his companion, Gordon does not cease to record and to measure. A full page is devoted to describing the dead lioness and a 'werewolf'.[13] He also takes time to relate a story about the resident farmer:

This morning Niewenhuisen, who was like an old Jewish patriarch in many ways, wanted to show me how he had got the lion with the trap, having set it to this purpose. When we arrived at it he wanted to walk into it in order to demonstrate how it went off. I asked him if the gun was not loaded? Whereupon he replied 'No'. I asked him once again and he said 'certainly not'. With this he walked into the cord and the shot went off with a powerful report. At first I thought he had been trying to surprise me. I laughed when he laughed, but having heard the whistle of the ball and seeing his astonishment, I saw that the gun had truly been loaded with a ball. Examining him I found that the ball had passed through his hide overcoat a hand's breadth from his thighs. Thus his stupidity nearly cost him his life.

It is a good story with a strong comic element but related flatly here. There are many reports of Gordon's geniality and surely this would have made a good tale to recount to friends back at the Cape. But in the journal it is as though the very act of writing it down had imposed a kind of woodenness to the account.

On 9 November Gordon set off on his travels again and by the next evening he had arrived at Brak River, the site of Aberdeen today. His delight in the plains of this region are manifest, his descriptions full of zest and enjoyment:

At about ten o'clock we reached a widely extended plain, which only a range of low-lying hills separates from the Camdabo. Here we saw the Sneeuw Bergen which surround the Camdabo like a long half-circle. Saw no snow on the chain of mountains and it appeared to me that it was not as high as the Rodesands mountains but the country itself is higher. Here we saw great herds of springbok, but they seemed few in comparison to the widely extended plain. I therefore believe that the story that one can kill them with sticks is a fable, except when one can drive these animals through the passes of these low-lying mountains which lie like round hills here on the plains. They were so wild that we could seldom get them within range of our guns even though we saw a good ten thousand, divided into several herds. We shot only two of these buck. They come to these parts about September, October and November for water, travelling south and always towards the wind. When the country becomes dry they return. They lamb once a year, one lamb, usually in August and September and in April as well. It is delicious game to eat.

Even lions perform a somewhat playful role in the following entry:

Our guide told me that a short time ago he came upon sixteen lions lying asleep in some small bushes on their backs with their legs in the air. He said that when they became aware of him they ran off and lay crouching in the bushes like cats, without moving. He said that generally they are not seen by day. They stay in the hills around the springbok but at night they are very confident and attack everything. To drive them away fire and the crack of an ox-whip are said to be better than a shot. The day before yesterday they were in the kraal at Basson's and killed several sheep.

It was from a small hill near Aberdeen that another magnificent panorama, this time of the Sneeuberg, was sketched on 11 November 1777.[14] The sketch is nearly six metres long. This hill has been identified and today, once again, bears the name of Gordon's Kop, the name it was originally given by a farmer called Basson at the time of Gordon's visit. In addition, the great range of the Sneeuberg facing the hill was called the Reuse Kasteel (Giant's Castle) by Gordon because, he wrote, the cliffs reminded him of the 'Giant's Causeway in Ireland'.[15]

Gordon's scientific curiosity is strongly roused by the geology of this range: 'In particular, there are very uniform, horizontal slabs, split perpendicularly like long, square pillars, all composed of the same igneous rock.' On the same day his curiosity is also attracted by a small animal that he calls a ground squirrel. The journal entry concerning this small mammal is here quoted in full to give some idea of Gordon's style and attention to detail in these matters.

Drew a ground squirrel: in Hottentot 'Gradow'.

	feet	inches
From head (snout) to tail	0	9
The tail	0	8

Had the usual black and grey tail. Three inches wide but could distend it as it ran, swinging it up and down. It also covers itself with it like a squirrel. The hair is hard and bristly. Cannot climb trees. Has four claws or fingers on the forefeet and a very short little thumb but without a nail. It holds things with it to eat but due to its short, blunt thumb must use the other forepaw to hold them. Can bend its tail over its back like a squirrel but the natural position is flat on the ground behind it. Its ears are just holes and do not stick out. It has five large fingers on the rear paw which has a heel like the dune-mole. Colour red-brown, has a yellowish-white horizontal stripe from the fore to the rear paw on each side. This is a sixth of an inch wide and under it is a dark reddish-brown stripe. Large black eyes on which there is a small white circle. White around and under the snout. Very large testicles. A split upper lip. Two incisors above and two below. The lower one a little longer and slightly apart. This animal becomes very tame. The head flattish. The eyes closer to the earholes than to the snout.[16]

Gordon arrived on the farm De Vrede, which is about twenty kilometres west of Graaff-Reinet, on the evening of 11 November. It was from here on the next day that he prepared his party for a journey, as he puts it, 'into the country of the Wild Bushmen. I intend to see what can be done to make peace with them and to see whether I can get any of them to hold talks with me.' This is the first specific statement we have of Gordon's mission.

From the opening entry for 13 November it is clear that Gordon is still preoccupied with his mission and with understanding the name and nature of the indigenous inhabitants. It is of particular interest that he gives these people their true name, as he understands it.

Departed northwards at ten o'clock on horseback and with an oxwagon, climbing the so-called Sneeuw Bergen, in Hottentot 'Noa Gore'. They could not say what it meant. This is the true land of the Hottentots who call themselves Oesjswana or also Saana, but called Bushmen or Chinese by us. Passed a round hill of stones half an hour from De Beer on the road.[17] It had a diameter of 20 feet and is the grave of one of the chiefs of the Camdabo Hottentots (called the Korana People). He was killed here by an elephant. There are none of these people here any more, except a few with the farmers.

In many ways this is a remarkable passage, which can yield significant clues to Gordon's cast of mind. We must understand that, in principle, he is trying to ascertain the original or 'true' name of the places he visits. In the first sentence he tells us that these mountains are the '*so-called* Sneeuw Bergen'. It is the Dutch colonists who have given them this name: that is why they are 'so-called'. In fact, they already have a name, the 'Hottentot' one: 'Noa Gore'. The implication of that 'so-called' is subtle but nevertheless clear: it is an alien name. The fact that 'They could not say what it meant' also has its ironies. Already, under the incursion of the colonists, names are losing their meaning as the people who would have understood the words have now disappeared. These are presumably the Korana people referred to in the concluding sentence. Tellingly, the 'few' that remain are 'with the farmers'. This can only mean that they are now servants of the colonists.

And what of the larger grouping known as the 'Oesjswana or also Saana'? Here again, Gordon is trying to ascertain their real name in their 'true land'. Given the confusion of the terms 'Hottentot' and 'Bushmen' both by Gordon and his contemporaries – a confusion that has lasted up to the present day – one can only applaud his desire to give the genuine, original name of these people. Their name for themselves is 'Oesjswana' or 'Saana', the latter term being spelt San today. But, having established that, Gordon adds that they are 'called Bushmen or Chinese by us'. In fact these colonist-imposed words are derogatory or absurd, or both. The appellation 'Bushman' needs no further comment here, but it should be noted that because the original inhabitants of this part of the country had 'slanted' eyes and high cheekbones they were also called Chinese – a manifestly absurd appellation that is also derogatory because it is wilfully inaccurate.[18]

It is not suggested that Gordon was consciously taking an 'anti-colonial' stance in this passage, though there were many men of the Age of Enlightenment in Europe who did vehemently take this position – witness Diderot for one. No, Gordon was, after all, firmly embedded in the 'establishment' of the Colony – an officer in its forces and soon to be their commander. Nevertheless, Gordon was also an enquiring man of science in the best ideals of that same Enlightenment. In this aspect of his personality he wants the facts – the truth. Ironically here, these facts undermine the legitimacy of the colonizers' names. By finding and recording the original names and by calling into doubt the labels imposed by colonialism, Gordon does, albeit unconsciously, help us to see the facts – the truth – more clearly.

Leaving De Vrede on 13 November the party arrived the same evening at the farm of a certain Carel van der Merwe. This man held the semi-official post of veld-wagtmeester, a civil position roughly equivalent to the rank of sergeant-major. Gordon consulted with him concerning the state of the frontier and the ensuing record of this conversation now comprises one of the most moving passages in the journal.

Found everything at peace here with regard to the Bushmen. I was told however that further east they had stolen sheep from a certain Villier and had killed the herdsman. These so-called Bushmen or Chinese have a famous chief called Ḱoeriḱei, or 'bullet-escaper'. Veld-Wagtmeester Van der Merwe told me that, after an action which he had commanded, this Ḱoeriḱei, standing on a cliff out of range, shouted out to him: 'What are you doing on my land? You have taken all the places where the eland and other game live. Why did you not stay where the sun goes down, where you first came from?' Van der Merwe asked why he did not live in peace as before, and why he did not go hunting with them and live with them (He had been living with the farmers) and whether he did not have enough country as it was? He replied that he did not want to lose the country of his birth and that he would kill their herdsmen, and that he would chase them all away. As he went off he added that it would be seen who would win.

Once more, one cannot expect that Gordon will show his emotions or partiality outright, but what is interesting is that he spontaneously puts the chieftain's words into direct speech, a mode of writing that Gordon rarely employs. The effect is to emphasize and dramatize the man's statement. In this way, unconsciously perhaps, the pathos of the situation is brought out. Though there is no overt expression of sympathy with the chieftain, or the plight of his people, there is also no condemnation of his defiance. From the words on the page it is not possible to gauge Gordon's true feelings about the incident. Ḱoeriḱei's speech, however, is so eloquent and deeply felt that it is fair to believe Gordon had a real measure of sympathy for this simple 'Bushman' who could so defy the encroaching farmers; a man who, after all, 'did not want to lose the country of his birth'.

Shortly after this incident Gordon records that he had seen another 'Hottentot apron' on the 12th, presumably while he was at De Vrede. It is clear that neither he nor the woman had any false modesty about the examination he conducted:[19]

On 12th examined a Hottentot woman. Found that it was formed approximately like the others but that the two labia hanging down were each three inches long. The skin was very elastic and hanging loose. They were each an inch wide and a quarter of an inch thick. However I was able by pulling to extend the width to an inch and a half without losing any of its length. It appeared like two wings.

The party continued its northward trek and arrived at a farm called Kraane Valey, which has been tentatively identified by Professor Forbes as lying eight kilometres south of The Willows. Gordon spent a few days here, clearly very interested in the remnants of the San or 'Bushmen' people. Once again he cites the farmers' name for them. They are the 'Oeswana Hottentot People or Chinese . . . . They speak Hottentot, but their dialect as well as many words, though pronounced with clicks, differs from the others, so that they do not understand each other much.'

Gordon examined the abandoned kraals of the 'Bushmen' as well as their rock paintings, which clearly did

14. *The black wildebeest or gnu.*

not impress him. As he recounts, he 'made a drawing' of some of the paintings. It depicts an elephant, an ostrich and men with prominent penises. Here is his description of the paintings:

Here for the first time I saw their drawings on the rocks. Some of them were fair but as a whole they were poor and exaggerated. They had drawn different animals, mostly in black or red and yellow; some people too. I can easily understand why it is said that they have drawn unknown animals because one had to make many guesses as to what they were. Made a drawing of the best, where the cave lay deep in baboon droppings and left for our wagons.

It is interesting to note at this point how the party has grown. It consists of twenty-five people: thirteen 'Hottentots', ten farmers, Gordon and Schoemaker. The narrative too assumes an exuberance now, as though Gordon was relishing life on this frontier. It is particularly noticeable in his descriptions of the animals, birds and flowers, and his delight in the antics of a herd of 'gnus' or wildebeest is clearly apparent: 'It is a pleasure to see these animals running, their white tails standing up in the air, kicking out backwards, as well as bounding entirely off the ground. They had a curious humour: for I saw one of the same chasing a springbok for half an hour.'

Such a prolonged sense of animation is nonetheless rare, his natural reticence usually restricting direct statements of pleasure to observations about the quality of the water or about the weather. For example: 'About noon we arrived at a delicious spring where, very hot and thirsty, we refreshed ourselves', or 'it was again delightful the whole day', or 'it is the finest weather in the world again, without a cloud in the sky'. These are the only overt expressions of his pleasure.

Essentially Gordon's mission on this frontier was to make contact with the 'Wild Bushmen' and he did not cease to watch all the signs and examine all the evidence of their presence in the country, taking note, whenever he could, of their customs and artefacts. In the following passage he describes the brave stand made by these people in a battle with a commando of colonists.[20] One of the farmers, a member of a prominent frontier family, was killed by a poisoned arrow in this engagement.

Seven of us left early on horseback in order to look at the battle field where Van der Walt was killed in June one year. It lay an hour out of our course. The same was a stony hill where they concealed themselves and although the farmers shot many of them dead they were still not able to take the hill. Here the Hottentots had piled up stones everywhere to serve as breastworks. When they hit one of their enemies, they shout: 'Hoi, Ha!' Found their abandoned kraal with about twelve or thirteen huts but nothing was standing except for dry bushes in a half-moon, protected from the south, and open to the east. Over these they hang mats. They lie in a circle round these bushes. There are as many as eight sleeping places in one hut. These are shallow cavities in the ground, eight inches deep in the middle, all close to one another, where they cover themselves over with their skins. Found some badly fired pieces of pots which were carved ornamentally on the outside. Van der Walt was shot at 74 paces. Saw no skeletons and only one grave which was a circular heap of stones.

15. *Gordon's drawing of selected 'Bushman' paintings.*

By 19 November the party had moved on to what is now the Zeekoei River and which Gordon named 'after His Excellency, the Plettenbergs River'. We can presume that they were approximately at the spot where Governor Van Plettenberg was to set his beacon the following year, some twenty kilometres west of present-day Colesberg and only fifty from the Orange.

The descriptions here of the hippopotamus are most lively and the observation of these animals is careful and detailed. Both a cow and a bull were measured and drawn. No less should be expected from this diligent and austere zoologist.

An entry of 20 November casually records that he only had one shirt. A trivial detail perhaps but evidence of how hard Gordon travelled. He was washing this shirt in the river when he heard

loud shouting downstream and not knowing if the wild people were there or whether it was something else, since I heard more than ten consecutive shots, I put my shirt on half-dry and rode towards the sound. When I arrived there was a large hippopotamus, lightly wounded coming out of the river on the other side among the reeds. I rode up the river where it was shallow, and as softly as possible, approached the animal that lay there roaring furiously. After I had observed it a little I got to within four or five paces. It was staring at the hunters who were on the other side of the river. Afterwards I saw that it had been shot many times through the head. It was certainly a wonderfully monstrous animal. I shot it between the eye and the ear and a great stream of blood flowed out. It opened its great muzzle wide and bit on all sides in the reeds, roaring all the time. It kept trying to get to me but having had the true death-shot, it plunged, floundering back into the water. We saw it sinking, dead.

It is not often that Gordon uses such vivid language as 'wonderfully monstrous', but he was clearly excited and impressed by these animals. It is manifest too that he had a true hunter's sympathy with the animals he was pursuing. Seeing a hippopotamus come out of the water he prefers, he says, 'to have the pleasure of seeing it run' to shooting it. Again, when the farmers continue killing eland and buffalo just because they need the skins, he pleads with them to halt the slaughter. To no avail – they probably thought him mad or over-refined. Nevertheless, what other man in that time and place would have even tried to halt the killing or have had that kind of sympathy in the first place?

No contact was made with the 'wild people' at the Zeekoei River, though evidence of their presence was all around the party in the form of hunting lairs, used fishing baskets made of rushes, old kraals and more than a few skulls. As Gordon tells us, they rode backwards and forwards looking for these people, but when they did eventually see one of them they could not catch up with him. The reason for their elusiveness is not difficult to understand. Gordon recounts the story of a notoriously cunning ambush carried out by a commando led by Adriaan van Jaarsveld in 1775:

We saw the skulls of several Hottentots who had been shot by a commando two years ago. They were unable to catch the wild people who crossed the river with stolen cattle, moving on further. The farmers shot some hippopotamus and made as if to return home, travelling back a few hours, whereupon the unhappy creatures came back for the remains of the hippopotamus and about 240 were killed. The farmers say, however, that it was they who first began to shoot at them with arrows.

Once more, there is no explicit sympathy for these people beyond, perhaps, the adjective 'unhappy'. But that one word, given Gordon's unforthcoming style, must be taken as some sort of evidence of his distaste for the massacre. Being Gordon, however, he does not scruple to record that he is taking back one of these skulls for 'Professor Camper', another of his scientific contacts in Europe.[21]

ℐt was on 22 November that the farmers decided to turn back. As Gordon writes:

Could not persuade my travelling companions to go any further. They said they were afraid the Bushmen would make off with their stock at home. For this reason, when we were ready in the afternoon, we departed S.S.W. We had been further out into this region than any commando even and our Hottentots had not seen more than one wild man.

Gordon, of course, had wanted to go on and, had the party agreed, they would have struck the Orange, only fifty kilometres to their north. His frustration must have been intense. Some consolation may have been that a spring and some mountains were named after him by his companions.

The party returned to Kraane Valey where they had previously gathered. By 25 November Gordon had moved back to De Vrede where he spent the next two days. Never

16. *These illustrations of a female (top) and male hippopotamus are taken from* Histoire Naturelle. *Both are based on drawings sent to Professor Allamand by Gordon in 1780.*

Previous page:
17. *Chief Coba and his wives. This is probably the painting that was referred to in Gordon's journal entry for 11 December.*

idle, he went hunting spring hares, worked on the hide of a hippopotamus he was trying to preserve, and all the time took notes and observed.

His next move was to Bruintjieshoogte. Here on the farm of Jacobus Potgieter he recounts meeting the 'committee members'. These were almost certainly the party that accompanied the surveyor, C. H. Leiste. This official had been instructed to inspect the country as far as it was occupied by Europeans and to draw up a map.[22]

Though Gordon does not mention Leiste's name, he does recount a short, droll story about 'the surveyor's son'. The first entry takes place on 30 November 1777:

We fired off many shots in the evening to help the surveyor's son who had got lost. We also sent Hottentots out but they could not trace him . . . . 1st December . . . . A farmer brought the lost youngster back in the morning. He arrived at a Hottentot herdsman's hut in the night. Neither could understand the other, were frightened of each other, together passed a terrible night.

This brief incident is told 'straight', with no further comments. It is therefore impossible to tell whether Gordon found it funny or not. If not, though, why did he write down the story in the first place? We are given no clues. Nothing need prevent us, however, from appreciating the bizarreness of this encounter between the herdsman and the surveyor's son – this mutual culture shock that took place in the wilds of Africa over two centuries ago.

Whatever the opacity of Gordon's style, we can take it that the meeting on this farm had been pre-arranged. He says he received his barometers here, so these must have been brought by the committee members from the Cape. He tested them on 2 December, though no height for Bruintjieshoogte is shown on his map. However, the height of the next place he stayed at is shown on a drawing made at the foot of the Bosberg.[23] This farm belonged to Willem Prinsloo and is the site of present-day Somerset East. Prinsloo was the first settler in the Agter Bruintjieshoogte, arriving there in 1771 without the permission of the governor. Both Sparrman and Swellengrebel had been to this farm before Gordon, and it was Swellengrebel who wrote that he talked to farmers here about the 'Great River' situated to the north-east. So it seems likely that one of Gordon's aims was to discuss this with the farmers of the area. We know that an elephant-hunting expedition had been mounted by a Jochem Prinsloo, together with three sons of Willem Prinsloo, some time before December 1777 (the month of Gordon's visit), and this was in a north-eastward direction towards the Great River. It was here, therefore, that Gordon would have found guides to take him to the Orange.[24]

Before making this journey, however, Gordon made contact with the AmaXhosa. The first meeting took place on Prinsloo's farm, and it was quite clearly a happy and cordial encounter.

Since Gordon's meetings with the Xhosa elicited some of the liveliest prose and most interesting observations, it is worth quoting from them at some length.[25] The first encounter took place on 4 December 1777:

... at sunset found three Caffers who begged us for every possible thing singing and dancing all the while. These were fine, large people with free, merry faces. Their chief is called Godissa.

5th December 1777.
Fine weather with a fresh north wind. Departed E.S.E. and afterwards E. and arrived at the farm of a certain Teunis Botha where we found three Caffer chiefs, Coba, Baberà and Godissa with some of their people. This farm lies an hour from the Great Fish River which has its source on the eastern side of the Rode Bergen, a branch of the Sneeuw Bergen. The Caffers appeared friendly and merry. They taught me several of their words and had a very ready wit. They pronounced my name clearly and appeared to make much of me. The three who went with us from Prinsloo's walked behind my horse for a while. I sang for one of them, called Goroe, a song in High Dutch. He managed to sing each line of the melody almost perfectly. When we had left Teunis Botha's for the Fish river one of them called Diensa pestered me to let him sit on my horse. In the end I gave up and helped him on to the horse. He galloped away briskly ahead of us to the Fish River to where the wagons had gone and left me with about thirty Caffers to tramp after him, and it was very hot. They are the freest, merriest people I have ever seen, and the most fond of begging but not, on the whole, thievish. Their language is liquid with almost no difficult words to pronounce. They speak very swiftly and in a heavy, manly tone, generally with a heavy emphasis on the last but one syllable of the word, usually long-drawn out.

From this first meeting with the Xhosa, specifically here the Gqunukhwebe tribe and their chieftains, one can see that Gordon's attitude is overwhelmingly positive. He responds with fine tact and genial courtesy to what the historian J. B. Peires recently has called 'the aggressive self-confidence of most Xhosas'. The same writer goes on to explain:

They did not envy the Caucasoid features and Christian religion of which the Boers were so proud. They presumed Europeans wore peculiar clothes because they had feeble and sickly bodies. They were surprised at many things white people did, 'but never think the white men are more wise and skilful than themselves, for they suppose they could do all that the white men do if they chose'. Initial respect for guns and horses gave way to a shrewd appreciation of their ineffectiveness in dense bush.[26]

Gordon, however, was an unusual European and was able to come to terms with these people easily and rapidly. He is clearly fascinated by them, and they by him. In these passages one soon perceives how he is not just an onlooker but an active participant. Not only does he closely observe their dancing but joins in the dance himself. He immediately sets about learning their language, and his word lists, made on the spot, form part of this journal. They sing to Gordon and Gordon sings to them. While he walks with the chief, Coba, learning Xhosa, they lean on each other's shoulders. But at the same time every custom is carefully watched and noted. The crops grown are specified and even the forging of assegais is recounted in detail.

Gordon's activity is astonishing as he rides from one kraal to another. His curiosity and delight in these people are reflected in all these entries, day after day, but little is said of the more serious intent of his mission. On 13 December 1777 mention is made in passing of 'a long conference with their chiefs' but that is virtually all. Whatever agreements were made or territorial claims discussed, nothing is recorded here. Nonetheless, these entries make for some of the liveliest writing in the journal, giving us not only a vivid description of the AmaXhosa at this period in their history but also revealing the generous spirit and enquiring mind of this man.

We return to Gordon's account of 5 December. He and his party had reached the Great Fish River, somewhere near present-day Cookhouse.

Sat in the middle of the Caffers with their chiefs, the greatest of whom is Coba. This particular man was about thirty-five years old, stocky and well built, with a truly martial face. He taught me various words and their names which I wrote down. Whereupon I repeated them which astonished them greatly, sticking their fingers into their mouths and laughing heartily. Then one of them came with some others and called out names, of some of their women and girls as well, and when I had written them down he took the paper and made as if he was reading, repeating some of their names by guess-work. At which the others gave a hearty laugh. I made a present of a fat wether to each chief and they also got some tobacco and presents from the committee members; in addition Coba got a grenadier's cap. They slaughtered the sheep by cutting their throats and began a dance which was most strange with its various changing movements. They formed up into a platoon with six or seven in a rank but the foremost ranks faced the next two, or turned right round. Most of them remained on their toes, singing while moving their bodies which they did by balancing heavily on their toes, and shaking their heads with jerks. One of them sang the words and directed the music, the others mostly hummed, strongly exhaling the breath from their chests, then all together, in time, they jumped off the ground. Then the ranks moved a little apart from each other and then together again whistling. Most of the time they kept close to one another, armed, pushing their sticks up and down. Then, when the dance which had been performed by males only had lasted some time, some women and also some men went clapping around the others, producing a sling or large figure of eight as they turned around. Some of them also left the platoon at times and made all kinds of movements, after which they again went back and began to dance with the greatest zeal. It was curious to hear some among them whistling while dancing and singing. They do this through the teeth, very sharply like the cry of a finch and I danced with them which gave them great pleasure. Some of their wives were dancing and singing all the time outside the wings of the platoon and made a pleasant melody with the beat of a contre-danse. When the sweat had broken out on all sides and one had a bleeding nose they broke away and after they had wished us 'Cabé' or 'Good day' went off to their kraal which lies half an hour to the north from here. I remained with the others . . . .

6th December 1777.
Fine weather. Fresh south wind. From morning we again had the Caffers with us. Gave them trinkets once more and for a prize let them throw their assegais at a sheep skin on a pole from 60 paces. This they did very badly: in general their throw reached only that far though some of them threw up to 80 paces. Their chief Coba threw about this distance and fairly close but in many throws none of them hit the skin. Eventually one, Diensa threw well over the measure, hitting the pole. The others missed it even at 30 paces. They also gave a display of how they hunted which consisted in running backwards and forwards, jumping, and throwing assegais. After this they portrayed the animal dead. They started their barbaric song in a round circle around it, all in a deep humming voice which is their usual tone but which is more affected when they sing. They keep to a measure but without much melody. They formed up again for their dance which is called 'Conlocanjati' and pulled me into it once more, holding me under the arms. They started to sing their 'Ombe Mackai' and as on the previous day we finished up the dance briskly. After this I went with them to Godissa's kraal who did not come today because Coba had been given more than him. Coba came with me, on foot, teaching Caffer, leaning on my shoulder now and then and I on his. When we approached the kraals two of his young wives walked behind us. There were thirteen huts in all, which stood here and there, made of wood, reeds and little mats, just like a Hottentot hut, round with low openings. Nevertheless they were so placed in the thorn-trees that each family was close to the other. They had five cattle-kraals close to their huts, made just like those of the Hottentots or farmers with thorn-branches and posts placed in a circle in order to prevent the cattle from getting out. Each family had its own cattle. Saw a Caffer woman playing on an instrument just like those that the Madagascans have, a circular bow made of reed or wood, strung with one string with a calabash on it. She struck the string with a little piece of wood and made some tunes. Since Godissa had not appeared I asked for him. Eventually he did come and I asked for something to drink. They brought me sour, thick milk in a little basket of closely woven rushes. Coba drank first out of a scoop which was woven in the same way, placing the same in the milk and then showed this to me whereupon I drank. It appeared that they had an order of rank because Diensa, whom I made much of, did not dare to serve himself but requested . . . a spoonful [from me], which I gave him. Godissa was enraged and ordered that I be asked why I had summoned him. I ordered that he be told that it was the custom in my land that when one was visited, one then paid a return visit, whereupon he said no more. Since it was already late I left their village for the Fish River. Saw some of their fields which are small dug-over gardens which they plant with pumpkins, maize, tobacco and dagga. Some of their daughters and wives with small boys walked along with us. They took great pleasure in our horses, especially in watching them go fast. (The Caffers use oxen as well for riding and use them even when they

18. *Chief Coba wearing a grenadier's cap – a gift from Gordon.*

are 2 years old.) When we reached the river there were still some Caffer women with us. I gave them a present of some tobacco and then some of the interpreters who were with us chased them off home.

7th December 1777.
Some drizzle, the air misty with a south east wind. Took leave of the Committee members who were travelling towards the sea in order to return once more to the Cape. In order to further continue the journey I had planned, I went to fetch my wagon which I had left five hours from here so as to rest the oxen a little. Went once more through the Caffer village giving Godissa and Coba some tobacco. Godissa is now better contented. Gave Coba two pieces of tobacco for the people in two of his kraals that lie over the river. I had promised to do this yesterday but had forgotten to give them. They were all astonished at this, as well as at my double-barrelled gun and pistols. After I had taken leave of them I rode off. After a slight delay Godissa and Coba again came towards me so that I stopped. Coba and Godissa shouted 'Cabé Gordon, Cabé!' and I grasped that they wanted some more sheep to eat but I showed them that I did not have any more. They said that lions had killed three oxen hereabouts in the night and then both turned back. Shortly afterwards I also saw the foot-print of a large male lion but arrived at Willem Prinsloo's farm in the afternoon without having seen anything.

The next two days (8 and 9 December) were spent at Prinsloo's farm. The following day's entry reads:

10th December 1777.
Travelled back towards the Fish River, somewhat S.W. Almost no wind or cloud, very hot. Again went to visit the Caffers and was received now in a very friendly manner but with begging as always. Went with Chief Godissa and his son Gona to see their crops which are up against the mountain. These are sown in places here and there between the thorn-trees. Their grain was still young and I did not recognize it. Also saw pumpkins, calabashes, watermelons and peas. Asked where they had their tobacco and they said they had not [yet] planted it. A girl looks after the plantings. Arriving at the kraal I saw Chief Coba was still paying a visit to this kraal. He was busy forging assegais with two or three of his people. Their hammer was made of iron and their anvil was a stone. One of his soldiers had a leather bag in each hand and at the front of this was a hollow cattle horn. Both of these were inserted into a pipe made of ants' nest (of clay therefore) which lay in the fire. When he pressed shut the bags, which were open at his hands, the fire burned more strongly from the blowing.

Drank some of their sour milk and we did a brisk dance. After this I left but a whole swarm of Caffers, with the chiefs and some of their wives accompanied me to the Fish River. Here they came and sat around me, smoking but in the end their continual begging was annoying. While we were sitting there a hen-harrier came flying over. I immediately took my musket and shot it. They admired this greatly and especially when I again hit a smaller bird with the other barrel. They were not pleased by the report of the gun. My Hottentots arrived with a beautiful blue crane, which I had shot this afternoon at the Little Fish River. Coba immediately asked for it and when I had given it to him he cut off its wings. These are remarkable because their rear feathers form the long tail of these birds.

He held these to his head and made all sorts of strange caprices and postures, saying that he wanted to use them in war. They returned [home] at sunset. It has been very hot today but towards evening there was a fresh S.W. wind.

The Swede, Mr. Sparrman reached the Fish River here with Potgieter and then went along the Bosjemans River. Returned to Cape Town the same way they had come.[27]

Tried out the barometer at the previous camp on Prinsloo's farm at ten o'clock in the morning. Fine weather, a soft S.W. wind, almost no clouds. Got 27 inches and 5 points.
N.B. If one asks them they say that their gardens belong to their chief, but they all eat from it. They shoot . . . [Incomplete in manuscript.]

11th December 1777.
Cleared up at sunrise. The two chiefs again came to visit me. Gave each of them a dog and a sheep. Had a painting done of myself and gave it to Coba. Had him and his wives painted.[28] Saw him washing his hands with fresh cowdung this morning.

Gordon spent the rest of this day alone on horseback, exploring beyond the Great Fish River in an E.N.E. direction. He was back briefly among the tribe on 12 December and writes:

... passed four Caffer chiefs with their kraals, Coba who was on a hill, Deca somewhat below him, Baberà further on and finally Serambane who was at the stream called Agha Lè. I planned to visit them when I passed back this way and in order not to be pestered too much I carried on riding at a gallop having only Hannes de Beer with me. Saw hosts of Caffer men, women and children. There were also very many head of cattle, the horns of which they fashion in all sorts of different ways, the skin on their head as well. Saw one of them riding a small ox through the countryside. Also saw a skull. They drag their dead into the countryside and cover them with a little grass. Only their chiefs are buried in their huts and this funeral has to be paid [for] in cattle. We saw many huts, cattle kraals and their planted lands. They came running up to us and around us stamping (many dogs too), and screamed out 'Cabé Tabeca!' Their faces were painted white and red. All had assegais in their hands. They quickly made way for us. I gestured to them that I would be coming back. They were happy, whistling and shrieking, as they saw the horses galloping by.

Gordon states that he then rode on 'east by south' to where he could see 'at a distance of three hours to the south, the place where Swellengrebel turned back'.[29] In other words, Gordon was again near Adelaide, on the Koonap River. When he returned in the evening there was a welcoming party: 'We were beset by whole swarms of them. We rode to Coba where we received in a friendly way. He showed me everything in his hut. We let off some shots, threw assegais, danced. They were astonished to the point of being frightened by the shooting yet this is what they requested for chasing off wild animals.'

The last entries regarding the Xhosa, made on this preliminary visit, are dated 13 December 1777:

Three chiefs and a great host of Caffers came to visit me. Made them a present of four sheep. They were very merry and when we had had a long conference with their chiefs I let them see how our sending of letters worked. Sent presents to Gagabe with one of Gagabe's[30] and Cobe's Caffers. The Caffers were utterly delighted.

*I*t was time now for Gordon to mount his expedition to the Orange River, though he does not say so explicitly. 'My intention is to go further north and see what more can be done,' he writes. As has been noted, he had probably discussed his plans at Prinsloo's farm early in December. It is a fair assumption that he also then arranged or contracted with three farmers of the area to act as guides; he gives their names as 'Jan Durand, Hannes de Beer and Hannes Meintjies'. As he tells us, 'we have my wagon, ten oxen, eight horses and eight Hottentots'. Thus, count-

19. *The confluence of the Orange River and the Caledon (Gordon's Wilhelmina's River) from a point south-west of present-day Bethulie. This view forms part of a six-metre-long panorama.*

ing Gordon and Schoemaker, the party consisted of thirteen people.

The expedition set off up the Great Fish River and then turned north-east along the Tarka.[31] On 16 December they passed 'the last farm', which was in the vicinity of present-day Cradock. They were entering 'Bushman' country once again, but none of the fear and hatred felt by the colonists towards these people is evident in Gordon's comments. This time he obviously believed he would make contact with them at an early stage and hoped, by his own conduct and authority, to effect some form of reconciliation. Here is how he discusses the 'Bushmen' and his intentions:

The Hottentots who are on the Sneeuw Bergen and Fish River with the farmers call themselves there nothing but Cora (thus Coranas in the plural). All these Hottentots are called 'Hei Hei Tini' which means 'People who go without a covering in front of their genitals'. Saw some of them with the Caffers and with our farmers but they were all true, so-called Bushmen-Hottentots. Beyond the Caffers there is a kraal whose chief they very much fear. He is called 'Aree', meaning 'Left', because he shoots from the left.

In general they were lean and small. All Bushmen (or Inland-Hottentots) are called 'Chinese' by the farmers and so far as I have been able to observe till now they are all the same people, differing in dialect according to their distance from one another. I have today seen several old Hottentot graves, which I also saw in Cafferland. In addition the rivers in Cafferland, the ones I have heard of, have Hottentot names. Think that the Caffers, as well as ourselves, have been spreading further out, for the Caffers say that they and all their stock come from the direction of the Mtamboenas.... Because these [wild] people are at war with us we are very much on our guard. I shall do all I can to confer with some of them and see if this savage war cannot be brought to an end. About a month ago the man who lives on this last farm was hunting with his half-caste Hottentot and encountered one of these Chinese who was also hunting. The man was wounded on the head by a poisoned arrow and the half-caste in the nose. After great difficulty the Chinese was shot dead.

Indeed, Gordon never underestimates the 'Bushmen'. He continually stresses that the party is on its guard. Again and again he records that the watch is sleepy or asleep and that there are signs of the 'Bushman' presence everywhere. But, despite his unrelenting efforts to meet them, they elude him.

His route continued up what is now the Vlekpoort River (Gordon's Oerebies[32]) and past the Bamboesberg to present-day Steynsberg. It is interesting that he named the place where this valley is now situated 'Sir Archibald Campbell's Valey' and another feature close by 'Lady Campbell's of Ramsay's Valey'. This Sir Archibald Campbell was a British officer on service in India and the only time Gordon could have met him was when he and Lady Campbell touched at the Cape on their return to England in 1789. But this was twelve years later than the ostensible date of entry. However, this puzzle may be solved by entries in the journal dated 20 and 21 December 1777, where Gordon states that he gave each place a fresh name 'later'. There are deletions in the text and the new appellations, together with the comment about later naming, are written above the crossings-out.

The names Gordon chose to call the places he passed have caused some speculation. It has been opined that he chose the names of influential people so that when his book of travels did come out sales would be boosted. This could be so but it cannot be wholly justified, for he also gave places the names of very humble people, people who in all probability could not even read. A case in point would be the three farmers who accompanied him to the Orange. We have H. Meintjies Fontein, H. de Beer's Vlakte and A Durand's Fontein. In addition, many of the names sprang naturally from incidents that occurred on the journey. The same farmer Durand, for example, named a place 'Schepmoedpoort' (roughly: 'Takeheart Pass') after they had just negotiated a difficult ascent. And when Gordon hit a crow on the wing on the banks of the Orange he called the spot 'De Fraaije Schoot' or 'Fine Shot'.

Again, Gordon was, I believe, merely demonstrating a worthy sense of duty when he called a spring after his mentor, Hendrik Fagel, to whom he also wrote many detailed letters discussing his travels and ideas about the Colony. Professor Allamand is also remembered. He was certainly an eminent man but he was also a respected and cherished friend, as we have seen. Nor is Buffon forgotten. On 22 December Gordon wrote: '. . . after a distance of three hours going steeply downhill over grassy countryside we arrived at a small river with pools of standing water. I called this Buffon's river after the great Buffon.' According to Professor Forbes this can be identified as a small stream called the Broekspruit today.

*L*eaving the Steynsburg Valley they continued north. They caught sight of 'Bushman' hunters but once more they could not make contact. They examined their hunting traps and even heard them singing at night but the wily people were always elusive. Eventually, on 23 December 1777, Gordon and his party struck the Orange:

Four of us rode ahead to look for water and saw some fires in front of us. The countryside, falling steeply away, promised nothing. Then in the flat stretch which was about five hours further on we saw some green shrubs half an hour away, past the edge of the mountain. These we found to be thorn-trees and all of a sudden we came upon the steep bank of a great river. It flowed from the east, a good hour to the west, through a gateway in these mountains. At its narrowest here it is about 225 paces wide as we saw from the flight of a bullet. In addition it flowed as strongly as the Meuse at Maastricht. The southern bank was about 40 feet high and steep, though it was possible to get to the water. There was reed growing in the direction of the gateway in places and there were high thorn-trees. The northern bank was lower, with reed and many willow and some thorn-trees. This bank had stony ridges and coarse, shining sand but the soil in the river itself was clayey and vegetal. There were reefs here and there stretching mostly from one bank to the other over which the stream rustled loudly. We called this river the Orange River; it is the same, we believe, that flows out at the Namacquas, the Garie or Great River. Since the sun was setting we rode rapidly back looking for the wagon and found the same at the tip of the mountain which I called Robertsons Macleods Bergen, after a friend. The gateway through which the river runs is in the same mountain. We found a good spring here which I also called Robertsons Fontein after a friend. Here we made camp ten or eleven hours N. by W. of Yorks Fontein.[33] We have seen many gnus and springbok today. Most beautiful weather but hot during the day with a cool S.E. breeze. There was an abandoned camp of the wild people at Rietbokke Fontein.'[34]

As has been previously noted, there are no cries of jubilation recorded as Gordon and his companions reach the 'Great River'. There is no break in the narrative, but Gordon does immediately compare the flow of the river to the 'Meuse at Maastricht', thus relating this discovery to his own past, to Europe and to what was, for him, the familiar and commonplace. And the facts and observations continue to pour out in a way that is almost obsessive: the rocks, the trees, the nature of the soil, even the 'reefs' in the river, all get their due attention. It must have been a moment of great triumph, yet there is nothing of this in Gordon's pragmatic recital, his compulsive litany of facts. There are times when one is unable to decide whether to praise the man's objectivity or deplore his apparent indifference.

The place they had reached was the great bend that the Orange makes south-west of Bethulie. It is significant too that Gordon named the mountains here the 'Robertson Strowan Bergen' on his map. (In the text he says he called a mountain 'Robertson Macleods' and a nearby spring 'Robertsons' but these appear to be referring to the same person.) It is significant because the name Robertson Strowan refers directly to his service in the Scots Brigade. This family had a long and honourable connection with the regiment, and Gordon stresses rather clumsily, twice, that he named these features 'after a friend'. There is no doubt that this friend is the same Alex Robertson of Strowan who became the godfather of Gordon's son Alexander when he was baptized in April 1786. It is therefore clear that this name was added later, as was the case with the Campbells, mentioned earlier. But the only record we have of this man is his name in a baptismal register.

There is something touching in the prominence given to this unknown friend. Not only is Gordon's strong attachment to an individual shown, but by implication, his erstwhile regiment is also honoured. Nevertheless, who exactly Alex Robertson was and what he was doing at the Cape at that time is a complete mystery – another Gordon mystery.

Gordon's fealty to the House of Orange is, of course, borne out by his naming of the river. His dedication is further emphasized in the names he gave other topographical features. On the map there is a 'Prins Willem's de V Berg' and 'Rivier', as well as a 'Princes Wilhelmina's Riv'. Today one can be grateful that the 'Great River' still bears the name Gordon gave it, considering how many of the names that he bestowed on this country have now disappeared. At least here clear evidence has survived of the unquestioning loyalty with which he served this dynasty.

20. *What appears to be a Cape wagtail perches on a branch of* Acacia karroo.

CHAPTER THREE

THE SECOND JOURNEY: THE EAST COAST EXPLORED

(DECEMBER 1777 – MARCH 1778)

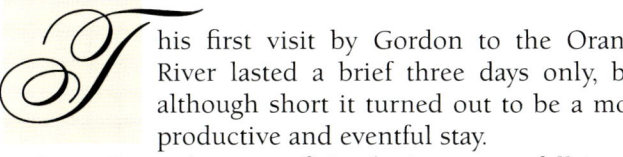

Three days at the Orange River; escape from a hippopotamus trap; the return journey begins; more evidence of the 'Bushmen'; the mouth of the Great Fish River; fresh contact with the Xhosa; the Histoire Naturelle hippopotamus anatomized; home via the Southern Cape coast

This first visit by Gordon to the Orange River lasted a brief three days only, but although short it turned out to be a most productive and eventful stay.

On 24 December one of Gordon's servants fell into a game trap laid by the 'wild people' along a hippopotamus path beside the river. Shortly afterwards the same thing happened to Gordon himself. This dramatic and frightening incident is quoted below within the fuller context of the day's journal entry in order to illustrate how Gordon's style of recording events tends to reduce the impact of such occurrences. Gordon has just shot a hippopotamus. The entry continues:

A remarkable thing is that these animals lie still in the strongest current where it is deep, apparently without floating [away] but they have their feet on a stone under the water. Stayed on this bank under the thorn-trees, lying and watching the animals for some time.

Everything here enchants with the beauty of this river and foliage. (One is accustomed to having torrents and brooks called rivers in this country.) Rode alone beside the river to the wagon. I had shot with my gun and wanted to clean it. I therefore gave it to the artist. After riding on for a while I saw some terra natal fowl (which is a guinea fowl in all respects) and several other beautiful birds and wanted to ride to a reef that showed a half-moon where the water foamed up against it, stretching from one bank to the other. I wanted to see if I could cross this river on horseback and spent some time looking at it. Eventually found this impossible to do on horseback. I then decided to ride away from the river and following a hippopotamus path through some reed on a hillock, fell unexpectedly into a pit which the wild people had made for a hippopotamus, my horse going with me. While falling, I pulled at the horse's bridle violently so that most of the underside of its body fell below. Dust and stones fell on me from all sides so that in order not to smother I struck up with both hands and made an opening. I gripped the horse, which started kicking and rearing violently, by both ears, closing them tightly, because I had heard that this was the right thing. The poor animal stood still, sweating in its deadly fear and suffocating in the pit. Being unhurt and completely in control of myself, I saw that the pit was eight feet high above me and that I had to make an attempt quickly because breathing had become very difficult. I therefore jumped as high as I could and fortunately remained hanging with my shoulders and feet in the hole above the horse that had started to thrash violently. I now gathered all my strength and worked myself upwards, with three or four thrusts like a chimney sweep. With one hand I snatched at one of the remaining sticks which was at the edge of the hole and where it was still firm enough to hold me and thus with every good fortune got free of the danger. I talked to my poor horse and the creature was calm once again. I then ran as fast as I could to the wagon and fetched people with a spade in order to save the creature but when we arrived at the hole we found that the animal had died of suffocation; the sweat stood like water on its body. It would also have taken us more than half a day to dig it out. Since the pit was about 16 feet deep, it appeared incomprehensible to my travelling companions and to me how I had got out of the hole without help. We let a Hottentot down into the hole to get the saddle and bridle out but it was so suffocating in there that he was unable to endure it until the saddle was loose. Eventually we did get the saddle and bridle out and nothing was broken. My pistols which were under the horse were also not damaged but the one had cocked itself . . . .

Went swimming in the river which was deep and uneven with stony ledges and holes. Found I could hardly progress against the current. Did not dare to risk going far for fear of hippopotamus which are very dangerous in the water. This animal should be called neither seacow nor hippopotamus but river-cow or -bull. It was very warm today, the most beautiful weather with a fresh S.E. wind, blowing like the S.E. trade wind. Lightning at nightfall far to the north and across to the south east. No dew.

It is characteristic of Gordon that, once out of the pit, his first concern is for his horse. It is in details like this that we can 'read' Gordon's concerned but unsentimental compassion. He had acted, we can well appreciate, with great presence of mind – 'completely in control of myself', he says – but that is the only comment he gives about his own feelings. He must have drawn on deep reserves of energy and strength to have extricated himself so fast. No wonder his companions were astonished.

We in our turn, however, may be astonished at how Gordon continues his entry by telling us that he next went swimming in the hippopotamus-infested river. As he comes to the end of this day he finds time to give his considered opinion on hippopotamus nomenclature. The concluding words end off with observations that are typical of his 'scientific' preoccupation with the weather. There is no further mention of the fall into the pit. It appears that, for Gordon, it was an incident like any other – to be recorded but not dwelt upon or made extraordinary.

Christmas Day comes and Gordon is still as active as ever. The day is not marked in any way and no allusion is made to its significance. Even accepting the fact that Christmas was not treated with the same hysteria in the eighteenth as it is in the twentieth century, it is interesting that overall in Gordon's writings there is scant attention paid to any religion, let alone to the reformed Protestant faith of his fathers.

On the following day he goes diving in the river for stones, which he says 'resembled jasper and agate'. He has to desist because 'While I was busy swimming and collecting stones, my Hottentot saw a river-cow (hippopotamus) on the opposite bank. With the result that we speedily retired. As we have not seen any at this place, I supposed that it had come to look for us.' After this mildly humourous comment and some more finely observed details about these animals, Gordon announces that he is turning back and, at the same time, commemorates the exact point of departure with a spectacular display of marksmanship:

Because there were no more observations to be made here and because we were unable to cross the river, we departed after midday on our journey back. As I was mounting my horse a bird of prey, here called a *witte kraai* [white crow] came flying above us and being asked to shoot it, my ball hit it right on the head, smashing it. They then called this place *De Fraaije Schoot* [The Fine Shot].

When Gordon and his party had reached the Orange on 23 December 1777 a rough sketch had been made at the place where they had had their first sight of it (a point on the south bank opposite present-day Bethulie). Almost certainly this sketch was the origin of a panorama which was worked up later into an impressive 'view' nearly six metres long, the largest of Gordon's panoramas. In fact, two very similar copies of the scene survive, one of which is dated 4 May 1778 in what appears to be Gordon's hand. According to Professor Forbes, 'the position occupied by the artist was on a rock-strewn knoll within 100 yds of the river and some 300 yds east of the homestead of the farm Eerste Stap'.

In an inscription below the drawing, Gordon repeats much of the information contained in the journal, quoted earlier, such as his belief that this is the same river that runs into the sea on the Namaqualand coast.

Turning once more to the journal, it would be reasonable to expect that a proposed work of such magnitude as the panorama would have elicited some specific comment from Gordon. Typically, however, the only hint we have of his intention to produce it is a laconic aside in his entry for 24 December. In it he merely mentions that he climbed a mountain with De Beer and 'the artist'.

At this stage it might be fruitful to look a little closer at the question of who actually made the drawings in the Gordon Atlas. This is a puzzle that has been the subject of conjecture for some time. Was the artist in the field Gordon or Schoemaker?

The only real evidence we have is that given by Mrs Gordon, whose words on the subject were quoted in the letter from Philip Gidley King to Sir Joseph Banks on 27 May 1797 (see page 11). The passage reads:

The second box contains a very full and large Book, in which are arranged upwards of 400 drawings of Natural History, appropriate to the Charts and Views. The Charts and Natural History Mrs Gordon informs me were all designed by her own husband, who drew every outline, and had them finished under his own eye.

This statement would seem to apply only to the charts, maps, zoological and botanical drawings and to exclude the 'Views' – presumably landscapes – from Gordon's intervention but there is no doubt that he was intimately concerned with the execution of the particular panorama discussed here. As has been noted, there is a long inscription below the drawing in Gordon's hand. It is therefore probable that, in this case too, he first 'outlined' and then 'finished' the sketch mentioned earlier and then went through the same process back in Cape Town when the panorama was drawn. It is highly unlikely that the six-metre-long panorama itself was made in the field. Indeed, it is possible, even probable, that other hands besides those of Gordon and Schoemaker were also involved in the panorama, though it is a safe assumption that all this work was done under the supervision of Gordon himself.[1]

Impressive though Gordon's pictorial records are it is important not to lose sight of his remarkable technical skill in the use of scientific instruments, a pertinent example of which is the barometer reading that he took just before his departure from the Orange. It was transferred to his map as 4 125 feet – precisely the height shown on a recently published map of the area. (Because his barometer was a Ramsden, Gordon always recorded the height in English feet.[2])

Travelling a little more to the west than on their previous course to the Orange, the party made its way back to the Greffier Fagel Fontein. Again, traces of the 'Bushmen' were seen but no contact could be made. The weather was fine and it would not be too fanciful to surmise that Gordon and his party were in a fairly exuberant mood. Light-heartedly, a spring was named after Gordon's green hat 'owing to its round, green formation'. A connection with the Scots Brigade is again made when Gordon calls another nearby fountain 'Graaf Benting's Fontein'. This Count Bentinck — as it is usually spelled — was almost certainly the colonel of that name, one of the few non-Scots who commanded a regiment of the Brigade during Gordon's service.

Though Gordon was not able to talk directly to any of the 'wild people', there are two descriptions of their abandoned camps which should be noted. On 27 December he wrote: 'Waited for the wagon by a stony hill where we saw many sleeping places of the Wild People. Called it "Het Wilde Casteel" [The Castle of the Wild People]. On the rocks there were some of the afore-mentioned Wild People paintings all of the same mettle.' And then, further south, on 28 December he has a fuller description:

Here we again found a sleeping-place of the wild people, but for five or six couples only. Their sleeping-places are like those of an animal: a pit three feet in diameter, seven inches deep in the middle, rising towards the sides. There was some reed in them and they each contained two people, one presumes a man and his wife. There were stones on which they had rubbed their paints and on which they had smashed bones to eat the marrow and there were also burnt reeds from their fire, since there is no wood here. Where there is wood there are three or four branched sticks on which they hang their provisions. When they move house, which they do daily, they take [the] mats with them, using them to cover the one side of their huts. Found some pieces of these here and there.

He arrived back at Van den Berg's farm on New Year's Eve.

Gordon writes that he is not apprehensive about a 'Bushman' attack because 'they are much too frightened'. But frightened or not, he had not succeeded in meeting and conferring with them and this meant that he had failed in one of the main stated aims of his mission to the north. It is difficult, however, to believe that his intervention could have brought peace to this frontier. The foes of the 'Bushmen' were too intractable. The colonists from the west and the black tribes from the east both wanted more grazing. The 'Bushmen', at once hated, feared and despised by both groups, were in the way. Where they had hunted for millennia, cattle would graze and houses be built. They were doomed and there was very little that Gordon could have done to have brought peace or to have saved them from extinction in this area.

Nonetheless, Gordon's expedition to the Orange was a triumph. It was an accomplishment that would only be surpassed by his journey to the mouth of the same river in 1780. It is probable that other white men (colonists) had been that far north in this region before him, but he was certainly the first man to record his visit, describing

Map 2. *The expanding frontiers of white colonists at the time of Gordon's second journey.*

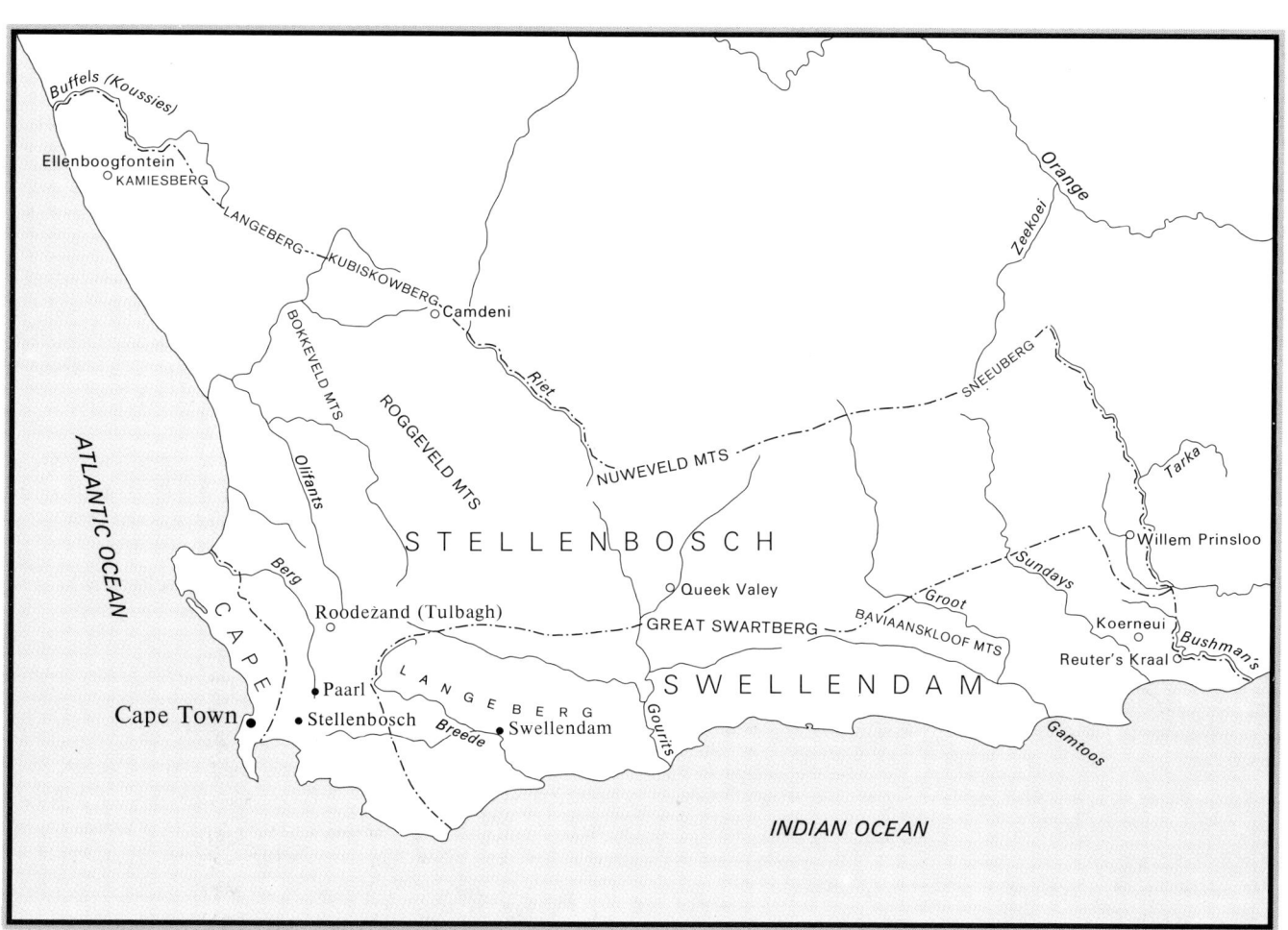

the region both in writing and by drawings. It was also incorporated into his 'great map'.³

The next stage of the journey was to take Gordon from the vicinity of today's town of Cradock to the mouth of the Bushman's River. By New Year's Day he had reached the banks of the Tarka River. His party had grown smaller, he explains (perhaps with a faint suggestion of relief): 'Treated the Hottentots to tobacco, a glassful and a full belly of mutton, and here we celebrated our New Year. The four Hottentots who were with my travelling companions had stayed behind, so that I was now alone with my own people.'

By 3 January he was once again at the farm of Jacob Erasmus, close to where Cookhouse stands today. Even here, in country already settled by the Xhosa and by some white farmers, the 'wild people' are active — lions too, it seems:

Passing Godissa's village on foot, at sunset, I met four Caffer women who asked me for tobacco, but not having any to give them they went off to their village. There are some lions around here; they again killed two head of cattle eight days ago. Three large males have been seen. Nevertheless I continued on my way without a gun, having only my pistols. I saw and heard nothing and arrived at the Fish River in the dark. Heard here that the Bushmen had murdered two herdsmen and taken about two hundred cattle. They are most careless about cattle here. The herdsmen fall asleep and I have come across many herds in this state. Then the wild men, who have seen what is happening from the mountains, come and murder them, never openly using violence.

Continuing south, Gordon comments wryly on one of the frontier farmers: 'Though he has many cattle, I have seen Hottentot huts better than his.' However, this remark should, perhaps, be seen in context. The whole area was in a state of flux and was to remain unstable well into the next century. There could be little motivation to build permanent structures while there was a possibility of open conflict with the Xhosa.

The confluence of the Great and Little Fish rivers was reached on 6 January and the next day Gordon arrived at the kraal of a petty chieftain called Sjomossi — somewhere near present-day Alicedale, according to Professor Forbes.⁴ On this day Gordon refers to the fact that Swellengrebel had also been there. Indeed it is remarkable how closely Gordon followed Swellengrebel's route of 1776. The journal entry reads:

I came upon Sjomossi's great Caffer kraal. This is the same as the one Mr. Swellengrebel was at, on the other side of the Coenap, where they were living at the time. He is the brother of Coba and thus Mahoti's son. He was sitting with some Caffers under a thorn-tree and after the usual 'Cabé' I gave him a piece of tobacco and some beads. I asked for some milk and he had this fetched and first even held the basket, not drinking first like the other Caffers, but last. He pointed out his wife and children and when I asked him why he had only one wife he said that this was enough for him. In a short while there was a great host of Caffers around me, some of them painted a red and yellowish colour. From my knapsack I gave each one of these a pipeful of tobacco until I had no more and they were well satisfied with this. After staying here for some time, it being very hot, I took my leave. When they say 'Cabé' they usually stick their right hand straight out. I rode back followed by a whole band of them. In among the thorn-trees in the valley to the east there were Caffer huts as far as I could see and large herds of cattle. None of them had bread, which they call 'Manassi'; they also had no 'Sana', their wheat, because they had left their country and those crops were not ripe.

As the party travelled on more lively encounters occurred:

A good hour before we arrived at Bosjesmans River we saw large herds of cattle and shortly afterwards four Caffers came up to us, their hands full of assegais, which is usual, and with some knobkerries as well. They asked for nothing and I spoke some Caffer words to them and repeated a snatch from their songs. Thereupon they began to sing and dance as they walked. Without being asked I gave them a piece of tobacco. At this they wanted to barter for cattle with me. I said that I came from far and had nothing. They offered me a head of cattle for my dog but when I told them I had only one and that I needed it to protect me at night from the 'Goronjama' (or lion in their language) they were satisfied. Nevertheless when I asked them for milk, they again asked for the dog and when I refused they left.

A further comment was added the next day:

The Caffers we saw yesterday were Chief Langa's, which means 'Sun' in Caffer. He is the brother of Gaggábe or Cambushi, and both of them are sons of the dead paramount chief Paró or Paló.⁵ He is by no means in the good graces of his brother. He lives behind the Bosjesmans Mountains on this side of the Great Fish River. We left him two or three hours away to our left-hand side yesterday.

It was now 9 January 1778 and in his entry for this day Gordon gives an account of his first meeting with the important chief, Ruiter:

Close to the river here we found the old chief, Ruiter, who has the Gonaquas and other half-breed Caffers under him. This man has a courteous manner and a very good appearance. He had a copper plate on his chest with the arms of the Company. His kraal is divided into two, the other lying more to the south-west. He had many cattle and sheep and I hear that he has a few hundred men under him. Gave him a breast-plate, some tobacco and a tot of drink (which Sjomossi would not take but which Coba liked). I also gave some gifts to his wife and children and he gave me delicious sour-milk, the same as the Caffers have, and a guide to take me to the sea. He was most gratified when I told him that my Great Chief liked him very much because he had always been an upright chief.

As Gordon relates, Ruiter's tribe, the Gonaqua, were of mixed 'Hottentot' and Xhosa origins. (More correctly, their name should be Hoengiqua.)[6] Visits to Ruiter were recorded by Swellengrebel, Paterson and Sparrman. Le Vaillant's dalliance with a young girl from this tribe, Narina, is amusingly related in his *Travels*. A further meeting between Gordon and Ruiter took place a few days later, at which point further matters concerning this chief's importance to Gordon were to be considered.

Ruiter's kraal has been located thirteen kilometres south-east from Rautenbachs Drift on the south bank of the Bushman's River. Gordon was thus not far from the sea. But he was still destined to meet many more of the Xhosa before reaching the mouth of the river. The next two passages record encounters which took place on 9 and 10 January:

Went past large herds of Caffer cattle and through a village where we attracted many flies and Caffers, men, women and children who ran alongside us in the best humour in the world. They belong under Chief Thaka.[7] They again wanted to give me an ox for my dog and to barter stock but without being impudent or begging. Gave them some tobacco. I wanted to barter a piece of copper wire for three assegais but after the Caffer had considered this for a long time, he decided that he wanted to give only two. In order to show that we did not always do what they wanted, I broke off the transaction. He ran to his village and brought three calves to exchange for the copper wire but I would not do this. Encountered more large bands of Caffers and when I wanted to plot our course from a high hill, they walked about me and gazed at the compass as it moved, astonished and frightened. I asked them to put their assegais away because the thing could not tolerate these and I would not be able to carry out my duties. They jumped back in fear and I took an assegai from the hands of one of them and altered the adjustment of the compass with it in order to demonstrate it to them. Since they did not understand much about this I had difficulty bringing them close again, as they were afraid they would be bewitched. ... We passed many Caffer kraals and herds of cattle and I was greatly entertained by the same; they danced and sang, running alongside the wagon. In the afternoon we saw a large kraal or town. It was black with Caffers who came to me, asking me to stop because their chief was approaching. I did this and shortly afterwards two old, grey men arrived with a large band of men, women and children, encircling me on all sides. These were the two chiefs Titi and Tsaka.[8] The first was the son of old Paro's brother. Gave them some tobacco and they asked where I came from and also asked for iron. I told them that I came from far over the country and that I had no iron. Tsaka, who spoke Hottentot, asked for a present which, he said, was what great people did when they met. Gave each chief a small bunch of beads and gave the people small pieces of tobacco. They sent for milk but I said that the sun was getting low and that I was in a hurry. They again asked for my dog but I refused. They walked a little more with us and then turned off to their town. Followed the same course, wounded a hartebeest and shot some duck. Arrived at a Caffer town at sunset. They were afraid of me at first but approaching them and giving them tobacco found that they were the best and merriest people in the world. They showed me their gardens and gave me milk and begged in a very moderate way. Saw them milking their cattle which are very tame. They

first talk to them, as though mindlessly rattling off a prayer then they whistle but they tie up the rear legs nevertheless. And so the man does his milking talking all the while. From this man, who was called Poemla, I bartered a small basket and a calabash. While the moon was still shining I heard them singing from their huts. I went back to the tent escorted by four Caffers who, when they had had a smoke, went back to their town. These were soldiers, or people of Chief Umsella [9] who lived across the river, 12 hours E. by N. of us. I had been in my tent for an hour when a Caffer arrived bringing me a basket of milk. My horse ran off to the Caffer town and they brought it back immediately.

On 11 January 1778 Gordon reached the mouth of the Bushman's River. The entry is typical of his journal at this point in his travels, with his interests reflected in the mixture of game notes, scientific observation and undisguised pleasure at the actions and reactions of the Xhosa. There is no attempt, it would seem, at keeping any sort of order or sequence in the entry. It is all written down as it occurs to him:

21. *A 'Hottentot' man in traditional dress.*
Smoking was a passion among these tribespeople.

A little dew. A misty sky. Strong W.N.W. wind still, which made the weather clear and most pleasant.

Gave some presents to the Caffers and their wives and children who brought me abundant milk, departed for the mouth of the river. At first all the Caffers came with me but later only seven stayed. After we travelled E.S.E. for two hours we came to dunes, a little higher than the ones in Holland but not wide and covered with thick bush. There are many buffalo and elephant in these. Looked in vain for a road for the wagon and then rode directly to the river where I had seen a gap from on top of the dunes. But it became so bushy again that the wagon could not get through and at the river there were high sandbanks caused by wind.... Passed very closely by two buffalo which I did not see. They were standing in a thicket as I passed. They came out and my Hottentot shot at them but missed and they ran away. Unyoked here, and went with the Caffers and my Hottentot to the beach which is less than quarter or an hour from here. The river was 80 to 100 paces wide at this place and ran through bushy hills which presented a fine prospect. There was a sandbank at the mouth where the buffalo cross and swim. This river could carry hippopotamus but not at the sea since they avoid salt water. Found the beach flat and sandy, without rocks and there were few breakers. The wind was blowing diagonally towards the beach. There was no bay. So far as I could see the shore extended E. by N. and W. half S. and from the left bank of the river a rocky dune stretched right into the sea, but half an hour to the west the shore was flat and unbroken. After this there was another rocky dune. Found no amber or fine shells. The barometer showed 29 inches 6 points. Because I lacked an horizon was unable to get a clear view with my marine octant. Got 77 degrees 30 minutes. All this amazed the Caffers and also that my fingers did not become wet from the quicksilver. Let them look at the sun through a dark glass which astonished them very much. Sketched the views of this place and left for the wagon. There I found a large band of different Caffers with bunches of assegais in their hands. Treated my six to a piece of meat and gave them a tot which they hardly tasted. The others laughed out loud at the faces they pulled while they were tasting. The whole band turned back. The other Caffers were Titi's soldiers from across the river, not from beside the shore. As it was my intention to travel on to the Sondags River if I could, I returned, and because for the most part the course was W.N.W., it was too much of a detour. Took leave of my friendly Caffers and made camp an hour before sunset at a valley which was three hours from the Caffers. Called this valley 'Douglas Valey' after Colonel Douglas.[10] Wanted to go to the river to shoot hippopotamus but found the bush too dense. There are low bushes everywhere at the river, full of elephant, buffalo and rhinoceros paths so that I could have got lost in the dark. Saw a hare here today, the first in this part of the country, as well as many hartebeest. Three hyenas came close to where we were in the morning but after a shot they went off.

During this whole section of his journey, from the vicinity of Cradock to the mouth of the Bushman's River, Gordon writes with obvious engagement and delight of his meeting with the Xhosa. The whole region was thickly populated by these tribespeople. Once more, Gordon does not tell us what he discussed with chieftains such as Sjomossi, but his pleasure in observing and conferring, the bartering and the giving of presents, is evident. He is always friendly when he meets a new group of Xhosa. He speaks to them in their tongue, hands out tobacco and sings snatches from their songs. He can be firm too, as when refusing to barter his dog for cattle, but it is the firmness of courtesy. Once more, he remarks 'they were the best and merriest people in the world'.

It is important to realize how unusual Gordon's attitude to the indigenous people was. Hardly more than a year earlier Swellengrebel had recounted how his farmer-guides regarded the Xhosa as 'black heathens, who only wished to do away with the Christians'. As a result he says the colonists' 'attitude towards this nation was rather gruff and rude'. Less reliably, but more emphatically, a few years later Le Vaillant records the same contempt and arrogance of the frontiersmen toward the tribes. No one can accuse Gordon of equivocation or sentimental indulgence in his dealing with the AmaXhosa, yet his humane and tolerant spirit, his civilized sang-froid shine through his dry observations. It was remarkable in an age of sharp class distinctions and religious intolerance. There could have been few colonists or officials at the Cape who shared his attitudes.

As Gordon had noted at the mouth of the Bushman's River, it was his intention to travel on to the Sondags (or Sundays) River. However, on 12 and 13 January he broke his journey again at Ruiter's camp.

The passage begins with a potential confrontation with an aggressive thief, which is handled decisively but with good humour by Gordon, as one has come to accept. However, he has far more important matters to attend to here. He has 'a long conference with Ruiter' and then the next day he states: 'I told the Caffers that our Great Chief wanted them to live on the other side of the Bushman's River and us on this side. They were surprised at this and dissatisfied, asking to know what harm they had done?' Indeed. Nevertheless, a little later in this same year of 1778, the 'Great Chief', Governor Van Plettenberg, was to make an agreement along these lines with the Xhosa. It is quite evident from Gordon's casual aside, quoted here, that he was attempting to discuss the basis for Van Plettenberg's subsequent proposal: namely that there should be a boundary running roughly along the Upper Fish, in a north-south line. It was an unsatisfactory arrangement that would lead to disputes and bloodshed in the future. But, manifestly, all this was prefigured in Gordon's 'conference' here in January 1778:

We came to a Caffer town belonging to Chief Conga.[11] (After we were given milk in a most friendly way by the other Caffers I gave them beads in exchange). At this town our guide from Ruiter told me that one of them had seized his shield and wanted to go to the wagon to fight with me and steal everything but that the others had stopped him. Laughed about this and told him to tell the Caffer that I had not come to do them any harm but that if they molested me in the slightest way he would not lightly try it again. Continued our journey and arrived at

Ruiter by sunset. Hyena came close again. Had a long conference with Ruiter.

Ruiter's name is 'Toena' in Hottentot. The Caffers call him 'Coosjoe'... near Ruiter's kraal there is a small kraal belonging to a Hottentot called Trompetter. He and two Caffers escorted me a part of the way. These Gounacas or Gounaqua Hottentots are larger than the other Hottentots. They are also almost completely fused and mixed with the Caffers.

His conference over, Gordon and his party resumed their journey, travelling westward along the Coerney River and then down to the mouth of the Coega, where a drawing was made of Algoa Bay on 15 January.

The meeting with Ruiter and his people was to be the last significant encounter that Gordon had with indigenous peoples on this journey. But shortly after leaving the 'Gonaqua' chief, Gordon reports that he 'crossed the first stock farm', which means that the colonists had already come this far in their search for grazing land. It is not surprising then that when Gordon did once more come across small groups of Gonaqua a day or two later in the vicinity of present-day Port Elizabeth they had tales of dispossession and ill treatment:

Found here the kraal of the Gounaqua chief, Nouka who had ten straw huts belonging to the people with him, among which some were true Caffers. Asked for some milk, giving beads and tobacco in return. Nouka complained that he always behaved well to the Hollanders, fetching their runaway slaves from the Caffers and that they had now driven him from Van Stadens River where he had always lived. I promised him that I would talk to His Excellency about this.... A Gounaqua came to complain to me here that a certain Pieter Buis had beaten him almost to death. He looked pitiful and could scarcely walk. Promised him that I would speak to His Excellency about this.

As we read, in both cases Gordon promised to report their complaints to the governor. But to what avail? The eastward thrust of the colonists was under way and they were not going to be impeded by a few Gonaqua. As with the 'wild people' to the north, their land would be taken and they would vanish as an identifiable tribe. Significantly, Gordon also records that in this area 'we arrived at a place where a farmer called Nouman had come to live. He was busy building a house, about half an hour from the sea.' Only some twenty years later the Englishman Barrow would report that there were only 'about a dozen people' left of this tribe. They were, he said, on the 'eve of oblivion'.[12] The same complaints of ill-usage and land-grabbing had been registered by Swellengrebel.[13]

As has been noted, Gordon saw these Gonaqua tribesmen in the area where Port Elizabeth now stands. Wild life too abounded here and he was assiduous in describing it. Clearly he was fascinated by the lives and habits of the game, though at the same time he did not neglect his mapping duties. To get the full tenor and variety of one day at this point in the journey, the entire entry for 18 January 1778 now follows:

Rained a little from the south east last night, the sky clearing up this morning. S.E. wind. Went E.N.E. across the large, grassy plain to the mouth of the Swartkops River. Passed a salt-pan; there is still another here, close to the one I passed yesterday but none as good as the first one. When I was not far from the small dunes I shot some duck on some marshy places formed by rain-water; whereupon going up to them I robbed a lion of his 'déjeuner', for seeing something lying there I went up to it and found a hartebeest (as it is here called) bull, fresh from the lion, with its throat bitten open. It was still not cold and not mutilated at all; the lion's teeth had gone well into the throat but had not torn anything. There was a large foot-print about seven inches long next to the animal, just as it had sprung on it. Sent someone who was with me back to get the animal slaughtered and to carry it away. Could not see the lion anywhere though it is completely flat here except for where there are low dunes with undergrowth nearby. This is where it must have gone to hide when it ran away at my shooting. In the meantime I went to the sea by the mouth of this river and here found some more hartebeest which had probably been chased off by the lion. Saw an ostrich too. Saw two animals approaching me which I did not at first recognize. They came closer until at fifty paces I saw that they were an eland bull and cow. Could have killed them both with one shot had I had my gun but had gone out with my shot-gun in order to shoot birds. After we had stared at each other for a long time they went off into the dunes. Coming to the mouth of the river which is one hundred paces wide here and in which the sea breaks violently I saw something black there. Coming closer I saw that it was an hippopotamus. It stayed up to fifty paces away from me and lay watching me for almost a quarter of an hour and, after submerging a few times, it stayed away. It was nearly low tide and I tasted the water and found it to be very salty, with the result that my opinion concerning this animal has again been changed through this experience. It was not even two hundred paces from the breakers. Trustworthy people have assured me that they have been seen beyond the breakers though not far from the shore. At Sitse Camma one was killed in the breakers, although in the mouth of the river. Have also been assured that they do indeed swim beside the shore in the sea, going from one river mouth to the other.

After I had taken bearings on the river and the beach and had them both drawn, found that it ran into the sea in an easterly direction, an hour from the innermost western corner. Also found that the land was very low with the result that the river flows far into the land at high tide. Along the shore the dunes are almost level with the land and there are heavy breakers on the shore. I left and found that my Hottentots had nearly finished slaughtering the hartebeest. In the short time that I had been away the vultures had torn a great deal off it. Reached my tent at sunset. Had a piece of the animal grilled and found it very good-tasting. It was the most beautiful weather today, it was not too hot on account of a cool S.E. wind. I set a trap with a gun to kill hyenas. A small brook runs into the sea alongside Nouman's farm. From Nouman's farm one can see the sea 40 degrees in the E. by N., at a distance of half an hour.

The next day, reporting that the trap did not go off, Gordon rode on to Kraggas Kamma and stayed there for the following three days. His main interest here was a shipwreck, which has been identified as that of the Portuguese ship *Sacramento*, which went down in 1647.[14]

Having heard from an old Hottentot living at Potgieter's that a great ship had been wrecked somewhere here and that there were some anchors, I sent for him. He said that this had happened in his grandfather's time and he was most confused in his story. Went to the beach with him, to a place between the western point of the great inlet and this farm. We found that it was almost high tide so that we were unable to see any anchors or any large piece of metal, or as he put it, 'copper' cannon. The unfortunate people had made some huts in the dunes and all died of hunger and hardship, an old man living the longest. Saw some skulls and skeletons which we buried. We found many rusty nails and some finely worked ivory, a ciborium, but it had all disintegrated. There were some pieces of ebony lying on the beach. Here from the soundness of the teeth in the skulls, I decided that it had been a French or Portuguese ship.

On 23 January Gordon was on his way again, travelling westward, on what appears to be the identical route taken by Swellengrebel in 1776. On 26 January he arrived at the farm of Jacob van Reenen near the mouth of the Kabeljous River. It was a well-known stopping place, which had been visited by Swellengrebel. Paterson stopped there a year later, in January 1779, calling it 'a pleasant river'.[15] Gordon stayed at the farm for the next three days. There is a vivid account of shooting a hippopotamus in the Gamtoos River, again with careful descriptions of its habits. He was obviously not pressed for time and so could take pains to slaughter it carefully and to examine it scientifically:

From the top of the dunes, across which we had to clamber on account of high tide, I saw something in the river that looked very much like a hippopotamus, and approaching the place found that it was one of them. At times just the back was above water and then nothing more than the bulges of its eyes and at times just one eye protruded in order to see. The overseer of Van Reenen's farm had brought his gun with him (I had left mine behind to be cleaned) and he sat forty paces from the animal which continued to lie in the same manner though our scent was heavy on the wind. He began to whistle and cough. It listened and stared at intervals from the same position. Then all at once it pushed its whole head out, but the overseer's gun refused to fire. The animal, which we now realized did not have enough water here, jumped up and, half out of the water, ran into the river. But the musket, which had been put right, went off and the stricken animal rolled with great force back and forth in the water for a good while; it stuck its feet upwards many times and it died thus under the water. We marked the place and rode to the shore. Found that the river here was somewhat smaller than the Swartkops River and that there were heavy breakers in the mouth. . . . There was a heavy swell along the whole coast though the wind was in the N.W. Found no shells or amber and returned to the hippopotamus that we had shot. In the course of an hour it had come floating up and, as is usual, it was on its side. The sea water pushing back left it lying halfway on a shoal. We sent for people but before they could arrive the water began to retreat and the hippopotamus became more buoyant and floated away. I did not want to let it drift into the sea so I went into the water with a leather strap from my horse and tied it around a foot. But because the current was so strong I would have had to let it slip away had the people we had summoned not come to help just in time. When we had pulled it from the deepest part, it took only four of us to roll it like a barrel, even though it was a fully-grown cow, to where the water on the shore was a hand's span deep. We made it fast there and left two Hottentots to guard it against wild animals. Because evening had begun to fall we rode back and arrived at Van Rhenen's farm when it was pitch dark. Hippopotamus feet though thick are very supple and it pushes the part next to its nails or rather its hooves into and against its body and this helps it greatly when swimming. One can fold its feet and its legs into its body as one folds one's hand and it was for this reason that we were able to roll it so easily.

Fine weather all day. Fresh N.W. wind.

28th January 1778.
Fine weather. Fresh S.E. wind.
Went to the hippopotamus and pulled it higher up the river through the water because the wagon was not able to get through the dunes. Occupied the day with drawing, examining and slicing. The skin was cut off in its entirety but had to leave it behind until tomorrow because the oxen could not carry everything at once on account of the difficult road. Estimate that the weight of the heaviest hippopotamus would be within three thousand pounds. This, which was only about eleven feet long, had an estimated live weight of two thousand, one hundred pounds. Left people with the skin.

29th January 1778.
Good weather, though hot. N.W. wind. When the skin and the bones had arrived we went on with the salting and drying.

As a scientist Gordon had the great gift of curiosity. This passage provides ample evidence of this quality. One can sense vividly a furious desire to *know*, to record in detail – to observe, measure and draw the dead mammal. He pours his energy into the task, desperate that he should not lose his prize, rescuing it from the retreating tide by going into the water himself and securing it by his own efforts. And again, how well he could describe the features of the animal when in this heightened pitch of enthusiasm, as witness his remarks on how the legs fold into the body 'as one folds one's hand'.

Indeed, this particular hippopotamus was to be used as the basis for a long article in *Histoire Naturelle* by Gordon's correspondent in Europe, Professor Allamand. Drawings of a male and female hippopotamus were made from specific animals 'just after they had been killed' and these, together with measurements and descriptions, were received by him at the beginning of 1780. Allamand quoted Gordon extensively in the eight-page 'Addition' to the encyclopaedia. Referring to the fact that Gordon had seen many of these animals 'in the interior of Africa where they are hardly disturbed by the inhabitants', Allamand does not conceal his admiration, citing his correspondent's 'indefatigable zeal for new discoveries and for the ad-

22. Phoenicopterus ruber: *the greater flamingo.*

vancement of Natural History'. Several details from the passage in the journal just quoted are to be found in the article, such as the fact that Gordon and his party could 'roll [the hippopotamus] like a barrel'. Justly, Allamand remarks that Gordon observed these animals with 'the eye of a true Naturalist'. The article concludes with the measurements, described thus: 'Dimensions of a female hippopotamus, killed 22 January 1778 by Captain Gordon in salt water, close to the mouth of the Gambous [sic] River.' The date is out by a couple of days and the Gamtoos River has suffered something of a sea change, but there can be no doubt that the same animal is indicated.[16]

It was time, however, for Gordon to travel on once more and on 30 January he moved to another, even more comfortable lodging, the farm of Jacob Kok, near present-day Aloe Ridge, which is five kilometres from the mouth of the Zeekoei River, E.S.E. of Humansdorp. 'On this farm found the first proper house,' Gordon writes. 'The grapes are beginning to ripen here. Slept in a bed here for the first time.' Kok has been described as an 'hospitable and industrious Hessian ... who was visited ... by the Boundary Commissioners, Faber and Mentz in 1770, and then successively by Thunberg and Masson, Sparrman, Swellengrebel, Van Plettenberg and by Paterson'.[17] We can now add Gordon to the list.

Predictably, no matter how comfortable his quarters, Gordon does not rest but rides to the mouth of the Kromme River and then back to Van Reenen's to see how his hippopotamus skin is faring. After collecting some oysters he diverts himself with a hyena hunt on 2 February:

The four of us[18] and some Hottentots rode to a place in a bushy kloof an hour west from here to hunt hyenas. For some nights now the hyenas have been killing many sheep in the area. We went through long undergrowth and marshy places to a wood, following the footprint of a lightly wounded hyena. After the dogs had crept off into the bush for a while, they began to bark loudly and approaching ourselves we found the animal fighting the dogs, who had all seized it from behind. It stuck its neck right out and roaring loudly bit the dogs off itself. One of the dogs had opened it at the thigh and in its rage I saw the animal bite into its own innards. I first threw a Caffer assegai into its body but hitting a bone it did not go in deeply. The hyena seized it in its mouth and bit it into pieces, upon which I shot it through the head. It was a large male. We slaughtered it and continued our hunt. We chased another four of these animals out of the wood. A Hottentot shot a male and the others only just escaped. One of the Hottentots threw an assegai at a wild pig and the animal ran off with the assegai in its body. We went on hunting till three o'clock in the afternoon and then returned to Van Rhenen's farm. We had set a trap for hyenas and when the shot went off at ten o'clock in the evening we approached well-armed and found that a dog had shot itself.

On 4 February 1778 Gordon took to his travels again, sending the wagon on ahead while he explored the seashore around the Kromme mouth and Cape St Francis. After riding west, observing the shoreline and interior, he rejoined his wagon by riding up the Kareedouw pass. He then travelled into the Langkloof on a well-used route, close to what is now known as Joubertina. Here he records that he 'was not feeling well. . . . My whole body was in pain and I was listless. I caught a cold by sitting on a rock a long while and reading after having sweated.' Gordon's remedy for his illness is unusual, though perhaps an accepted Boer 'middel' at the time. On 9 February he writes: 'Drank a great quantity of tea.' The next day he reflects: 'Found drinking tea has been a great help because I have not been used to drinking it daily and I am much better.'

By 11 February he had reached Avontuur, where the village of the same name stands today. He is 'not well again'. Nevertheless the next day he dutifully climbs the mountain there in order to take his bearings. When he descends, however, he finds that he is 'not at all well, very dizzy in the head', but ill as he is, he still writes up his journal for the day and finds the energy to record this narrative of eighteenth-century frontier life:

Saw a certain Lindequast or Lindeque who had been badly wounded in the thumb by a lion last December. Father and son went in pursuit of three lions which had killed some of their cattle. The son shot one of them, breaking its jaw, whereupon one of the others that they were pursuing came towards them and the father stuck his gun into its mouth but it did not fire. At this the lion bit the barrel of the gun and the father in the thumb. He then fell down a slope and the lion fell on top of him. The son going to free his father, stumbled and the gun went off. At this the lion left the father and sprang on to the son who stuck the stock of his gun into its mouth. He was driven against a rock by the lion but held it off in this way. Because the lion could not draw breath or because of its pain, it could not harm him and, seeing their people approaching with guns and dogs, it took flight. Fourteen days after this the wounded lion was killed in a trap by the son.

On 13 February Gordon 'was much better'. His next move was to ride down what is now presumably Prince Alfred's Pass. The entry is illuminating:

Hazy weather from the south in the morning. Found I was much better. Departed S.E. in order to cross the Outeniqua chain to Algoa or Plettenberg Bay. This was on a difficult road for Mattys Sondag had given me wrong directions and I had got on to one of the stoniest and steepest of roads.[19] Schoemaker, the artist, who was the only person with me, quite gave up hope with the result that I was at a loss to know what to do with him. However at the top of the range I discovered another road with my spyglass. After having lost my way for a long time in this place, I crossed the Keurbooms River which was also flowing S.E. It was low and full of round pebbles. Here I found a Hottentot, Berkhousen's herdsman, who took me over another mountain, first S. and then S.E., to another Hottentot named Jakhals who was living on his own. After this we went on to the Witte Drift, half an hour from the bay on the Keurbooms River mouth, arriving at ten o'clock in the evening. It was a distance of six hours but took much more on account of the mountains.

Poor Schoemaker! Every time Gordon deigns to mention him, it is with exasperation, an emotion he seldom registers with any of his other travelling companions.

Of interest too in this entry, is that Gordon talks of making his way down the Outeniqua Mountains to 'Algoa or Plettenberg Bay'. What is now Plettenberg Bay had been known as Algoa or Formosa Bay before getting its present name. On a map drawn at this time Gordon claims that he named the place Plettenberg Bay and this entry would seem to confirm his claim. However, in the original manuscript the word Plettenberg's (or Plettenberg) is added above the line and the legend on the map could also have been added later. It would therefore appear to be impossible to confirm or refute his statement.

While exploring the shore and interior of Plettenberg Bay for the next two days, Gordon stayed at Wittedrift – still called this – on the Keurbooms River. Most of the time the entries refer to the various bearings he took of this area. He foresaw too that 'It would be possible to let wood float down the river and to load in the bay'. However, breaking off from these dry and essentially practical notes, he does also remark that he saw 'a baboon ... which was the largest I have ever seen; thought at first that it was a human being. It stood on its rear feet far off in the hollow looking at me, then it gave a cry and ran off.'

On 16 February he again set off, riding towards Knysna or what Gordon called Neisenas. Here he also met with a minor adventure, as he tells us:

I went over large hills and deep kloofs with many turns and after about three hours (mostly S.W.) reached Neisenas mouth which is on the farm of Stefanus Terblanche. Went to the Neisenas mouth, to the shore which extends east and west. It is high, with cliffs so that one can only reach the shore at one narrow place. This river, which flows with many bends from the Outeniqua Mountains in the N.W., is very wide at this place and the tide, flowing strongly for an hour and a half up the river, makes the water salty. It goes into the sea through a gap that is a hundred paces wide and very steep. It was low tide and I saw the swell breaking every three or four minutes in the gap, although it was calm weather with a light westerly wind. It would be impossible for even a hooker to enter here. The French Captain who wanted to enter here and who said he had seen the light of one of the two houses around here, must have seen some other fire, since none of the houses at this place or around it are in the line of vision. On my return I took bearings on and drew a view of the Neisenas.

A fairly large yellow snake was lying on a bush and Terblanche who was riding behind me took great fright and called out 'a snake!' for I was almost touching it with my hand as it lay there, watching. At this I stopped and asked 'where?' and when he had shown me I saw the snake lying there motionless, watching me. Riding a little to one side, I shot it dead. These snakes lie in this manner watching for birds and are dangerous if one steps on them.

Continuing his journey, Gordon was held up for a day at a farm called De Kleine Hoge Craal, of the same name today. He was forced to shelter in 'the wretched hut of a certain Meyer .... Could not cross the torrents (rivers),' he writes the next day, 'and for this reason had to stay here. Last night it rained into the house everywhere through the roof so that most of the night I had to sit by a smoking fire to warm myself.' Never idle, Gordon used his enforced stay to explore what is now Swartvlei, Sedgefield and the Wilderness.

When he was able to resume his route westward, he passed through the newly-established Company Post or 'woodcutters' Post' at present-day George, reaching Mossel Bay on 21 February. Here he comments that there are 'two very good, extensive, sandy landing places'. It is probable that Gordon was considering the possibility of a military force landing here. As future commander of the Castle garrison, he was obviously taking his military duties seriously, though a seaborne invasion of the Colony at this remote spot would seem unlikely.

Continuing westward he arrived at the farm The Egypt on 25 February 1778. This was where he had been the previous year, before crossing the Plattekloof. Here, four months to the day, he had botanized, sketched the farm and had received a most friendly reception. It is clear that all those who travelled in this area made for certain farms or places, knowing that the hospitality would be good. Gordon usually only gives generalities about these places, but a real feeling of relief and delight can be sensed when he arrives at these havens.

The last week of his journey, as he travelled through long-settled country, he was plagued by delays due to rain-swollen rivers. Trying to cross the Duivenhoks River he became 'almost chilled to death' and then developed 'a fever'. But he was able to shrug this off and finally crossed the Duivenhoks on 3 March, arriving in Swellendam on 4 March.

One last detail of this journal remains unexplained. Why did Gordon decide to delay his return to Cape Town by making a detour to Essenbos, the farm of Martin Melck at Franschhoek? But this is only one of the mysteries confronting the Gordon scholar, and a small one at that.

On 8 March 1778 Gordon arrived back in Cape Town. He had been on his travels for just over five months.

23. Lachenalia bulbifera.

CHAPTER FOUR

THE THIRD JOURNEY: AN AMBITIOUS PLAN THWARTED

(AUGUST 1778 – JANUARY 1779)

With Van Plettenberg to the Zeekoei river; Van Plettenberg's Beacon; agreement with the Xhosa; Gordon falls ill; the Histoire Naturelle rhinoceros anatomized; the Bokkeveld; the Roggeveld; the north-western Cape; contact with the 'Bushmen'; return to Cape Town

A little less than six months after the completion of his second journey, Gordon again set out for the Eastern Cape – this time travelling in the company of the governor, Joachim van Plettenberg. But before turning to the record of this journey, it is worth noting an event that took place during the brief interval between the two expeditions.

In either March or April 1778 Gordon met the Dutch rear-admiral J. S. Stavorinus and told him of his discovery of the Orange River.[1] Many of the details recorded by Stavorinus of this conversation with Gordon correspond closely to the journal of the second journey, so it is likely that Gordon either showed him the journal or read from it while the rear-admiral took notes. This may not appear to be particularly remarkable or worthy of note, but the fact that the record of this meeting was only published twenty years later, is; for it is possible that Gordon told very few people of his discovery. We know that he told Paterson because his friend was also to record the discovery in his *Narrative* of 1790, twelve years after the event. Further consideration of this matter will be given later.

Gordon started his next journey on 28 August 1778. For some reason he went to stay once more at Vergelegen. In the manuscript the first page records the title, the dates of the journey, the usual details of weather and temperature, and the bare fact that he arrived at the farm in the dark. On the next page, however, crammed in above the following entry, is the curious fact that his servant could not rouse him and that he eventually woke at one o'clock. He also says he went to sleep at four in the morning. Does this mean that his host, De Waal, entertained him rather well? It would be nice to think that this was so, thus relieving the picture of the almost unmitigated austerity displayed by Gordon in this and all the following journals.[2]

Presumably he spent the next ten days or so at Vergelegen, but there are no entries in the journal for this period. Van Plettenberg and his retinue left Cape Town on 3 September 1778, and we know that Gordon only joined the party on 6 September as it travelled through the Hex River Mountains. We owe this information to the account of Van Plettenberg's journey which was kept by Olof Godlieb de Wet, a Company official.[3] Gordon's journal only resumes on 18 September when the party had reached the Traka River, about eighty kilometres east of present-day Prince Albert.

On the whole, this journal is terser and more factual than the previous one. It abounds in compass bearings and details of rivers and mountains, essential information for map-making. Perhaps the presence of the governor acted as some kind of restraint on Gordon. There is a further gap from 22-27 September in the opening pages of the journal. Again, this hiatus is unusual in Gordon's journal-keeping. Generally each day is meticulously recorded. He had, of course, passed this way on his previous journey, but he gives no indication why he took up his narrative once more when the party left the farm De Vrede, some twenty kilometres west of where Graaff-Reinet stands today. It will be recalled that it was from here that Gordon had set forth to 'make peace' with the 'Bushmen' the previous November, and it is clear that the governor's party now followed very much the same path north that he had taken then.

To give something of the flavour of this third journey, at least in its earlier parts, here is the entire entry for the day 30 September 1778. (The 'last farm' referred to in this extract is in the 'Kraane Valey' where Gordon had been on 15 November the previous year. It lies forty-odd kilometres west of Middelberg in the vicinity of the place now known as The Willows.)

Last night standing water was frozen into ½ inch of ice, and it was white everywhere with a clear sky and a southerly wind which blew briskly. Otherwise it would have frozen harder here. It began to get coldest in the morning, about two hours before daybreak. Half an hour before dawn the thermometer stood at 30 deg. and at sunrise at 32 deg. Left at half past six. We have got a Chinese or Bushman called Carel who used to live at a certain Van der Walt's. He is meant to accompany me into the interior. The Gov-

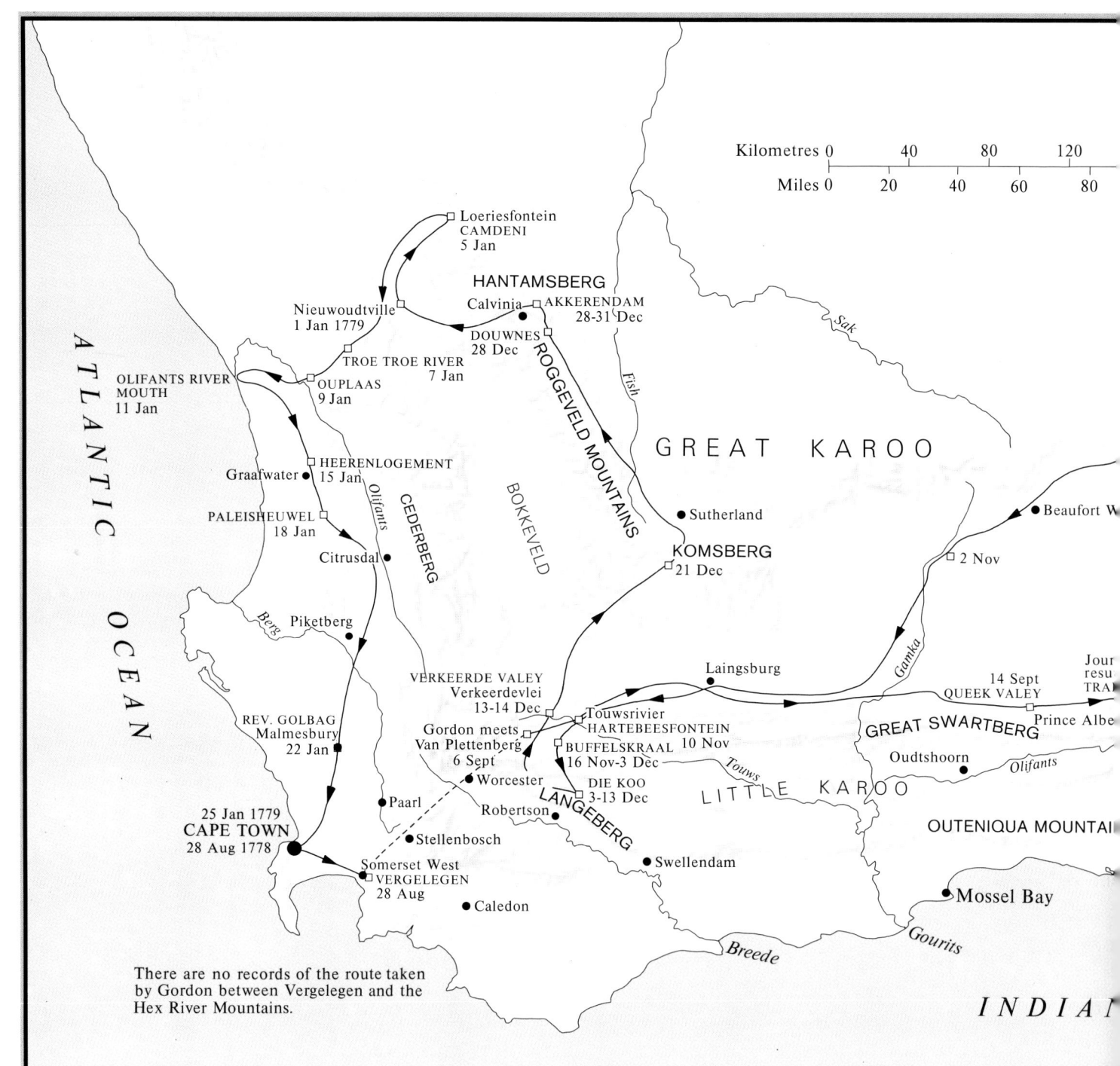

Map 3. *Gordon's third journey: to the Zeekoei River with Governor Van Plettenberg and thereafter with his own party to the west coast.*

ernor and I rode ahead on horseback and taking my previous course, we arrived after two and a half hours at Stephanus Smit's the last farm. We saw some bush pigs[4] (sanglier d'Afrique), bubalis[5] and springbok. On our left we passed three streams which come into the Plettenberg River from the Sneeuwberg. At Burger's, on the 17th last, three thousand sheep were smothered and killed by the great snow which lay 3 feet deep. 5 to 600 were still lying there in his kraal. Barometer at Smit's: 25-3. Thermometer midday 63 deg. afternoon 73 deg. sunset 63 deg. Clear weather. Fresh S.E. wind. Departed N.E. by N. and after four hours ride came to a spring overgrown with reed. It had good water in it and we made camp. We saw some gnus,[6] springbok and bontebok, but these do not have as much white as those at the Cape; however they are the same animal. Barometer 25-4: therefore has dropped almost not at all. The country is drier than last year, it being also two months earlier. The ridges still all lie in the same direction, namely S. Easterly and N.W.: but sometimes N. Easterly and S.W. We called this place Van Heijden's Fontein after Captain-Lieutenant Van Heijden. Course today four miles N.E. by N.

Captain-Lieutenant Van Heijden was an officer in the governor's retinue and he was not the only member of the party to have a geographical feature named after him.

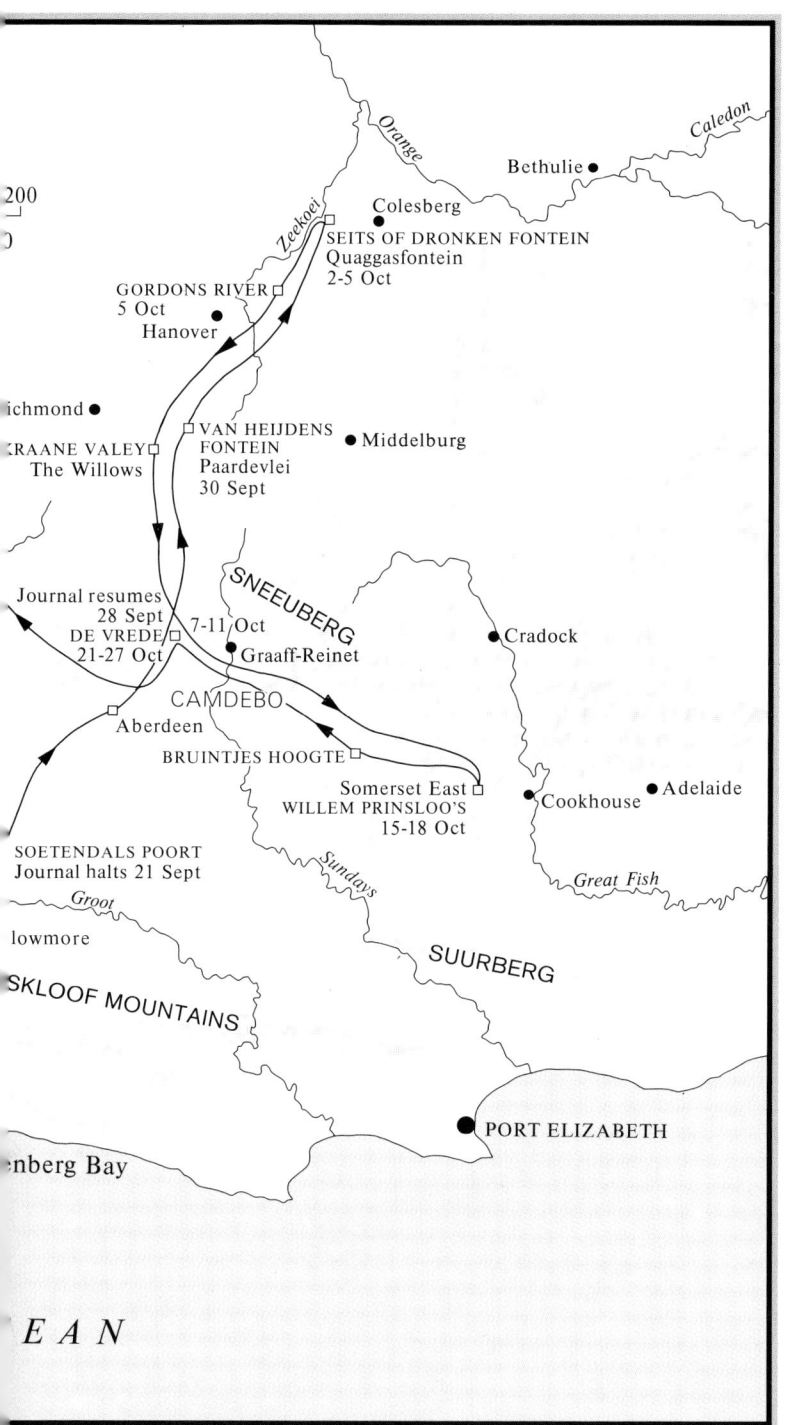

font'. But how this second whimsical appellation came about, the journal does not relate. Perhaps there was some celebration after the killing of the animals. Or perhaps the drinking had to do with the erection of 'a stone in commemoration of the Governor's visit' – in other words, the object known as Van Plettenberg's Beacon.

The erection of this beacon brings us to another enigma. Why was it placed here at all? This question has been thoroughly explored by Professor Forbes in *Pioneer Travellers in South Africa*. Briefly stated, however, the problem is this: the beacon was meant to mark the northernmost boundary of the Colony in these parts, so why was it placed in this remote spot and not at the natural boundary, the Orange River, which was only fifty-odd kilometres to the north-east?

It was at this point that Gordon had been forced to turn back on his previous journey. But he had struck the Orange subsequently and not so far to the west, less than 100 kilometres. So Gordon must have known how close they were to the river. Apart from Gordon, there were other members of the party – farmers – who knew of the existence of the river, which was hardly more than a day's ride away.

It has been posited, therefore, that Gordon did not want the governor to visit the river. According to Professor Forbes, this may have been because Gordon wished to preserve the name for his Prince, fearing that Van Plettenberg would call it after himself.[8] This is certainly feasible, knowing, as we do, how loyal Gordon was to the House of Orange. However, Gordon never admitted this in writing. Indeed, in a draft letter to Hendrik Fagel,[9] composed shortly after his return from this journey, Gordon stated that the reason they did not follow the river north to the Orange was because the governor had allowed only ten days for this part of the expedition. There was therefore no time to go to the 'Great River'. He also added that the burghers comprising the escort were frightened of the 'Bushmen' and were in a hurry to return south.

The journal entry for 5 October 1778 would appear to confirm the governor's haste to return. Gordon writes:

Departed, going back on our old course. We unyoked a while at Schuijlhoek and at sunset arrived at Gordon's River (or Brack River) and there we camped. All these rivulets run into the Plettenbergs River. Thermometer 37 deg., rose at its hottest to 73 deg. and dropped to 57 deg. after sunset. We took the skin of a hippopotamus bull with us. I saw Mercury before sunrise; it was very beautiful. We saw some of the aforementioned game but did not hunt as his Excellency the Governor would like to be back over the Sneeuwberg within the next four days. Fresh S.E. wind. Fine weather.

As we have seen, one of Gordon's main aims the previous year had been to negotiate some kind of peace with the 'Bushmen' in this area. It was almost certainly why Van Plettenberg was also here at this time. No contact was made, however, and the party decided to retrace its steps, Gordon riding ahead to De Beer's farm, De Vrede.

Gordon himself was modestly assigned a brack rivulet in his name. The Seacow, or Zeekoei River of today, had already been named the Plettenbergs River on Gordon's first visit and it was to this site that the party made its way. Apparently, one of their objectives was to shoot hippopotamus and on 3 October an appropriate slaughter took place. One can sense in the entry for that day that Gordon found this wholesale massacre as distasteful now as he had the year before: 'so many,' he writes, 'that we were weary of shooting: many were killed'.

The spring at their camp was named after the accompanying surgeon, receiving thus the name of Seit's Fontein. On the map,[7] however, the name is given as 'Seit's of Dronken

24. *The governor's hippopotamus hunt:
'. . . we were weary of shooting: so many were killed'.*

Following Gordon, the governor had more excitement to add to the hippopotamus hunt. Three male lions had been spotted:

His Excellency the Governor and his company also saw them [the lions] hunting gnus. Some of the company fired several shots at them from 4 to 500 paces. Two ran away but one kept turning back after each shot with its tail high. It lay down but then got up and walked away again. They considered this lion to be very ferocious so they left it alone.

After a short break of three days Gordon was again on his way, this time travelling east, with the governor once more following him at a more leisurely pace. As he says, he followed the same course he had taken on his previous journey, and on 15 October he reached his immediate destination, Willem Prinsloo's farm – now the site of Somerset East.

The object of this visit was to negotiate once more with the Xhosa tribesmen, but this time with the authority of the governor's presence. The frontier area was very unsettled. The 'Bushmen', the Xhosa and the colonists were all fighting for the same territory, hence Gordon's terse notes that 'the farmers of the Sneeuwberg and from this part fled before the Bushmen'. There was also the individual complaint of 'a certain Joubert' whom the 'caffers wanted to murder'. The whole entry for this day, 15 October, is worth looking at closely, for it illustrates in its tantalizing way so many of the facets of Gordon himself and how he presents himself in his journal:

We left east for Prinsloo, but in a turn going round the Bos Berg. From Bruintjes Hoogte measured the angle of the Sneeuwberg from Lottering W. Half N. De Beer W.N.W. Good weather today. Soft west wind. Arrived at Prinsloo before noon. Therm. 67 deg. to 84 and dropping to 78 deg. We heard from the farmers that there were some thousand Caffers in the mountains, waiting to fight us. Jacob Joubert also came and complained greatly. I had doubts about the case and I rode alone to the Caffers. (Asked a man called Durand, who went with me to the Caffers last year, whether he would go with me again, but he declined). I came upon them only two hours from here; they were under the leadership of Chief Coba. In the beginning he remained lying on the ground and appeared suspicious. But when I asked him if he no longer knew his brother, Gordon, he jumped up happily and gave me his hand in a friendly way. I proposed that he should come with me to our great Chief which he accepted; 39 of his people also accepted. They did not want to take their assegais with them.

The first sentence tells us the direction he took on leaving Bruintjieshoogte for Prinsloo's. But he does not simply ride 'east'. He must record that he made a 'turn going round the Bos Berg'. He then remembers that he took certain compass bearings on the Sneeuberg from Bruintjieshoogte and duly records these. Then he observes that the weather is good and that there is a 'soft west wind'. The temperatures at morning, noon and evening are noted, and without any break in the progression of his writing he tells us that the farmers report that there are those 'Caffers in the mountains waiting to fight us'. The matter of Jacob Joubert who 'complained greatly' now follows.[10] It is a fact, and is simply recorded as such. The sentence that ensues, however, is Gordon at his most enigmatic: 'I had doubts about the case and I rode alone to the Caffers.' He does not record why he has these doubts, or indeed what the case is beyond the fact that it concerns Joubert's complaint. But what are we to make of the second half of the sentence 'and I rode alone to the Caffers'? We must imagine this extraordinary man hearing out some dubious story from a farmer and then riding off into the mountains to confront a large gathering of angry tribesmen.

What is astonishing is that both matters — the complaint and the confrontation — are given equal weight in the sentence. In the original Dutch this juxtaposition of the trivial and dramatic is even more marked. This is because the parenthesis about Durand's declining to accompany him is clumsily inserted into the body of the main sentence, thus further diminishing the dramatic aspect of his riding alone into the mountains. Furthermore, he in no way places any emphasis on the fact that he meets Chief Coba, the leader he had befriended the previous year. It is only in the remaining few sentences of this entry that the scene suddenly springs vividly to life — and this happens almost by chance as it were, because Gordon actually allows us to see what he is recording: Coba does not rise when Gordon approaches. Initially suspicious, the chief continues to lie on the ground. Only when Gordon refers to himself as Coba's 'brother' does he respond and jump up happily to greet him. The confrontation ends cheerfully and they agree to go with Gordon to meet 'our great Chief', Van Plettenberg.

This whole entry demonstrates the curious quirks of Gordon's style — the way facts crowd upon facts with only the slightest hint of his own opinion intruding. ('I had doubts about the case.') Above all, we can see how often in Gordon's narrative the momentous and trivial are presented as equivalent. This demonstrates either an amazing sang-froid or an almost total indifference to the value of words. It could be argued that in a journal a man has a right to express himself as he wishes, and that had Gordon decided to write and publish a book of his travels the niceties of style and emphasis would have been present. That may be, but the very fact that this is a journal — in effect an *aide-mémoire* only — allows us to see how his mind worked when not constrained by formal demands.

Once more there are no entries for a couple of days, namely 16 and 17 October. We know, however, from De Wet's records that Gordon brought Coba and twenty-eight of his men to Prinsloo's farm on 15 October (Gordon says that thirty-nine 'accepted' the invitation but some may have dropped out on the way). The meeting with the governor was cordial and De Wet states that the Xhosa showed great trust and affection for Gordon who discoursed with them in their own tongue. They sang and danced to entertain the governor and were treated to tobacco and arrack. The next two days (missing from Gordon's journal) were spent visiting the tribespeople, observing their ceremonies and discussing their withdrawal to the eastern side of the Great Fish River. This they promised to do once they had brought in their crops.

The party moved south alongside the Great Fish on 18 October, and on 19 October Gordon took leave of the governor, riding west to Bruintjieshoogte where he spent that night. He says nothing here of what his intention was. According to De Wet he left to return to the Camdeboo in order to pursue his journey to the north and north-west. But De Wet also omits to say why Gordon is making this journey. This matter will be addressed shortly.

On 21 October we find Gordon back at De Vrede. Again we have a series of disparate observations and notes, haphazardly recorded and juxtaposed without regard for any order or symmetry. It is curious that so 'scientific' a mind could be so random. At times, entries such as the one below evoke an eerie feeling that Gordon is anticipating the stream-of-consciousness mode of writing pioneered by the novelists Joyce and Woolf, where mundane and significant moments mingle in the prose just as they tend to do in real life:

Arrived at De Beer's. Good weather. Thermometer 59 deg.–80 deg. dropping to 63 deg. Soft west wind. I was not at all well. Just as we arrived a Hottentot woman sang a song of welcome for her son, who leads the team of oxen for our wagon. (It does happen that children are cast out, but not generally, and not in every tribe. It is only done for reasons of hunger or great affliction. Otherwise most Hottentots are very fond of their children).

Here are the first signs that Gordon was falling ill, and from later entries it seems that he had contracted dysentery. However, he still has time to remark on the mother singing to her son and then to comment on the custom that aroused some interest among the travellers of the time, namely that 'Hottentots' abandoned their children in times of need. Conceding that it did happen occasionally (who gave him this information?), he is nevertheless quick to remark that 'most Hottentots are very fond of their children'. It often seems, in these odd comments, that he is attempting to correct current prejudices about the indigenous inhabitants of the country. It is typical that he should try to do this by noting the facts as he observed them and not by indulging in fanciful or sentimental speculation. The practice of abandoning the old (instead of children) is clearly linked to this passage and is discussed later.[11]

From the entry for 25 October a reasonably clear idea of Gordon's plans begins to emerge:

Clear weather, cool. A little wind from S.E. Last night it froze white. Thermom. was on freezing point. I am getting worse rather than better and have no medicines. As two of my best Hottentots, Iteki and Platje, are also sick, I resolved to pursue my intended journey north no further but to survey the land west of here and then, if I get better, to act according to circumstances.

We have got a female gerbo here which is pregnant and tame already. Took an accurate latitude here and got 32 deg.–5 min; error 25 deg. N.W. The vineyard, which already had young grapes, was totally ruined by the frost last night. At about 10 o'clock in the morning the leaves were already withered by the sun. This is late frost and unusual.

It is in the entry of 27 October 1778, as he left De Vrede, that we finally hear, with greater exactness, just where Gordon was intending to go. This is also where we have the first mention that he had a boat with him:

Left with the greatest regret in the world, seeing that I had brought my boat and other supplies to this point. But, having no medicines, and not knowing if I might become sicker, already so far away, I decided that my health and that of my people would not allow me to set forth on my intended journey over the Orange, north and then further west.

Thus illness prevented him from making this journey. 'North' would have taken him back to the Orange, probably close to the debouchment of the Zeekoei into the 'Great River'; while 'west' would have taken him to the mouth of the Orange. Presumably he would then have returned south to Cape Town either along the coast or inland. This would have been a journey unprecedented in the annals of eighteenth-century travel – a matter of thousands, not hundreds, of kilometres if the round journey from and back to Cape Town is considered. Ill though he was, he nevertheless left the De Beers, 'his friendly host, his wife and family', on the same day 'in order to survey the land west of here and then, if I get better, to act according to circumstances'. There is a note of great sadness in his words as he leaves De Vrede 'with the greatest regret in the world'. He had obviously planned this expedition with high hopes and great care, even to the extent of bringing a boat, though it seems to argue a lack of foresight that he had brought no medicines.

𝒢ordon's course west took him past the site of present-day Aberdeen and, as usual in this journal, there is a multitude of compass bearings which testify to his plans to survey the land he was travelling through. He records and travels on despite ill-health, taking frequent readings on his barometer and, as on 2 November, using his astrolabe to ascertain longitude. It is on this same day that he describes the shooting of a rhinoceros bull near the source of the Gamka or Leeuwen River.

This morning just as I was adjusting my instruments, a rhinoceros came close to our wagons but as soon as it caught our scent it turned away. Two of my Hottentots tried to shoot it but after sniffing the ground twice it trotted off fast. We saw three hunters go after it. It went up wind and they rode after it, almost alongside it, without it seeing them. At last from the high place where I had gone I saw powder flashes and shortly afterwards

25. *The* Histoire Naturelle *black rhinoceros.*

young Mr. Viljoen, J. Jacob Kruger, and Dolf Bronkhorst came up. They told us they had shot a rhinoceros bull. Viljoen had given him the mortal shot at 118 paces. However, when it fell after walking a short distance, they did not trust it, for they consider it to be one of the most ferocious of animals, so they fired another four shots at it. We rode over to it. I made a drawing of it, and wrote a description of this wonderful animal. I came back late in the evening. I left my Hottentots to skin the animal in the morning. It had already begun to swell up. It is of medium size but nevertheless an adult animal.

This animal was almost certainly the one that Gordon described in detail to Professor Allamand – the one in fact that appears in the *Supplément* to *Histoire Naturelle*.[12] This is borne out by Gordon's remark in the journal that on 3 November, despite the fact that the bull's body was fast deteriorating, they were trying 'to preserve the skin as a specimen'. Professor Allamand acknowledged that he had received the drawing, description and skin from Gordon and was using them for the basis of his article. Interestingly, he ascribed the shooting of the rhinoceros to Gordon himself, claiming that Gordon had shot it at a distance of 118 paces 'close to the source of the River Gamka or River of the Lions'. It would seem that Gordon indulged in a mild but unimportant deception in claiming he shot it himself. Nevertheless, he quoted the same distance for the shot.

The good professor also poured scorn on the writer Kolb who stated as a fact that if poison was poured into a rhinoceros horn it would crack open. Allamand, that true man of science, confessed, 'almost with shame', how he had experimented by pouring wine into a rhinoceros-horn cup and then adding a strong dose of arsenic: '… the horn received not the slightest crack,' he dryly remarked.

Still unwell, but meticulously recording day by day, Gordon continues his journey, south-west down the Gamka River and then more westerly towards present-day Laingsburg. It was in this vicinity, on 12 November 1778, that he made some rough notes in the journal concerning the gestures and words of a 'Chinese-Bushman'. We can infer that one of his aims in making this journey was to try to make contact once more with these people. The message he gets – on this occasion at least – is hostile: 'They say we are evil, and come in the night like wolves and have hair like lions.' This poetic phrase contrasts most sharply with the surrounding compass bearings and latitude calculations of Gordon's text. It is likely, however, that Gordon recorded those words not because they contained picturesque images but because they were what were spoken at the time and because he wanted a true reflection of their attitudes.

His route continued in very much the same direction and location as the national road today, until he reached Hartebeestfontein, a farm in the area of present-day Touws River. He then diverged slightly from the course along the modern road to reach the farm of Wouter de Vos, Buffelskraal, at the head of the Hex River Valley, on 16 November. Swellengrebel had stayed there barely two years before and had remarked upon its comfort. It is likely that Gordon regarded this hospitable farm as a haven to make for until his recovery, because the next day he 'sent a man on horseback to the Cape for some medicine'.

Clearly weakened by his condition, Gordon continues to write up his journal but the entries are short. On 22 November he remarks that he is still feeling unwell; yet even illness does not deter his scientific curiosity, and he sends Schoemaker (mentioned here for the first time in the journal) and two of his 'Hottentot' servants up 'the mountain' (almost certainly the Matroosberg) to record the temperatures of the snow that had recently fallen. It must have been a hard day for his servants and the artist, though if Schoemaker complained it is not on record here. Apart from the temperatures, a barometer reading was taken. Gordon's notes also contain fairly technical details about rock formations, so it can be assumed that the artist did his work well.

The entries continue to be brief and mainly concerned with the weather. Even on 30 November Gordon writes: 'Still not at all well. Have bad diarrhoea.' Then, with the new month, his health suddenly begins to improve and he starts to make plans to continue his journey. Here is his entry in full for 1 December 1778:

Fine warm weather. Calm in the morning; at midday a fresh west wind, somewhat cloudy. Thermometer 65 deg.–80 deg.–70 deg.

Am much better. We are making ready to go into the country once more. The Sak River, Vis and Riet Rivers run into the Great River.

Namaquas always milk at noon. They hold their hands high before drinking milk. Many have the first joint of their fingers cut off (like Bushmen). One seldom sees small children with the first joint of their little finger. Sometimes two joints of the middle finger are missing. They say they do this for a sickness. Most of the Great Namaquas have one testicle cut out.

In the evening Captain de Lille, the Botanist Paterson and Van Reenen came from the Cape to visit me. They had heard of my illness.

Gordon's remarks for this day convey the usual mixture of facts and information. (The subject of testicle excision, first mentioned here, is pursued in much greater detail on Gordon's following journey.) It can be assumed that his servant had returned from Cape Town with the medicines before the arrival of his friends, for although Gordon was still not better on the 30th, he was 'much better' the following day and confident that he was now fit enough to continue his journey. He postponed his departure – planned for the next day – apparently to enjoy the company of his friends.

It is perhaps appropriate to consider here some curious contemporary speculation concerning Gordon's journey from De Vrede to Buffelskraal. It is contained in a letter written by Hendrik Cloete, a well-known burgher at the Cape, to the younger Swellengrebel in the Netherlands.[13] The letter is headed 'Kaapsche Nouvelles (Cape News) 19.3.1778 – 15.2.1779' and the passage concerning Gordon starts from the time he parted from Van Plettenberg:

Gordon took his leave [of the Governor] and returned to the farm of De Beer, intending to return across the Great River to the North. Two sons of De Beer, two Van der Walts and three others had promised to accompany him, but De Beer, no longer being Veld Commandant, retracted his promise and Gordon had to give up his plans. He pretended to be sick and returned to the Hex River, where he secretly arranged for fresh supplies to be sent to him and departed for the Hantam and the Sak River returning via the Kamiesberge across the Olifants River to the Cape.

The painter Schumacher, well known to you, spent some time with Gordon on this trip, but not being satisfied with the way he was treated, he left by agreement.

The passage is perplexing. It is far from clear why Gordon should have 'pretended to be sick' or why he should have sent for supplies 'secretly'. Furthermore, if Schoemaker (Schumacher) left his service, Gordon certainly does not mention it – a startling omission. Finally, the visit of De Lille (an officer in the garrison), Paterson (a conspicuous foreigner), and Van Reenen (a prominent burgher) hardly justifies Cloete's allegation of secrecy. However, perhaps one fact might be of interest concerning the identification of the paintings and drawings made on the rest of this trip. If Schoemaker had left, then they could only have been made by Gordon.

On 3 December Gordon set off for 'De Ko', while his friends returned to the Cape. 'Die Koo' is still a regional name for an area approximately fifteen kilometres north of Robertson, and 'Conradie's farm, Harmonie' is still marked there on the topographical sheet for Worcester, 3319. It is situated between the Langeberge and the Kooberg.

It was, he says, an 'excellent place to complete my triangulation' – in other words, to continue with his map-making activities. The highest point on the Kooberg, on the same topographical sheet, is marked as 1 089 metres, so we can speculate that it was from somewhere near this site that he made his observations. Indeed, the entries from 3 to 11 December contain a great many compass bearings and remarks on the topography of the area.

While there, he also visited two mineral baths, which are surely those just north of Ashton, some twenty kilometres east. However, of far more interest to us today is the account which follows of an 'old Hottentot sorcerer'. It reveals a genuine curiosity as to how the practice of sorcery was conducted, coupled with an amused scepticism at the superstitions of the participants. Even in the privacy of his journal Gordon appears to maintain his 'scientific' principles, but at the same time there is nothing malicious in his scorn. Indeed, he displays a certain degree of pride in the fact that he had been allowed to wit-

26. *Gordon at the 'Bushman kraal of Chiefs Gronjam and Doerop, with their way of offering peace'.*

ness the event, as his host, Gideon Joubert, had never been granted the privilege. The ceremony took place on 8 December 1778:

Saw an old Hottentot sorcerer who did not want to acknowledge what he was, making *goudeni*. He sometimes strikes fully grown Hottentots and they do not dare to defend themselves. He was frightened of me. The others did not dare to refuse him, whatever he demanded of them. In the evening I saw him, in their own manner, doctoring and practising his sorcery on a sick boy. He did this after refusing many times and mostly because he was frightened of me, for I had let him see the sun through a smoked glass. He thought that I would bewitch him. He ordered the youth to come naked to his hut in the twilight. My Hottentot, Iteki, was also frightened of him and he sat by the fire showing great attention, alongside the sorcerer's wife and a young Hottentot girl. I had a candle lighted in order to see better, whereupon he went and sat by the youth who had a pain in his foot. He rubbed the thighs and the leg, and, holding the foot to his head, he roared and snorted like a lion and a tiger. Then he held his hand to the head and the heart of the boy, and did this several times. Then sneezing three or four times, he opened his hand showing some insects, like beetles, which he said he had pulled out of the leg. Having smeared some mutton fat on the leg he rubbed the rest over himself. After this he took some roots (from thorn and mimosa trees) which were hollow and tied together and filled with stones that rattled inside. Then he began his sorcerer's song, all the time sitting, but twisting his body continually and striking the bundles on the ground, often singing furiously and shaking his head while his wife accompanied him, clapping her hands all the time. We could not understand him, even Iteki was not able to; he said it was Bushman sorcerer's language. When he broke off, sweating, I asked him several questions but all I could get out of him was that *touqua* (God) had taught him this in a dream. Joubert said that he must have been very frightened of me to have practised sorcery in my presence, since they say it never goes well if there is a white skin present and that they would never practise sorcery in front of him. The whole time I kept a most serious demeanour though often I could hardly stop myself from bursting into laughter at his cures and the terror of my Hottentot. They say that they have jackals and other animals in their service, that these take messages to other sorcerers for them. Bought his magic rattle for a tinderbox.

On 13 December Gordon returned north to stay with the widow Jacobs at Verkeerdevlei. This is the stretch of water some twelve kilometres west of Touws River. It was presumably another of those havens, hospitable places where travellers knew they would receive a measure of comfort. (Van Plettenberg and his entourage, including Gordon, had stopped at this same place on their outward journey east in September.)

Gordon was not there to rest, however, as may be seen from the next day's entry with its long list of compass bearings and other geographical observations. On the following day he was off on his travels again, this time north to the Roggeveld, the Hantam, and thereafter southwards to the Olifants River and home to Cape Town.

As his records show, he first returned to De Straat (near present-day Touws River), and then made his way in a north-easterly direction up the 'Namgas Riviertje' to 'Pinar's stock farm'. (Today the river is known as the Pienaarskloof River — a name perhaps derived from this same earlier Pienaar.) It then took him another day to reach Smitswinkel, near the river of the same name, before entering the Klein Roggeveld.

It was at this point that Gordon rode ahead, doubtless to scout the road before them. When he returned to the camp he found 'all in confusion because the drink had been badly guarded'. But this does not seem to shake his equanimity or provoke his anger, as his next sentence concerns the source of a stream.

In an eloquent passage discussing this journey, Professor Forbes has pointed out how many of the farms marked on Gordon's map bear the same names today.[14] Gordon's progress into the Roggeveld can in fact be traced by names such as De Fortuin, Brand Fortuin, Brand Valeij, Bonne Esperance, Standvastifheid and Oranje Fonteijn. Obviously such reliable pointers enable historians to track a traveller's route with far greater confidence, as well as supporting the argument against the haphazard changing of place-names.

By 21 December Gordon had ascended the Komsberg, making many barometric observations and compass bearings en route. He was having trouble with his wagon, and this recurred as he travelled north into the Groot Roggeveld on Christmas Day 1778. It appears that to Gordon it was a day like any other day, for the journal contains the usual careful description of the course taken, compass bearings and notes on the state of the weather. He also notes that on the 'Aape Berg' (Monkey Mountain) there are 'N.B. no monkeys'.

On 28 December Gordon left the Roggeveld at Downes — another place which bears the same name today — to make his way to Adriaan van Zyl's farm, Akkerendam, at the foot of the Hantamsberg, just north of present-day Calvinia. As usual, he omits to record that before leaving the uplands of the Roggeveld a fine drawing was made of the area from the vicinity of Downes, looking back to the mountains he had just left.[15]

Why these impressive works — whether made by Gordon or Schoemaker — are seldom referred to in the journal deserves some consideration. It may be because they were regarded as routine records, where accuracy in conveying the look of a place was more important than artistic merit. Sometimes the need to get the 'look' of a place was taken beyond mere accuracy. Many of the drawings in the Gordon Atlas are composite — that is to say, the most impressive features of a landscape were included even if their topographical relationship to one another had to be distorted to do so. If making drawings was a routine for most travellers, as it was, then it is understandable that they are seldom referred to in the narrative. One further point that bears mention is that it need come as no surprise that a military man, such as Gordon, could draw so well. Accurate sketching would play an important role in his duties and form part of normal military intelligence techniques, such as the drawing of fortifications and so forth.

Somewhat uncharacteristically, Gordon spent 29 and 30 December resting at Akkerendam, but he did not stay to celebrate New Year there and on the 31st we find him at his 'Soet Waterfontein' — probably the Soetwater which is just north of the road between Calvinia and Nieuwoudtville and about halfway between the two towns. He was travelling along the Oorlogskloof River — which he calls the 'Douwnes' — and reached the Bokkeveld a little south of Nieuwoudtville on New Year's Day 1779. Here we have his notes about the 'Bushmen' leaders he hoped to meet in the next few days, to which end he travelled on to 'a farm belonging to Mrs Ryk'. This has been identified by Professor Forbes as 'Swellengrebelsfontein on the northern parts of the Bokkeveld', though this is not absolutely clear from the journal.

On 4 January Gordon records that he was visited by the 'Bushman Chief Doerop'. Significantly, he reminds Gordon of Chief Ruiter whom he had met in January 1778 near the Sundays River. The relevant passage reads: 'In the morning the Bushman Chief Doerop and one of his tribe came to fetch me. He was very like Chief Reuter. He spoke very well and had a good physiognomy. Had a long talk with him. Departed travelling further N.E. and after a seven-hour journey reached the Bushmen on the Camdeni.' (It may be recalled that Gordon had also had a 'long conference' with Chief Ruiter — or Reuter as he calls him here — who was of mixed 'Hottentot'-Xhosa origins.)

Gordon's journey to the Camdeni (or Kamdanie as it is called now) is not marked on Map 3 of the Gordon Atlas, but there is a well-known and interesting drawing made at the time that has a subscript which partly translates as 'the view of the Bushman kraal of Chiefs Gronjam and Doeroep, with their way of offering peace which I made with them on 5 January 1779 at Camdeni Spring'.[16]

The site of this ceremony was in the vicinity of what is now Loeriesfontein and the Kamdanie River. (The source of the Kamdanie lies just north of Loeriesfontein.) Although the journal tells us nothing of the peace-offering, the drawing depicts a dead ox lying with its feet in the air and surrounded by small figures. Gordon is also shown at the entrance to his tent handing out gifts from a case at his feet, while other figures remove a sack from the back of his wagon (see illustration 26).

In none of the entries for the days when he made contact with the 'Bushmen' does Gordon say that he was there to make peace. Only the drawing mentions this indirectly. Nonetheless, we know from his previous expedition that this was his clear intention, and we can assume that he was under orders from the governor to perform this mission which ties in with the peace-making undertaken with the Xhosa earlier.

From a few remarks made on 5 January we can see that he was trying to sort out the identity of the various tribes about which he had been told. The distinction between 'Hottentot' and 'Bushmen' had never been very clear, but his mention of the Briqua is significant for it is the first time the name occurs in his journal: 'The Ein Eip people,' he writes, 'are bastard Namaquas. The Nou Eik are different Bushmen. The Briqua are still another kind of people. They are Caffers who own cattle, sheep and large goats. N.B. These Bushmen repeat the last words of those who are speaking to them: many at the same time.' As we shall see from the ensuing journal he had a great desire to visit these 'Caffers who own cattle sheep and large goats'.

The most interesting journal entry is that of 6 January:

27. *The Heerenlogement as depicted by Le Vaillant, whose name can still be seen inscribed on a wall of the cave.*

I was very much amused by the Bushmen who are good people. Saw an old woman performing sorcery. From her son's body she snorted forth a devil (evil spirit) which she said she could see and it was like a cobra. The snorting made her nose bleed. She walked away drunkenly with the evil spirit. One of them held her under the arms. Quickly she was given a stick which she used to walk on her own. She also beat the ground with it. She snorted once more upon her son's nose. She rubbed his belly with buchu. At the same time some of the women sitting there were smoking buchu through the nose.

This passage about the sorcerer undoubtedly portrays a trance state as defined and described by Professor Lewis-Williams and others.[17] The snorting forth of the 'devil', the nasal trance blood, the walking away 'drunkenly with the evil spirit' all testify to this. Gordon's amusement is therefore somewhat ironic, since he was not really aware of what he was witnessing. His statement, however, that they were 'good people' needs some qualification. It is not a mere commonplace — bland if not patronizing. Its significance only becomes apparent when the prevalent contemporary opinion concerning these people is taken into consideration: they were detested, and were hunted down and killed like vermin by both the colonists and the Xhosa. Seen in this light, Gordon's remark is astonishing. It is obvious that he really liked them. If he found their customs and superstitions amusing, this is understandable, given his 'scientific' approach and cast of mind. However, what emerges most forcefully from this and his earlier encounter at Die Koo with the 'sorcerer' — indeed from his attitude to the Xhosa as well — is that Gordon was a rational and civilized man. He was humane but never sentimental — in essence, a true exemplar of most of the qualities admired in eighteenth-century Europe. He was, after all, a son of the Age of Reason and the Age of Enlightenment. Indeed, this remark from his journal echoes his sentiments about the 'Hottentots' which he had communicated to Diderot in 1774. But in Africa at this time there were few men who felt as Gordon did.

He rode back to Mrs Ryk's on the evening of 6 January, and the next day set off on a journey of sixteen hours to bring him to the Troe Troe River in the vicinity of present-day Van Rhynsdorp. After spending the whole of the following day there — no doubt to rest the oxen — on 9 January they crossed the Olifants River and 'made camp at Van Zyl's on the southern side of the river'. This site has been positively identified as Ouplaas, about seven kilometres W.N.W. of Klawer.[18] (It and its owner, Pieter van Zyl, figured in the writings of several travellers of the time.)

The next day was spent travelling to the mouth of the Olifants River and 11 January in exploring the area. Returning to Van Zyl's, Gordon continued his journey south and by 15 January he had arrived at the Heerenlogement, which can be translated as 'The Gentlemen's Lodgings'.[19] As Gordon says, it was just a cave, but it was also a well-known halting-place for travellers who appreciated the fresh springwater. Many wrote their names on the walls of this cave: typically Le Vaillant did and, as typically, Gordon did not.

What remained of Gordon's journey need not detain us long. He was at the Langvlei River for a day, then at his 'Swartbaaskraal', which appears to be Swartboskraal today. On 18 January 1779, in this vicinity, he records that he 'climbed about in the mountain in order to see the so-called drawings and strange characters which I had been told of and found this to be a false report. The characters were some scratches and the drawings were worse than those of the Bushmen, but the hollow rock looked like the entrance to a great church . . . .' This mountain, with its unimpressive 'scratches', was almost certainly the place known as Paleisheuwel today. He then continued his journey by well-beaten roads to the Piketberg region, where he stayed with a Gerrit Smit whose farm, Drooge Rijst Kloof, still bears the Afrikaans form of this name.

By 22 January he had reached the 'Reverend Golbag in the Swartland', which is where Malmesbury is situated today. On 25 January 1779 Gordon rode back into Cape Town. His journey had lasted just under five months.

28. *Male ostrich,* Struthio camelus –
widely distributed but first recorded by Gordon in November 1777.

CHAPTER FIVE

The Fourth Journey: to the Mouth of the Orange River
(June – August 1779)

A rendezvous with Pienaar the hunter and Paterson; through Namaqualand to Ellenboogfontein; a meeting with Wikar; contact with the Namaquas; the mouth of the Orange River; encounters with the Strandlopers; Gordon's first elephant

Very little is known of how Gordon occupied himself for the next five months of his life. Presumably there were military duties to perform at the Castle; but more to our purpose, in April 1779, shortly after his return, he wrote a long letter to his patron and friend, Hendrik Fagel.[1] It testifies – if further testimony were needed – to Gordon's steadfast diligence and exceptional powers of observation. It contains descriptions of his travels and his views on the state of the Colony, as well as detailed particulars of his ethnological, zoological, geographical, geological and military interests. It makes abundantly clear that Gordon's principal objective was to become a zealous expert on his new country, and in this connection he talks of accomplishing 'one more journey . . . before I can arrange everything into a correct order'. This would seem to argue that he saw his journeys as part of some specific design.

Indeed, if one follows the route taken in Gordon's second, third and fourth journeys, an overall plan becomes apparent: he was tracing the boundaries of the Cape Province as we know it today, excluding only the area east of the Fish River that is now mostly taken up by Ciskei and Transkei.

As we have seen, on his third journey (August 1778-January 1779) he did not accomplish what he had set out to do: namely, to follow the course of the Orange River from the site of present-day Colesberg to the mouth, and from there presumably make his way back to Cape Town via the west coast. Had he succeeded he would have completed a rough circuit of the Colony, alluded to above as the 'overall plan'. Sickness, unfortunately, prevented him from doing this on his third journey, which is why he told Fagel he needed 'one more journey'.

If we accept that Gordon had this plan ('to arrange everything in a correct order'), then his fourth journey can be seen as having a specific end in view. He was seeking to achieve what his previous venture had failed to do – to complete his round journey – but this time by travelling from Cape Town up the west coast to the mouth of the Orange, then proceeding roughly east along the course of the river all the way to present-day Colesberg. In other words, Gordon would seek to complete his circuit the other way round.

Whether we accept this idea of an overall plan depends very much on how we assess the workings of Gordon's mind. He does not spell it out for us. Yet we know sufficient about his nature, his hardihood and his sense of purpose to at least allow that it is a strong possibility. Whatever our assessment, however, we cannot deny the evidence of the journeys and what he did in fact accomplish.

Gordon's fourth journey – which deserves close examination on a map in order to fully appreciate its daring and originality – must be considered his crowning achievement in the field of exploration. In terms of distance travelled he went further than he had ever been before, and although he had suffered a measure of hardship on his earlier travels, physically and mentally this venture was to be far more testing than any of his previous expeditions.

He was almost certainly the first European to see the mouth of the Orange from inland and to reach as far upstream along the Orange as he did. He was certainly the first to record these specific visits and to do so in a way that can be described as 'scientific'.[2] No less remarkable and no less useful to the store of contemporary knowledge were his drawings and descriptions of little-known and little-understood animals, such as the African elephant, rhinoceros and hippopotamus – to name but a few. His most notable feat in the field of zoology, though, was his encounter with the giraffe, which will be considered more fully later in this account.

The journal of the fourth journey also contains a great deal more physical description, as opposed to technical recording, than the previous journals. This applies not only to animals and geographical features but also to the people Gordon encountered, whether they were white pastoralists or Korana tribesmen. The names of his dogs, his servants and of the people who accompanied him

ROBERT JACOB GORDON

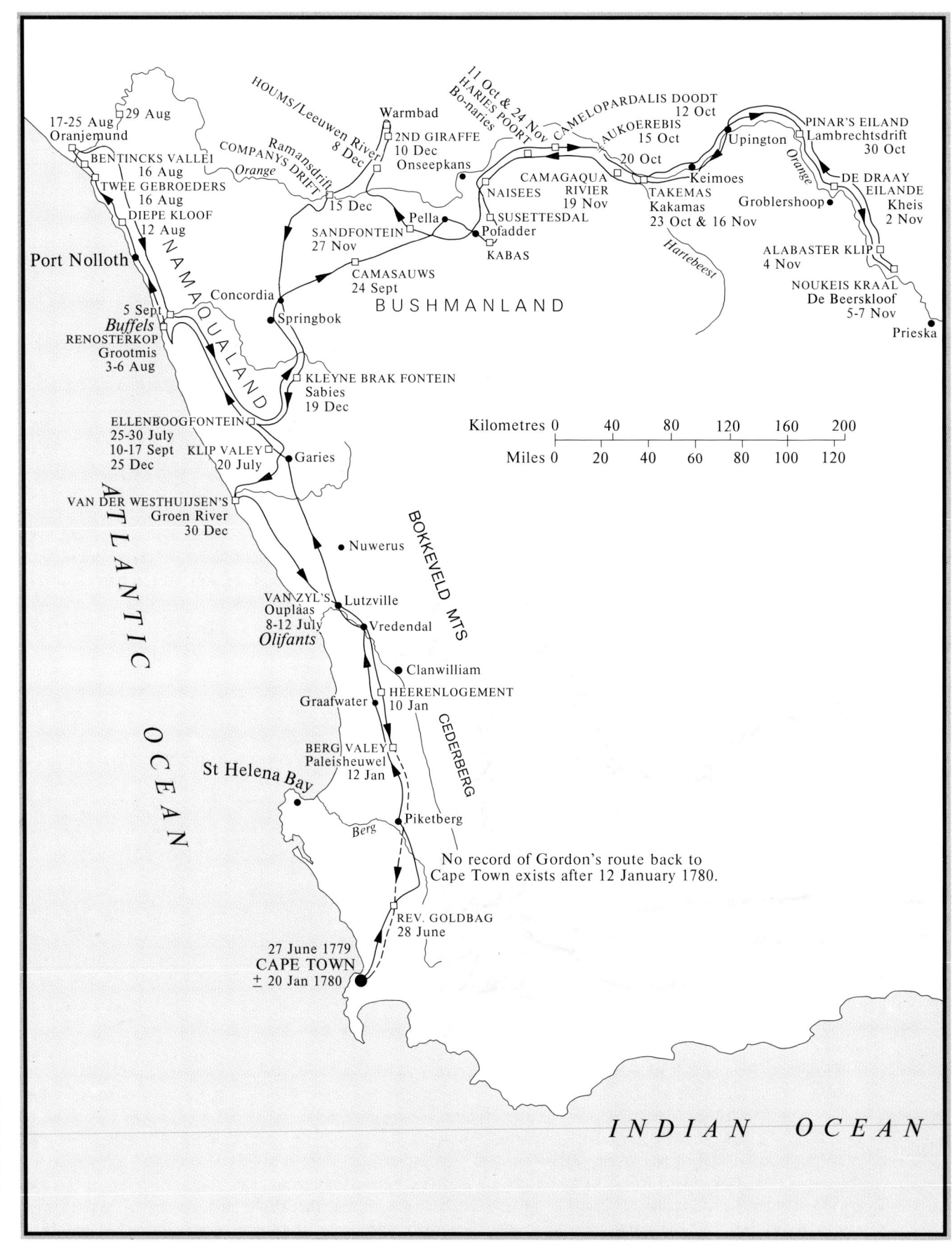

Map 4. *Gordon's fourth journey: to the mouth of the Orange River and west along its course towards present-day Prieska.*

appear more frequently too this time, and it is details such as these which make this journal a far more personal record — though this aspect should not be overemphasized; it is hardly an intimate account. Nonetheless, he takes time to record how he cooked and ate an ostrich egg, and it is interesting to know that he carried a microscope with him and that he 'made merry' on the banks of the Olifants River on 11 July 1779.

The entries in the journal tend to be of greater length than before and this is particularly marked in comparison to the previous journal (of the third journey). There is also a feeling that there is more time, more space to enlarge on subjects that he finds of interest. For instance, his encounter with the 'Strandlopers' on 20 August 1779 is over 2 000 words long, or three closely written folio pages in the original manuscript. Of course, the entry is of this length because the subject and manner of the discovery of these people fascinated the writer. But consider how long it would have taken to write those three folio pages of absorbed description, probably by candlelight and using a goose-quill pen.

Turning now to the journal itself, it will again be our task to try to see how much of Gordon's personality is revealed in this document, once more examining diverse quotations from the text. Even the title, subtitle and first sentence can tell us something:

Journal of the Fourth Journey of Captain R.J. Gordon in the Southern Part of Africa.

Started on 27th June 1779 from the Cape of Good Hope.

The thermometer observations are taken at sunrise; again at the greatest heat of the day, which is generally in the afternoon about two o'clock; and finally at sunset.

These opening words are interesting, not for any intrinsic value, but because they show how important Gordon considered these observations to be. With this traveller, the 'scientific' always takes precedence over the personal, and although this can be frustrating for the general reader, in the light of what we have observed in the two previous journals, at least it can be said that Gordon is consistent.

*A*ccompanied by some friends from the garrison and by his young servant Koerikei, Gordon set forth on 27 June 1779.[3] He was making for the Reverend Goldbag's house where he had stayed in January of this same year, at the end of his previous journey. (As previously noted, this was located in the area where Malmesbury is today.) He states that he has two wagons, one of which carries his boat. What he does not say is that the artist Schoemaker is also accompanying him. In fact it is some time before this is revealed. As we have observed from the previous journals, Gordon's attitude to Schoemaker seems to have been a compound of indifference and irritation, and, true to form, at this point in the journal he does not consider the man's presence worth mentioning.

While at the Reverend Goldbag's (or Goldbach as it is usually spelt) Gordon notes that he is running a temperature and that he 'had been feverish for some time at the Cape'. No other symptoms are mentioned, but the question of Gordon's health will recur again in this journal. One can only speculate that the illness he suffered from in November of the previous year was still dogging him, though after a few days he does record that he was beginning to feel better.

Taking leave of his military companions and the Reverend Goldbag, Gordon then followed much the same track as that of his previous journey, visiting the same farms and mentioning the same names as he made his way northwards. However, on his arrival at the Olifants River on 8 July 1779, we learn that he has been joined by a further travelling companion, a certain 'Pinar'. This was certainly no chance arrangement or encounter. The man who was now joining Gordon was the well-known hunter, trader and farmer Pieter Pienaar. To some, such as Le Vaillant, he was not so much well known as infamous. By all accounts he was a rough-and-ready individual — the sort of personality any sparsely colonized frontier will produce; but whatever his moral 'attributes', his talents in hunting and survival must have been sorely needed and welcomed by Gordon.

Gordon's journal entry leaves no doubt that the meeting with Pienaar on the Olifants River had been planned, as had the rendezvous with Paterson and Sebastiaan van Reenen: 'After riding for seven and a half hours reached Van Zyl's on the Olifants River, here I found my travelling companion Pinar, a burgher from Rodesandland, as well as the botanist Mr. Paterson, who wants to accompany a certain Van Reenen to the Orange River. But they are first riding to the Bokke Veld.'

It is also clear from Paterson's journal that the meeting was not haphazard. However, Paterson adds that 'as he [Gordon] was going a different course we appointed to meet in the Small Nemiquas Land and then to keep company together along the shore of the Atlantic Ocean as far as we could possibly come to the northward'.[4]

The next stage of Gordon's journey — to Ellenboogfontein in the Kamiesberg, the farm of Hermanus Engelbrecht — took place without undue excitement. It was a journey of approximately thirteen days and Gordon, clearly with plenty of time at his disposal, observed and discussed a fine variety of subjects on his way. Setting out on 12 July he passes a casual remark that 'The greatest unpleasantness about travelling in this country is this unavoidable overturning of the oxwagons'. Interestingly, it is a fact not generally recorded by other travellers.

A day later he had these complex observations to make about the topography of the countryside, plainly echoing Buffon's theories on the formation of the earth:[5]

This is a very poor region. The longer I observe the more strongly it strikes me that all the angles or tips of these hills fit into each other, but with this peculiarity: every two hundred paces the hills lie in such a way that there are four gaps in them, one East, one West, one South and one North. But all the tops fit between each other in whatever direction they may be: That is to say the gaps in the hills lying East and West have tops or

29. *'Meerhof's Casteel' where Simon van der Stel chiselled his initials on a rock. The cloud of dots is a swarm of bees.*

rather roots in the North and South and the roots lying North and South have angles in the East and West. This region, consisting entirely of such hills, is the same in all directions. Thus though I am sure this area was once covered by water this particular phenomenon could not have been caused by this, i.e. not by normal currents, because one cannot logically suppose that two currents could flow in opposite directions so close to each other.

Continuing in this vein a little longer, he then turns to a curious description of the common 'dassie', or rock hyrax:

Shot a bergrot [mountain rat] today which is wrongly called a dasje in this country.[6] It has the teeth of a rat, and a tail which is not visible but which can just be felt. It has four toes in front, the smallest of which is hardly visible, and three behind. The shape of its back foot is very like that of a human being. It lives on herbs and on grass and is good eating. It has four teats. Pelt brown and soft. It is said that they have the *écoulement périodique*.[7] This may well explain the oily crust which is known as dasje's piss.

The next day Gordon visited Meerhof's Casteel where he came upon the traces of an earlier visitor:

Pinar went hunting yesterday morning. Has not yet returned. He came back in the afternoon but had seen nothing. Much elephant dung around here. Left in the afternoon and arrived at Meerhof's Casteel after riding for five hours N.W. It is a rocky cavity 15 ft deep, 24 ft wide and 12 ft high. It is made of *Cos*, white with pieces of quartz in it.[8] The elephants come here to scratch themselves. Looking at the opening there is a spring on the right-hand side. It has quite good but rather brackish water, but not in abundance. Although this used to be a stock farm belonging to a man called Warnek it has now been abandoned. Opposite this rock, on the other side of this shallow basin among low hills, there is a similar but smaller cave on the left-hand side as one enters the cavity. On a rock, faintly chiselled, are the letters *de: E.H:S:V:de:S. A.S.* 1684. The 16 is hard to make out. This must be the Honourable Simon van der Stel, probably the son of Adriaan, who was the Governor anno 1684 and who travelled to the Koper Bergen.[9]

Travelling on northwards, Gordon remarks on 19 July that he has been looking for 'the cattle post of a certain Van der Westhuizen' but that he could not find him. The next day he finds the farm and records meeting an audacious woman, Van der Westhuizen's wife, who was of French Huguenot descent, as the text makes clear:

At daybreak heard the bleating of stock and half an hour ahead of us found the farm, which is the first on the way from the Oliphants River to here. Sent there for some milk. The wife was alone with only her children at home. They come here in the rainy season when there is grass. They had one room, a round hut built of sticks and covered with mats and without a chair or table. There was no bread to be had here. The husband was ploughing on his lower farm beside the river. Stayed here. Pinar rode over to him ... the wife of the house is quite a heroine and can shoot well. Her mother's name is Guilliaume, from France, but her father is an Amsterdamer called Engelbrecht. She hates the French deeply. She told us that she had once fired at a lion and that it nearly leapt on her after the shot but, it being almost dark, she escaped to a hut. The lion pursuing her into their Hottentot shepherd's hut jumped with its front paws into the fire and burning itself sprang back again. Just before this a Hottentot had shot it in the paw with a poisoned arrow. This caused its death the next day.

This woman, born Claudina Engelbrecht, was the sister of Hermanus Engelbrecht, whose farm Gordon was making for. She is certainly the same 'widow Van der Westhuizen' of the farm known as Klipvlei and who was described by the missionary John Campbell in 1813. In his account too she appears to have been a lady of spirit, telling Campbell that she had travelled together with François le Vaillant to the Cape and had 'given him a good drubbing with a sambuck ... for speaking improperly of her daughters'. The missionary added: 'She is a tall and still strong woman, though in her 75th year.' Understandably, no mention of this alleged sjambok-beating from the lady appears in Le Vaillant's account![10]

A few days later, on 24 July, Gordon's interest in the customs and practices of the 'Hottentots' is aroused by an encounter with a man in the foothills of the Kamiesberg. He is described as one of the 'Kleine Namaquas', meaning that he lived south of the Orange. ('The Groote Namaquas' were the tribes that lived north of the river.)

One of the Kleine Namaquas has the knucklebone of a small buck on his right hand. It was tied on to him by the kind of sorcerer they call *kai ouw* or *Garap* at Wiltschut's kraal. A hole had been worked through it. The *Garap* had dreamed that Canseep would become sick. He therefore went to him and made *camie* for him, which means to make lucky and did it so well that the danger was warded off. This is a different ceremony from *dro* when a man is 'made' or 'made different'. It is when pissing by the old hottentots is regarded as fitting (not at their weddings as has been said).[11] He wears it round his hand until it drops off. He then sticks it down a mouse hole, believing it would be unlucky for him if someone were to find his knucklebone (it is the same kind our children use when they play knucklebones). At these ceremonies they slaughter something or other which they eat and finish, all together. While making *dro* they have to carry the peritoneum round their necks.

The next day, referring once more to Simon van der Stel's expedition of 1685, Gordon describes the mountain known today as Vyemonds se Berg:

It is certainly the mountain of 'The forty eight days' ride', although I make it higher than Table Mountain. Perhaps van der Stel said 'the mountain range 48 days' ride from the Cape' because in the beginning of the Colony they were not able to ride so far in one day because of the roads. Although I have now been travelling for nearly four weeks, an East Indiaman with a good wind could easily sail this distance in twenty-four hours.

The quotation here is from the Jesuit missionary and scientist, Father Guy Tachard, who had met Simon van der Stel at the Cape in 1685 and 1686 while travelling to and from China and Siam. Gordon had certainly read the account of his stay at the Cape, contained in Tachard's book

30. *Ellenboogfontein near present-day Kamieskroon – a haven to Gordon and many other travellers.*

31. *Tribespeople of Namaqualand.*
Note that these faces have been duplicated in illustration 42.

Voyage de Siam which was published in 1689. We know this because Gordon alludes to the book and 'the 48 days' ride' in an inscription to be found on his 'great map' (no. 3 in the Gordon Atlas).

Eventually, on 25 July 1779, Gordon arrived at his first real 'base' on this journey. It was the farm Ellenboogfontein belonging to Hermanus Engelbrecht, situated 'six kilometres W.S.W. of Kamieskroon and one kilometre S.S.W. of the present farmstead of Ellenboogfontein', according to Professor Forbes.[12]

Paterson had rejoined Gordon on 23 July and they had travelled together to the farm which was another of those havens mentioned by traveller after traveller. A few years later Le Vaillant was to write of this place: 'I received many real proofs of friendship, and experienced some degree of pleasure. We drank punch, we had music, and the greater part of every night was spent in dancing.'[13] Neither Gordon nor Paterson mentioned such festivities, but both of them made drawings of the farm which was to become their base for the next part of the journey.

Of Hermanus Engelbrecht Gordon writes: 'He has a Christian wife, crops, and lives in a walled house.' The fact that the wife was Christian almost certainly meant that she was white. (As we shall see from a later entry in the journal concerning the farmers of this area, this was somewhat unusual.[14])

At Ellenboogfontein Gordon was again subject to a high fever. This had been brought on by a septic wound when 'something poisonous' had stung him in his right leg on the night of 22 July. He treated it, he tells us, by placing beeswax 'on the swelling where I was bitten, having bathed it there in warm vinegar first'. His entry on 26 July records the 'high fever' but also adds 'my leg is drawing well and is somewhat better'. On the 27th he mentions putting a plaster on the leg, saying laconically 'I was better'. He also tells us that he rode for four hours that same day, so perhaps it is not surprising that in his entry for the 28th he remarks: 'Had a fever yesterday and today.' However, no further mention is made of the illness other than on the 30th when he writes finally that he is 'much better'.

The only point to be made here is that the painful, septic leg and the high temperature did nothing to stop Gordon from engaging vigorously in a wide range of activities during this period at Ellenboogfontein, as his journal well testifies. On 26 July, for example, we have this entry:

Engelbrecht took me in his horsecart to the Lange Klip where my wagons were. Took two hours. Found here a runaway Swede called *Vicar* who was a year with the Namaquas. He claims to be the cousin of Merchant Hasselgreen of Amsterdam. He was formerly a schoolmaster in the Swart- and Sneeuwberg. Ran away from the Cape seven years ago but has now got a pardon. He was thirty days' journey up the right bank of the river. His account is on the reverse side. He had the skin of a female giraffe with him.

Found Mr. Paterson here again and we ate together.

Originally stationed at the Cape as a clerk to the Dutch East India Company's hospital, Wikar (the usual spelling) had incurred heavy gambling debts. According to E. E. Mossop, the editor of the English translation of Wikar's account (of which there are several versions[15]), 'Overcome by shame and desperate, he deserted the Company's service on April 4th, 1774' and fled to the Orange, admitting later that he had not anticipated 'all the peril and wretchedness I must encounter during the 4 years and 6 months I remained undetected'.[16] After writing a petition to the governor, Wikar was eventually pardoned and it was on his journey back to the Cape that Gordon, with great good fortune, encountered him.

Gordon took immediate advantage of this meeting to question Wikar on the tribes and topography of the country he intended exploring, as did Paterson. The English translation of the account has this to say of the occasion:

'Mr Gordon came ... the following day ... to see my curiosities and to get information about some matters which might be useful to that gentleman on the journey he had begun. I did all in my power in my simple way to be of service to this gentleman.'[17]

As will be seen during the course of this journey, Gordon made thorough use of Wikar's written and spoken accounts.

Despite continued fever, Gordon persisted in visiting various Namaqua settlements around Ellenboogfontein, recording what he saw with manifest interest and pleasure. On the same day that he met Wikar he wrote:

Again heard a tale from one Chief Cupido, saying that the evil spirits are angry with the Kleine Namaquas and that the Hare has said that they must die and stay dead and that he has told a lie about this. Therefore he must summon the *gowaaps* of certain spirits in order that they should come over the sea together, with all their livestock and animals. For this reason they have a strong feeling of hate for the Hare.
At their *Cami* or good-fortune-making neither children nor woman join in the eating.
Cupido had some knucklebones around his right hand and his right leg.

It is interesting to find that this same 'tale', or a version of it, was recorded in 1875, and again as late as 1971.[18]
The next day he was off again:

I went to Chief Wiltschut's kraal with the Chief. The kraal lay a quarter of an hour off the road. It consisted of nine straw – or rather mat – huts. There were about fifty men, women and children. Observed that those who had the most children had not more than four and that each man had only one wife. Saw two women from the Groote Namaqua Land. Married here. Each had the first joint of the right-hand little finger cut off. They said that their parents had done this when they were still young – for beauty. But when this took place there was a slaughtering: therefore a ceremony. They said that this was not done by everyone. Some said it was done because they were ill, as a way of bloodletting.'[19]

On 29 July Gordon had a musical interlude:

Enquired about the Amaquas but was told that the Kleine-Namaquas and the Amaquas are the same; that there are, apart from Wiltschut, four more chiefs and that this whole tribe consists of about four hundred men, women and children. None of these people cut out a testicle or a finger-joint.[20] Heard however from a Groote Namaqua that some of his people did do this, sometimes because of illness. Another said: so that they can run faster. These Namaquas make long pipes from reed or thorn-tree bark, and then block it at one end so that only one note is produced when they blow in from the top. Each has a longer or shorter pipe thus producing a different note. Then they form themselves into a circle and each in turn blows his note, like threshers or smiths, and it goes very pleasantly. They maintain a sort of melody while dancing, or rather bending very low (which is their manner of dancing) while stamping on the beat and turning, while others, just as with the Caffers jump around them singing and clapping hands all the while. They pour milk into their flutes to keep them moist and sound. The tone comes out mostly as a minor third (which sounds much like a quarter tone) but there is little diversity.
Also saw a *goura* which was as tall as I was, and in the place of a bird's feather quill at the top, as with the other Hottentots, it had a thinly scraped cattle horn.[21] They make a sound on this which, though softer, is just like the noise one gets on a second attempt at learning the french horn.

On 30 July 1779, feeling 'much better', Gordon set off on his journey to the mouth of the Orange. One wagon, 'under the supervision of my trusty Hottentot Iteki', was sent due north; in other words, it went on the road that had been taken by other travellers to the river and which was relatively well known. Gordon rode west and northwest to the seashore.

A curious and revealing episode completes the entry for this day. Once more it concerns the ineptitude of Paterson. Apparently some sort of challenge was involved concerning Gordon's high-spirited horse 'Snel'. Inevitably it is Paterson who falls into a ditch, luckily not hurting himself. But why does Gordon always tell these odd stories about the Scot? So often, when Paterson is mentioned, he is made to look a fool.

Gordon left without Paterson and his party, though he does not say so. The agreement, according to Paterson, was to travel separately. Characteristically, Gordon says nothing of the dangers ahead. Thus, in order to get some idea of the situation awaiting the travellers, it is worth quoting from Paterson's account.

We were much advised by the natives not to proceed, that we had an uninhabited desert to pass where there was neither man nor beast to be seen and great scarcity of water and hardly a blade of grass to support our cattle. We however resolved to go as far as possible so we agreed one to go a few days before the other and if possible to meet at the mouth of the Great River.

Accordingly, Captain Gordon parted with us and proceeded on his intended journey entirely without a guide, all the natives refusing to accompany us.[22]

Guide or no guide, on 31 July, the second day out, Gordon in fact becomes positively lyrical for a few lines before returning to his usual sober narrative mode:

We found it warmer at first and the country on all sides blazed with flowers, the most beautiful colours in the world: yellow oxalis, orange arctotis, red, yellow and bluish-purple mesembryanthemums etc. There were many Kokerbooms (agave) in bloom here. (There were three kinds of geranium). We called this place the Floraas- or Bloeme Kloof. After a seven and a half hour journey came to a spring but a Hottentot said it was not the Kooks Fontein which we were trying to reach. He was mistaken however. We therefore went on travelling for a further seven hours along an uneven track and beside a dry rivulet. Eventually we found a fairly good supply of water and so we made camp. Shot a hare and my dog caught a porcupine, all the dogs getting themselves badly wounded from its quills. Because our servants complained of hunger, I called this place Honger Kloof. We slaughtered a sheep for them. Everywhere sandy, poor karoo-country. Brack water as well.

It was no accident, of course, that Gordon was able to provide mutton for his servants at Honger Kloof. All expeditions into the interior had domestic stock travelling with the wagons. As we know from these journals, as well as other accounts before and after Gordon, game was by no means always available for the pot.

The first week's travelling to the vicinity of Grootmis (Gordon's 'Renoster kop') passed without any untoward incidents or undue hardship. Gordon, however, is indefatigably active and meticulous in writing down his observations in the journal. Early on he mentions his fears that, without his guidance, the wagons would overturn. At the same time the horses get lost, but this does not prevent him noting that he 'Caught an animal that looks like a field mouse. Called it an elephant mouse because it had a long, very flexible trunk or snout'.[23] Later, with the rising of the moon, two 'Hottentots' are sent to track the horses and we are told that Pienaar and his servants are off hunting elephants. From this entry, and from many other similar ones occurring throughout the journal, it is evident that Pienaar's main role was to provide meat for the party. This would have freed Gordon to concentrate more vigorously on his scientific activities and explains — at least in part — why he was able to make longer and more detailed journal entries.

On 3 August they came to the 'Groote Sand River (called the Kouwsie)' — now named the Buffels River — but, he records dourly, 'All water in these parts barely quenches one's thirst' because it is 'sweet' but 'brack'. He comments too on the presence of lions. And still interested in the geology of the area, he continues to make his familiar observations based on Buffon. The shells fascinate him too:

After an hour's ride heard the sea in the west. Rode down the

Above, **32**, *Carpobrotus sauerae*
(*also known as 'Hottentot fig'*) *and right,* **33**, *Sarcocaulon l'heritieri*
(*often referred to as 'Bushman's candles'*).

river and found Pinar and his servants on a rise and saw the sea hardly an hour's ride away from me. Found many shells on these ridges and though some appeared to be sea-wrack many of them seemed to have been brought here by people or baboons. Also heard that shore-Hottentots had spent some time here.[24] They eat only whale or shellfish. There were also big heaps of shells, too recent to have been left over from the time when the sea was here. Found whitish, chalky soil and salty, white earth and the rock is now beginning to lie in strata. Many of these very brittle and sandy, and although they lean to the N.W. their angles fit into one another. Found the loose stones very hard; much pebble and quartz in same so that if one strikes them they sound like an anvil. Because it was getting late, returned to the wagons which were in camp a good hour from the shore.

One of our Hottentots found a dead elephant cow and calf. He brought the tusks along, each of which weighed about twelve pounds. Saw many elephant tracks and the slides where they descend from higher places, slipping down on their heels. N.B. the front teeth of eland etc., are loose. Found the river water better here than higher up.

On 6 August he again meets up with Paterson near the site of present-day Grootmis/Kleinsee. Two days later he refers to abundant signs of there having been Strandlopers in the area and that they have seen jackal traps and huts made out of right whale bones as they travel 'along an elephant track, mostly N.N.W. Course always beside the sea'. But of the fact that they are finding the journey heavy going Gordon gives only the barest hint – as in his fleeting comment on their making camp 'after ten hours' difficult travelling for the oxen'. In contrast, Paterson's account is much more dramatic. He talks of 'the most barren coun-

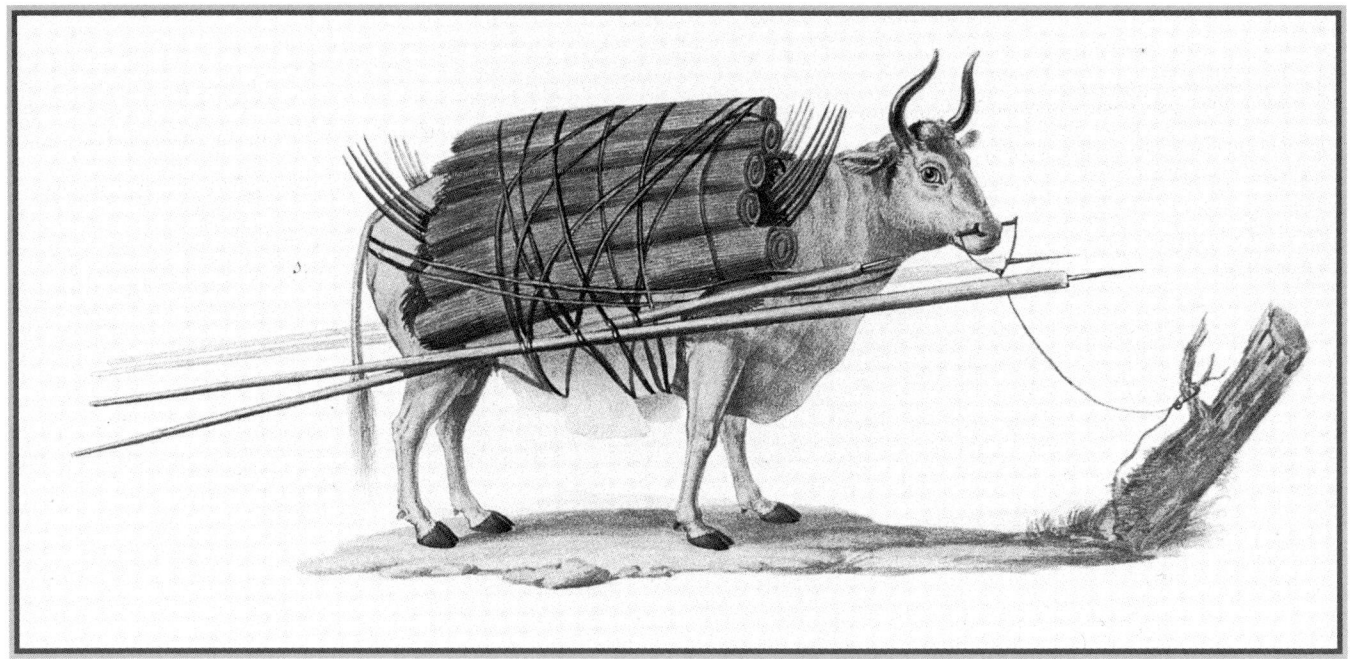

34. *A pack-ox laden for a journey.*

try I ever saw, several of our Hottentots complained and wanted much to return'.

Of such matters Gordon has nothing to say. Nevertheless, he has plenty to observe. He had written earlier of the flowers: 'mesembryanthemums and euphorbias and a beautiful kind of red ixia'. Now he turns to a wild, local inhabitant and to larks, among other matters:

A Hottentot, called Pedro by the farmers, said there was fresh water around here but we could not find it because of the dark. Shared out the little water that we had brought along in a barrel. Between these two places there was not a drop of water to be had. At the top of the *Kouwsie* mouth there is a small spring, half an hour's walk away. In the dark a hyena came close to the wagon and my dogs caught hold of it but before we could get to it with our guns it was gone.

Pedro the Hottentot has the wildest appearance one can imagine. He was utterly amazed at my spyglass, compass and watch. Van Reenen said I knew by my watch whether he had put us on the right road to water. He said that in order to see this proved he wanted to go the wrong way but when I showed him the compass and how the needle still showed our course, through deviation, he was greatly astonished.

Only one of our servants could easily converse with him. Although it is still the Hottentot language, it is a different dialect.

This is a very poor region. Found seashells everywhere, apparently brought by Hottentots. Went hunting but saw nothing except a steenbok. In the morning I heard the flutter of wings: larks as in the Cape, but none of them were singing as they do in the interior. Saw mountain swallows at the *Kouwsie*. The sea is everywhere very choppy and I can see some low rocks a few musket shots from the shore.

As the two parties made their way northwards, Gordon frequently referred to 'slow travelling' and to the 'heavy going' nature of the journey. Water was a continual problem for beast and man alike. But there were signs that other people had been on the shore ahead of them. Pedro, who seems to have been acting as some sort of guide, told them that the tracks they saw were of 'Hunting Bushmen' and that these people 'had drunk all the water'.

On the evening of 12 August Gordon wrote that the oxen 'would not move' because they had no water and had been travelling in deep sand. However, they did find water the next day at a camp which he called 'Diepe Kloof' and which has been identified as a point on the dry bed of the Holgat River, some ten kilometres inland and about thirty kilometres to the north of Port Nolloth.[25] Here they had to dig out the sand, so allowing the water to seep into the hole they had made. It was a slow process and the teams of oxen had to drink in turn, one after the other. They had had no water for fifty hours.

On the night of 14 August, still at 'Diepe Kloof', Paterson was in trouble again: 'Last night about twelve o'clock, it being my watch, they called for help from Paterson's tent. Found him nearly unconscious and very ill, but after heavy vomiting he became better. He had, against my advice, drunk too much water when hot and thirsty and then eaten a piece of very fat mutton.'

Typically, Gordon had no personal comment to make on this incident – neither a hint of pity, nor irritation, nor even humour in his account. Paterson himself, incidentally, says nothing of this overindulgence in his entry for the same day.

The parties trekked on again, though Gordon once more writes of the 'weariness' of his oxen. But they were close to the 'Great River' now. Gordon and Paterson climbed two hills which were named the 'Twee Gebroeders'[26] by Gordon, and he was able to estimate that the smaller hill was three miles from the mouth of the river. He named the 'valey' or vlei where they camped after Count Charles Bentinck of Sorgvliet.[27]

The next day, 17 August 1779, they rode up to the 'steep southern bank' of the Orange. It is worth quoting the entire entry for the day in order to once again experience this lively mind with its non-hierarchical variety of interests — a mind which, despite the momentous nature of the occasion, can pay as much attention to the habits of the ostrich as to the river itself:

Fine weather. S.E. wind. Therm. 56–74–60.
Departed at daybreak to give the horses water since they have had none for fifty hours; also to have a good drink myself. Mr. Paterson and van Reenen rode with me and as we came over the rise an ostrich sprang up and we found a nest with 34 fresh eggs. Since everything is so scarce it was a great treasure for us to find. The nest was a round place scraped in the sand, round and ten feet in diameter, raised slightly in the middle. Here in a shallow little hollow were 22 eggs where the male had been sitting. Around this bare place or circle there was another circular ridge as though dug out to the depth of a hand (thus surrounding the nest) and in this lay twelve eggs. It is said they always keep these to feed their young with when they are hatched. They say that one can find up to 84, even more in a single nest where five or six females each sit. Some say that when the female has hatched some of her eggs she goes off with the chicks and rolls the remaining eggs into the nest; and that they do not feed their young with those of other females which have been left in the nest.

Once over these rises we came upon country as hard as gravel with small, sharp, hard pebbles. They were of every kind of colour and facet also many beautiful geraniums (spinosa). Ugly, barren country everywhere, We saw some zebra and two springbok. We have seen hardly any game as large as this since leaving the Cape, though we have seen tracks. Wounded a zebra but it got away. We saw that the land rises across the river and that it has the same sandy appearance as the place where we were. Saw seven fresh lion tracks and after half an hour's ride from the wagons arrived at the river. This is the same river that I was at in December 1777 and which has its source to the North, beyond the Caffers. It was low and about four hundred paces wide, not flowing fast and with a steep southern bank. There are large sand-banks with a few small thorn and willow trees. We found elephant and lion tracks. Cooked one of our ostrich eggs. We buried the rest in the ground and left a coat on some piled up shrubs at the nest as a mark for our wagon, should it pass this way. Went a short distance up the river, letting the horses graze the meagre grass that was there.

We imagined that we could see a band of wild people so we returned to the horses, having but one gun with us. Then we rode to the place but found that our eyes had deceived us. We had sought so hard for various stones and had been staring so intently that our eyes grew dim from looking at the sand (also from the atmospheric phenomenon common in these regions). In this way we made several blunders which we had to laugh about. Because we were waiting impatiently and in vain for our wagons, not knowing whether they would make camp below or above us, rode up to the rise but saw nothing more than a herd of eland. When evening fell therefore, we decided to ride across the countryside, first to the west to look for the wagon tracks, and then at the shore to turn east and do the same thing. Mr. Paterson saw the wagons at a great distance but because we had all seen so many optical illusions this day we could not be sure until I found the tracks close beside the shore. Soon after this we found the wagons camped close to the river where it makes a large marsh one hour from the mouth. This marsh changes completely at high tide when it is one and a half hours' wide, with an island against the left bank. At ebb-tide however it runs very shallow, revealing many sand-banks and one can then go to the island on foot. So far as I can discover the sea breaks strongly at the mouth and the opening is not wide. Found many water-fowl here: pelicans, ducks, two different kinds of flamingo etc. To our astonishment we found that the water was very sweet, though ebbing and flowing strongly. It surprised me that I saw no hippopotamus and only one animal foot-print; however there is not much to graze on here.

Brought the boat to the water, hoisted the Prince's flag and we drank to the health of His Highness. We bade welcome to the river to which I gave its name in 1777. Said more concerning the welfare of the Company, and all done to the accompaniment of some shots. We have still heard nothing from Pinar and his four Hottentots from Goewaap. A stiff N.W. wind this evening. Sky overcast.

What is so baffling here is that the main episode of the day — a day of great historical importance — is given remarkably little prominence, with the actual ceremony on the river restricted to a few lines. Worse still is the clumsy and off-hand way in which Gordon describes the event. Yet it must have been a wonderful sight to see. These travellers and explorers in a small boat, drinking toasts to the Prince of Orange while the flag was hoisted above them and the strange, wide African river rolled by as evening closed in. 'All done,' says Gordon, 'to the accompaniment of some shots.' And that is that.

This episode is arguably the high point of Gordon's exploring career, but the drama of it must be created in our imaginations, for Gordon gives only the facts.

It is interesting to be able to compare Gordon's entry for this day with that of Paterson. On the whole, Paterson's prose is austere and matter-of-fact, but next to Gordon's his account seems positively eloquent. Paterson writes:

At ten in the forenoon we arrived at the river which seemed at once to be a new creation to us. We had been nine days before crossing a dry sultry desert where no living animal was to be seen and during which time our cattle had had no water but twice. We here unsaddled our horses and refreshed ourselves by the side of the river under the shadow of a willow which hung over the banks . . . .[28]

By contrast, Gordon scarcely alludes to the hardships that they had been through, and he certainly has no phrase like Paterson's 'new creation' to offer us.

The last entry of the day concerns Pienaar who had gone off five days earlier and had not returned. It is strange that this is Gordon's first mention of the fact and that he makes no reference to being worried about the missing hunter. He merely states that he has 'heard nothing' from him. Paterson, on the other hand, voiced his

35. *The 'moggel' or mud mullet (Labeo umbratus) – a common Cape fish found in river mouths.*

alarm several times in his journal, saying on 15 August: 'By this time we lost all hopes of ever seeing them.'

It is evident that the absence of Pienaar and his four Hottentots in fact caused great anxiety in the party. However, when they arrive the next day, Gordon merely records 'our joy', but Paterson is a great deal more graphic about the event: 'Mr Pinar arrived with three of the Hottentots who were dreadful to look at . . . their eyes were sunk in their heads and appeared more like dead than living ones.'[29]

The fourth 'Hottentot' servant, whom they had given up for dead, arrived the next day – 'to our great joy' says Gordon. However, it is worth noting that Gordon records refreshing the man 'with a tot and . . . food to eat'. It is from small details like this that we can see that Gordon had the welfare of these people very much at heart. It was simply not part of his personality, however, to say this in his journal.

As might be expected, once at the river, Gordon threw himself into a number of activities. Food for the party was his first concern:

We started fishing. At first we did not seem likely to succeed because of the strong wind and turbulence of the water but on the second cast [of the net] we caught enough for all our people. This caused great rejoicing, the catch consisting of so-called harders and some barbel.[30] In his hunger, my dog Keiser swam over to the sand-bank where we were fishing and greedily ate up a live fish, surely for the first time in his life.

On 19 August he explored the mouth in his boat, ingeniously converting a wagon tent to make a sail. They did some more fishing and Gordon examined the nature of the river sand, fascinated by certain ruby-like particles which he observed under his microscope. He did not neglect to take bearings on both the Twee Gebroeders and 'the northern tip of the river mouth'. On returning to camp he 'received the good news that our Hottentots had shot a zebra and that they had found 12 ostrich eggs. So now, once more, both dogs and men had food.'

It was on 20 August, the following day, that Gordon had his first encounter with the Strandlopers. As noted earlier in the chapter, this account of their meeting is full of interest, with moments of real drama and tension created by Gordon, despite himself, through a quickening tempo in style. As this was a significant episode in the journey, the whole entry for this day now follows.

Therm. 48–55–52. Fine weather. S.E. wind. Dew tonight. Misty in the evening and the wind at the sea was again a fresh S.W. Crossed the river to see how things looked on the other side and to see whether we could track down any people. There is a sandbank in the mouth which lies right in the way. It took us more than half an hour to cross the river because our boat kept on running aground on the sandbanks. There were eleven of us in it and we had to keep on jumping out to lift it. With our fishing net we were much too heavy for the boat, thus making our journey across dangerous. Once on the other side our people went fishing. Before this, on the sandbank in the river we made one cast and caught some harders. Mr. Paterson and I went due north into the country; a Hottentot as well as my young Koerikei came with us. It was low-lying country; the soil of clay, with a few small fleshy shrubs. Thereafter the soil at the river was entirely sand, without any water. There were low dunes on our left-hand side. (Resin is given off by Cacativas). After we had been going for an hour we came to a rain-water marsh. Beside this we found the small and large footprints of people, very fresh. We also found large, dry, washed-up trees here. Soil had been washed over these and shrubs were growing on them; this means that the river must have been very high some years back or that there was a heavy storm at sea. We followed the footprints which led to the dunes, being most curious to see these people.

We first set our course a short half hour landwards and then turned once more towards the dunes in order to get there before them. When we reached the dunes we found a well-trodden track and saw first one and then three of the wild people rising from the ground. After looking at us for a moment, they dashed off, like deer. In order to stop them I stood and waved my hat as hard as I could but they ran down the dune and along the shore. Upon this I sent my Hottentot after them, with a gun, but he could not catch up with them. We then followed the footpath which brought us right to their huts, where we found their fire burning and a puppy which, though very young, was very vicious.

There was one large hut, different from the kind the Hottentots make, with two high doors or rather openings facing east. It was made of wood (washed-up trees, right-whale or whale ribs) and was thatched with grass and undergrowth, very warm. In same there were 9 to 10 sleeping places on which lay dassie and jackal skins. The other hut was smaller and had only one opening and had yet another place made for sitting in the daytime. They were all in a row and joined together so that one wall served for two. There were pouches made of skins hanging in the huts and horns (Canna or Cape eland) with buchu and fat and a pot made of baked earth. There were many ostrich egg-shells, some empty, some filled with water in store, and the fireplace was in the middle of the hut, which was not quite high enough for a man to stand upright. They had stuck dry, washed-up trees in front of the door and on the branches were hanging pieces of raw right-whale meat which they had cut off. They broil or cook this for their food. We found two, beautifully dressed seal-skins.

We left everything in the same place and in order to get these people to come and talk decided to leave them something as a present; to place it there and to come back the following day. Having brought nothing, I cut all the copper buttons off my coat, save one, and added these to the copper tinderboxes which Mr. Paterson and the Hottentot had placed on a skin where these people were drying herbs, such as buchu, in the sun. I also left a piece of biscuit, which we had baked, next to them.

Before we decided to go, however, I ordered the Hottentot to make a fire in front of the huts so that we could first cook and eat an ostrich egg which we had brought for food. (First one makes a hole in the top, since otherwise the expanding air would make it burst open violently, then it is cooked in the shell, as though in a pot. Having done this one makes a spoon from a piece of the shell and one eats it thus in the Hottentot manner.) After we had cooked the egg and were busy eating we saw three of the wild people coming on to a dune not so very far from us. Once more I waved and sent the Hottentot to them, letting him show them that we had no gun, by throwing off his sheepskin and holding his hands high. The Hottentot was frightened to go near them so I encouraged him by loading my gun and showing that I was on the alert for the wild people; (they had bows and arrows and thick assegais, 7 to 8 feet long). He went rather reluctantly towards them and when he reached them, they all sat down. After we had spent some time waiting Paterson said he would like to accompany me to them without

36. Equus zebra (*mountain zebra*) *was indigenous to the Orange River region in Gordon's day.*

taking a gun; however I judged it more prudent that one of us should keep the gun because they could surprise us by coming from behind the dune. Whereupon the botanist stayed with the guns and I went up to the foot of the hill with a bottle and a jug held high in my hands. Finding that their number had grown to seven, and judging it inadvisable to go amongst these people without a gun, I sent Koerikei to them with a bottle and a jug in order to make them a present of some brandy but he came back and said they did not know what it was and did not want to drink it. Upon this I sent him with a tinderbox, a flint and a flint-stone (about which they also knew nothing) for the chief. I said that two of them should come to me without weapons seeing that I too had no weapon. While they were talking to each other, I saw some more of the wild people on a dune to my left-hand side. After Koerikei had delivered his message, two of them came down without weapons. In the meantime another, who at closer hand turned out to be a woman, was jabbering most violently on top of the dune, pointing with her hands to the river. When I saw that they had voluntarily laid down their weapons I went out to meet them and found the three men suspicious and frightened. But the women were talkative and merrier. They had a child with them that appeared to be the bastard of a slave (but later found otherwise) because his hair was curlier than the Hottentots', it was still however, woolly. But closer saw that this was from being smeared. There was also something different about his features.

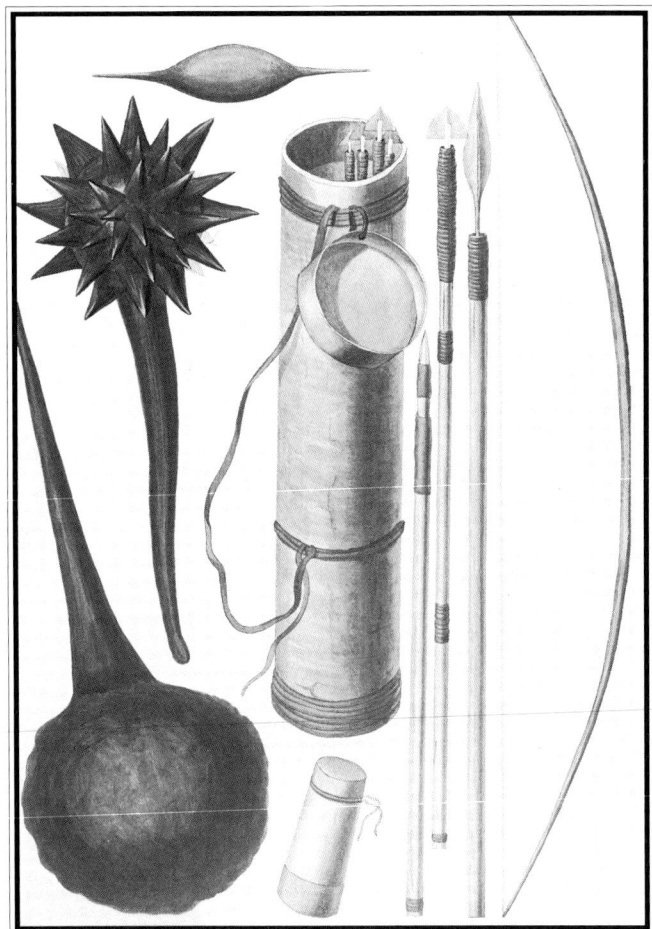

37. *'Bushman' and 'Hottentot' weapons.*

These creatures had the same posture and shape as Bushmen (their dress etc.) but their teeth are short and bad. Their women too carry ostrich shells filled with water in just such nets, also wood. I counted that one of them was carrying 24 full shells on her back. Gave them the aforementioned buttons and they immediately became bolder, but they would drink no brandy even though I did so first. Gave them some tobacco which they smoked out of our Hottentots' pipes (later from a buffalo horn using water).

So we all went together to their huts and we showed them that we had left everything in order, and they were happy about this. They speak a Hottentot dialect of which our Hottentots were able to understand a fair amount. One woman showed us the belly of her husband. He had been wounded with a knife by Hottentots from the other side of the river a long time ago. That was why they distrusted people from the other side and why they had been frightened of us. Told them that they should not fear us but that they should go with us; I also said we had nothing now with us to give them. They said yes, that they had already seen us yesterday on the other side of the river and that they were utterly astonished at our boat and its sails (at first they took it for an animal). Found a piece of deal there. They said they found it on the beach, but that they had never seen a ship. One of their women was born in Kleine Namaqua Land and she had seen Dutchmen and guns before – as a result she was frightened to touch my gun.

Asked them if there was water further north or a river. They said No, and that they had always lived here and that they had gone far along the shore in search of food. But they knew of no other people, such as Bushmen, along the river. They all had very short, flat, small teeth and only one young fellow had good ones and his were rather small. Of average figure and thin. Two women had the first joint cut off their left-hand little finger. They said that this was because of 'Other Making' or *Canie* when they were ill. Gave each of them a European name which they were pleased about and they laughed. They had their wool plaited: one of them as though it was a wig in curlers – with thorn-wood pins. Some also with little pig-tails. They had a few beads and copper ear-rings which they said they had had for a long time, passed down from hand to hand.

Their chief was a young fellow, his nose frightfully disfigured by a lion. He had an uncle, a mother, a wife and children. He was called Koet, his mother is also called Koet. His father had also been the chief of this band. The people that used to live on this side of the river died out but for two women who are now here. They denied that it was through eating poisoned fish, but they said that once one of their girls had died from eating what had been washed up (they called it this 'evil spirit'). The uncle was called Hanni, the other one Cabesi, the women – Camaz, San ga, Nauta, and Carouta. Four other of their menfolk were out hunting and some of their wives and children did not dare approach us. They had a puppy and an old bitch, black and yellow, much resembling a jackal. They showed me two beautifully dressed seal-skins. Exchanged the one for the last button that I had on the front of my coat and I cut off another from my sleeve in order to obtain a skin for Mr. Paterson.

Went along the shore to the Northern side of the mouth, followed by nine of these people. Took bearings on the shore: N.W. by N. as far as I can see. The sea is very rough for half an hour out from the shore, though I could see no rock and the shore is completely sandy without shells. Returned to our fishermen following the right bank of the river, completely certain now that no skiff or boat could ever enter here, because the breakers are too rough and start too far out. Also, when the river is full it flows out too far. The greatest depth in the river was two and a half fathom but this did not last for long. When we reached our fishermen, who had caught a fair amount of harders, I gave the wild people some fish which they first grilled and then ate. I ordered another cast to be made so that they returned to their huts with some fish, very happy, and they promised to cross the river to us next day.

Because the party was eleven strong and had caught many fish, we started back for the camp leaving our net on the bank, the moon shining now. Mist began to come up and because we had to pass many sandbanks, the boat being heavily laden with no free-board, the crossing over was dangerous. At times we shipped water on account of the rippling of the river but guided by the fires on the bank towards which I steered we did at last, fortunately, reach our camp; but not without often going aground.

It is very hazy along the shore though the weather is fine.

Once Gordon, Paterson and their two servants had reached the deserted huts of the Strandlopers, it is interesting how much detail the journal gives us, not just about the encampment but also of such matters as 'the puppy which though very young was very vicious'. It is as though Gordon does not wish to forget or leave out anything that happened on this day.

The impulse to cut off all the copper buttons on his coat 'save one' is indeed unforgettable and reveals a spontaneity in Gordon not often found in the journals. It also shows us how very engrossed he was in getting to know this new group of people, and anxious too that they should have some present as a witness of his good faith. But it is also characteristic of Gordon that, having described this dramatic gesture, he immediately goes on to explain how they cooked an ostrich egg in its shell. This detail is also important for him and the story must wait while he discusses this matter.

He notes that once contact has been made with the Strandlopers — not without suspicion and due caution on both sides — it is the women who are 'talkative and merrier'. Gordon and his party are clearly adept at convincing the tribe of their good intentions, and all apprehension is soon forgotten.

As incident succeeds incident, and detail follows detail, it is easy to forget what an extraordinary encounter this was. For all, bar one, of the tribespeople this was their first sight of white men, and for Gordon and his party this was their first meeting with the Strandlopers — a type of people little known until then. Although Gordon does not comment directly on this aspect, his awareness of the fact is manifested in the length and detail of his entries regarding this band.

There is a drawing of these people and of their huts in Gordon's 'great map'.[31] It even shows their dogs and a dead beached whale in the background with the 'wild people' feeding off it (see page 118). He calls them 'Strand Bosjemans' or 'Sea-shore Bushmen', adding that they are 'fish-eating and Hunter-Hottentots'.

The Strandlopers continued to fascinate Gordon and it is fair to assume that he, in turn, continued to fascinate them. The following quotations show how readily they had accepted his goodwill and his generous, if circumscribed, hospitality. It will also be seen that although the 'wild people' occupied most of the journal at this juncture, neither Gordon's 'scientific' duties nor matters of zoological interest were neglected. Again, the entries for 21 and 22 August merit being quoted in their entirety.

21st August 1779.
Sky overcast, hazy weather. Wind N.W. Therm: 48–65–56. Weather clearing in the evening.

Because visibility was not good, stayed on this side. The wild people came to us. They numbered three men, four women and one child. They had gone upstream a little and crossed, the water up to their bellies, by a route known to them. I gave them some fish and tobacco and when we had had a talk about this country, they departed happy towards sunset.

Took a latitude but not accurate because of the misty weather. Got 28 deg.–32 min.

Most of us had pains in our body today. We attributed this to eating a lot of fish without bread.

The Bushmen said that there were never many hippopotamus at the mouth of the river but that they were plentiful two or three days' journey upstream. Saw the wild people make fire. They had two little sticks of a light wood and thickness of a little finger and about two feet long; it grows alongside the water (of this river). The wood is very dry. They place one of these sticks on a skin or on one of their shoes made of hide, put a foot upon it to hold it still, then they push the other wood into it, and, spitting on their hands, they twirl the stick as rapidly as they can between their flattened hands. Thereupon one sees smoke issuing from the stick and afterwards fire. They always have these kinds of sticks tied to their quivers; the wood is called *Goerop*, almost the same name a white flint-stone is given.

22nd August 1779.
Therm: 50–65–53. Sky overcast. Light N.W. wind. A little drizzle in the evening.

Crossed the river, rowing for an hour and caught some harders. Mr. Paterson and I went to the Hottentots once more and there we had our midday meal of ostrich egg and a piece of grilled zebra meat we had brought; and very good it tasted, although the Dutch inhabitants will not eat it; they say it is unclean. Took a few shots at a skin with the Bushmen. Examined some of their jackal traps. Two of them accompanied us a little further inland. Low-lying, sandy country everywhere, although the sea has retreated for good. The wild people said that there was absolutely no water for as far as they had been and they said that when they went hunting they took water in shoulder bags, also in seal-bladders. We bartered for one of these and the water from it tasted very good.

We turned towards the shore. On the way a so-called horned-snake ran out in front of us.[32] I took one of the wild men's assegais and lifted up the bush under which it had crept, sitting

TO THE MOUTH OF THE ORANGE RIVER

Previous page:
38. *The 'so-called Strandlopers' were clearly related to the other indigenous peoples of the west coast.*

there hissing. As I lifted, it struck the blade of the assegai. I hit and killed it and took it with me. It was about a foot long, with two small fleshy knobs just visible above the eyes which were split like cats' eyes.

Because of this it is known as *hoornmannetje*, in these regions. Here one can see how wrong Kolbe was who gave it two proper horns.[33] In the upper jaw and high to the side it has two canines which bend slightly inwards below; it has no incisors. In addition it has six upper molars on each side. No canines or incisors below but also six side-teeth on each side (much like a fish) slightly crooked and bent backwards. It is said to be very poisonous. Its colour is grey and it is flecked. Its tail ends in a sharp point. We saw another longer thin snake but we could not catch it.

We reached the sea and found that the shore was the same as the day before yesterday, not a single rock though the sea broke heavily. The wild people said that the shore had this same feature for as far as they had been along it; no rivers and no rocks so that they had to cross the river at low tide to get shell fish. They said that it was their footprints we had seen at the Kouwsie River and that they had also killed an eland then. Returned to their huts, gave them some tobacco and drew the picture of their huts.

Returned, crossing the river in the afternoon. We sailed back with a fairly brisk N.W. wind in half an hour, and had to turn many times going through the sandbanks; even so ran aground twice.

These people with men, women and children are about 20 strong. They appear to be concerned about their children, since most of them were always away somewhere. They said: looking for food in the veld, roots, bulbs etc.

From this last entry we have a statement that seems to imply that Gordon himself 'drew the picture of their huts'. Up to this point in the journey he has not mentioned Schoemaker at all, so in all probability the drawing was made in Gordon's own hand and was not his by proxy, as it were. We cannot be certain, however, that the picture on the map, obviously made much later in Cape Town, is identical or close to the one that was made on this day. The particular problem of who drew what in the Gordon Atlas therefore remains, to a large extent, problematical.

On 23 August Gordon wrote that he had made a 'map for Pinar so that he could go up the river, it being impossible for the wagons to do this'. This is an interesting statement. Gordon could only have got the information for this map from Wikar's 'account', discussed earlier in this chapter, as well as from the Swede's crude sketch of the Orange which was attached to the account. (The sketch showed the river from its mouth to the vicinity of Koegas, 'which lies between Upington and Prieska'.[34]) The wagons were, indeed, only able to travel a day's journey upriver due to the rough terrain they encountered there, as was noted a little later in the journal.

However, before leaving to go upstream, Gordon was once more visited by the Strandlopers who were so hungry that they asked

our servants for two worn-out shoes made of eland hide, whereupon they rubbed the hair off with a stone and then grilled and ate them. Gave them some fish and tobacco. One of our party who had found a dead, washed-up right whale, told them of it, whereupon they rejoiced greatly. They said they would go to it tomorrow and would not come with us up river since they were suffering the greatest hunger.

On 25 August 1779 Gordon and his party did eventually leave the mouth to journey upstream, eastward along the river. On his first day out there is a lively description of a hippopotamus:

After going upriver for three hours (to the place where we first reached it) we ate a grilled duck which we had brought with us and cooked an ostrich egg. While we were eating, a hippopotamus came to have a look at us, sticking only its nose and eyes out, but we had no gun. He did this again and again and in the same place the whole time we were eating. As he stuck his head half out in this way he did look somewhat like a horse and this could be the reason that the ancients called it a river horse. The Hottentots have told me that there is a sort of wagtail at the drift higher up the river, which, when the hippopotamus sticks its head out, flies on to it.[35] When it goes under again they fly to another head which has come up, without the animals (and there are many of them there) paying any attention. It may be that these little birds pick ticks off these animals for they are full of them. It surprised me that there are so many of these animals upriver where there are more people. They are so shy here where they are never disturbed. That there is little grazing is probably the reason why there are so few here. It is also said that they are much smaller here than they are beyond the Sneeuwberg. The wild people here did not know of the giraffe.

Though it is not mentioned in the journal, evidently Pieter Pienaar and his hunters shot an elephant on this or the previous day. Accordingly, Gordon rode along the river to where the dead animal lay. It is on this day then, 26 August, that we have his first recorded encounter with an elephant. As usual, his description, which follows here, is packed with information. It also contains a respectful, if not awed, impression of the power of the African lion:

The Hottentots told us that they had found a pride of lions by the dead elephant. My dogs chased a large band of baboons in the thickets beside the river, and most probably killed one because their muzzles were bloody when they returned but, because of the undergrowth, could find nothing. When we reached the elephant it was lying in thick undergrowth between high thorn-trees and it stank greatly. We went with our guns at the ready in case of lions. Although the Hottentots had lighted a fire at the elephant, a pride of six lions had walked through the smouldering ash so that now we saw only that there was a great deal of their black dung around and that they had eaten into the

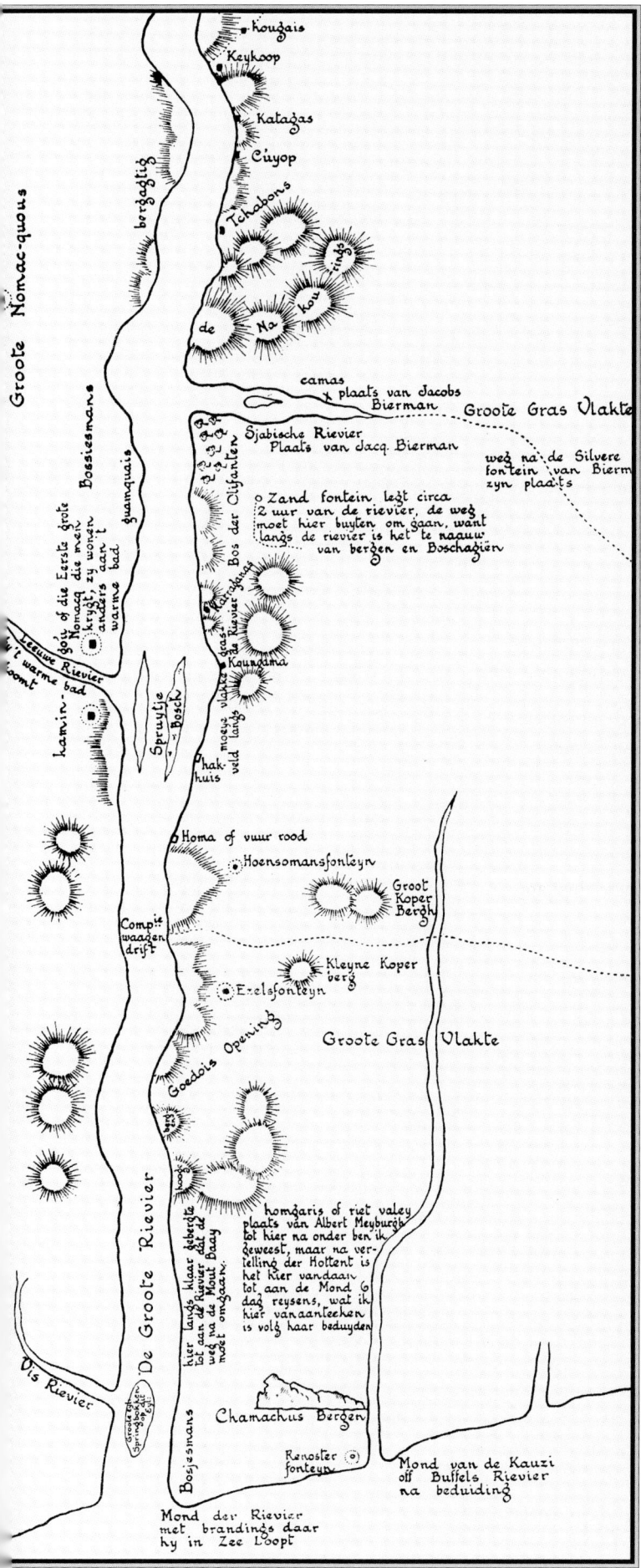

elephant's head and eaten part of the brains, in addition to a piece of the ear, which in this animal covers the whole shoulder. Measured it as much as I could: its height in front, in a straight line was 10 feet and 2 inches (Rhineland); it was the same height behind, from above its anus (it slopes sharply away below the tail). Its length in a straight line was 12 feet 4 inches. The sole of its front foot was 18 inches in diameter. Its rear foot had a diameter 2 inches longer and was just as wide. Since it was a bull its tusks stuck out three feet, therefore a young animal. An elephant can trample down a large thorn-tree and feed itself along this river where there are still a fair amount of these. It eats the foliage and bark of the trees, especially the thorn-trees (mimosa). This greatly stunts the growth of the trees.

This elephant was hit by four or five heavy, half-tin balls before it died. Following this, a herd of elephants was here again but they went off. These thorn-trees produce a good gum which is eaten by the Hottentots.[36] On a thorn-tree which was a good seventy feet high saw an ape like those in Outeniqua Land. Today also saw some quail, turtle doves and so-called pheasant.

Because I had forgotten my cloak I first took bearings (though it was in the evening) and then rode back to my tent with one Hottentot. Arrived there in moonshine after three hours' riding without noticing any lions. Made one turn to the left across the range or rather the high ridge.

Our Hottentots who had not shot anything while hunting were very hungry; they went to the elephant and found its paw or lower foot still very good eating but the eight hungry men were still not able to finish it. Pinar and the two van Rhenens stayed at the elephant to forestall the lion, but this evening it got too late. The lions came roaring half an hour after I had left the elephant. Next day they found that one foot had been dragged a very long way off, showing the great strength of this animal.

Gordon also had a taste of the elephant's foot, which he found 'very good though somewhat harder than calf's foot'. On this same day Gordon again mentions the 'map' or 'sketch' that he sent to Pienaar: '. . . also a pocket-compass and some provisions. He is to go along the river to Companys Drift and wait for me there. Five Hottentots go with him. I am most sorry that I cannot be of the party. This is because my presence is needed most at the wagons.'

It is not immediately clear why Pienaar was to make this journey to what is now known as Ramans Drift. But, as we shall see, Gordon was now preparing to return to Ellenboogfontein with the wagons. In the meantime he suffered another mishap: 'Got a thorn in my finger which developed into a bad sore; it has troubled me greatly. Bad water and an irregular way of living make a bagatelle of a wound develop into something highly malignant.' In other words, Gordon was fully aware of the dangers of blood poisoning in this situation, though there was not much he could do to prevent it occurring.

Map 5. *A section of Wikar's map, copied from the original.*

39. Giraffa camelopardalis. *Something of the awe felt by Gordon and contemporary zoologists for this great quadruped is clearly evident in the tribesman's eyes.*

CHAPTER SIX

The Fourth Journey:
The Land of the Cameloparns

(August – October 1779)

Return to Ellenboogfontein; blood poisoning; back to the Orange; 'Hottentot' marriages; the first giraffe; the Augrabies Falls; tribespeople of the Orange

Unable to continue along the river bank with the wagons, Gordon's decision to return to Ellenboogfontein must have been taken on two main counts: firstly, to refurbish his party, and secondly, to use a known wagon road to reach the river higher up at Companys Drift – the rendezvous place with Pienaar.

Leaving the river on 29 August, it is revealing to see how carefully Gordon had to plan his journey. The way he presents this in the journal allows us to hear him 'thinking aloud', as it were. A vigorous moonlit zebra hunt rounds off the entry for this day:

Had the fever last night and my whole hand was swollen. Made everything ready for our return, filled our barrels with water. Because of the scarcity of water we will now have to travel back for 80 hours with the ox wagons. Also because it is impossible for a wagon to go further up river at this point – the cliffs are so steep – although not as high as one is given to believe, it will again be one degree, sixteen minutes due north before I reach the river where I want to cross. It will still take a good 58 hours' travel with the ox wagons and that in bad country where there is almost no water and what there is will be brack (not much game as well). It would take six days to where I was, a reasonable journey by wagon, with water, to the drift. (Or so I imagined then). We travelled back along the path we had previously taken with the horses and reached Bentinck's Valey where we rejoined our wagon road. We decided to travel by night since we now knew the road and where there was water and to let our stock graze during the day. Also to so arrange things that our stock will drink every second day, until we get to Kouwsie and to let them rest a day at each watering place, there being but two of these for cattle. . . .

Departed south at six o'clock in the dusk, saluting the river with a discharge of guns and with a tot of brandy. This is almost finished so that we have to share a ration of two or three tots a day. After we had been travelling for three hours and the moon had been up for about an hour there was a loud barking from the dogs. We ran to them and found some zebras, six I think. A Hottentot had shot a mare before we got there and the rest of the zebras were being harried by our dogs, in particular my Keiser and Koning. The zebras ran with open muzzles towards van Reenen and Pedro who evaded them. They ran down a hill and Kobus van Rhenen wounded one in its foreleg so that the dogs were able to pull it to the ground repeatedly. It bit several of the dogs even though it was wounded. More than once my gun which had got wet would not fire but at last among all the dogs I was able to shoot it. It was also a young mare. While this was happening we heard the remaining zebras calling their companions. I heard this sound for the first time: a grating noise as when a stone is thrown over freshly frozen ice and differing greatly from that of the kwagga. The largest mare was in a straight line 6 feet 2 inches long (Rhineland). The height in front three feet nine and a half inches; behind two inches higher. We cut off as much [flesh] as we could take and since we could not linger because we were short of water for our cattle, we travelled on, having delayed a good hour there. We made camp at four o'clock in the morning after nine hours' good travelling. We were now a half mile W.N.W. of the Twee Gebroeders, at the smallest of the two, by the sea. While chasing the zebras the wound on my hand burst open and is still painful and swollen.

For the greater part of this return journey Gordon was in considerable pain from the infected sore on his hand. On 30 August he wrote: 'My hand was very painful and swollen; this is chiefly because my dog Keiser was hungry and when I was going to give him a piece of meat, he, in his haste took my hand with it. This made my young Koerikei laugh and got him a few cuffs over the ear.' This is the only time in the journals that Gordon records a reaction of this nature. Equally interesting is that he even records this trivial incident. Was he slightly uneasy about his quite justified bout of temper?

The wound continued to deteriorate and the day after the punishment of Koerikei, Gordon wrote in the journal: 'Stayed here, lying down. My hand has become so bad that I have caught a fever as well. Used a lancet to cut open the finger and found that a growth had formed. Much blood and pus came out. I could not walk because of the great pain.'

Despite his illness, however, Gordon continued writing up his journal for the day – recording, speculating, observing:

The abundance of big, white periwinkle shells which are found everywhere in the veld must originate from the wild people or animals who feed on them otherwise one would not find so many dead ones and so seldom the living. Their colour is somewhat grey and one sees them here and there under the euphorbia bushes, crawling suddenly into the earth.

The abundance of seashells to be found here can only come from the wild people and with time will probably become covered with earth. Under the euphorbias (or what are here called melkbosjes) there is a fungus or growth like a mushroom which has a taste something like that between a potato and fish roe (because of its small seed).[1] It is not unpleasant and is eaten by the Hottentots and called *kaniep*. It also grows in the Roggeveld. We also found a small spider whose nest contained many insects. The material of this nest most resembles the little nests that the kapok bird makes.[2] Inside were threads resembling thin darning wool: they were thick and very strong. Koerikei brought me good honey which he had scooped out.

Eventually, Gordon was unable to leave until 2 September. Even then, at the end of his entry for that day, he wrote that his hand was 'still not better'. Notwithstanding this, the wagons continued to travel seven hours or more each day under punishing, parched conditions. Only on 5 September did they reach Kouwsies River, near present-day Grootmis: 'Found no spring there; drank the river-water which was sweetish-brack and hardly slaked one's thirst.[3] My supply of Orange River water came to an end today. One of my oxen collapsed. We are having a hard time of it.'

For Gordon to admit to having a hard time is unusual. Given his habitual reticence about such matters, we can assume that they were suffering greatly. Indeed Paterson, in his *Narrative*, records that on this same day, 6 September, 'Our provision began to be short; but one of the Hottentots determined, notwithstanding this circumstance, not to be deprived of his meal, contrived during the night to rob the others of their shoes, which he completely devoured'.[4]

On the same night they again broke camp and sustained an accident: 'Through the negligence of the leaders, Mr. Paterson's wagon overturned as we were travelling along the bank of the river by starlight. I was sitting up in front, there were three of us in it, and we were hardly harmed, but some boxes were broken.'

It is surely revealing that Gordon was sitting in the wagon. Most of the time, as we are given to understand from the journal, he preferred to travel on horseback or on foot. It therefore seems probable that he was using this more leisurely form of transport because his hand was still troubling him.

However, things began to improve after this and, riding ahead, Gordon reached the haven of Ellenboogfontein on 10 September. He does not mention his hand again and we can assume that by then it had nearly healed. But it is worth noting that he left Paterson and Van Reenen to come after him with the wagons. They only reached Engelbrecht's two days later. Perhaps Gordon needed this time to rest and to convalesce. Certainly it was unlike him to spend, as he did here, a whole week in one place with such little activity recorded.

Before reaching Ellenboogfontein Gordon stopped to watch the singular way in which milking was performed by certain 'Hottentots': '... I saw for the first time that after they have milked a while they grip the labia of the cow's vagina in both hands and then blow strongly into it. Shortly afterwards the cow pisses and they go on milking. They say they do this if the cow withholds its milk.'

This practice, it should be mentioned, was also recorded by earlier travellers.[5]

Once again, on 17 September, Gordon was to witness a dance by local tribespeople, this time the 'Gam or Kleine Namaquas'.

Seven sit down in a circle close to each other. Each had a thin cylindrical tube made of thorn-tree bark with a diameter of half an inch and more; each differed in length as well; from 2 and 3 to 4 and 5 feet long. A chewed-up plug of thorn-tree bark is then pushed in, after it has been moistened with milk. After this they tune their flutes: it is often a fourth but not always. They push the plug higher or lower with a thin stick, according to the song to be played. Thus tuned, each maintains his individual tone by blowing into it from above, through the vent. Each generally produces his tone twice in succession, after that they carry on one after the other like smiths or threshers. It produces a very wild melody. Each begins by making his tone twice and at the same time stamping with his right leg putting it down slightly to the right and the left leg follows behind in the same way. Whereupon they start the same thing again, following one upon the other, all of them bending forwards so that their heads come together. (The Hottentots always bend forward in their dances, the Caffers never). And so they stamp, always to the right in the same circle until their dance is over. The women stand up at a distance of ten paces, skipping and singing 'Ho, ho, ho: ha, ha, ha!' clapping their hands and going up to the men from time to time, as if to rouse them, turning quickly back to their former place, sometimes turning once round the men and then away. When the men who are blowing are a little apart, one or two of the women go between them and then the men make as if to catch them. One of these women, going through the circle, fell upside down in such a way that we all had to laugh, and, she ran off ashamed. This was one of the prettiest Hottentot women that I have ever seen. She was almost white and although she had a Hottentot face, she had fine features.

The sudden change to moist, cold weather inconvenienced us.

The latter part of this entry deserves some comment. The remarks about 'the prettiest Hottentot woman I have ever seen' seem oddly personal and thus out of keeping with Gordon's normal style. There seems to be just the slightest deviation from his habitual, empirical detachment, as though, for a moment, he was betraying some degree of sexual interest. But, as if correcting this momentary lapse, the final sentence is abrupt, matter of fact and once more 'scientific'. The change in the weather that he records has almost become an admonition.

There is a lively drawing of a 'Hottentot' dance in the Gordon Atlas (see overleaf) which appears to be an illustration of the ceremony described in this passage. For example, the way the men are said to bend forward while playing their 'flutes' and stamping their feet is accurately portrayed in this drawing. There is even a female figure entering the circle of males – a detail that perfectly corresponds with the journal account, in which the women are said to be 'going up to the men from time to time as if to rouse them'. The drawing obviously depicts real people: each face is different, and the skirts, karosses and beads are all carefully, even affectionately, detailed. It is a charming scene and more than likely was drawn by Gordon himself.[6]

The next day, 18 September 1779, Gordon again set off for the Orange River. Paterson and his party did not join him, preferring to return to the Orange at Ramansdrift, to enter Namibia via the Houms River, and later to return to the Cape in December 1779. According to Paterson, 'he [Gordon] intended to direct his course to the eastward in search of a nation called Briquas[7] which is a sort of Cafferes'. Gordon himself makes no mention of such intentions at this point in the journal; nor does he inform us of where he is going or who is accompanying him. But the search for the 'Briquas' was not the only aim in his mind.

According to Professor Forbes there were several other considerations which must have occupied him. There was the question of whether the Orange River which he had just 'baptized' was the same river that he had struck near present-day Bethulie in December 1777. He could not be absolutely sure of this until he had reconnoitered considerably more to the east of the mouth. Furthermore, there was the information that he would have received from Wikar of a great cataract and of other rivers flowing into the 'Great River'. This he most certainly would wish to confirm, as well as see those tribes, other than the 'Briqua', that the Swedish deserter had described. He would also want to know, for military and trade reasons, how navigable the river was, and he would want to map it as accurately as possible. In short, he wanted to complete the circuit touched upon at the beginning of chapter five. Finally, there was the desire to see new animals and plants – above all the giraffes which, according to Wikar, were to be found in the vicinity of Coboopfontein, west of Pella and twenty-odd kilometres south of Onseepkans.

In 1760 a certain Jacob Coetsee Jansz had also sighted giraffes, describing them as 'a sort of camel', north of the 'Great River' and had shot two females.[8] It was his report (which Gordon had read) that had led to the official expedition in 1761-2 under the command of Hendrik Hop, captain of the Stellenbosch Burgher Militia.[9] Gordon had obviously read the account of Hop's expedition as well, which had been written up by the Company's surveyor, C. F. Brink, and indeed, to some extent, Gordon was now to follow the same track to the Orange.

It is interesting to note that the route Gordon took at the beginning of the journey followed closely what is now the main road between Kamieskroon and Springbok. For instance, Gordon's Aloes Kloof, reached on the night of 18 September, has been positively identified as joining the 'Buffels River 1 km upstream from the bridge of the national road and 9 km east of Wolwepoort'.[10] He reached the vicinity of Springbok on 22 September 1779 and there visited 'the copper mine' discovered and worked by Simon van der Stel's expedition of 1685-6. His next move was east through the area of present-day Concordia and then on to the place he called Queekfontein (today spelt Kweekfontein). Next, Gordon's course veered E.N.E. and took him in turn to Naip (his Huib or Heip on the map), then on to Komasoas, which is his Camasauws. On 26 September he reached Pieter Pienaar's stock farm, Sandfontein, which has the identical name today.

The journal entries from Ellenboogfontein to Sandfontein deserve some comment. Firstly, it is clear that Gordon had not recovered from the illness and fever that had dogged him from the very beginning of this journey. On 20 September he tersely records that he 'was not well and was feverish', yet he must have been feeling very ill indeed, for he only took the latitude of their position the next day, having been 'prevented' by 'nausea' from doing so the day before.

It is easy enough to miss or overlook these entries, and so forget how often they occurred and how uncomplaining and conscientious Gordon remained. The fact of his illness was noted – that is all. His tasks were performed, the journey continued. Every day he recorded what he observed.

The entry on 23 September 1779 is of great interest as it concerns the marriage customs of the 'Hottentots' in that part of the country. (Most of this material is taken from Wikar's account of the same ceremony.) As has already been noted, Wikar gave Gordon a copy of this account when the two met near Ellenboogfontein in July,[11] so the details had been known to anthropologists and historians for many years before the discovery of Gordon's journals. Here is the relevant passage:

Yesterday I rode to the cattle post of a man called Beukes. There was a lot of stock there and many shiny-haired or wool sheep. This is excellent sheep country.

From Groene River there are nineteen stock farms in Namaqualand. On these there are five married farmers; the rest mostly take a Hottentot woman or two, which, so I hear, they marry according to their custom. In the Hottentot marriage ceremony no pissing is used (but this they do in their 'Man-making').[12] It is the most natural way of doing things in the world. If a young man takes a liking to a young girl he seeks her company without declaring his love or speaking of anything [to do with it]; he is too shy. However, since a family usually lives together pell-mell in one hut, the young man crawls across to the girl, even if this is just for his own amusement and she is willing (which it is said hardly ever happens). He [then] goes back to his sleeping place. But when the girl is modest she stands up and goes to lie in another place, well outside the hut.

THE LAND OF THE CAMELOPARDS

Previous page:
40. A skilfully executed painting of a 'Hottentot' dance – probably illustrating Gordon's journal entry for 17 September 1779.

If now the young man has serious intentions he stays in the sleeping place of the young girl until full daylight so that everyone can see this. So it goes on until she consents or until he gets tired and sees that she will not have him. If she consents she continues to lie there but this seldom happens at the first proposal. Once he has got her to sleep with him he stays with her so that everybody can see this and even if the parents hear something they let nothing show, saying that it is embarrassing, even if the marriage is not to their liking. In the morning the bridegroom or man stands up and takes off the beads from around his waist and throws them on the parents' sleeping-place. If these are accepted the marriage has been concluded. But if they do not want to consent (and they almost never refuse) the daughter remains with her parents, even if she is pregnant and they live as before, without scandal. However if the beads have been accepted the young man fetches his cattle and generally gives them cows and calves, mixed together as he chooses. In addition he must also slaughter for his wife and some of them hang the stomach fat around their necks and the gall-bladder on their heads. They also mix some other fat together with buchu from [the hair of] the head (one of the elders does this) and they (the man and wife) eat it from each other's hands. And so everything is completed. However, nine of the oxen are a kind of a loan and one is for the parents for having brought the girl up. After three or four years the remaining nine, or others in their place, must be given back. The Hottentots have daughters willingly because they get stock at their wedding. A poor young man is in as bad a way as he would be in Europe; and a Hottentot who owns a lot of stock very often has two or three wives; which causes them more trouble than pleasure. The wives quarrel among themselves, first one running away and then the other. Then, the Hottentot who gets no satisfaction in being without his wives, must go after them and bring them back again. One of these, who had both an old and a young wife, was asked why he did not let his young wife go since she was always running away, replied that although it was certainly true that his old wife cared for him better he still liked the young one. Their 'Other-Making' occurs at births, marriages, (becoming man and woman) deaths and at other events. (Sometimes just for diversion). They never tie knuckle bones around their hands but almost always tie a gall-bladder in their hair until it falls off in one piece. Hottentots marry very young, a Namaqua told me, and that is why they are so weak.

From here took bearing on Brakfontein Berg: N. by E. 3 deg. E. Our course to here yesterday: N. 3 deg. W.

What is of singular interest here is the offhand remark that prefaces the account of the marriage practices: 'From Groene River there are nineteen stock farms in Namaqualand. On these there are five married farmers; the rest mostly take a Hottentot woman or two, which, so I hear, they marry according to their custom.' From the context of the passage it is clear that Gordon in no way considers it unusual or sensational that this is how the frontier farmers set up their homes and families. The passage comes after a comment that 'This is excellent sheep country' and is followed by an entry concerning compass bearings. Presumably his remark that there were five 'married' farmers would imply that they were married according to Christian custom only and has nothing to do with the race of the wives or of the farmers. It is indeed refreshing to note from this description how free from racial prejudice the tribespeople and the early Dutch settlers of this area were.[13]

We know from previous intimations that Gordon himself was most open-minded, indeed often affectionate, towards the indigenous inhabitants of the country, and so his attitude – his matter-of-fact recital of the ceremonies – can come as no surprise. What is betrayed here in the tone of the narrative is a certain humour, especially when we consider how the marriage customs would apply to a young Dutch colonist. The mere fact that the journal says 'no pissing is used' is funny because it implies that it very well might have been used. And then all the details about living 'pell-mell' in the hut, and the hanging of cattle innards around their necks and on their heads and in their hair – all have a ludicrous element when applied to people of European stock. Gordon must have recorded this passage because he saw this implication and it amused him. And what of the concluding sentence ('Hottentots marry very young, a Namaqua told me, and that is why they are so weak')? This shows humour of another kind.

As Gordon approaches his immediate destination – Pienaar's farm, Sandfontein – he encounters new faces. The entire entry for 27 September 1779 now follows, showing the tone and tenor of Gordon's journal at this time:

The same weather and wind which generally becomes light easterly three to four hours after sunset. Very hot on account of the loose, hot reddish-brown karoo sand. The wind fresh, veered with the sun. Therm: 68–100–80. Barometer gave 2165 feet.

	62 de.	– 12 min.
	27	– 48 from the zenith
giving	90	– 0
	1	– 16 southerly declination
	29 deg.	– 4 min. Latitude.

N.B. The course therefore fell in a more northerly direction.

As the sun was setting yesterday saw an animal that looked like a rhinoceros; it was standing against a hill but it was too far and the sun was going down. (My young Koerikei sees as well with the naked eye as I can with my pocket spyglass.)

The great change in the heat since Engelbrecht's has caused my nose to bleed from time to time. Yesterday I ate a beautiful wild cucumber which was so bitter that I became ill from it and vomited. This also happened to a Hottentot.

There were four robust young fellows of middling stature among these Bushmen: brothers. They arrived here from the east yesterday. They were very open and friendly and brought me milk this morning. There were only three children and a young girl and two older people. Had never seen people like me.

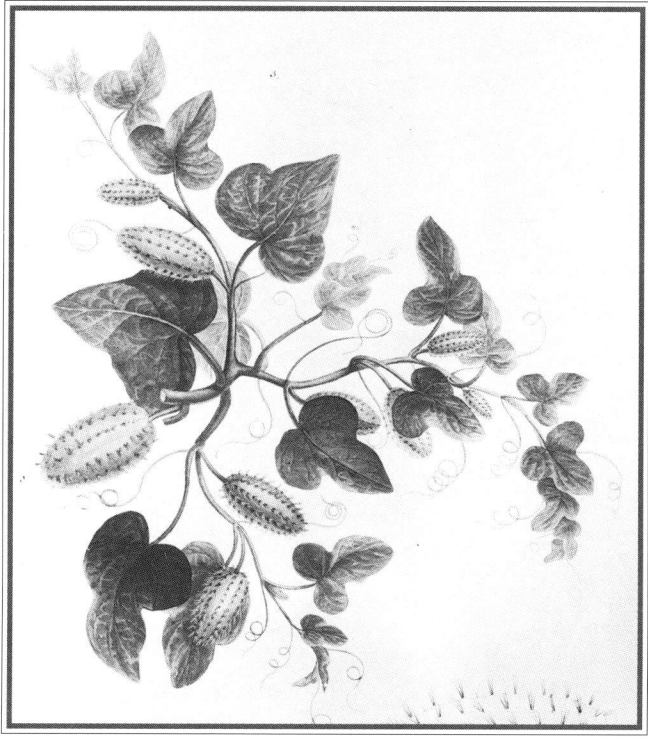

41. *The spiny, or wild, cucumber.*

Gave them some tobacco and they searched the countryside around here for stones for me; different kinds of pebbles and flints. The sand in this veld is looser: grass-country, bushman grass-country, or *Taaneina*. Plotted course ahead: E.N.E. 3 deg. N. Have used the compass to travel over this country; a Hottentot has been showing me the only waterholes. He has learned this from the Bushmen.

Last night, while travelling over this flat country by moonlight we found an ostrich nest which had twelve eggs which had been sat on for a time but were still good. In the outside circle however (as in the previous description of the ostrich nest) there were seven very fresh ones. The male, even though he also sits on them, makes himself a nest in the sand close beside the nest containing the eggs. There is a scarcity of water here and it does not taste good (but not brack). We have to let the oxen drink two at a time, digging and letting it fill up each time.

Departed E.N.E. 3 deg. N. and reached Sandfontein, Pinar's cattle-post after ten and a half hours' travel and found him there. It took him twenty-one days to reach here from the dead elephant. He had shot two elephants and thirteen hippopotamus along the left bank of the river. It has no waterfalls but it does have rapids over the reefs and very large bends. Found my two Hottentots and my wagon all in order. Because I am the first to come this way by wagon they were not expecting me to come from this direction. Until a mile short of Camasauws we had difficult, reddish brown, sandy ridges; thereafter hard, pebble-strewn, flat stretches and more than half of the way to Sandfontein we had loose reddish-brown and gravelly karoo sand. Shrubs everywhere and more stony hills up to 400 feet high. Saw where the river lay, one and a half miles to the north east, between a mountain range which is not, however, high. Runs E. ½. S. thus Brink's map is totally inaccurate on this.

The wagon Gordon found here was, of course, the one he had sent 'due north' from Ellenboogfontein at the end of July 'under the supervision of my trusty Hottentot Iteki'. Pienaar was also waiting for him, as previously agreed.

It had taken the hunter 'twenty-one days to reach here from the dead elephant,' Gordon notes carefully, and he also reports what Pienaar had to say about the topography of the river between the two points. All this was, no doubt, important for his mapping of the river. Pienaar, it should be noted, had completed a vital portion of Gordon's journey by proxy, as it were; but his record was by no means perfect and Gordon's resulting map hardly indicates the deep sweep to the north taken by the Orange between modern-day Beesbank and Vioolsdrif.

*N*ow that the party had come together once more, two days were spent resting on the farm and preparing for the arduous journey ahead. Most of the entries comprise information about the tribespeople encountered here, and in particular the male custom of excising one testicle[14] – a subject that seems to have fascinated Gordon, since it recurs many times in the course of his narrative. It is clear that he spent these two days gathering all the information he could about the tribes, the subsidiary rivers and other features he would meet along the river. Although he does not say so, it is clear that he intended to go as far east as possible, hoping, one can be sure, to map the river up to where he had last struck it in December 1777, near present-day Bethulie, and so complete his 'circuit'. Thus his entry for 28 September is again of great interest and is quoted here with few omissions:

Saw today for the first time two old *Eini* or *Einiqua*.[15] Both had one ball cut out, the one on the right and the other on the left. The remaining ball was slightly larger than usual and filled the pouch so that it did not swing loose at all. They were called Naugaap and Oegaap. They were married and lived with the Bushmen who frequent these parts and are called *Haussa eip*. Naugaap's was cut out by the Einiquas when he was an adult and he said it was because he had a pain in his loins and because it would make him run faster. He had four children and a wife. Oegaap's was cut out when he was still a young boy. It happened casually and not in the normal course of the cutting out custom. He was not obliged to do it. It appeared to be partly superstition and partly an old way of treating sickness; it happens at slaughtering as well, always with two head of stock or at 'Other Making'. For as long as Naugaap could remember only one of his people had died of it. Oegaap had nine children. Naugaap was sorry he had let himself be cut since he now lived with the Bushmen who never did it. It had made him very ill. He did not want his children to be cut. Laughingly, he said that he was now almost an ox. His wife was pregnant with her first child when he let himself be cut which was done by a man called Caumaap who did this at their kraal. At most there were two who could cut and they often do this to many men together at the same time in the rainy season. Then those who have been cut rub themselves with red paint, also about June. They must then each sit apart without letting any woman come to them until they are healed.

The first joint of the finger next to the little finger on Oegaap's right hand was cut off, for sickness; their parents do it if they are very ill, also the head-woman or head-man.[16] In each kraal of the Einiquas (which is the name of all the kraals though every kraal has its particular name) which lies on this river as many do not have the ball cut as do have it cut. They say that these uncut ones are too afraid but do not despise them or consider them to be different from the others. The women make no distinction between them and everything stays the same. They are all Hottentots and their speech varies only slightly from the Namaquas.

These people are called Hoensing eib meaning Spider Kraal.[17] Some of the *Einiquas* (the Ein comes from the name of the River) — those who live almost behind the Sneeuwberg on this side of the river, have much stock. The Coraqua are somewhat further up on the other side of the river.[18] They, the *Hoensing eib* are good friends of the Bushmen who fight with the Sneeuwberg farmers.

Klaas and Piet Bastart are living on Pinar's farm; they went with Vicar but have now returned.[19]

Two good days' journey to the north of them the black Briqua or Brinas begin. Saw a Kouqua (or One-of-the-people-who-cut-kraal)[20], an Einiqua too who had been to the Briquas and he called their corn *semica* just as the Caffers do. Earlier they did not use the bow but now they do. The *Kouqua* also had his left ball cut out and said that all the people in his kraal had this done according to an old custom, excepting only a few who were too timid. The Briquas cut as well.

The river that runs behind the Orange River is called Koeroemana by the Briquas.[21] It runs from the east to the N.W. and somewhat more north-westerly than parallel to this river.

We are making everything ready to go east upriver in the moonlight. We are making a wagon ready and are leaving the boat here since we are not able to travel very far with the wagon; after that we are taking pack-oxen. I long very much to see the so-called Briquas.

These concluding words are significant, for this is the first time Gordon hints that finding the Briquas is one of the aims of the journey. It will be recalled that Paterson had given this as the sole reason for Gordon's journey 'to go eastward along the river'. Here Gordon makes what, for him, is a strongly emotional statement about meeting these people. The reason is plain. He might perhaps be able to establish a link between those African people — the Xhosa — whom he had met in the east, and the Africans who were living here in the west, known as the Briqua, Brina or Batswana.

𝒯he next stage of his journey, lasting from 29 September to 22 October 1779, was to be made with one wagon. The terrain ahead was known to be rugged and for this reason the boat was left behind. So far as one can make out from scattered notes in the journal, the company was, in the beginning, made up of Gordon and Pienaar, the two 'Boland Hottentot' servants, Iteki and Koerikei, Schoemaker the artist, and the brothers Klaas and Piet Bastert, as well as Klaas Barend — all three excellent hunters and shots. In addition, there was a small group of Einiqua tribespeople — five or so men and women — but this element of 'wild people' would swell and diminish haphazardly, as the journey continued.

The route that the party took for the next three weeks or so has also been convincingly plotted by Professor Forbes.[22] From Sandfontein the company passed through Klein Pella, which Gordon called Soubiesjes, and made camp at Pella itself (his Commas). His next camp at Cabas Riviertje still has the name of Kabas. (It is approximately eight kilometres north of Pofadder.) Gordon's Cabouws and Naisees are almost certainly Koboop and Nanseep respectively, just as his Samoep and Aiaas must be our Samoeprivier and Eyas. Travelling east along the bank of the river, with a few camps in-between, Gordon came to a place he called Haries or Garies Poort on 11 October. This can only be the Bo-Naries shown on our maps today. The permanent spring at Gomnuip would accord very closely with Gordon's Gam Ey, though it should be mentioned that he described it as a 'brack underground waterhole' with no water then;[23] and of course there can be no uncertainty about his 'Aukoerebis of groote Watervall' (the Augrabies Falls) which he first saw on Friday 15 October 1779.

The subsequent camps made after the falls were at the 'Eerste Namaneijqua Kraal' and the 'Tweede Namaijqua', and given the fact that these were temporary dwelling places of tribespeople, they cannot be identified etymologically, though an *in situ* examination using the journal would very likely yield their location.[24] The last place on this stage of the journey is marked as Takemas and this can only be present-day Kakamas. (Professor Forbes has stated that the T and K in both spellings are approximations for a click sound still used in pronouncing the name by local people of Korana extraction.)

The first few days of the journey passed without much incident. From the entries we can see that Gordon spent some time talking to members of the group of 'Einiqua', who were accompanying them. Once more Gordon's interest in these people — his admiration even — is manifest. 'Noeroep,' he records, '... is a small elderly Hottentot who is swift and courageous and as a result all are respectful of him.' Gordon ends this passage by remarking wryly: 'These Bushmen serve our farmers and are good herdsmen but they do not tolerate bad treatment.'

The entry for 2 October 1779 is of particular interest. The party had been joined by a stock farmer called Model who drew an amused comment from Gordon:[25]

Departed first E. by S. half a mile until we reached a small hollow in the branch of mountains that extend to this point. Half-way we crossed the dry Cabas rivulet which runs S.E. from the plain in thunderstorms. After one and a half miles we came on to a bad, stony road going downhill: first a quarter of a mile N.E. then E. through a flat ravine through which a dry river ran, which I called Susannadal. There were many kouw[26] trees and much Bushman grass making it very pleasant.[27] But, looking for water, we found none and travelling on for a further quarter of an hour we made camp without water, after four and a half hours' brisk travel. In this valley we saw many giraffe tracks;

42. Wrapped in his kaross, a male 'Hottentot' lies ready to be buried.

they had grazed on every kouw tree and looking at their tracks I was astonished to see that, when they stand still, the rear hoofs can only be a foot away from the fore hoofs. We saw rhinoceros tracks as well.

We travelled now like the Children of Israel, since Model, due to the fact that the water on his farm had run out, had loaded his hut and his household goods on to pack-oxen and a pack-sled and was moving with us, which, together with all his stock produced a great hubbub of sheep and cattle. Some of the ewes lambed on the way; the lambs were then picked up and carried or placed on the sled as well.

At the end of the kloof we saw a great, flat country in front of us (lying between N.E. and S.E.) as far as we could see, broken only here and there by small irregularities.

First, we should take note of the name Gordon gives this 'flat ravine'. Who is this Susanna or Susette? (On Map 3 of the Gordon Atlas the place is called Susettedal.) Who is this lady who gave her name to this 'pleasant' spot?

On 4 October 1779, two days after Gordon had written about Susannadal, the Here XVII met in Amsterdam, and among the resolutions passed on that day was one concerning a certain Susanna Nicolet of 'Leijnerolle in Zwitserland'.[28] She was permitted to travel to the Cape of Good Hope on one of the ships from Amsterdam, and in addition she was allowed to take a maidservant to attend upon her. There was to be no charge for this.

Now Susanna Nicolet was the lady that Gordon was to marry in April of the following year, an event which will be discussed later in this account. There can be no doubt that it was after her that the kloof, with its abundance of grass and trees, was named on this day. Indeed, there is an agreeable degree of synchronism in that the naming of Susannadal and the permission for Susanna Nicolet to travel to the Cape occur within a couple of days of each other. But how typical it is of Gordon that he gives us no hint as to why he gave the kloof that name. It does show, however, that he knew she would be coming to join him at the Cape.

In this same passage we should also note Gordon's remark about the giraffe tracks. Clearly he was fascinated by these animals and was longing to encounter them, but for the moment he had to content himself with other creatures. On 4 October there is a vivid account of a rhinoceros hunt. The whole passage attests to Gordon's zeal for precise detail in the way things are done: the positioning of the hunters, the distraction of the hartebeest bull, the agility and bravery of his dog, the measuring and account of the dead animal's eyes, limbs and hide, all testify to the care Gordon took to get the facts right. The whole episode has a descriptive vigour which derives, surely, from the sheer pleasure Gordon himself took in these activities:

Therm: 56–76–68. At dawn a fresh east wind (calmer two

hours later). Fine weather, somewhat cloudy on the horizon. Very fine all day with a light east wind. There is little dew here and seldom.

Departed north over the plain downhill and after half an hour's travel we were out of the kokerbooms[29] and going uphill over difficult reddish-brown and stony sandhills. We made a small turn to get through the rises and thereafter followed our course on a hard road. Ahead of us we saw many rhinoceros tracks. They had been cutting all sorts of capers and running round in circles. At every place where they had dunged they had scratched two furrows, had kicked their dung and uprooted shrubs from the ground. Was nowhere able to find traces of horns in the ground but everywhere the scratching where they had dunged.

After we had been travelling for four hours, it being one o'clock in the afternoon, we saw two rhinoceros standing at about 1000 paces away on the plain between caan and kouw thickets ten to twelve feet high. We loaded our guns and the three of us went towards them, the Hottentot Klaas Barend, Model, (an off-duty soldier, a German) and I. They went off to the right, into the thicket, in order to stalk the animals from down wind and I stayed up in front in case they intended to come forth there. The rhinoceros were standing facing me, their ears flapping up and down. Before we had left the wagon to go into the thicket a hartebeest (bubalis) bull came right up to us, about 80 paces distant. It appeared to fear nothing nor to be aware of us. However, while we were on the plain we did not want to shoot it since we did not wish to disturb the [two] rhinoceros. It would, I believe, have come right up to us had my dog Keiser not seen it and flown at it. Fortunately it took a course away from the rhinoceros, bounding off in the most beautiful way, making beautiful jumps like a springbok, which caused the dogs to aim too short.

The rhinoceros had not been aware of anything and we went to the places mentioned before. Model and the Hottentot crept to within a good hundred paces of them but were then unable to see them well in the thicket. They had still not become aware of me because I saw them calmly lying down with the result that the two hunters were unable to shoot them. I went about fifty paces nearer, whereupon one of the animals stood up; shortly afterwards the Hottentot shot and the animal fell down dead. The shot, as we afterwards found, had gone close to or into the heart. The other received the ball high in the foreleg, in the body, and limped off. My dog Keiser, however, who respects no animal, flew at it on the first shot and attacked the rhinoceros from in front and from behind. It tried to gore the dog but Keiser was too quick for it and, before I could get to it, Model shot it dead.

We found that both were cows with two teats that were much bigger than those of a hippopotamus and with light, pendulous udders very much like a horse's. They were almost the same length and height and were fully grown. The largest was four feet ten inches high in a straight line in front and one and a half inches lower behind. It was eight feet, four inches long, measured in a straight line just as the animal lay there. We placed it in the same position it would have had were it alive and as if we were seeing it from the side. The other differed by one inch from the above measurements. The largest horn was 15 inches long and that of the smallest 8 inches, thus differing from last year's bull by one inch.[30] The thickness also hardly differed and with these the head was 23 inches long. The eye lies just between the tip of the nose and the middle of the ears, below the posterior horn, nine inches above the lower jawbone and only six beneath the posterior horn. Its muzzle is very pliable and loose (probably so that it can be extended and retracted) and the lower part as well; its tongue is not hard but very soft, although it is rough higher up towards the back. It can see forwards without turning its head. Although the eyes are placed as they are and the opening is one inch in diameter, the pupil is clear and protuberant and not sunken. The thick horns on the nose allow room for the line of sight to pass completely unimpeded also since the hindmost part of the eye at the side of the ears is much wider than the foremost part of the eye, this exposes more of the eye. Thus I was wrong in suggesting that the rhinoceros cannot see straight ahead but it was the hot weather that misled me last year. Also because it was the first rhinoceros I had seen I was busy with everything at the same time. An animal shot in the heat will swell up in less than an hour. Because of this its muzzle and fold around the eye were so swollen that one could see no movement in the muzzle and almost no eyes from sideways on, let alone from the front. The drawing is accurate as the animal then was. However since one of these rhinoceros was dying as I came up to it I saw, looking closely at the face, that it could see well in front of it and I saw that the eyes did not look inward but sat straight under the lids. It had a dark blue pupil, a darker iris; the white of the eyes was clear as well. I also saw that although the rhinoceros sometimes stands and looks as it does in the drawing, its more natural position however is with its head held lower down so that the horns form an angle of forty-five degrees to the horizon.

For the rest, both these animals had no folds in their hide, only at the flank; and only a slight fold on the foreleg and on the neck. They also had a much smoother hide and not as furry as last year's bull. Still do not know whether it is common for cows to have no folds. For the rest they are somewhat smaller than the bulls but they have the same stance. Both the horns were loose. Although they have no incisors the teeth do however come together in the front of the mouth in such a way that for a space of two inches there are no teeth.

The journey east continued without noteworthy incident for the ensuing four or five days. On 7 October a tribesman called Toenema, whom Gordon had befriended, estimated that they were 'two days from the great waterfall'. This was optimistic for they were now at Samoeprivier, a good eighty to ninety kilometres west of the Augrabies Falls. In fact it was to take them more than a week to reach this destination.

The next day Gordon wrote of his continuing, happy relations with the Einiquas, also stating how his immediate party was now constituted:

The *Einiquas* with me were delighted that their fellow countrymen would be astonished at me. They asked especially that I should wear my long hair loose when with them. There were now two male Einiquas and three women of that nation with us, as well as a Hottentot and good shot called Claas Barend. In addition there were another four Hottentots, one of whom was Koerikei and that, with Schoemaker, was all our company; the

Bushmen having gone with Pinar along the river. We have missed them this sixth day although our agreement was to meet on the first evening.

On 10 October something out of the ordinary occurred when Gordon received a new addition to his party:

Left at seven o'clock and had to travel S. and S.E. for three and a half hours with many turns around the range before we came to the underground water-hole *Haries*. It had good water but little of it. The whole range is the same; there are underground water-holes in the rivulets which only flow in thunderstorms. Found Pinar here; we had been looking for each other. Saw many giraffe and rhinoceros tracks and yesterday a herd of zebra, about 30, but could not get within range. They had shot four rhinoceros, two hippopotamus, killed an elephant and severely wounded another. They found a Bushman kraal the other side of Samoep. A woman gave him two young Hottentots about eight years old. One ran away again, the other stayed with me; his name was Cabas or Red.

No further details are given except this additional note made a day later:

Returned to the wagon in the afternoon. Was most astonished at young Cabas who is only three feet, four inches high. (Koerikei is four feet high). He carried the copper measuring stick of the barometer and he was always as close to me as a dog although I walked very fast and it was very hot. He paid close attention to everything and did everything to win my favour.

It was, of course, common practice for the colonists to take captured 'Bushmen' children by force into their service, but here there is no question of violence: the child Cabas was a gift. A probable reason for this handing over was that the 'Bushmen' were short of food and believed that the boy would be better off under the protection of these efficient hunters and powerful men from the west.

From the start of this stage of the journey Gordon had been recording the sighting of giraffe tracks, and it is clear that it was a prime ambition of his to bag one of these animals as the giraffe was a great rarity in the annals of eighteenth-century zoology.[31]

The first recorded sighting of giraffes had occurred in 1663 when two 'camels' (short for 'camelopards') had been seen by European travellers some 190 kilometres south of the Orange River. After that date, however, no further sightings south of the river were reported until the events described in Gordon's journal entry of 12 October 1779, quoted below.

As mentioned earlier, in 1760 Jacobus Coetsé Jansz shot two females in what is now southern Namibia and brought the skin of another young animal back to Cape Town. Then in 1762, during the expedition under Hop – also mentioned before – a female and bull giraffe were shot in the vicinity of Warmbad. The skin of the female's calf, which had died, was subsequently sent to Professor Allamand at the University of Leiden. It was the first example of this species to reach Europe in the eighteenth century and attracted considerable attention. Professor Allamand produced a short description of the animal and, together with a drawing of the skin, this was published in Buffon's *Histoire Naturelle*.

It can be safely assumed that Gordon knew of this account and, given his close ties with the professor, we can also assume that they had discussed this rare and wonderful creature – perhaps examined the skin too – before Gordon's second departure for the Cape.

William Paterson had examined a giraffe shot by Sebastiaan van Reenen in 1778 north of the Orange. This trophy would also have been discussed by Gordon when he and Paterson were together in the earlier stages of this journey. Finally, Gordon twice had occasion to mention giraffe skins in this journal: once when he met the deserter Wikar, who 'had the skin of a female giraffe with him', and secondly, when he returned to Ellenboogfontein from the mouth of the river, tersely remarking 'I had been given the skin of a young bull giraffe at the drift'. On this latter occasion he described the 'horns' and the head of the hide, adding that he had put it in water to soften it.

From all these facts we can see that the giraffe was of absorbing interest not only to the anatomists and zoologists of Europe but also to Gordon and his fellow explorers. With this in mind we come to the moment when Gordon meets his own first giraffe:

About sunset (N.B. after travelling for six hours) I saw the first giraffe but far off and I used my pocket spyglass. He came towards us in this course to the river, at times standing still and waving his neck from one side to the other like the mast of a ship that heels over strongly at sea. One of my Hottentots had already seen it and, stalking it, wounded it slightly but it got away. Pinar, who had been hunting two rhinoceros, came from behind, right into its path. Following the animal and setting my dogs upon same, I then heard barking and two shots. Although dusk was already drawing in, I left my horse and went on foot to the barking and came upon Pinar who was making signals by shooting and with fires, being an hour from the wagon. There I found this handsome and extraordinary animal, one of the most beautiful formed by nature, dead. Lighted by burning brands I could not inspect it enough for my satisfaction. Young Kabas and Koerikei had followed and stayed by me up hill and down dale; as full as it was of thorn bushes. I told two Hottentots to fetch the wagon although the other Hottentots said it would be dangerous in the dark, on account of rhinoceros of which there are many around here. It arrived at midnight. My upcountry Hottentots were the most astonished at this animal. In the evening a cold, brisk southerly wind came up and since I had become hot from walking, and being thinly clad, I suffered greatly from the cold until the wagon came. Had no water but for that in my water barrel.

Gordon's language is fired with excitement as he describes this exotic creature. His comments, if not poetic, are certainly unexpected in their metaphoric intensity, going far beyond the terse sobriety of his usual style. For once, it seems, he allows his delighted curiosity and enthusiasm to burst out on to the page. It is oddly moving, too, when he confesses 'I could not inspect it enough for my satisfaction'.

The whole of the next day, 13 October 1779, was spent 'measuring and examining this beautiful animal' which was a 'fully-grown bull giraffe'. Gordon makes no idle claim: there are no fewer than seventy-eight different external measurements of the animal – all in Rhineland feet. In addition there are many further details given of the head, hide, sexual organs, neck, hooves and tail, etc. From time to time he breaks off to describe some facet of the anatomy or to recount some curious anecdote, such as that of 'the wife of a certain Visagie' who rides unharmed among the creatures, 'being dressed in striped clothing'!

Gordon is giraffe-mad – obsessed with the animal. The entry for the day takes up almost four folio- or foolscap-size pages of the journal, while his Atlas contains no fewer than nine drawings of giraffes, and only one of these is not in Gordon's or Schoemaker's hand.

The final result of all this measuring and description was to be an article in one of the supplements to Buffon's *Histoire Naturelle* contributed by Professor Allamand and published in 1781. In the article the professor freely and warmly acknowledges his debt to Gordon:

He has seen several of them [i.e. giraffes] and has even killed some. He has examined them with all the attention of a judicious naturalist: he has sent me an accurate drawing of them which I have had engraved ... and his letters to me have given me a fairly extensive description, thus clarifying at last what one should think of the animals .... [32]

That 'fairly extensive description' is undoubtedly taken from this journal, but the measurements and observations on the anatomy of the animal are of little interest to the general reader and therefore are not quoted here. The following short passage, however, is a little more digestible than the pages of figures in Rhineland feet and inches that precede it and gives some idea of Gordon's diligence as a zoologist:

The shoulder of this animal is placed as though the breast formed part of the neck. It moves the neck backwards and forwards, slowly as it walks like an ostrich, and this must be, as it were, to keep its balance, and this causes it to appear low behind. Otherwise the chest and crupper are level. The crupper forms a rather narrow and pointed peak on the back and the two breasts are curved in front as well. When this animal stands the shortness of its body and the neck and shoulders sticking right up erect make it seem very much like an ostrich. Indeed some Bushmen call it the fourlegged ostrich.

As stated, most of the measurements given by Allamand in the *Supplément* agree with those shown in this journal entry. But the hide and skeleton received by Allamand and finally mounted in the attic of the Prince of Orange's 'Cabinet' came from a different giraffe, shot by one of Gordon's party near Warmbad in southern Namibia on 10 December of this same year, an incident that will be examined later. It is not clear why or how this confusion of giraffes arose, but it is strange that two such dedicated men of science should have allowed the mistake to creep in and then not have attempted to correct it.

Another mistake that remained uncorrected was the statement by Allamand that Gordon had himself killed giraffes. According to Gordon's own journal this is not the case. The first giraffe was shot by Pienaar, as we have seen,

and the second was hit and wounded by Afrikaander, one of the 'Hottentots' who were with Gordon. Its throat was cut as it lay wounded on the ground. So in neither case could the dead animal be claimed as Gordon's own trophy.

There are one or two further points in the article that deserve attention for the light they throw on the attitudes and feelings of the men involved. Allamand states: 'The illustration of a skeleton which I append here, Plate XX, was sent to me by Mr Gordon. It had been drawn by a man who had little knowledge of anatomy, as one can easily perceive....' And the Professor continues: '[The skeleton] is a monument to the zeal with which Mr Gordon applies himself to all that concerns Natural History. In order to do

43. *A giraffe hunt – one of the finest 'narrative' paintings in the Gordon Atlas.*

this he had no other help but that of several Hottentots who had attached themselves to him, as well as a soldier who served him as a draughtsman. Yes, those were the people who helped him to anatomize this great quadruped in the middle of the African deserts.'[33]

From these passages it can be seen how valued Gordon's contribution was and how deeply admired his exploits in pursuit of natural history were. Allamand was a most distinguished figure in the world of zoology at the time and his words would not have been taken lightly. But of interest too are the remarks that apply to Schoemaker, the soldier-artist, who had such a poor knowledge of anatomy. It appears that it occurred to neither the Professor nor to Gordon to give him any praise whatsoever for sharing in the trials and hardships of the journey.

This raises an issue that must be faced squarely, not just about Gordon, but generally about the facts of class distinction in the eighteenth century. The gap between an officer such as Gordon and a private soldier such as Schoemaker was indeed wide and would remain so even under the shared hardships of a journey like this. It was easier, paradoxically, for Gordon to become friends with a Xhosa or 'Bushman' than with one of his own people of a lower social station. The European and 'Bushman'/Xhosa cultures were so remote from each other that there could be no meaningful class distinctions between them.

It is thus quite comprehensible that Professor Allamand would ascribe this whole enterprise to the leader's glory alone. Not unnaturally, Gordon also believed that the giraffes were 'his'. He had initiated the journey, he had the necessary knowledge to observe and anatomize the animals and, finally, he was leading the expedition.

𝐵efore returning to the journey, there is a further comment, made by Gordon concerning giraffes, which deserves notice here. It is written on a loose piece of paper, in his handwriting, and slipped between the pages of this journal. The note concerns the giraffe that Le Vaillant claimed to have shot north of the Orange on his *Second Voyage* [English Title: *New Travels*] of 1783-1784:[34]

Barend Vrije shot Vaillant's giraffe.[35] He crossed the Great River only for a short while. Barend Vrije's dogs held the giraffe at bay towards noon and Vaillant took Barend Vry's horse for a giraffe and stalked it and nearly shot it dead, taking it for a giraffe. And Vailliand has never seen a live giraffe and this giraffe was smaller than mine, so Pinar told me who saw both of them. Klaas Bastert also confirms that this is so and says that Vailliant himself never saw it being killed, much less measured it and that he only could have seen it from afar while it was alive. However, he says he cannot be absolutely sure that when Barend Vry hunted the giraffe on horseback Valliant stayed behind and went back because of the heat. He said that it was an old animal and as Klaas expressed it 'a miserable cow'. Klaas and three other Hottentots slaughtered it in the presence of Barend Vry and Swanepoel and then brought it across the river to Valliant the next day, and Klaas said that it was not nearly as large as mine which he also helped to slaughter. In addition mine was a bull giraffe which had black patches.

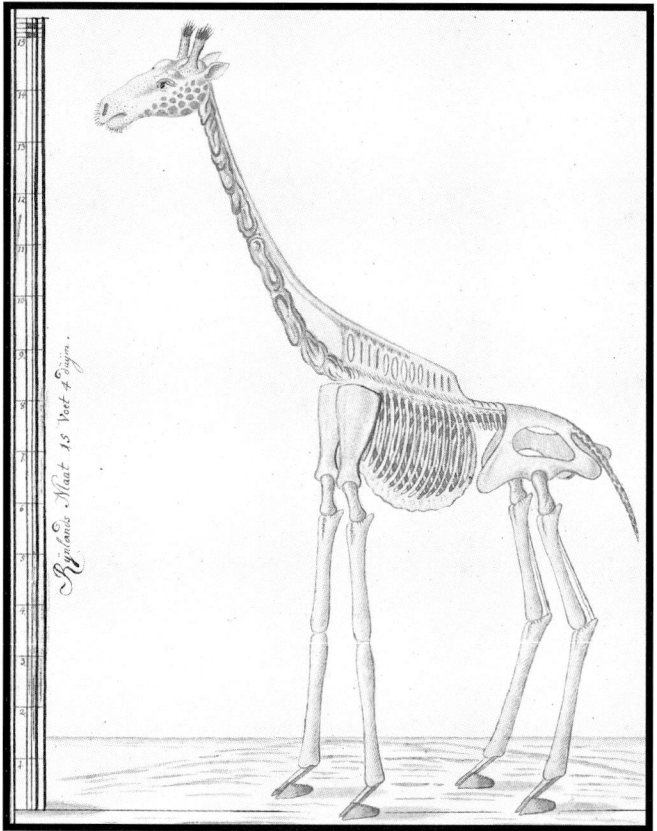

44. *The giraffe skeleton sent to Willem V.*

This is, of course, unintentionally humorous. Gordon was clearly more than indignant when he wrote it. The repetition of how Le Vaillant took Barend Vry's horse for a giraffe, and the fact that this giraffe was smaller than his (on the somewhat dubious testimony of Pienaar and Klaas Bastert) are comic enough, but when we add to this that Gordon manages to spell Le Vaillant's name differently three times in this short passage, the unwitting humour is richly enhanced.

But what occasioned this outburst about 'a miserable cow'? It is just possible that Gordon could have seen a copy of Le Vaillant's *Second Voyage* which appeared between September 1794 and August 1795. As noted, it was in this account that Le Vaillant claimed to have shot a giraffe.[36] Could it have been this claim that caused Gordon's fury? If so, he must have written the note in the last year of his life. However, it is far more likely that Gordon read about Le Vaillant's giraffe in that traveller's first French publication, *Voyage de Monsieur Le Vaillant dans l'intérieur de l'Afrique*, which appeared in 1790. At the end of the book Le Vaillant appended a commentary or 'supplément', as he called it.[37] In it he states, somewhat coyly and mysteriously, that this 'is a kind of anticipation that may appear irregular, but to which I have in some measure been constrained by solicitations which I ought to consider as commands'.

While discussing 'the natural history of the animals', he remarks: 'Many and various accounts have been published of the giraffe; but, notwithstanding all the elegant and scientific dissertations written on this subject, no just or precise idea hath been hitherto formed of its configuration, much less of its manners, its tastes, its character, and its organization.' This would have enraged Gordon, for in the dismissal of former 'dissertations' his own 'elegant and scientific' contribution to Buffon's *Histoire Naturelle* would have been included. Indeed, Le Vaillant remarks a little further on that 'the figures of this animal given in Buffon and Vosmar, are in general defective'.[38]

Perhaps, however, it was the Frenchman's claim, casually stated, that he personally had killed 'a number of these animals' that finally drove Gordon to write his note. His choler is manifest: Le Vaillant had lied not only about the size of his giraffe but also about who had killed the animal or animals. The interesting point here is: had Gordon forgotten who had shot 'his' giraffes?

Before breaking camp on 14 October 1779, a few final tasks were carried out on the remains of the giraffe. In recording these, Gordon also gives us a glimpse of how his activities struck the local tribespeople. It is easy to forget that they were as fascinated by Gordon's customs and rites as he was by theirs:

Cut up the whole skeleton of the giraffe. Succeeded in making an accurate drawing. On account of wild animals buried the bones in the ground until our return. Nothing could equal the surprise of the Bushmen and Einiquas on seeing the drawing. They said that we were extraordinary people and that they now saw that I could *coeroeo* everything (this was the word for imitating and writing.) They said they now saw why it was I always walk so far, backwards and forwards, looking, because at first they could make no sense of this.

When they made camp the same day Schoemaker was again in trouble: 'Without, it seems, taking account of the dry state of the grass nor of the direction of the wind, he made a fire upwind to grill meat.' Quite calmly Gordon records that they had difficulty in putting out the fire which could have destroyed 'the entire wagon'. This surely would have been a disaster for the expedition, but having recorded the event, Gordon does not speculate on this, nor does he demonstrate any irritation with Schoemaker. He closes the day's entry with a description of the countryside they are passing through.

The next day, Friday 15 October, is full of incident and interest. Once more giraffes were encountered which gave Gordon the chance to observe and record their ways of moving. This occurred 'at the underground water hole Koekabassi' which is shown just downriver from the Augrabies on Gordon's map. Indeed, he wrote that they were 'half an hour from the waterfall . . . the Einiquas call Aukoerebies or Holleplaats [sunken place]'. There is a sense of complete absorption in his description of the giraffes and so great was his fascination — and passion for accuracy — that he even felt it necessary to make a small outline drawing to illustrate a detail.

Saw at last what I had desired for so long: six giraffes close by so that we were able to examine them thoroughly. One of them (had blacker patches being a bull) was, at an estimate, half a foot higher than the others but probably not higher than about fifteen or sixteen feet at the most. They stood and grazed off the low trees. Then, because they had become aware of us, they paced ahead slowly, one after the other, like flamingoes.

I now saw that although, while standing, they sometimes hold their necks completely straight in a line with their feet, when they walk their posture is such that their necks form an angle of thirty degrees in a straight line from the zenith to the horizon. This means that the extension of the neck, shoulder and rear part of the body appears to make a slanting line, thus: The head and mouth bend down. While walking their neck moves forward and down but not being able to trot (so it is said and I did not see them doing this) they fell into a hand-gallop when chased by my dogs. Every time the front part of the body came down the neck also went backwards and forwards; most curious to see. Nevertheless this animal runs as fast as an eland, but both can be overtaken by the average horse.

It is said that they can give a fearful kick and that they fight each other thus. The one we shot still bore scars from this. One dog could not keep it at bay, not daring to approach its feet, and unable to get at its body. We were most anxious to shoot one but the dogs were on it too quickly. Also, wanting to spare my horse Snel, I left it behind. (It could have chased and circled them). Furthermore, I planned to shoot one closer to the place where I left my boat so that I would be able to take the skin back with me. There is nothing ungainly about the legs, which are well-proportioned. It can eat from the ground without bending the knees but it mostly grazes off the leaves and branches of trees where its horns play a part. Without the dogs they would have remained standing, within shot, looking inquisitively at the wagon because they were not used to seeing anything like it.

The comparison of the pacing giraffes to flamingoes is both novel and illuminating. It was made, no doubt, in a spirit of scientific accuracy, of wanting to get that movement exactly right, yet the comparison gives the passage a lyrical quality which is unusual in Gordon's writings. But giraffes had this effect on him, as we have seen. Nor was his excitement confined to his journal.

In the Gordon Atlas there is a drawing which surely reflects this episode, although it appears to have been elaborated on slightly in order to make it a more 'typical' scene: eight and not six giraffes are pictured, and two hunters are seen shooting at the herd while a third follows on horseback, accompanied by two dark human figures on foot. The drawing is full of naive vigour in the depiction of the people but, significantly, the giraffes themselves are most lifelike, as though drawn by someone who truly understood their anatomy (see pages 102-3[39]).

Beneath the drawing is an inscription by Gordon which conveys so much about the man and his capacity for delight in the animals he encountered — latent and restrained though that passion may be — that it merits quoting here:

View of the country at 28 degrees, 32 minutes, latitude and 3 degrees east longitude of the Cape of Good Hope; below the

Great Waterfall Aukoerebis in the Orange or Garieb River in the country of the Einiquas. Here I saw the most beautiful and singular sight in all my journeys, seeing, all at one glance through a semi-circle: twelve giraffes, about fifty elephants, 5 rhinoceros, a flock of 20 ostriches, a herd of 13 kudu, and one great herd of zebra. Saw hippopotamus in the river below, swimming and playing together.

There is more excitement to follow. On the same day Gordon records his first sight of the Augrabies Falls. Gordon apparently drew, or had a view drawn of the falls as seen from the south bank of the river[40] ('at a point about 1½ miles in a direct line downstream from the main falls', according to Professor Forbes).

The description of the falls is carefully and accurately made in Gordon's usual manner, but what the somewhat exotic 'legend of the enchantress' refers to has not been recorded for posterity:

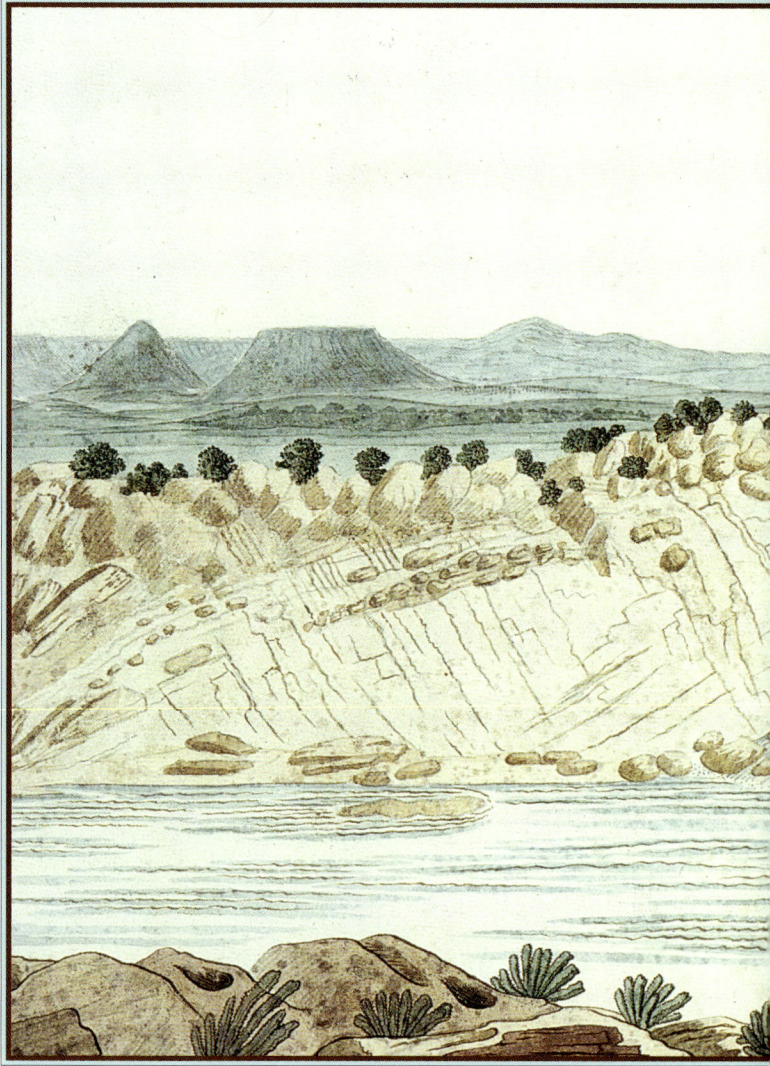

Went to the river to look at the waterfall which I could neither hear nor see although when the river is full the spray can be seen a day's travel away and can be heard from even further off. Because the countryside is flat around here found that the river forms deep clefts, entirely of rock, which are about ten to twenty feet wide below but a good fifty feet above. In some places they are 200-300 feet deep. As far as I know at present, the river divides here and forms three long rectangular, stony islands but with some shrubs on them. This lasts about a mile before the next confluence of the river.

Was fortunate that the river was now at low water, otherwise I could not have reached the islands and thus the deepest crevice (although I missed the fine view of the spray and the rainbow). From this arises the legend of the enchantress who sits in the middle and stirs it all up.

The concluding entry for this day, 15 October 1779, is particularly revealing. It is true Gordon and absolutely reflects his unruffled, calmly civilized temperament. The last sentence in particular is really only a confirmation of the feeling that underlies the whole of this journal, demonstrating his rejection of fantasy and his confidence in reason:

Have been surprised by the Bushmen; though all our things lie unguarded before them they will never touch anything with the intention of removing it. Although we are so vulnerable in this distant, savage country, full of wild animals, we are quite at ease in our minds, as in the middle of Cape Town, even though on our guard. When one compares this with the descriptions of people who even in the surroundings of Cape Town, find all kinds of danger, one can see how little danger there really is because it is only in the minds of men.

Exploration of the river continued and more human encounters took place. It all proceeded happily, as Gordon records in genial detail:

Fine weather. Normal heat. Cool easterly breeze.

Went to the river to take latitude. Bushmen and some of my people carried the barometer and the astrolabe. Between the second and third streams, which are further apart from each other, there are many trees and bushes . . . . Come midday obtained the latitude: 28 deg. 31 min. Error: 22½ deg. N.W. to here. We had grilled rhinoceros tongue to eat and went on a good half hour northwards across stony ridges and uneven places with the same trees. Here I again saw a crevice through which the water ran as in a powerful watermill. Coming from a more easterly direction saw that this stream is formed from four others. Standing here in order to look round, I saw some Bushmen running away. I waved and called to them but they continued on their way until Toenema saw them and knowing that they were his friends he called one of them by name and said that he should not be frightened but should come to us across the river.[41] This the others then did, showing however that they were most timid, and astonished by me. Gave them some tobacco and Toenema, greatly praising my kindness towards them said that he was like a child to me and told them everything that I could do. This the others repeated almost word for word, or the latter half of the sentence only, which is their way. This has an extraordinary effect if there are many of them together; everything that one says is mimicked by way of approval. The Bushman stayed close to my side repeating often to the others: 'This is my *Hoenequai* or Master or Lord.' Then

45. *Gordon's view of the Augrabies Falls from a point 2,5 km downstream of the main falls.*

another two of them came up. These two or three Kraals are the *Anoe eis* (or bright kraal) and they stay here by the river.[42] Three of the four, since they had been joined by yet another, lacked, like Toenema, one ball, but not one old man. Thus most of them are half-castrated.... Returned to the wagon with the Bushmen. Found some of the others busy filling my water-barrel. These Bushmen catch fish and live by hunting, digging pits on the side of the river in order to catch hippopotamus and rhinoceros. These pits are just like the one I and my horse fell into on a previous journey. On this kind of island saw many baboons and not many birds, but saw some ducks and divers. These Anoe Eijs are Einiquas who, because of a quarrel with the Namneyqua Kraal have lost all their stock but they are once more good friends. The Namneyqua live a day further on. The Anoe Eijs stay mostly on the other side of the river or on these unusual types of island when it is low water. But when it is the season of thunder and rain and the river is full they stay on this side. The Hottentots who half cut themselves call this ceremony *Tabie*. So far as we know there are more Bushmen living north of here: they told me these were called *Noe Eis* and *Ei Eis*.[43]

The party renewed its journey with the wagon on 18 October 1779, travelling E.S.E.. After four and a half hours they arrived at an island 'one and a half hours wide'. This could only be present-day Perde Eiland. Gordon's gift for making friends with the tribespeople, who had never seen a white person before, is yet again convincingly demonstrated here. He encounters a small band of 'Hottentots' who have, he writes, 'ten mat-huts among the trees and I estimate there are five to six people in each hut'. This day and the next day were spent among them. His observations are full of interest and bear quoting at some length:

Two came to me and I went with them across the stream which was about 20 feet wide and less than a foot deep and reached their island, which they abandon when the river covers most of it at high water. Found this a most beautiful place. The trees and the foliage below which we walked and of which there is so little in this land made it delightful. The change from the parched, ugly, stony and poor countryside made the difference all the greater.

I was received in the most friendly manner by a cousin of one of the chiefs which they call *Ghawoep*. His name was *Tamega* and he was much whiter than the others. Thundery weather coming up I took shelter in his hut. There, however, the rain

46. *A 'Hottentot' chief's grave.*

poured in so heavily that I had to cloak myself with their large oval bedding-skin of cattle-hide. The opening or door was so narrow and low that one could scarcely creep in or out of it. The storm over, I went to take the altitude of the river with the barometer, getting 2 000 feet. Tamega, the son of Aboegoeb, who showed me the way through the forest, could make no sense of my work although I explained it to him. Like all wild people the quicksilver astonished him the most; how it is wet and yet dry.[44]

Found Pinar here. Yesterday he and his people shot five elephants (these forests are full of them). They shot three cows, a young calf and a young bull from a herd of 20. We heard them shooting close to us and saw the brightly burning fire that they had lit in order to keep the live elephants at bay and to guard the carcasses. This is an old custom; Tamega told me too that they often have to burn wood to keep the elephants away from their huts. The elephants chase them as well when they encounter them. These Hottentots possess cattle; though not very many, also sheep and goats and are great hunters. (The sheep are smooth-haired like goats and have long thin tails. N.B. They milk their sheep). Met some of them in the forest; their pack-oxen and cows were laden with elephant meat and they were most satisfied.

Returned to my tent which was pitched a little distance from the stream, accompanied still by thunder, hail and rain. Tamega was astonished at my house. Gave him some meat but he wanted no biscuit or the bread which we had baked with some flour. When the heavy thunderstorm was over, the two kinds of chief each brought me a wooden cylinder of milk and I gave them some tobacco. They said that they had continual arguments and war with the *Kau Heys Kaw Eis* (Cutting Kraal) and the Ogoqua or Agokwa (Narrow Cheeks.)[45] These are actually the Einiqua.) They said that they were always stealing each others' cattle and killing each other. A nephew of Aboegoeb walked with a limp from a poisoned-arrow in the knee which he had got two years previously. They mostly complained of the Ogoqua but they owed each other nothing. I told them that our great Chief wanted them all to live in peace and that I would also discuss this with the Ogoqua, upon which they were delighted. Nothing astonished them more than my long hair which I was wearing loose at the request of Toenema, my thick beard as well. No king in Europe could have received more respect than that which they gave me in their own manner.

These woods are full of birds: Guinea fowl or Camdebo chickens as well as pheasant, (francolin). Saw a most beautiful woodpecker, but only one, which, to their amazement, I shot.[46] But further saw nothing of the usual birds of the river. I traded a sheep-skin for two of jackal and *Coerak Coelak*, as well as some smaller skins of animals I had not seen but which only exist here. It is reported that there are again four elephants dead though this is not certain because of the thundery weather. (If an elephant falls down and there are others with it they push and trample it hard in order to get it to stand again.) We are now 2 degrees, 9 minutes east from the latitude of the Cape and 4 degrees, 4 minutes from the mouth of the river which is now to the west of us.

19th October 1779.
Fine weather. Light easterly breeze. The air much cooler but sultry once more in the afternoon.

Again went to the kraal and the river which are on the same path. Would have fallen into a pit, dug out for hippopotamus, had I not been forewarned by the *Ghawoep* and his son Goroe who were walking ahead. They were very wary going through the forest on account of the elephants which, they told me, were liable to chase and trample them to death, although they never hunt them. As they showed me from their tracks, the elephants often come to their kraal, which they called by the name of *Comm*. In addition a short while before an elephant had trampled one of their young girls to death while she was walking in the forest looking for food.

For some time we wandered through the forest and along the river where I found some beautiful blue stones as transparent as sapphire, also some orange, speckled, green ones. Saw fresh tracks of elephant which according to the Hottentots, had passed 50 paces away yesterday. Six elephants had gone that way, one of which was wounded and they advised me not to use this path to venture through the forest. It is certain that one cannot see far in this thickly wooded place and that the animals can be upon one before one knows it. The Hottentots say that in a bad thunderstorm an elephant will stand still in the same place from fear. Till now these people have not found any of the elephants that have been shot.

Arriving at the kraal I saw a Hottentot who lacked an eye. I asked him how he had lost it and he told me, in the presence of the kraal, that a star had fallen out of the sky on to his head and in this way had wounded him badly. Enquiring further I found that superstition was mixed up in it and that he had probably had a kind of stroke. Asking how the star had fallen from the sky he and an old woman said that it looked like a porcupine, and that three girls had caught the thing. He said that although he was a very rich man and had already slaughtered much stock (this being 'other-making') he had not been able to become strong and healthy again. Thus all their customs end up in eating, as indeed with most peoples, who also add drinking. When a rich Hottentot dies many cattle and sheep are slaughtered and eaten at his grave. The bones and joints are left there as a memorial. I presented the two Ghawoeps or headmen with some beads and two little mirrors (one each) for their favourite wives and we were good friends. They warned me to be on our guard with the other Hottentots saying that they were treacherous.

Today again saw some hippopotamus in the river which here runs S.E. and N.W. Saw some blue ixias as well; and otherwise up to here there have been few flowers, and also much honey.

It can be noted from this passage how Gordon in no way patronizes the tribespeople. He does not sneer condescendingly at their astonishment but obviously delights in their naive surprise at the quicksilver, 'wet and yet dry'. Clearly, he is only too happy to oblige his friend Toenema by wearing his long hair loose. Furthermore, his sincerity and appreciation shine through when he remarks on the respect he receives from these people 'in their own manner'. Even the account of the star like a porcupine, wounding the 'rich' man's eye, is related without mockery. It is, after all, a good story but balanced by Gordon's explanation, so characteristically rational, that it was 'probably . . . a kind of stroke'.

As the narrative flows, it is easy to ignore or forget the vital part that Pienaar and his followers played in the expedition, since Gordon himself does not often refer to their activities. They were, of course, constantly hunting for game, thus providing the main source of food for the party. By doing so, they freed Gordon to carry on his exploring and observing and recording. Without Pienaar and his half-caste marksmen, Gordon would not have been able to take and record so many measurements or to supervise and make such a wide variety of drawings, to name just some of his many activities. On this particular day Pienaar and his men provided a substantial amount of elephant meat, so much that they were able to give the tribesmen a feast as well. Their 'pack-oxen and cows were laden,' Gordon records, '. . . and they were most satisfied'. Such gifts no doubt helped greatly to strengthen the good relationship that had sprung up between these diverse strangers in the wilderness.

They travelled on with the wagon the next day, 20 October, and made their camp on the dry river bed of the Camagaqua or Hartebeest River, which still bears that name today. A hippopotamus was shot and the tribesmen appear to have appreciated this treat as much as they did the elephant meat. It is a savage scene which Gordon records as they slaughter one of these animals 'wildly prattling and screaming as they cut the flesh off with their assegais'. Later he entertained them by lighting 'their pipes of tobacco with a burning glass' and by playing 'upon the cithern for them'.[47] This is the first time that we learn that he had such an instrument with him or that he had any musical gifts. Though perhaps his detailed descriptions of indigenous music, mentioned earlier, should have alerted us that Gordon had a musical bent. What, one wonders, did he play for them, here on the remote reaches of the Orange? Xhosa songs, marching tunes, or Celtic melodies are all possibilities, as we know from the few accounts we have of Gordon's musical diversions. At all accounts it is an entertaining tableau to reflect upon, before following this exceptional man across to the northern bank of the Orange, on this last stage of his eastward exploration of the river.

It was at this point that Gordon decided to continue his journey without the wagon and pursue his course on the other bank, 'taking only as much as four pack-oxen could carry'. He decided to abandon his barometer but to take his astrolabe. This gives us an interesting insight into his priorities: it was more important to know his latitude than to register the heights of places on the journey. It is also interesting that he changed his journal notebook from the large folio size he had been using up to now for a smaller, quarto size book. Obviously this was easier to carry and to handle for a man going, for the most part, on foot: for, although we know from some remarks later in the journal that the party did cross the river with horses, it is evident that Gordon foresaw, correctly, that the terrain would be rough and unsuitable for extended riding.

At no time in the narrative does Gordon say what his destination was on this northern bank of the river. It can readily be supposed that, at most, he hoped to get to that part of the Orange near Bethulie that he had struck in December 1777, thus completing the circuit alluded to earlier. However, one can at least opine that he wanted to confirm that it was indeed the same river and, from the casual remarks in the journal, it is clear that, in Gordon's mind, this minimum aspiration was met. In fact he and his party were to travel approximately 150 kilometres upstream to the vicinity of present-day Koegasbrug which is about forty kilometres downstream from the town of Prieska.

On 22 October — the day before crossing to the northern bank — Gordon wrote in the journal that his party now consisted of 'three Europeans and nine Hottentot marksmen, as well as my two young servants and some Bushmen'. The 'Europeans' could only be Gordon, Pieter Pienaar and Schoemaker. The two young servants must have been Koerikei and the newly enlisted Cabas. Disappointingly, Gordon does not tell us who the marksmen were. From the evidence in the journal, Piet and Klaas Bastert, Klaas Barend and 'Afrikaander' were probably among those nine men mentioned.

47. Pachypodium namaquanarum
(a member of the Num-Num family) from the western banks of the Orange River. It is also known as the 'halfmens'.

CHAPTER SEVEN

THE FOURTH JOURNEY: A TRIUMPHANT RETURN

(OCTOBER 1779 – JANUARY 1780)

On foot along the north bank; news of the Briqua; the Alabaster Rock; Gordon's turning point; loss of the first giraffe; the road to Sandfontein; return to Great Namaqualand; the second giraffe; farewell to the 'mountains of the Great River'

The crossing was made upstream from a place Gordon called Takemas, which is clearly the modern village of Kakamas. The next day, after some tense moments with some 'Bushmen' whom they encountered, they passed alongside an island which Gordon says he 'later' named after 'my friend Sir John Macpherson, former Governor of the English Indies'. Indeed, this Sir John was the governor-general of Bengal and was, in 1787, to become godfather to Gordon's daughter Johanna who died in infancy. The friendship between the two men must have occurred when Sir John stopped at the Cape on his return to Britain after relinquishing his Indian post.[1] One wonders too whether there were not direct or at least indirect connections with the Scots Brigade. As we have seen, many of Gordon's place names stem from this source and Macpherson was a name well represented on the regimental lists.

On 24 October 1779 the party passed the vicinity of modern Keimoes which Gordon mapped as Moebees, drawing a small hill to mark the place.[2] This is certainly the distinctive koppie known as the Tierberg just outside that village.

All along the river, as the party moved eastward, small groups of tribesmen were encountered. There were tense moments from time to time but generally speaking the people were friendly, and despite the rough going and hard conditions Gordon maintained his easy, pragmatic attitude to each incident and each person that he met.

A visit to a band called the Ogoqua[3] on 26 October gives some idea of how the expedition was proceeding. Gordon's continued interest in all that concerns the tribespeople is most evident here. The custom of excising testicles, 'cutting' as he puts it, is again discussed; but his enquiries at this stage always tend towards the 'Briqua', and here he meets people who have at least a partial knowledge of their language. He can at once see that there are similarities with Xhosa words:

Departed at one o'clock and after three quarters of a mile arrived opposite the Ogoqua because they had moved further up. Their *Gauwaap* called Naba noe, touw oab, or Touw oab naba noeb came to meet me with four of his people, bringing me two sheep and a pot of milk as a present. He was an old man who walked with a limp because of an arrow wound in his knee, which he had got from the Bushmen. The Bushmen call those who lie to the south of them Aw nameiqua.[4] He seemed to be a good-natured man and to have more brains than the rest. He as well complained of the Geisiqua which he also called Combe-coe or -qua[5]. Thus one kraal complains about the other. They were all cut but said that they do not do it any more now because they said it made them weak. They said this probably because they saw that I did not think it a good thing. Among them, however, there are some who are not cut.

They said they had friends among the Briqua but that the children's disease[6] was always with this people and that for this reason they had no more dealings with them. The river called Koeroemana is a small river without running water.

On consideration therefore this must be the Keinkaap or Kaikaap or some such river because we have seen no other running river and have heard of no other from the Bushmen people.[7]

N.B. Have since learned that it is half the size of the Orange River, always contains water, and runs into the sea in the furthest part of Namaqualand.

Nou ei koe and Hoekeikoe lie to the north of the Ogoqua and are Bushmen.[8] Asked the Gauwaap about the Briquas and he said that he spoke a little of their language. Found some words that were most similar to the Caffers' language but water he called *betsi*.[9] Matsiboa was one of their chiefs and kept many women. Mocodoe was another chief. Kakobaab lies to the furthest part of the Briqua.[10]

We went to the second stream of the river which we found to be very deep and very wide and full of hippopotamus. N.B. the *Gauwaap* told me that while one of his people was swimming in it one of these animals had bitten off his leg; he was still alive but another had died. The forest was very wide at this place so that we could not see anything except when close to the water. Wounded some hippopotamus with my hand-pistol and let off a shot close to the Gauwaap and three of his people so that they

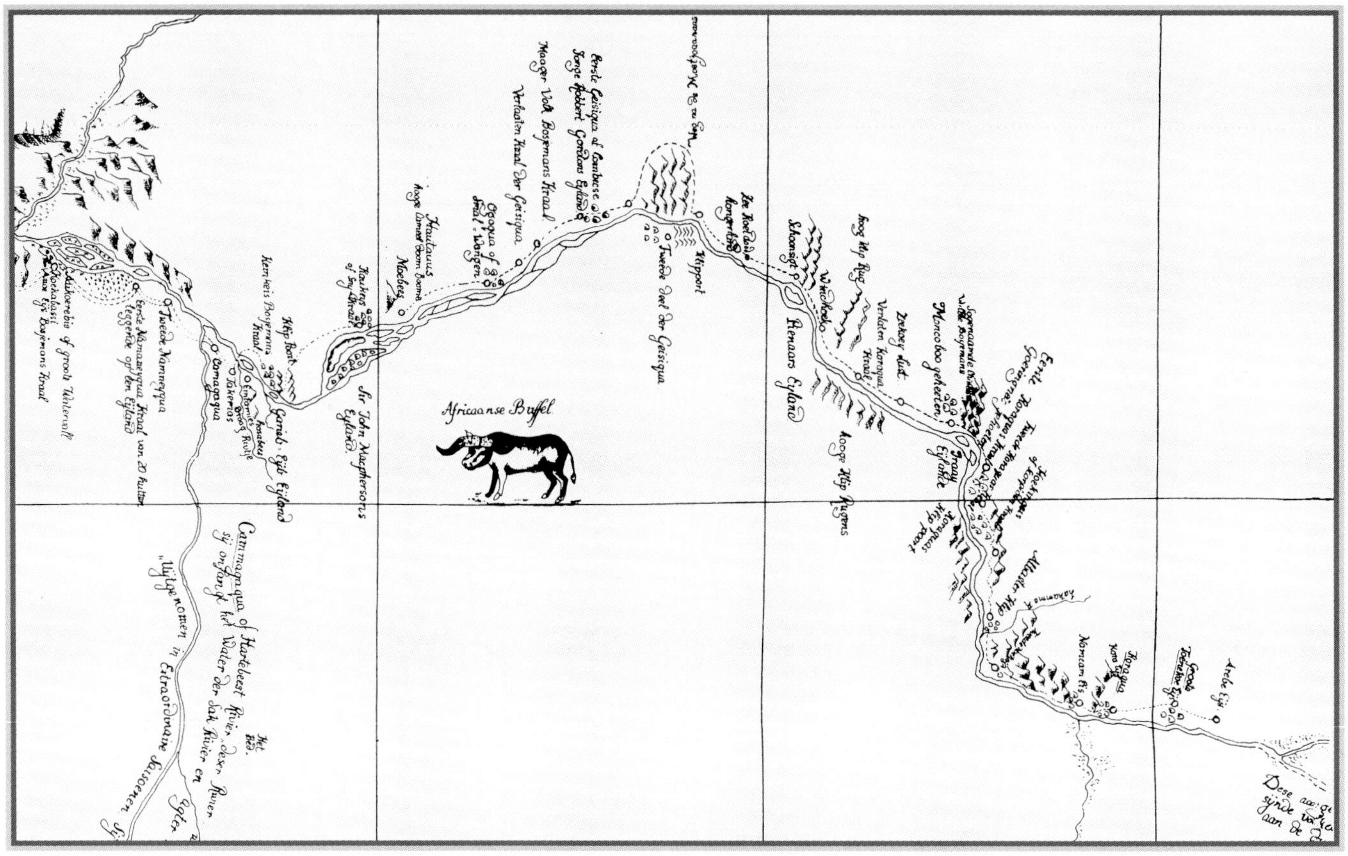

Map 6. *A redrawn section of Gordon's 'great map', showing where he crossed to the north bank of the Orange River and his later turning point.*

nearly tumbled over. They came back with me and slept at our camp. We kept strict watch. Shortly before we got there three lions had settled down: they jumped up and ran away. On our return they showed me where the Geisiqua and Koraqua kraal had stalked them and attacked them and stolen their cattle. Two or three on each side were left dead. If possible, even while fighting, they bury their dead, in case they have to retire. They kill prisoners and the wounded, even women and children. But the Ogoqua say they do not harm the last two but keep them with them. They are well protected on these islands and in these forests and that is why they live there. Besides which everywhere here beyond the banks of the river, there is very fine grass; it is a delightful place. Many of the islands here are so high that they are seldom overrun at high water. They showed me one on which there was a high hill where they repair at that time. Some of their people had gone to the Briquas. We saw about twenty of them on the other side. There are about a hundred, men, women and children in all. There are more than 23 huts; four on a small island and 19 on a larger one. They had a fair amount of stock: cows, sheep and goats, all of the same kind as the Namneyqua.

However, it was on 28 October at the kraal of the Geisiqua (about ten kilometres downstream of present-day Upington) that Gordon was able to make contact with people who were significantly more familiar and interbred with the 'Briqua':

This kraal had fled the rising water and I found them putting up their huts, which they complete in a few hours. Went to them again in the afternoon as well as in the evening when the cattle were in the kraal. They milk in the afternoon and also in the evening like all Namaquas; seldom however in the morning. During the day each was busy on his own work in front of his hut. These stood, almost forming a circle, with three large, live thorn-trees in the middle. They make fish traps and milking pails which they hollow out with a bent scraping iron. They also dress skins by rubbing them with stones. In addition many of the women sat hammering red buchu from camelthorn bark. Saw several Caffer-like faces among them (these are also the Bitsiana or Briquas) and one very old man. I asked him about counting-words and many other words, which were perfect Caffer, but others did differ. They were amazed at me; most of all my long hair and burning glass, the taking of latitude and my speaking Briqua which, they said, I could easily get by with. They recounted to me that the Briquas had lived in these parts until now. N.B. the description of their huts is just like those of the Caffers, everything else as well. However they prepare many Hartebeest skins the way we do: all the hair off, but they let the tail hang down by the side of their neck. This is very much their dress. Previously they never carried bow and arrow, only the assegai. But because this weapon could not prevail against the arrow and bow they were soon using the poisoned arrow and bow. Their name is Bitjoana and not Birina or Briqua as they are called by the Hottentots. The Koraqua and Einiqua drove them from here but some of them now live among the Bitjoana. They dwell on the Koeroemana river which, they say, comes from the Gharie[11] which flows off beyond and beside the Nabobequa Namaquas.[12] But that is to say it has its source close to the

Gharie since it would be impossible that such a small river as this would be flowing so strongly. This Koeroemana is half as big as the Gharie and always contains water, has no hippopotamus, some thorn-trees and much reed. Across the same live the Caffers whom they call Cabeticoe but who call themselves Borroeniana or Morroena.[13] Beyond them is a large river, bigger than the Gharie. It is called Koeang, is full of hippopotamus and runs west beyond Namaqualand until the river and also beyond the Koeroemana.[14] There are Bushmen between the Namaquas and the Briquas, but for how far they do not know. It is flat country, poor in water but Briqualand which lies to the north of the Wilhelmina River has mountains and many springs.[15] In the interior are giraffes, gnus, hartebeest, zebras, kwaggas, elephants, rhinoceros, buffalo, eland etc., and the game known to us. (Brink's aueroks are gnus, which they call ghaúwp or the master; and the white horse is a pale kwagga.)[16]

The Geisiquas are about two hundred strong and were very friendly, bringing us milk in abundance. As is usual they were not good friends with their neighbours. Hamma Gamma Toeroebeep was an old man but I found that Eiheep had more influence. Went to their kraal in the evening where they had about 200 cattle, sheep and goats. They perform their dances just like the other Hottentots.

They were astonished at my whiteness when I went bathing in the river. Many of them stood peering through the trees.

As the text tells us, Gordon was able to confirm that the true name of these 'Briqua' was in fact 'Bitjoana' – in other words, the Batswana. Indeed the people he was enquiring about were a sub-tribe of the Batswana, called the Batlaping. They were of mixed Tswana and Korana blood, as Professor Forbes established when he examined the text of an inset entitled 'Moetjoaanaas Huijshouding', which appears on Gordon's 'great map' (Map 3 in the Gordon Atlas).[17] Most of that text is taken from the entry Gordon made on this day. There is one addition in the inset that should be noticed here: Gordon says that these people 'are the most civilized of all those I have found in my journeys in the southern part of Africa'. It is a statement that is not immediately justifiable from the information in the journal and must have been an afterthought. His acquaintance with the Batlaping was, after all, a little scant.

The final entry for this day also deserves our attention. Gordon is always delighted to 'astonish' the tribespeople and this time it is with his whiteness when he went bathing in the river. 'Many of them stood peering through the trees,' he writes. There is something wholly charming about these naive voyeurs and they seem to have amused the pale-skinned traveller – enough anyway for him to have thought the scene worth recording.

*S*ometime after the birth of his first son, Robert, in 1781, Gordon gave an island in this vicinity the name of 'Jonge Robbert Gordons Eijland'. Today, so far as one can tell, it is the one known as Kanoneiland. Obviously the naming of this island is not mentioned in the text of the journal, but nor is there a later note in the margin, as there is in the instance of Sir John Macpherson's island, and one wonders why such a prominent feature went unmarked origi-

nally. Did Gordon leave it unnamed for just such an eventuality? Not that he could have known that he would father a son sometime in the future; but he could have left 'gaps' to be filled in with appropriate names when the right occasion presented itself.

The party continued its journey eastward along the northern bank of the river. Schoemaker managed to lose himself for a whole day at this point but appeared again on 30 October. Gordon merely records that 'we looked hard for him and were worried'. No more is said of the incident.

Both written and cartographical evidence of Gordon's continuing interest in the Batswana occurs on this day. In the journal he wrote of 'large grassy plains towards the Moetjoana, on our left-hand side to the north', while on the map this feature appears as 'Weg na de Moetjoaanaa' (Road to the Moetjoana). This is 'Some 20 miles N.E. of Upington', according to Professor Forbes.[18]

As has already been seen, Gordon clearly derived a certain measure of delight in giving places appropriate names, but the next name was probably a communal decision, as Gordon explains: 'Because they had nothing to eat for two days it was a great sorrow to our people and we called this place Hongerland.' However, in contrast to this place of hunger, on the next day (31 October) three hippopotamus were shot, and Gordon writes: '. . . since one was in a shallow place we immediately dragged it out. While our people were dancing for joy we slaughtered it on the spot and grilled it. Even without salt or bread it tasted very good. Called this place Zeekoeidood.' Thus a dead hippopotamus gives its name to one spot on the river, and there is still more naming to take place this day. Resuming the hard trudge of his journey, Gordon writes:

48. *The* Histoire Naturelle *hartebeest.*

49. *'Moetjoaanaas Huishouding'. An artist's impression of a Batswana kraal, taken from Gordon's 'great map'.*

'. . . after every three and a half hours of brisk walking we lay down and rested close to the river on account of the heat. It flows southwards here and forms another long island which I named Pinar's island . . . .' This name, a tribute no doubt to his chief hunter, also went on the map with the others. (As far as can be determined, this is the island a few kilometres above present-day Lambrechtsdrift.)

By 2 November 1779 they had reached a spot on the river where 'On the angle of the turn there were two or three small islands which we called De Draay Eijlande'. This place has been confidently identified as the bend in the river at Kheis, which is a few kilometres upstream from Groblershoop.[19] An hour or so on from here there was a tense confrontation with a band of 'Bushmen'. It is one of the few places in the journals where Gordon allows himself to break into direct speech, thus immediately bringing home the drama of the situation.

Left in the afternoon to the sound of some hippopotamus bellowing like steers; first mistaking the noise for a Koraqua cattle kraal. We heard this for the first time. (It is said they do this when they are on heat, otherwise their sound is a snort). After walking for an hour we saw a band of Bushmen with arrows, bows and assegais. We sent a Bushman without a weapon to meet them. Four of them came with bow and arrow down a hill to one side of us, their bow hands full of arrows and threatening to shoot. Pinar and I held our course obliquely towards them; I with my double-barrelled gun at the ready. When we came opposite each other at a distance of about thirty paces, they held their bows and arrows at the ready, their bodies quivering, and I waited for the first shot. Koerikei who was walking behind me was deadly frightened and called out: 'Sir, oh Sir, they will shoot, they will shoot!' But our Bushman kept on calling: 'do not shoot!' and in this way we came up to the foremost ones. They were the ugliest creatures I have ever seen. The other two, not wanting to approach, we gave them some tobacco and they filled their stone pipes but it was a good while before they laid down their arrows and bows. They spoke the Namaqua dialect, said they were good friends of the Koraquas and that their Eis or tribe was called Moncoboo.[20] Some of them live across and some on our side of the river. One of Buffon's Jokkos, the Gibbon as I remember, has the exact physiognomy of these two, with hardly a nose. They were about five feet tall; the skin on their bellies had elongated wrinkles caused, we supposed, from hunger when they bind themselves with a leather strap, and then from eating too much when they have shot something. They appeared to be about forty years old. They said that the other two would not approach because they were tracking steenbok. These animals, fast as they are, run far on their first lap. After this they [the Bushmen] follow their tracks and chase them for the second lap; and so on, further. In hot weather they usually catch them on the third lap; the animal having worn its hoofs through as well.[21]

It is interesting to see here how Gordon succeeds in relieving — even dismissing — the tension of the initial encounter. This he does by adopting a jocular tone to describe the tribesmen and then going on to present them in quasi-scientific terms by referring to Jocko chimpanzees in Buffon's *Histoire Naturelle*.[22] But it is well to also take note that Gordon does not seem to express any contempt by these remarks and comparisons. The fact is that these men are ugly in his eyes and they do look distinctly simian. But having made this observation, Gordon lets the matter rest there.

Departing at daybreak on 3 November, the party travelled towards what are now known as the Boegoeberge and which Gordon called the 'Koraquas klip poort' on his map. Of these 'Koraqua' he wrote:

Saw a few that had slight Caffer traits in the physiognomy. Several were exactly like Jews; but no high nose. Called two of them Moses and Aron and this made them well content. They smear themselves with red paint and fat in which they put shining, broken fragments of stones such as mica. They get this from the Briquas or Caffers.

The same afternoon, at a place he called 'The Second Goeringneis'[23] kraal, Gordon recounts an incident which, though small, nevertheless tells us something of the authority he was able to command, even over complete strangers: '. . . there was a quarrel between two of them.

They took to their sticks and to their bows but I ordered them to be told that I did not want them to fight, whereupon they left off.'

At this point Gordon reported that 'our people' were bartering cattle and sheep with the tribesmen. Presumably 'our people' were the nine 'Hottentot marksmen' mentioned earlier as being in the party. Gordon is obviously irritated by this development and records that he is having trouble keeping these followers in order. They were, he says, 'very annoyed that the Hottentots had hidden their cattle and had offered us neither sheep nor cattle'.

The next day, 4 November 1779, the party reached a prominent feature on the river bank which Gordon called the 'Albaster Klip' on his map and in his journal. (This translates as Alabaster Rock or Cliff in English.) Very recently (June 1990) this feature was positively identified by Professor A. Smith of the Archaeology Department at the University of Cape Town.[24] It is, he writes, a 'huge white rock of vein quartz, more than 30 m high . . . right at the water's edge and forms a slight overhang'. (It is on the farm Bovenseekoebaart near a bend in the river at 29°7.3′S : 22°15.4′E.) 'Today,' he adds, 'river silts have formed at the base of the overhang. Some rock paintings of parallel red lines in red ochre disappear below the silts, suggesting the overhang was greater before the [Boegoeberg] dam raised the level of the river, and may have been an important reference point for San trancing activity.' Here is how Gordon described coming upon the rock in his journal:

We tramped beside . . . [the river] . . . for a total of four and a quarter hours from our sleeping place until we came to the Hoekingeis which is the Scorpion Kraal;[25] of 20 huts; a very sturdy, well set-up people, all like the ones before. They were more willing than the previous kraals and we traded some beads and tobacco for a pack-ox. Once they had done their trading they wanted us to stay on but, when we had drunk some milk and rested, we set forth, again across the flat stretches of this pass, south beside the river. One of our Hottentots had a sore leg and three sorcerer women snorted on it in the same way I have described in my previous journal.[26]

After two hours' going the river again ran close to the mountains, for that reason we sent the pack-oxen around them. There was a very large white alabaster rock here with bluish veins, but very intermingled. N.B. The Hoekingeis kraal was situated at this spot when Vicar and the two half-breeds were here but across the river, which is narrow here, and it is where they turned round. After we had tramped for three and a half hours and, after having left the river for the last half hour on account

50. *This Namaqua bull was painted, surprisingly, in the Camdebo at De Beer's farm, De Vrede.*

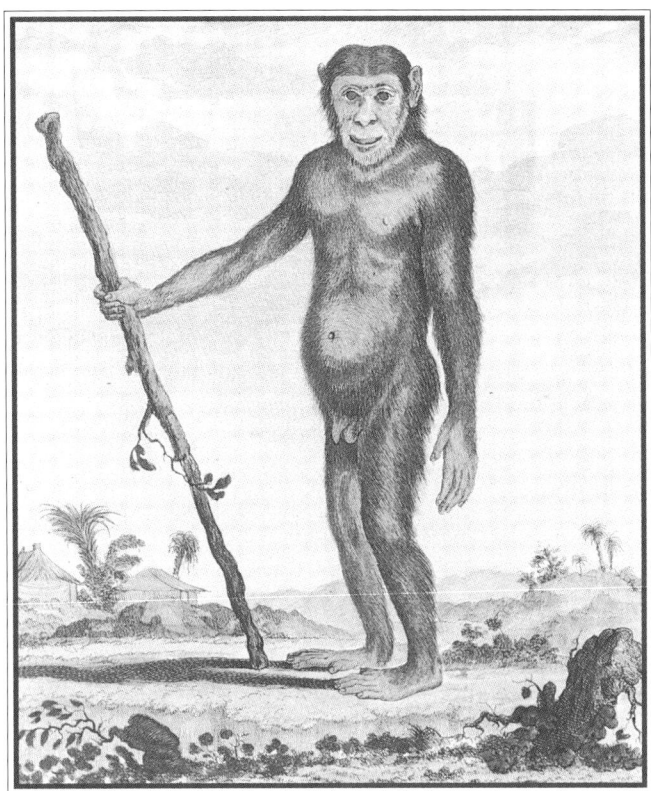

51. *Two 'Moncaboo' tribesmen reminded Gordon of this Gibbon ape ('Jokko') in Buffon's* Histoire Naturelle.

of a turn to the S.S.W., we lay down to rest at nightfall by the river again.

As was noted earlier, Gordon had with him Wikar's report, but Wikar referred to his turning point as being at the 'Husingais or Spiderweb kraal'.[27] In fact Wikar did not mention the Hoekingeis kraal at all. The slight similarity in the names does not allow an identification because Gordon specifically qualified Hoekingeis as the 'Scorpion kraal', making no mention of the 'Spiderweb kraal'.

In his journal entry for 5 November Gordon again breaks into direct speech. (This is the only occasion when two such passages occur so close to one another.) Here, as opposed to the confrontation with the 'Bushmen' on 2 November, direct quotation is used to emphasize the dramatically humorous quality of the man he calls Hansworst or, in English, the jester. Gordon's rendering of the speech makes it clear that a kind of praise poem of himself (in the interests of the cattle trade!) is taking place:

Departed at dawn, south again and still alongside the river. After an hour's going we reached the Noekeis kraal. These people had never seen anything from our Colony and were very afraid. However we had an old man from Hoekingeis with us whom we called Hansworst and he said to them: 'This is another child of man; look at his hair! He comes from far. Be not afraid! He is good. Bring cattle for barter!' He screamed himself hoarse. He jabbered so many good things about us that they became tamer and over a hundred men, women and children came to us.

After spending the rest of the 5th and the whole of the 6th at the Noekeis Kraal, on 7 November Gordon decided not to continue the journey and to turn back at this spot. Professor Smith has also been able to identify this site with some confidence, since he was able to use the Alabaster Rock as an accurate reference point. Using the Raper and Boucher translation of this journal, he refers to Noekeis as Nokukeis, a reading of the manuscript I must question.[28] The site of the kraal, Professor Smith states, is

where Debeerskloof kloof comes into the Orange River. There is a large flat area of river silts along the river used for farming today that could easily have accommodated a kraal of 'over a hundred men, women and children' (Raper & Boucher, 1988:348). Gordon obviously spent the morning with the Nokukeis, before climbing up the mountain behind the kraal and walking southwards along the ridge for two hours. From the top he was able to see the river running southwards for 2 miles (one Dutch mile was 7km = 14km) before turning ESE. We climbed the mountain called Knypgat se Berg, south of Debeerskloof. It took us less than half an hour to get onto the ridge and we estimate another hour would have taken us all the way along. We climbed to the highest point (29°12.5′ S: 22°17.5′ E) and we were able to see the river exactly as described by Gordon.

As we shall see, Gordon took the latitude of the camp and recorded it as '29 deg.–14 min'. Professor Smith reckons that he was within 2 minutes' accuracy with this figure, so there can now be little doubt that the camp was, as he says, 'at the mouth of Debeerskloof (just to the west of the Witberg)'. What is confusing is that the site is not marked on the map. However, there is a *'Tweede* Noekeis' marked on the map where the river makes a bend to the E.S.E., confirming Professor Smith's description and Gordon's words: 'Saw here that the river still runs southward for two miles and thereafter at the Noekeis Kraal makes its way E.S.E. At this second section of the Hoekingeis a small rivulet of reeds runs from the east into the Orange River.'

The most probable explanation for the confusion of 'Noekeis', 'Tweede Noekeis' and 'this second section of the Hoekingeis' is that these people were, in reality, of the same kind and the distinctions between one kraal (or clan) and the other were geographical only. When the map came to be drawn at a later time these minor differences were blurred and some degree of confusion arose. What matters is that we now have a firm identification of the Alabaster Rock and hence of Gordon's turning point.

Gordon's remarks about the 'Briqua' and the Korana hold great interest, therefore the remainder of the entry for 5 November and the whole of the next day's entry are given here:

Saw two Briqua at this place. The one was a true Caffer, the other a half-breed. As I have long suspected their language is the same as the Xhosa's, but a different dialect and without any click of the tongue. He was most astonished at the words I spoke in his language which he repeated on their own with a very slight variation. He understood but not if I spoke continuously.

Took latitude: 29 deg.–14 min.

Went up a mountain in the afternoon, going southwards for two hours from one peak across to another. Saw here that the river still runs southward for two miles and thereafter at the Noekeis kraal makes its way E.S.E. At this second section of the Hoekingeis a small rivulet of reeds runs from the east into the Orange River. So far as I could see the country was the same on both sides but the mountains continue still further on the northern bank. They brought us a slaughter animal for barter. They asked me to show them how a gun shoots. I shot it with my gun, felling it. But since I hit too high it got up and ran off but we told them to bring it back and we slaughtered it. They were most frightened at the shot.

6th November 1779.
Last night the wild people were up the whole night at their huts and, because we lay right close to them, I stayed awake all night. Their dogs troubled us greatly. Because they allow them to suffer great hunger, they carried off everything made of skin.

Generally the whole race of Koraquas are big, well-developed Hottentots, though not as burly as the Caffers, with many Jewish and Chinese traits of physiognomy. They had many Briqua Karosses. On many of them the hair on the front part of the head had been shaven as though they were wearing wigs. The Briquas or Moetjoana wear a smaller skin, from a calf or young animal, under the large cloak which is the skin of a hartebeest, the tail hanging against the neck. The skin goes over the shoulders and is fastened at the breast like a cloak. Most of the second skin hangs behind under the large one and not lower than the thighs. The cloak hangs to the heels. They only have Caffer ornaments on their heads. They are 'cut' and call this Goesigha. Their entire genitals are held in the scrotum of a goat or calf, the hair on the outside. They fasten it round the hips and through the legs behind to the belt again. It is not loose but bound very firmly. Like the Hottentots they have shoes that cover the soles (veldschoen). There was a fellow five feet, ten inches (Rhineland) tall with very broad shoulders, a powerful head and limbs and a face just like the Caffers. He knew nothing of the Tamboekies or of a sea to the east.[29] They get their iron from far in the north.[30] They have had a children's disease which they call Sequawquaan as well as Quaripane. This disease did not often come to their country but caused great carnage among them when it did. It came from the north. Apart from the Moetjoana he gave me these names: The Barolo, The Shounarreba Capii, The Bapouru Boucana.[31] However it is just the same as with the Hottentots: one people but in different kraals. His chief was Massepa and so he said: 'Masepa Moetjoana Incosji' which in the Caffer tongue would be expressed: 'Masepa, chief of the Moetjoana Kraal.'

When our people had bartered beads and tobacco for some cattle, something they were not willing to do before, we made ready to return. I gave them a little mirror for the women and girls of the kraal. I gave it to the oldest woman to keep in case they should want to paint themselves. They were most astonished and happy at this. Hearing me sing, one of them asked if we always sang without dancing.

It surprised me greatly that the Moetjoana who get iron and copper from the Europeans do not have beads. They make only iron beads for themselves as well as for trade with the Hottentots. Their huts are of the same kind as the other Caffers. But they are large so that they can wander about to and fro within them. There is only one family in each hut. As soon as the children grow up they have to make another house. They have no windows, however, but shelves where they put their possessions. The larger door or opening is also covered with wood just like the others. They plant tobacco and smoke stone pipes which are just like the Namaqua pipes. If the ground is made of clay they make two tubular holes in it, which are made opposite each other and lead into each other. Then they put the tobacco in one hole and suck through the other with their mouth, there being water in the middle. Koraquas, Geisiqua and Einiquas smoke with or through the horn of an ox and in this they differ from the Gonaquas who place a tube in the horn which contains water. On this tube is a long pipe-bowl which they light. Then with a hand or an arm they close the mouth of the horn as much as to allow them to suck with their mouth and in this way they gulp themselves drunk on the smoke. When they have gulped most of it down they sit for a while afterwards as though shocked, without being able to speak or stand up. They will walk for hours on end for a pipe of tobacco, swim across the river, or fetch milk, etc. Besides beads, therefore, it is the best money here. One of the Koraquas had the figure of a snake burned on to his thighs; almost life-size.

The supposition has been advanced that since Gordon had learned enough about the 'Briqua' by his questioning of individuals, it was not necessary for him to visit their actual country. Perhaps this supposition is partly true, but it will be recalled that earlier in this journal Gordon had recorded his great longing to meet these people. It is therefore questionable whether the few encounters he mentions here could really have satisfied his desire to see them. On

52. *The* Histoire Naturelle *aardvaark.*

53. A detail from Gordon's 'great map', showing a 'Bushman' settlement.

the other hand, he had gathered a substantial amount of information and his party was no doubt urging him to turn back. They were all surely tired of travelling so far and so hard. They had collected a store of cattle and they were probably also worried that the advent of the rainy season would make the river impassable, thus cutting them off from their homes. But whatever the reason – or reasons – for turning back at this point, Gordon does not say.

Another possible explanation for Gordon's unexpected and puzzling decision has been submitted by Professor Forbes:

It can be suggested that . . . he felt positive that he had established that the river whose banks he was on, was the same he had visited near where Bethulie now stands. His exaggerated estimate of the distance he had travelled eastward must have supported this conviction. It was no doubt the arduous travel over difficult country that principally led to overestimates in the dead reckoning of his longitude positions, whose excess becomes progressively greater as he travelled upstream.

Professor Forbes also shows that neither Gordon nor Wikar realized 'how great a northward bend the river makes above Prieska . . . [Gordon] drew its course continuing upstream in an E.S.E. direction to accord with its direction of flow mapped near Bethulie'. On the map Gordon wrote: 'This dotted portion is the further supposed course of the river, which is of the exact same width and with the same vegetation where I have been at the double lined parts [*i.e.* near Bethulie].'[32]

Assuming that the theory of a complete encirclement of the Cape, advanced earlier, has some validity, it is likely that Gordon believed it to be unnecessary to physically reach the Bethulie location. In other words, the course of the Orange was now pretty well established in his mind.

One other matter of relative importance concludes Professor Forbes's discussion of this part of Gordon's journey. Referring to the map, he writes:

Gordon's record of the names of the tribes of Bantu stock in and near the region now called Bechuanaland is perhaps more valuable than his mention or mapping of the Korana tribes along the Orange, since the latter work was largely forestalled by that of Wikar. This list of Bantu tribal names [such as those given in the entry for 6 November 1779] is probably the earliest available for this region of which otherwise practically nothing is known save from Native traditions. Hence his record has a singular ethno-geographical significance.[33]

The actual day on which the party started its return journey was 7 November 1779. The journal entry for this date, though comparatively short, has moments of humour – caused more by surprise than by wit:

The same weather. The western wind rose at about 10 o'clock. Our people arrived at about 8 o'clock with another band of the Hoekingeis and Noekeis kraals with cattle to barter.

Departed along the way we had come and arrived at the first Hoekingeis at noon and so got milk immediately since that is the first milking time just as with the Namaquas. These people also make Tabie[34] (at first they did not want to admit it). They are just like the Einiquas and probably spring from the Namaquas as do all Hottentots.

The river is still falling.

The biggest Hottentots I have yet seen were at this kraal. Many that we saw looked like Spaniards but with flatter noses (probably already cross-bred with Briquas). They were very afraid of us and probably thought we would put a spell on them. A big fellow whom I looked at several times sheltered behind the others and when I again looked at him he said, in fear mixed with anger, that I was always looking. Another was very like my brother, the Prebendary, but was more burly and just as large in stature. I wanted to stand next to him to see how tall he was but he shuddered when I touched him, though I showed him all friendliness. At this place, as at all the kraals, I gave a little mirror to the women. That everything they see about us is taken for sorcery is demonstrated by the fact that our afore-mentioned Hottentot, Swarteboy (who had a spell lifted from his leg by the sorceresses when we were on our up journey), said that he had bumped against one of our guns and that this had made his leg sore. The sorceresses told him that powder from the musket had entered the leg and that they had finally sucked it out as black as charcoal and that it had made them vomit. N.B. He gave them a necklace, the value of a cow, in return for this. The fellow firmly believed it and got better. The women had probably asked him what was in our guns and so by bumping against same it [the powder] had gone into his leg.

It may be recalled that the second son of old Jacob Gordon, a certain Adam Bernard, became a minister of religion.[35] Hence the reference here to 'my brother, the Prebendary'. But what exactly prompted Gordon to make this droll connection is a mystery. There seems to be a degree of jocular malice present, but the strangeness is emphasized by the fact that, presumably, the joke would be shared by no one but himself. Or did he read this pas-

54. *A young quagga, abundant in 1780, now extinct.*

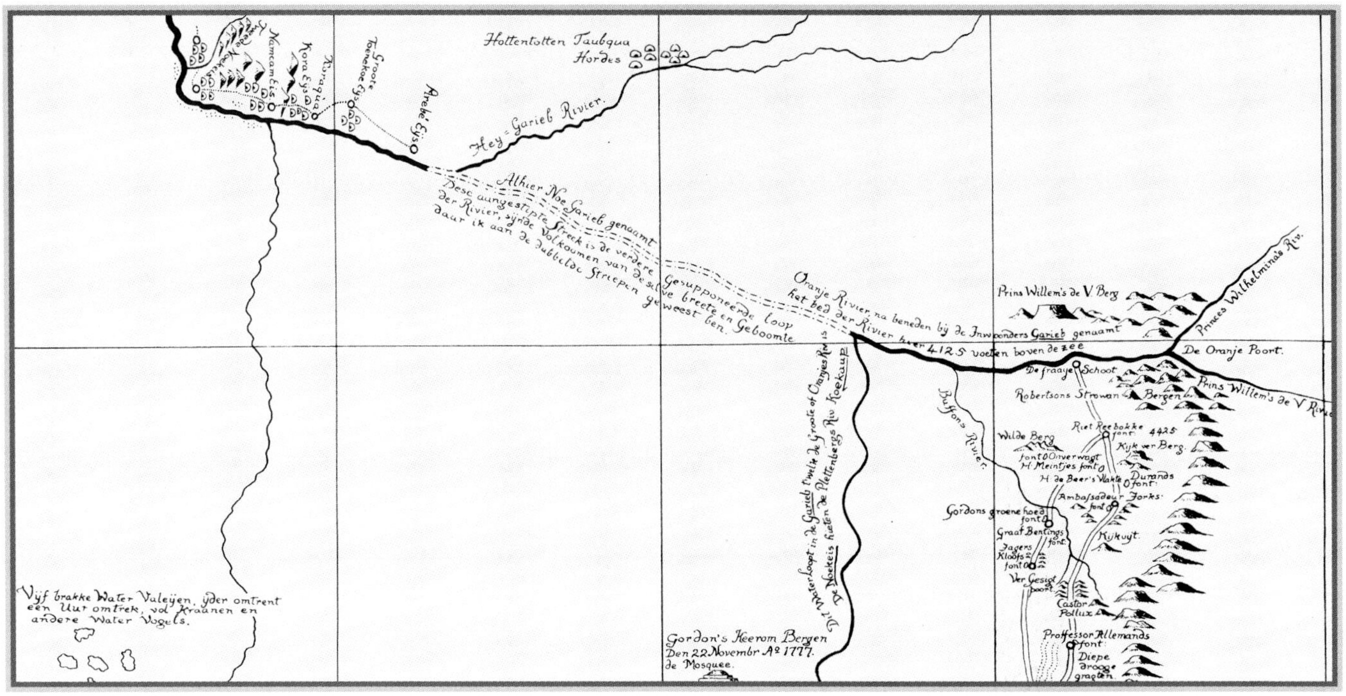

Map 7. *Gordon's perception of the unexplored section of the Orange River, from a redrawing of his 'great map'.*

sage out aloud to his family and those friends who might have known his brother? The incident is made even more striking, of course, by the 'burly' man's fear of Gordon, as well as by the context of tribal sorcery and superstition.

No time was lost as the party retraced its steps. The entries here become short and involve less speculation. On 10 November a somewhat familiar event is recorded: 'Schoemaker, following the bend of the river, got left behind.' The next day the subject is resumed: 'Because Schoemaker had not come, sent three Hottentots back. At midday we had our meal close to the red-sand country where we had previously cut up the hippopotamus. Schoemaker joined us again and we slept one hour short of the Geisiqua Klip Poort.' As before, whatever irritation Gordon must have felt gets no comment and the journal maintains its calm tenor.

*B*y the evening of 12 November Gordon had arrived back at the kraal where the pack-oxen and horses had been left. He had gone ahead of the main party and probably had more time than usual for reflection:

Overcast sky. Sunshine now and then. Cool weather. Some raindrops in the morning.
  Strong west wind that turned S.W. in the afternoon and was brisk. Was not cold last night; this was fortunate since I had to sleep in the open without a coat because the party had still not arrived. Yesterday and today heard much sorcerer snorting – there are some sick people in the kraal. It was as if they did this from time to time in the same way we take medicine. The snorting resembled the sound heard when sleeping at a certain distance from a dove-cot, where the doves are continually cooing. Our people arrived in the afternoon. They had shot a buffalo, a rhinoceros and two hippopotamus and this was the reason they had stayed behind. One does not easily get a Hottentot away from dead game. This kraal also found a hartebeest that had been killed by a lion, and they brought the meat back to the kraal with great rejoicing.
  Departed about four o'clock and slept at the place where we had slept on our outward journey. Called this place Gielquin's Island after Major Gielquin.[36] Saw a place where lions had killed a deer and [there were] many lion tracks. Here among hard flint-stone one finds lime-like patches at places in the veld. Gave the Geisiquas who had been with us some presents and to Eiheep a Grenadier's cap. He made some objection to accepting this from fear of his own people: thus an elder or Kawkawp has little authority. It was as if his authority would be too great if he had the cap. However he did take it and wanted to come with us to the wagon.

As we have seen, from time to time Gordon introduces remarkable similes into the mundane flow of his journal. A good recent example from this journey would be that of the giraffes compared to flamingoes. In the above passage another curious but striking comparison is drawn, likening the snorting of a sorcerer to the cooing of doves – which he hastens to qualify by adding 'when sleeping at a certain distance'. It is difficult, perhaps, for modern urban readers to imagine exactly what this sound is like. But obviously Gordon had thought carefully about this simile and one can be sure that it is as accurate as it is singular.

The business of the grenadier's cap and the delicate status of the Kawkawp is further evidence of how careful he is in observing the nuances of tribal custom. The meticulous note-taking is again evident the following day:

We passed five Bushman huts this afternoon which were not there on our outward journey. They came to us: the tip of their poisoned arrows can be bent in so as not to hurt themselves, as well as to preserve the poison longer. They did not have that small barb that they have at the Agter Sneeuwberg. Eiheep showed me where he had been shot eleven times by arrows and how he had been healed by cutting them open and sucking at them. Thus the strongest poison is here curable. They are cruel to their prisoners in war; they slaughter them like cattle. They cut their bellies open, put their hand in and break the main artery, leaving them to lie like that. They seldom spare women or children. The Moetjoana do the same.

The next day also provided important practices to record, even though it is evident that Gordon was in a hurry to get back to his wagon. He sees a 'Bushman' sitting on a hill:

Going a little nearer we spoke to him. (Had with me two Bushmen, my little Bushman Cabas and another three Hottentots, as well as my instruments that I wanted to take across myself). He came to us but was frightened. I gave him some tobacco and as he had his bow and arrow I asked him if he had shot anything. He said no, but that he was looking for kwaggas that had drunk of a certain small spring which he had poisoned. He had done this with several ostrich egg shells full of milk from the thorny six-sided euphorbia when it had its yellow bloom. He also used the bruised branch of the same tree. Generally they die close to the water but if there is a lot of water then they die the following night; their stomach rots but the flesh remains good food. He went with us to his kraal which was the same [one] we had seen previously, on the other side. I saw much zebra meat here, poisoned in the same way. Gave him some tobacco and we went to sleep on the other side of the mountain, almost at the start of the pass, beside the water. These three days the road has been very stony so that our raw-hide shoes[37] are in pieces. I have already worn out one pair.

On 16 November 1779 Gordon again reached the vicinity of present-day Kakamas, making his crossing here to the southern bank of the river. But as will be seen, *how* he performed this feat is a curious matter:

The wind whirled round with the course of the sun all day. Little wind, blowing lightly, bearing slightly from the east. A thundery sky in the morning, hot. Not cold last night which was fortunate since I had only my Scottish cloak which was worn threadbare. A hippopotamus was blowing close to us all night and the small waterfall was very noisy. Departed at dawn and was at Hosabees in two and a half hours. All formed one cliff through which the river comes together in a narrow passage, except for two small streams on the south side. Found some dark crystal here which has a blue vein. We looked for a place [to cross] and found one in the cliff. It was neither wide nor swift but it was deep. The momentum of the water had been broken up by the dividing and cascading of the stream higher up. It was a good place also because the slope was not steep here. Went across with my machine to the greatest astonishment of the Hottentots and, when everything was over, told the people here to make a raft and went off with two of them and my little Cabas to the wagon. Crossed the two streams, much stony country and two dry

---

55. *This scene is captioned by Gordon: 'Another sketch of a Bushman household. They are sitting next to a pot eating soup with a brush, their customary spoon.'*

56. *The gifboom or 'poison tree'* (Euphorbia virosa).

rivers, one of which is normally a tributary of the Orange River and the second was the Camagga, or Camagaqua or Zak River. Here for the first time on the whole journey I put myself on a horse, being anxious to see how matters stood with the wagon and our people at the Namneyqua. Although I lost my way, I rode along to the wagon in two and a half hours and found it in good order. My people praised the Namneyqua. Found some of these people at the wagon and they showed as much joy at my return as my own three Hottentots. They said that the other people must have been dishonest since I had come back so thin. I said no; it was because I had had to walk so hard. Tamega brought out milk for me at once and truly it was as though I had come to friends of my own kith and kin, so affectionately did these people conduct themselves.[38] They asked openly about everything and blamed each other because it took them so long to see me, not before I was right upon them. They were also astonished that I had come alone.

After five hours' going my little servant and my two Hottentots arrived. Today gave Cabas the name of Hector, because of his courage. He was very set upon having a Dutch name. The young fellow walked as hard as the best man, swam first through rivers, knew no fear and was always attentive and cheerful.

What exactly this 'machine' was is a mystery. The word in the original Dutch is spelt in the same way, as though written in English, but there is no further clue as to what it was. It does not seem to have been a raft since he specifically says that he told his people to make a raft, as though contrasting it with the 'machine'. Again, we appear to have an insoluble Gordon mystery.

Next, Gordon tells us that 'for the first time on the whole journey I put myself on a horse'. Presumably he means that while on the northern bank he did not ride but went on foot, which is what one would infer from the text. This can only be because he wished to save the horses in the rough terrain of those parts.

Gordon's eventual return to the wagon is most affecting since the language he uses is unusually warm and emotive. His likening the welcome he received from the people awaiting him there to one by 'friends of my own kith and kin' is evidence of their high regard and affection for him — and his for them. Note too how strongly he praises young Cabas. Yet all these statements are written without any embellishments — his blunt, even awkward, style seeming to emphasize the sincerity of his emotion. It is of course revealing that he found it necessary to record his feelings at all, and it is moving still to read them after the lapse of over two centuries.

Over the next two days first Pienaar and then the rest of the party caught up with Gordon. Odd pieces of information continue to fascinate him, as he notes on 18 November:

The same weather and wind. S.E. in the early part of the night. Our people arrived in the evening and we made ready to leave tomorrow. In the afternoon a large swarm of locusts, on the move, came from the east, whirling off towards the river, being very hungry. They were just like the ones last year at the Sneeuwberg. They serve as food for men, fishes, lions, springbuck and even horses eat them readily; so Pinar assured me.

These Hottentots do not eat of the hare or drink sheep's milk after they have been made 'men'.

On 19 November 1779 the party set off once more, at first resolutely retracing the tracks of its outward journey. However, the next day brings bitter disappointment for Gordon when he finds that the bones of the giraffe that he had buried so carefully had been dug up and destroyed by wild animals. Exercising his usual control, he talks only of his 'great displeasure', but it is easy to guess the frustration he must have felt, especially in view of his unmitigated joy when this 'handsome and extraordinary' animal was first shot. Yet the terse entry does no more than hint at what must have been to Gordon not only a personal disaster but a serious loss to the science of natural history.

The next entry (21 November) reflects something of the tensions induced by such a long and arduous journey and the hardships which they continued to endure:

57. *Great Namaqua and Strandloper kraals — a detail from the 'great map'.*

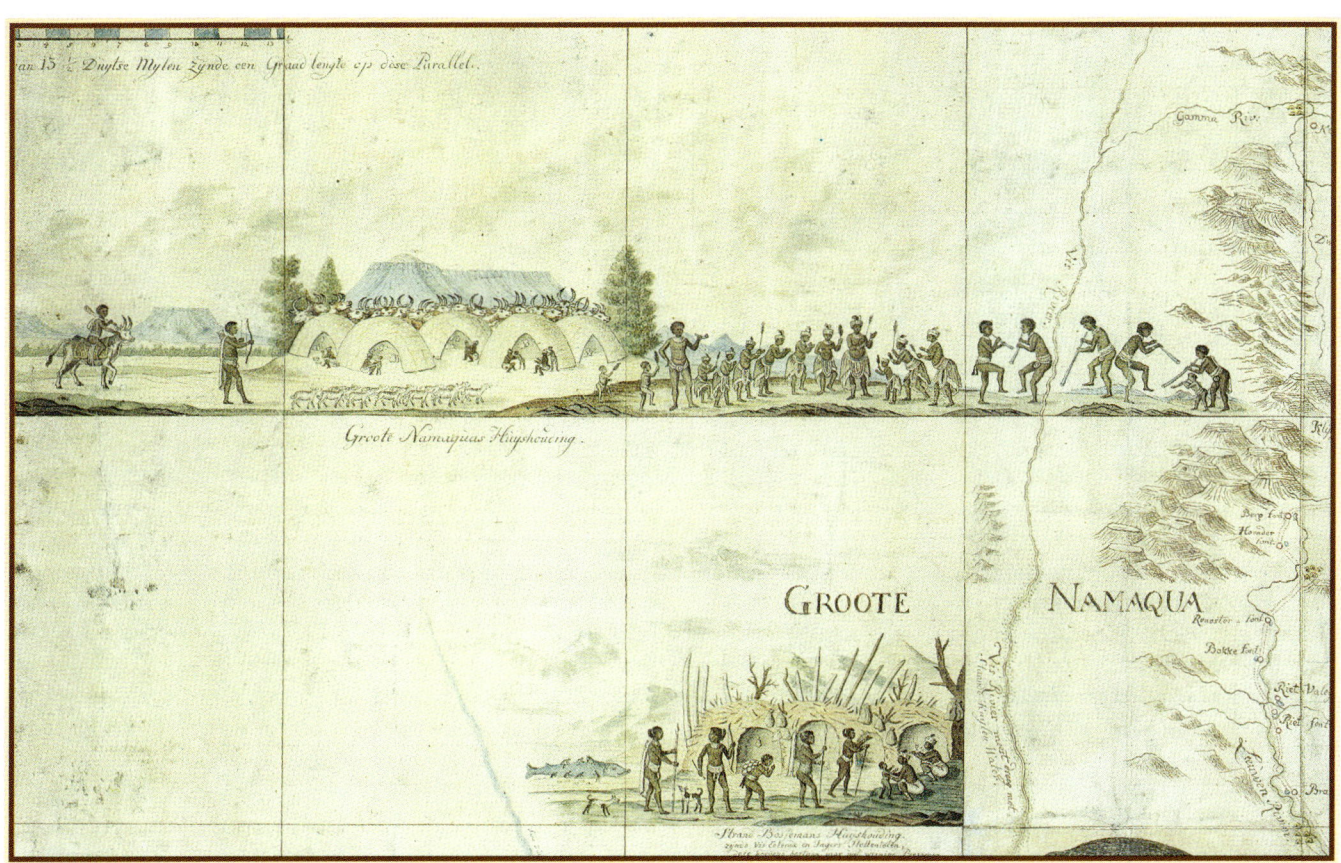

East wind and cool in the morning but at noon blew from the west again and was hot. Cloudy in the afternoon.

Pinar, longing for home, rode ahead. I gave him Schoemaker for company because his wits are astray; as much from lack of drink as from the length of the journey. Was alone now with my four Hottentots (as well as the two boys), happy to have rid myself of Schoemaker who was impatience itself. Rode straight across the countryside and after travelling for five hours arrived at our previous camp, Garies. Saw a giraffe but far off. We had to dig for water and let the oxen drink one after the other. We noticed several scorpions and it was a wonder that we were not stung since we just threw ourselves on the ground, exhausted.

One can feel a certain measure of sympathy for Schoemaker. He obviously had none of Gordon's interest in fauna and flora and all things scientific. He was on this expedition because he had been ordered to be on it. Gordon says Schoemaker was 'impatience itself', but one wonders who was the more impatient of the two. In any event, there is no mistaking the relief that Gordon feels now that, as he puts it, he is 'alone . . . with [his] four Hottentots (as well as the two boys)'.

Continuing on roughly the same track that he took on his outward journey, Gordon had cause to name a 'prominent mountain range' the Hendrik de IV Berg. These were probably the mountains around present-day Skuitdrift, and the name was prompted, Gordon tells us, by his having just finished reading the *Mémoires* of the Maréchal de Sully, the Protestant statesman and loyal supporter of Henry IV of France in the late sixteenth and early seventeenth century. What is interesting here is that this chance remark tells us not only that Gordon took books with him on his journeys but also what kind of books they were. It also shows us that his mind was not completely dominated by scientific and empirical modes of thought.

On 23 and 24 November the journal again emphasizes the rough going, especially hard now that they had not only to maintain the wagon in working order but also to clear the road ahead. And there is another unforeseen development:

The same weather and wind but very clear and hot.

Came through this stony pass with much difficulty. We had to work on the road everywhere and hold the wagons steady. There are only four of us travelling now. The wheels of my wagon have become so bad that we have had to tie in the tholepins. At noon Cabas disappeared; his kraal is on the river, close to here.[39] We had our midday meal a little beyond Honceib, a dry and sandy river, and in the afternoon went on to just opposite Samoep. Not wanting to travel the hard road to the river, I sent the oxen on to the water.

In the evening, the sky without a cloud, there was a beautiful total eclipse of the moon. My Hottentots were most astonished as I had told them about it some time before. It was a pity I had no time-piece, for both at the start and the finish and throughout the night it was very clear. At the finish there was a strong S.E. wind which became calmer with dawn.

I was asleep and my Koerikei woke me because Cabas and an old Bushman had arrived. He made many signs of friendship and said that he had been at his kraal. I gave the Bushman some tobacco and something to eat and he went off. I said that I did not wish to keep Cabas if he did not want to accompany me of his own free will. He protested that he was going with me of his own free will and he went off to lie down and sleep.

24th November 1779.
S.E. wind in the morning, veering slightly to the west. Strong S.W. wind in the night. Weather fine but very hot.

At dawn rode along the small stony hills higher up, looking for a better road with Cabas going ahead to see where the wagon could get through. Going round one of these small hills and not seeing Cabas I again came to the wagons and found that the boy had once more run away. It was probably so the day before as well and the old Bushman had forced him to go back to me, which is most unusual; coming to my fire at night in order to find me. In addition this Bushman had never seen me before because Cabas was with Pinar's Hottentots along the river on our outward journey and only came to me at Garies, attaching himself to me there of his own accord.

Given the warm remarks about Cabas, written a few days before, Gordon's equanimity about the boy's disappearance, is, at first glance, puzzling. Perhaps his apparently phlegmatic response lies in the fact that he genuinely did not want Cabas to stay with him under duress. As he says, 'I did not wish to keep Cabas if he did not want to accompany me of his own free will'. A sentiment that surely reflects both humanity and respect for the boy.

The condition of the wagon's wheels continued to cause anxiety and Gordon decided to let the party travel on to Sandfontein, a stock farm belonging to Pienaar where they had stayed earlier on this journey (27 and 28 September 1779), and which is about ten kilometres to the west of present-day Klein Pella. Gordon decided to go on ahead to the same destination, using a short cut through the mountains and riding through the night to arrive there on the morning of 27 November. He writes: 'Found Pinar and his people still at Sandfontein. Forthwith sent nails and hoop iron back to the wagon.'

As Gordon records, the wagon was indeed having great difficulty reaching the farm, and as though reflecting his anxiety, the journal entries are unusually brief at this point.

28th November 1779.
Easterly wind in the morning, veering round with the progress of the sun. Fresh west wind in the afternoon. Hot. Thundery weather in the east. We had a few drops of rain in the night.

Am sleeping next to my boat under a black ebony tree.[40] Everything except my scotch cloak is at the wagon. It is a great wonder that one can sleep thus on the bare earth and still be free of snakes and scorpions.

29th November 1779.
Westerly wind. Overcast, thundery sky.

Got news that the wagon had broken down in the stones the other side of Cabas.[41] Sent help forthwith. A fresh thunderstorm from the west in the afternoon, with fresh wind and rain which cooled the air and which the parched countryside badly needed.

*I*t was only on 2 December 1779 that the wagon arrived. After soaking the wheels in water to counter the shrinking effect of the great dryness, the party was able to set off once more on the afternoon of 4 December. The course taken was generally westward, travelling downstream along the southern side of the river, towards 'Great Namaqualand'.

But why westward at this time and from this place?

In his journal Gordon is always reticent about his future movements and only occasionally is there some hint as to where he is going and for what reason. This is understandable enough: journals are primarily for recording happenings, not intentions. Nevertheless it would have been of great assistance had Gordon given some rough outline of his plans.

This move westward is not explained at all. Instead of returning to Ellenboogfontein by the way he came and then travelling back to Cape Town, Gordon struck out west and then north into Great Namaqualand to what we know as southern Namibia, crossing the river approximately ten kilometres east of Ramansdrif. Once more we must guess why he did this. One reason was possibly to improve the mapping of the area which had been started under Hop's expedition, mentioned at the beginning of this journey. We can infer this by one or two remarks he makes as to correcting the earlier observations. Nevertheless, given his interest in the 'Briqua' (or Tswana) it seems odd that he should choose to make his expedition to the north at this point and not where he had mapped the 'Weg na de Moetjoaanaas' near present-day Upington. That was country totally unknown to any white man at the time.

Another even more compelling reason has recently been advanced.[42] Up until Sandfontein Gordon had been retracing his tracks and was presumably making for Ellenboogfontein, as noted. However, his grievous loss of the giraffe skeleton, recorded on 20 November, just a week before he reached Sandfontein, should not be overlooked. And even though he speaks only of his 'great displeasure' at the loss, his deep disappointment cannot be ignored. This was a disaster of significant proportions, and what man with Gordon's devotion to the pursuit of knowledge could simply resign himself to the loss without a second thought? (Such was its importance that when Gordon eventually got a giraffe skeleton to Europe it was hailed as both a personal triumph for him and a great gain for the science of natural history.)

It is highly probable, therefore, that Gordon decided either before or during his stay at Sandfontein to make his excursion to 'Groote Namaqualand' — to go first west and then north across the Orange to Warmbad in Namibia. It was in this vicinity, it will be recalled, that a female and a bull giraffe had been killed in 1762 by members of Hop's expedition. Furthermore, it was north of the Orange, in the same region that Sebastiaan van Reenen, Paterson's companion, had killed a giraffe in September 1778, just nine months before.

It also makes sense of a seemingly casual remark made by Gordon on 4 December that 'Afrikaander, our best shot … wished to accompany me into Namaqualand'. The fact that he did not say '*Groote* Namaqualand' makes it impossible to assert categorically that it was his intention to go north of the Orange, but the possibility that this is what he meant is strong. After all, Gordon did not proceed to Kleine Namaqualand anyway. And the comment about Afrikaander being 'our best shot' is surely relevant. In fact, as we shall see, it was this same Afrikaander who eventually shot the giraffe. We must also remember that Gordon no longer had the encumbrance of Schoemaker, nor of Pienaar's large party. He could now act without having to concern himself with their needs.

Considering what the giraffe represented to Gordon, there can be little doubt that bagging this trophy was the overriding motive for making this detour.

*O*n 6 December they reached a spot near the confluence of the Orange and the Hom or Houms River, which Gordon calls the Leeuwen River. (Paterson's name for the same dry river bed was the Lions River.)

The next day as they prepared to cross the river with pack-oxen, the wagons being sent on to the 'drift' at Goodhouse, Cabas once more makes his appearance:

In the morning I was astonished to see Cabas and two Bushmen approaching. It seemed that one was his father and the other was one of the Bushmen who took me through the Caboes mountains and to whom I had said that I was sorry Cabas had run away.[43] The father told me that he was bringing Cabas back to me and that he had scolded him for running away from me especially since he had heard that Cabas had such good treatment and that I had wanted so much to take him to my country. Cabas was quiet and fearful. I asked the bushman, who was a small, alert fellow, if Cabas was his son. He said 'I made him'. I asked him if he was giving Cabas to me then. He said: 'yes'. I told him that I would take Cabas to the Cape and would let him see everything. If then he wanted to return to his country, I would have him brought back. He asked for some beads and tobacco and said that he had not much to eat at the kraal and that it was therefore better for Cabas to be with me than with him. Cabas said nothing and thus father and son parted. It was at least five days' walk from his kraal. The oxen ran away so we had to remain at this place today. A man called Schoenmaker arrived. He is presently ten miles to the west on this river and is to take my wagon with him, since I shall have to go that way again.

The return of Cabas is strangely moving for a variety of reasons. In the first place there is the conflict in Gordon's own mind of whether to take him back or not. Despite, or indeed because of, his affection for the boy — reflected in several earlier remarks — Gordon does not want him to come against his will. (He writes this down more than once.) Now he states that Cabas is 'quiet and fearful'. But the father has walked for five days to return him and this time explicitly 'gives' him to Gordon, acknowledging with a degree of pride: 'I made him'. The journal here finely conveys the differing emotional states and, by implication, the tension between the three people involved: Cabas, the father and Gordon. At the conclusion of the episode, the laconic eloquence of the passage is as telling as it is understated: 'Cabas said nothing and thus father and son parted.'

It should be noted that the 'man called Schoenmaker' who arrived at this juncture had no connection with the artist but was in fact a deserter from the Company. He was later to act as a guide to Le Vaillant who described him as 'a little man in a red cap and the dress of a Dutch sailor'. When Le Vaillant, bearing a letter from Gordon, met him in these parts, the Frenchman stated: 'At the name of Gordon, joy sparkled in his . . . countenance: he beheld me as a friend . . . .' Yet there is nothing in Gordon's narrative to testify to this man's admiration for him, nor indeed is there any description whatsoever of his appearance or character. Nothing could better demonstrate the difference in approach of these two travellers than their treatment of this figure. Le Vaillant is effusive and emotional; Gordon is terse and unrevealing.[44]

With the wagon despatched along the southern bank to Goodhouse (or Goedhous as he called it on his map), Gordon's small party crossed to the northern side of the Orange River on 8 December 1779:

The same weather but less wind and somewhat cloudy in the morning. Very hot. Although it is cloudy from time to time it is never so much so that the sun does not shine unless it rains. Thus in this country the sun shines almost every day. Departed for the river with the two half-breed Hottentots Claas and Piet, and the Hottentot Afrikaander, who had been upriver with me. Set off down the river. Took five pack-oxen in the event I could obtain a giraffe skin and skeleton. After tramping along the river for two hours we crossed same by way of a stony ridge where there were two streams. We did not have to off-load the pack-oxen. The water came up to my hips and the current was so strong in the second stream that I had great difficulty. This was caused by the abundance of stones and having Cabas by the one hand. I had to bear him up because the water was deeper than he was tall. In the other hand I had my paper so that I almost fell upside down, not imagining beforehand that this drift would be so dangerous. On the other side we found four Great Namaquas

58. Pterocles namaqua – *Gordon's 'Namaqua partridge'.*

strongly flowing river. In one hand he is bearing up a tiny black boy above the waters and in the other he is holding a quarto-sized notebook. Besides being a singular sight, it also says much about Gordon – his consideration for a weaker companion and his desire to keep his means of recording intact. Both concerns are strong, they go together in him.

Once across the Orange the party started to make its way up the dry river-bed of the Houms or Leeuwen River. As already mentioned, it was most likely that Gordon wished to verify the mapping that was undertaken on Hop's journey. There are frequent allusions to this, and for the most part Gordon was following the same route, though he was not to penetrate as far north as the earlier travellers. The reference, however, to the five pack-oxen, 'in the event I could obtain a giraffe skin and skeleton' is surely further confirmation of the main motivation for this detour.

It was on 10 December 1779, the third day after crossing the river, that Afrikaander shot a great bull giraffe.

Making our way half an hour north beside a mountain we once more found a small kraal of five Caminoekwa huts and after going up the river for two hours we reached Vogels or Loeri Fonteyn, the water brack and bad. Saw fresh lion and giraffe tracks. The same stony terrain everywhere. Stopped for our midday meal and saw two giraffes. Started hunting the giraffes but not having good horses we put our trust in stalking them. (N.B. Sometimes this animal sticks its head into a tree and in this manner, especially in the heat, it sleeps standing. It sometimes eats from the ground and does this without having to bend its knees.)

We continued our way northwards to the Bad but while we were crossing a stony ridge Afrikaander came to tell me that he had shot and broken the fore-leg of a large giraffe bull, a quarter of an hour from there. He had stalked it in the thickets of the river. Went there immediately and sent for the oxen, which had stayed behind, to come there. Found the animal still alive, and lying still though it had been struggling hard as I saw from the loose stones. There was a black scorpion moving across its body. (N.B. They are a little larger than and different from the yellow ones and are considered more poisonous.) The giraffe lay there and behaved as though dead. We went close to it and it seemed to be a mild animal. We cut its throat whereupon a great deal of blood came, *ceteris paribus*, from this great animal. Then it began to kick so violently that I believe that there can be few animals with more power in their legs. Ascertained that it was a bull and that it was two inches larger than the previous one; thus it was 15 feet, four inches and the horns were 8 inches. It was one of the largest of these animals and fully grown. From muzzle to tail it was 13 feet, one inch long, following the curve. Its proportions differed slightly (almost not at all) from the previous one. Although there was no water here, we stayed and slept in the stones and were badly inconvenienced by the ticks from the giraffe. It had already got dark by then and we removed its bowels to prevent it from rotting.

The giraffe was killed in the vicinity of Warmbad, which Gordon called by the same name. He visited these min-

59. Asclepias fruticosa.

of the Caminoekwas tribe.[45] Because of the drought there are a few small kraals of them living here beside the river. I hired these to accompany us and to drive the oxen. N.B. This band is the same that was called Comeinacqua in Hop's journey, after a mountain called Comma, but they know of no Comma mountain and called themselves Caminoekwas saying that they did not know why their forefathers had called themselves this. They live about the same distance down the Leeuwen River as from the Bad[46] and were now divided into ten small kraals. They did have a Kauwaup but counted him for nothing. His name is Owbeep and he lives close to Warm Bad which they call Eibees, the Leeuwen River is called the same too.

It is well worth pausing a while to recreate episodes like this in the mind's eye. It is a wonderful, truly strange scene: in this wild corner of Africa in the year 1779 a tall, long-haired, bearded white man is struggling to ford a

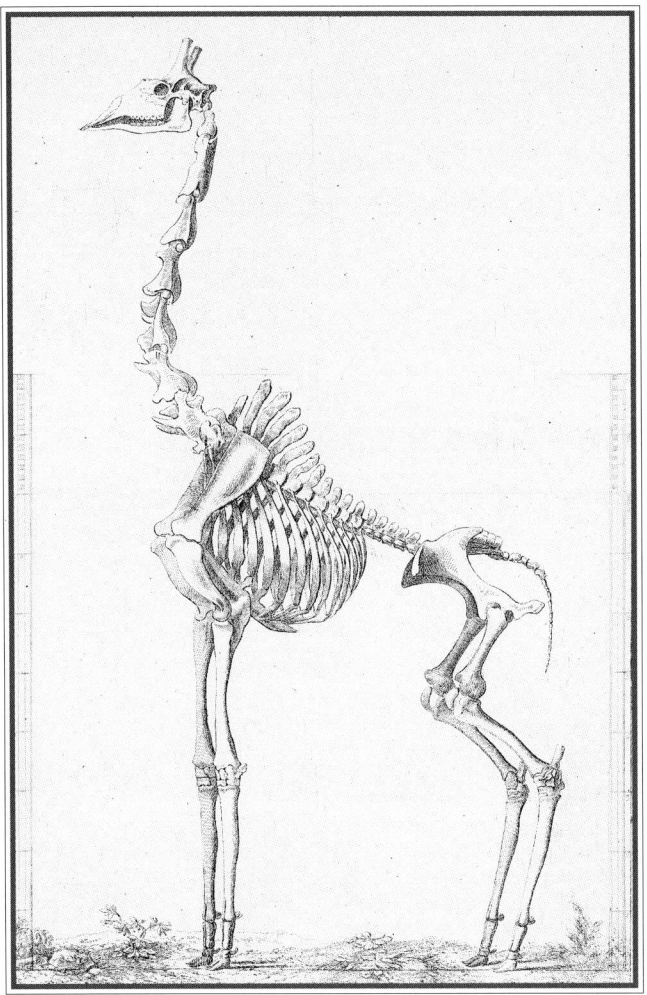

60. *A second drawing of the giraffe skeleton sent to Willem V.*

eral springs on the next day and even bathed in them, which he found 'very agreeable'. But this was to be the limit of his journey north. On 13 December he decided that it was time to return to the Cape, the 'season being so advanced'. In other words, he was worried that he would be caught by the summer rains of the interior and perhaps prevented from recrossing the Orange.

*H*is course back to the river took him in a more westerly direction, and on 15 December he struck and crossed 'a fine sandy drift, without unloading'. It was hip deep and with little current. This was the Compagnies Drift, Garragas or Bustard in 'Hottentot'.[47] Here the sand on the banks was 'so hot it burned through shoes'. He continues:

Departed S. in the evening making a turn around the mountains and, after walking hard for four hours, again reached the river, having one and a half miles west still to go. Found the wagons here and everything in order. My Hottentots had pitched my tent. Attended to my giraffe skin and its bones. Found Schoenmaker here who had come from his lower farm. This drift is called Gotoows or Sheep-path and the one below is called Homnaries.[48] These river farms had abundant grass but have now been grazed down and because little rain has fallen they are now very sandy and with scant grass. The river runs too deep to water the land thus it cannot be led out for gardens or planting wheat. This is a good drift which was only two hours to our right, had we but known.

The party stayed at this camp for the next three days – mainly, it seems, for Gordon to work at preserving the giraffe skin and to effect repairs to the wagon. He writes of the stifling heat, as on 17 December:

The same weather. Later in the evening a brisk west wind. Remained drying the skin out of the sun. Had great difficulty keeping the head from going bad. The savage heat of the sand between the mountains makes me long now for the sun to go down; the flies are a great nuisance too so that one cannot read or write.

They set off again on the evening of 19 December, travelling at night because of the great heat. The next day they reached Kleine Brak Fonteyn which has been identified as Sabies, lying at 29°17′.20″.[49] The countryside began to change here and by 21 December they struck the first farms, which prompted Gordon to write:

It was pleasant to see how green it was here and to see the stacks of freshly reaped wheat, as well as to drink good, fresh water.
  Last night there was heavy thunder and rain at the river and ahead of us but we got nothing. This was good for the giraffe skin which was packed into my boat and had been well cared for.

It was on 22 December that Cabas made his last attempt to run away:

My young boy, Cabas, seeing that we were leaving the river and his country did everything he could to run away (although he would now have to go through an unknown and almost waterless country. Nevertheless they live off lizards, mice and other food from the countryside). But I kept a close watch on him because I wanted to let him first see the Cape. While we were at this place however, he must have recognized the mountains of the Great River; thus while I was taking bearings, seeing no other chance, he ran off down the stones with all his might and would have been lost to us but that the half-breed Klaas who was with me ran after him and got in his way. Like a klipspringer he ran up the opposite hill in order to escape across it and crept into a dassie hole. However, another Hottentot, one who lived here, coming in answer to our cries, pulled him out of it. Whereupon Klaas whipped him a few times with a leather strap and as soon as he was out of his hands, he ran to me and climbed up my body, hand and foot. Whereupon I saved him from the beating and made friends with him again and said that he must see the Cape and that I would then send him back to his country.

It is not difficult to imagine the turmoil and confusion in the boy's mind as he realized he was leaving 'the river and his country'. Similarly, one can appreciate his panic as he saw the 'mountains of the Great River' disappearing behind him. Once more, however, Gordon's patience and the quality of his affection are finely demonstrated in this passage. There is surely both humour and pathos when he describes how Cabas 'climbed up my body, hand and foot' in flight from Klaas's strap. Inevitably the question arises: did Cabas see his homeland again? Certainly the bond between these two disparate personalities was maintained for at least another six years. This is learned from the very first entry in Gordon's journal of the fifth journey (1785-6) in which both Cabas and Koerikei are listed as being in the party. Unfortunately there is no further mention of the boy in Gordon's other papers, so it seems we shall never know whether he did eventually return to his mountains and his river.

Resting for a day at Jan van der Hever's farm, Silver Fontein, which has been identified as being '10 kilometres east of the Droedap'[50] — that is, just north of Kamieskroon — Gordon rode south once more on 24 December, reaching Ellenboogfontein that same day. Something comforting is surely conveyed by the entry on Christmas Day 1779 in which he records that they 'were bringing the harvest in'. Crude though the farm undoubtedly was, if we are to judge by the drawings of it, it must have provided a welcome contrast to the desert and wild places which Gordon had now left behind him.

Little time, however, was spent resting. On 27 December the wagons were sent on to 'Klip Valey' — a farm near present-day Garies that was well known to many of the eighteenth-century travellers. Meanwhile Gordon spent the next few days riding round this district, mapping and generally observing various phenomena, such as geological formations, 100-year-old inhabitants, and the characteristics of puff-adders.

By 30 December he was close to the mouth of the Groene River, on 'Van der Westhuijsen's lower farm'. This is almost certainly Cornelis van der Westhuijsen whose wife was Claudina, the 'heroine' whom Gordon had encountered in July of this same year. Now this memorable year was coming to an end, yet there is no account of any celebrations, nor even any mention of the fact that a new year was about to start. The only factor that is somewhat unusual is that the entry for 31 December is hardly more than a line long — indicating, perhaps, that at least he was taking some rest.

On the first day of January 1780 Gordon was at his observations once more, taking bearings and noting the lie of the coast and the countryside. He even records a small diversion involving Cabas: 'It was a delight to see the astonishment of the little Bushman Cabas when he saw the sea. He was told this was where we got our wine. He laid himself down on a stone to drink but he soon stopped.'

Gordon's homeward journey need not detain us much longer. On 2 January, using a well-travelled road, he continued south, reaching the Heerenlogement on 10 January where he took further bearings for his map. The last entry in the journal is dated 12 January 1780 and was penned at 'Josias Engelbrecht in the Berg Valey', a farm he had first passed early in July 1779 on his way north.

Evidently there was nothing new or of note to observe on the remainder of his journey back to Cape Town, and there is therefore no record of the route he took. However, we can safely assume that Gordon reached Cape Town before 23 January 1780, as he wrote a letter to Hendrik Fagel on that day.[51]

As a conclusion to this journey it is interesting to read how Gordon's contemporaries viewed him at this time. Some idea of Gordon's current reputation can be gathered from a letter to the famous naturalist, Sir Joseph Banks, in London. It was written from Cape Town in October 1779 by a certain James Lind, MD. As will be noted, Gordon was still on this journey when it was penned.

Captain Gordon, who was formerly in the Scotch Dutch, is the man that has gone furthest into the interior parts of this country — Paterson and he set out together; but he [Gordon] propose [sic] this time to go as far as he can: he has two faithful Hottentots who go thro' everything with him: he has killed several Lyons and Tigers with his own hands; and in this expedition, in Lat. 30, he shote [sic] a camelo paradalis twenty two feet high: he has been obliged to return back so far, in this trip, having got into a part of the country where he could find no water.[52]

61. *Susanna Nicolet, married on 23 April 1780 to Captain Robert Jacob Gordon, commander of the garrison at the Cape.*

CHAPTER EIGHT

COMMAND OF THE GARRISON

(1780-1785)

Appointment as commander of the garrison, with later promotion to the rank of colonel; membership of the Councils of Policy and Justice; marriage to Susannah Nicolet; at loggerheads with Governor Van Plettenberg; threat of invasion; visitors to the Cape; Van Plettenberg replaced

Gordon's achievements during the scant three years since his second arrival in southern Africa had been remarkable. It is true that various Europeans who had undertaken hunting and other expeditions had been to the same remote places that Gordon had reached, but only a few had attempted to record their journeys and none could equal the total distance travelled, nor the wealth of information that he gathered. Certainly some contemporaries, such as Captain James King, an English naval officer who was visiting the Cape at this time, saw Gordon's achievements in terms verging on the hyperbolic:

Captain Gordon ... was absent on a journey into the interior of Africa, but returned before our departure. He had, on this occasion, penetrated farther up the country than any other traveller had done before him, and made great additions to the valuable collection of natural curiosities with which he has enriched the Museum of the Prince of Orange. Indeed, a long residence at the Cape, and the powerful assistance he has derived from his rank and situation there, joined to an active and indefatigable spirit, and an eager thirst after knowledge have enabled him to acquire a more intimate and perfect knowledge of this part of Africa than could have fallen to the lot of any other person ....

With unconscious but poignant irony Captain King concludes his accolade by adding: '... it is with great pleasure I can congratulate the Public on the information I have received of his intentions to give the world, from his own hand, a history of his travels'.[1]

The British admiral, Sir Thomas Pasley, who was at the Cape in May 1780, was also full of praise for Gordon. He found him

a most ingenious, intelligent, sensible and agreeable acquaintance.... He speaks Dutch, English, French, Hottentots, Caffree and Erse; has collected innumerable curiosities as a Virtuoso; has travelled over a great part of this vast Tract of Africa; met with a race of men very little superior to Baboons, and one

nation that never before saw a European in the heart of Africa.[2]

Another visitor at this time – the French naturalist, Pierre Sonnerat – was equally impressed.

One of the most interesting people to know is Mr Gordon ... who has just completed three journeys into these lands. To him one owes not only some knowledge of the country and the people who live in it, but also some knowledge of a quantity of plants and of several unknown animals which he has studied and described being finely observed by him. Apart from the Hottentots he has discovered a new kind of people, who greatly resemble the Caffers, and who live in small villages ....

Sonnerat also concludes his remarks by implying that Gordon would be publishing his journals, providing fuller details of these matters.[3]

Gordon, in 1780, was now in his 37th year. As we have seen, his reputation as a traveller and a savant, an agreeable 'virtuoso' and a fine naturalist was now established and recognized. But with all this behind him, the year 1780 was notable in Gordon's life for two further reasons: his assumption of the Cape garrison command and his marriage to Susanna Nicolet.

On 22 February 1780 Lieutenant Colonel Prehn, the officer commanding the garrison at the Cape, retired from active service, and Gordon – as promised before he left Holland – was appointed to the post in his place. Assuming command of the garrison entailed several new duties for Gordon, among them: responsibility for the armoury and the Company's military equipment at the Cape, and the position of president of the Burgher Council of War.[4]

Writing to the Here XVII at this time, the Council of Policy strongly recommended that Gordon's appointment should be confirmed. Interestingly, they emphasized that 'the post could be entrusted to him with full confidence, the more so since he has travelled in the interior as far as has never been done by anyone before, and thus thereby obtained a thorough experience'. In addition

– and at Gordon's request – they also recommended that he should be given the same rank as Prehn. However, when Gordon eventually received confirmation of his promotion – two years later – it was not to the rank of lieutenant colonel but to the full rank of colonel. His new post also gave him automatic membership of the Council of Policy and Council of Justice.[5]

It will be recollected that during the course of his fourth journey, Gordon named a kloof near the Orange River Susannadal, and that two days later, on 4 October 1779, a certain Susanna Nicolet from Switzerland was given permission to travel to the Cape from Amsterdam on one of the Company's ships, together with a maidservant. It is therefore beyond all reasonable doubt that the kloof was named for Gordon's bride-to-be and that he knew she would be coming to the Cape.

There is some speculation, however, as to when and where Gordon met his future wife. It has been suggested that they met in Holland some time after Gordon's first visit to the Cape (1773-4). There is another suggestion too – plainly wrong – that she came out with the Swiss regiment, Meuron, in January 1783. Unfortunately there are no firm facts available. However, in a letter written in 1789 – most probably to the noted Swiss geologist and scientist H.B. de Saussure[6] – Gordon refers to the two men having been on a strenuous walk together sometime in the past. Since De Saussure never visited the Cape we can be certain that the walk took place in Switzerland – probably in the vicinity of Lake Geneva, where he lived. What we do know for certain about Susanna Nicolet is that she came from Lignerolle in the Canton of Vaud, whose capital is Lausanne, situated, of course, on the banks of Lake Geneva. Lausanne, therefore, would seem to be the likeliest place for Gordon to have met his future wife. There is absolutely no evidence as to when this meeting could have taken place, but the most likely supposition is that it was after his first visit to the Cape – in other words, some time between 1774 and 1777.

Susanna Nicolet arrived on the ship *de Parel* on 14 April 1780[7] and was married to Robert Jacob Gordon nine days later, on 23 April.[8] He was thirty-seven years old and his

62. *A groundplan of the Castle as it was in the late eighteenth century.*

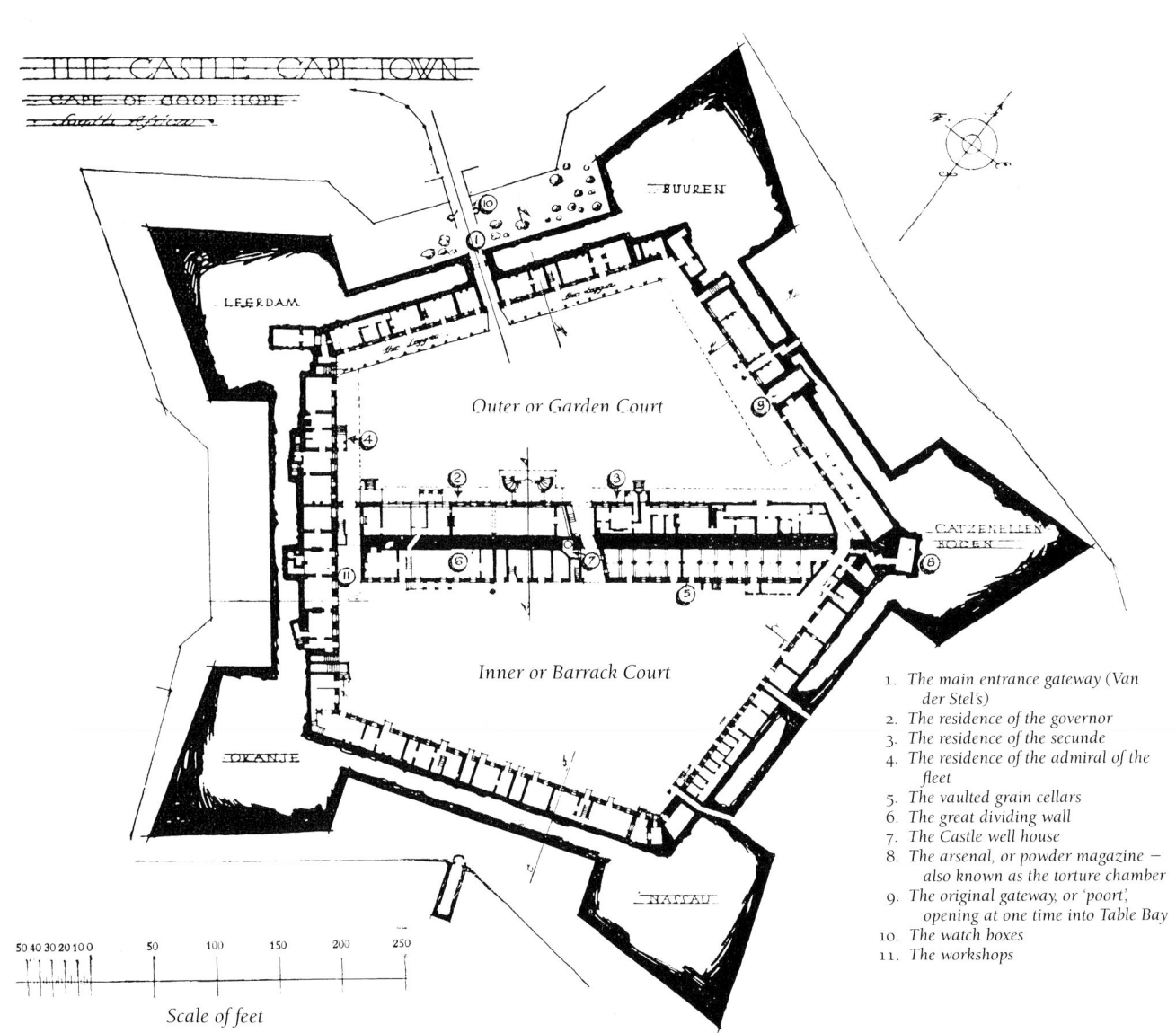

1. The main entrance gateway (Van der Stel's)
2. The residence of the governor
3. The residence of the secunde
4. The residence of the admiral of the fleet
5. The vaulted grain cellars
6. The great dividing wall
7. The Castle well house
8. The arsenal, or powder magazine – also known as the torture chamber
9. The original gateway, or 'poort', opening at one time into Table Bay
10. The watch boxes
11. The workshops

bride was thirty-one. Two portraits were painted of them at this time and they can now be seen in the William Fehr Collection at the Castle in Cape Town. Gordon is wearing the uniform of the commander of the garrison – a vigorous and confident air about him. Mrs Gordon, a slight smile on her face, is shown seated, plucking some musical instrument – probably a harp. She was a very beautiful woman.

*I*n December of the same year Great Britain declared war on the United Provinces (or Dutch Republic) which was now in alliance with France, though news of this only reached the Cape on 31 March the following year. Great activity ensued as the Colony endeavoured to mobilize men against a threatened British invasion. But in July 1781 French troops were landed and consequently no invasion took place, though a British fleet, under the command of Commodore Johnstone, did manage to capture four merchantmen lying at Saldanha Bay and another – the *Held Woltemade* – on the open sea.

At this stage we may perhaps ask of what Gordon's command consisted.[9] Surprisingly, such had been the organization of the militia at the Cape that Gordon himself was most unclear as to whom he commanded and where they were. On paper there were 530 troops in the garrison force. But, as was then the custom in peacetime, many of the soldiers were in the employ of local farmers, and it was by no means certain that they could be re-mustered in time of war. Apart from this, the organization of the garrison force was very poor. Even the usual hierarchy of military rank was uncertain. It was so uncertain that when Gordon became commander he was unable to determine exactly what his post authorized him to do or not do. He was appointed head of the garrison with the rank of a mere captain, but the head of the artillery force, P.H. Gilquin, was a major.

This perplexing contradiction of rank and authority was compounded when a regiment of mercenaries, recruited by the Company, arrived at the Cape in May 1782. This brought matters to a head as far as Gordon was concerned. Was this regiment – the Luxemburg – which formed a part of the garrison, under his command or not, he could well ask.

It is not difficult to imagine Gordon's feelings. These doubts were not just unsatisfactory, they were humiliating as well. On 25 May 1782 he made a determined move to right matters and end the equivocation and uncertainty. At his request an extraordinary meeting of the Council of Policy was held. Here Gordon demanded that he be given a clear answer as to whether the Luxemburg Regiment fell under him or not. He also brought up the position of the artillery command. Since being appointed as commander he had had no lists or reports on the state of the artillery. What was his position? Did he command it or not?

But Governor Van Plettenberg and his Council of Policy were not going to be compelled to make a clear reply. On 28 May a meeting decided that the regiment fell under the direct control of the governor. To this Gordon had to acquiesce. He was able, however, to have his salary raised to that of the colonel of the Luxemburg Regiment – a sum of 200 guilders, as opposed to his former pay of 150 guilders – justifying the raise by claiming that his status with his soldiers would suffer if he received less.

The matter of his salary was some sort of triumph but he was given little satisfaction in the business of the artillery. Van Plettenberg merely ruled that the head of the garrison artillery was responsible to Gordon 'in all matters relating to military service'. Such ambiguity did not satisfy Gordon. He therefore requested permission to write personally to the Company's directors – the Here XVII – regarding his authority over the artillery. His request was granted and the assurance given that it would be sent with the first homeward-bound ship.

Gordon's battles with the governor and his council over the issue of authority and command continued into the year of 1783. Frustration and scarcely suppressed anger underlie all Gordon's communications with them. And who could blame him? In January 1783 the Luxemburg had been replaced by a Swiss regiment, known as the Meuron. It had been landed, Gordon declared, without his knowledge and without him hearing anything further about these troops. Were they under his command or not? The reply was predictable: the regiment fell under the direct control of the governor.

Bearing in mind that all this uncertainty was taking place in a time of war, and that the Cape was under a real threat of invasion, one cannot help but sympathize with Gordon, as well as speculate as to how an invasion would have been met under these circumstances. But even more confusion was added to the picture when a French regiment – the Waldener – arrived at the Cape for a few months, in transit to Batavia. This time it was placed under Gordon's command.

With understandable and manifest impatience he again addressed the Council of Policy on 18 February 1783. He was writing, he said, simply to know with what position he had been entrusted and charged in this government? He then went on to assert that he had not been given the status of his predecessors; that in fact the status of commander of the garrison had been altered in his case, and for no apparent reason, for no such order had been received from Europe. In case of military operations, was he in charge of the combined forces of the Company or was he not? It was the Meuron Regiment in particular that he had in mind here, he said. Finally, he requested that his position regarding further regiments sent to the Cape should be clarified and settled.

Once more Van Plettenberg's reply was vague and equivocating. As he understood the military structure at the Cape, he, as governor, was responsible for the overall defence and command of the Colony. In his opinion Gordon was only in charge of the permanent Cape troops. Likewise, the commanders of the foreign regiments were in charge of their individual units. In the event of military action he, Van Plettenberg, would co-ordinate the operations of all these units.

As far as other regiments in the Company's service were

concerned, he continued, it all depended on the terms of their recruitment as to whether Gordon would command them or not. And there was no change in the respective positions of Gordon and Gilquin over the artillery and sappers. Gordon remained in charge on all matters 'relating to military service', but for the rest the command remained with Gilquin. In conclusion, Van Plettenberg again referred the whole matter of Gordon's status to the Here XVII.

When the war against England came to an end in September 1783, Gordon was still uncertain of his duties. As Barnard notes in his study of this period of Gordon's life, the official documents at the Cape Archives contain no mention of Gordon's military role, though much is said of the French troops and their activities in improving the defence of the Cape. In fact, Gordon's name is conspicuous by its absence.

There is no doubt that all this petty quibbling as well as the indecision and vagueness of the governor, was having its effect on Gordon – a humiliating effect. On 30 June 1784 he took what must have been a most unusual, if not daring, step: he wrote to his Prince, Willem V, in the language of the court (French):

Finally, Sir, I am unable to hide from you that all these troubles have made my service here disgusting to me, to the extent that if I am required to remain in my present position I have determined to quit the service, and, as I would not be able to live in Europe, having a wife and children, I would prefer to drive a plough in some remote district of Africa in order to maintain them, rather than see this disorder any longer, which I have neither the power nor the authority to remedy.[10]

On the following day, 1 July, he wrote to his highly respected friend, Hendrik Fagel, enclosing, it would seem, the letter to the Prince of Orange:

I have ... had the most unpleasant life here, which has been prolonged by the regiments which the Company has been forced to suddenly recruit in these unhappy times and from which one has nothing but unpleasantness. ... I [therefore] request your excellency to deliver the enclosed to His Highness. I have made him aware of my intention of quitting the service of the Company if nothing is done to remedy all these disorders.[11]

Whatever the effect of these letters, it was only in February 1786 – three years after Van Plettenberg's rulings and six years after Gordon had been appointed commander of the garrison – that a reply was received from the Company's directors. It vindicated Gordon completely, declaring that he was to have complete authority over *all* the Company's troops in the Cape. Even foreign regiments like the Luxemburg and Meuron were all to fall under his command 'without exception'. The same held good for the artillery. Daily reports were to be handed to him and he could carry out inspections at any time, with the permission of the governor. It was specially emphasized that removals of powder and ammunition from the magazine, intended for the batteries, were to be made known to Gordon.

In effect, Gordon was now chief of staff to the governor, commander of all the Company's troops at the Cape and, in time of war, the co-ordinator of all military operations.

It is evident that during the trouble-racked years of his garrison command Gordon had little time for his scientific pursuits, but his family life appears to have been happy. His first son, Robert, was born in September 1781, to be followed by another son, Pieter, in November 1783.[12]

Some idea of what life at the Cape was like at this time can be gathered from the account of the French traveller, François le Vaillant. He arrived in 1782, and after making two journeys into the interior, departed towards the end of 1784. He also grew to know and admire both Gordon and his wife. A brief examination of some of his observations is illuminating, despite the extravagance of his style and the questionable veracity of some of his claims.[13]

He mentions Gordon early in his narrative, thanking him before he sets out on his first journey for 'the services he had in his power to render me and of which he was not sparing.... I am particularly indebted to him for a number of valuable details ... for the instructions and advice I received from him ....'[14] According to Le Vaillant, Gordon warned him of the dangers he would encounter on the Eastern frontier, 'especially at a time when the Caffres were at war with the Dutch planters.'[15]

On his safe return from his first journey, Le Vaillant renewed his friendship with the Gordons. In an amusing introduction to his *New Travels into the Interior*, he paints a lively picture of Cape Town in 1783 – a town which had fallen to the charms of the French officers in the Pondicherry, Meuron and Luxemburg regiments:

In the course of six months a great change had taken place. It was no longer the French modes that the women copied; it was a caricature of the French. Plumes, feathers, ribbons, and tawdry ornaments heaped together without taste on every head.... The French ... soon acquire a sort of empire over every thing that surrounds them ... [and] though an attack from the English fleet was every moment expected, the French officers had already introduced a taste for pleasure. Employed in the morning at their exercise, the French soldiers in the evening acted plays.[16]

Le Vaillant could see the incongruity of all this and noted: 'These ingenious diversions afforded me ... much amusement; but the idea that most pleased me was to see them transferred to Africa; that is to say in the neighbourhood of lions, panthers and hyenas.'

All, however, was not pleasure in the town. An attack from the British was expected and many good citizens set about helping bodily to construct the new fortifications. It was not long, however, before the realities of colonial life asserted themselves – as Le Vaillant noted:

Under pretence of sparing their strength, and that they might not weary themselves to no purpose, they soon caused their slaves to follow them with the tools and implements. In a little

63. *Doughty Le Vaillant, on a remarkable craft, undergoes a 'dangerous crossing of the Olifants River'.*

time they contented themselves with sending their slaves only; and at last these substitutes themselves, in imitation of the masters, or perhaps by their secret orders gave over going also. Their enthusiasm, in short, from the first moment of its breaking out till the period when it was thus entirely cooled, had been the affair of something less then a fortnight.[17]

From Table Mountain to False Bay, from 'the Lion's Rump' to Hout Bay, the Peninsula 'was defended by new works of every kind'. One of these new forts was a 'subject of considerable pleasantry', the inhabitants believing that the contractors were working in their own interest and not for the good of the Colony. Le Vaillant adds – without perhaps being conscious of the irony – that Gordon called this fort 'in derision Fort Gusset'. As was noted earlier, it appears that Gordon, even though he was commander of the garrison, had nothing to do with this fortification activity, since the governor did not consider it to lie within his field of responsibility.

Le Vaillant, coming across the training exercises of 'Hottentot' levies on the parade ground, was considerably

64. *The corner of Strand and Burg streets, Cape Town, in 1790.*

amused at what were called their 'military evolutions'. 'I had never before laughed so heartily, and have never thought of them since without the same conclusive merriment.... [On] the arrival of the first bullet... the whole corps would have dispersed, like a flock of starlings, and never would it have been possible to rally them.'

Later Le Vaillant stayed with the Gordons, and despite a somewhat patronizing tone, he expresses his 'esteem... without bounds' for Gordon. He also comments on Gordon's work, stating that he should 'extend his reputation by publishing his discoveries. He owes to Europe an account of such complete researches, and which relate to so interesting a part of Africa. They are the property of the science that would then no longer be buried in oblivion.'[18]

The Gordons, husband and wife, helped Le Vaillant equip himself for his new expedition, lending him 'four excellent oxen'. Mrs Gordon 'reserved to herself the exclusive privilege of supplying me with sugar, and other necessary provisions for my table; while her husband, military even in his gifts, begged me to accept a new marquee, and the services of the armourer of his regiment to repair my fusees [guns]'. The 'Colonel' also gave Le Vaillant three grenadier caps, telling him that they 'were highly gratifying to the savages....'[19]

More important, however, than these material gifts was the information and advice that Gordon was able to give Le Vaillant. Generously, 'the Colonel ... sketched out, point by point, the course I ought to pursue. Having himself made the same expedition with Lieutenant Paterson, he knew the places where water was to be found, and he obligingly pointed them out.'[20]

Gordon also supplied the Frenchman with two letters, one to the Company deserter, Schoenmaker, and the other to Klaas Baster, 'a mulatto Hottentot'. These introductions proved to be of great use to Le Vaillant, saving both him and his party from death, as this rather sententious passage attests:

How ingenious are the devices of friendship! And can I ever sufficiently acknowledge my obligations to that of Colonel Gordon in this instance, to which I owe not only my own life, but the lives of all my people? It was in the midst of a dry and burning desert, when obliged to abandon my wagons and effects, after seeing all my oxen, one after another, perish with thirst, when reduced with my poor comrades, to the destitute situation of having no other drink than the milk of my goats, and when inevitable death seemed to await alike both them and me ... it was in this extremity I called to mind the planter and Hottentot to whom his provident kindness had recommended me. Guided by his instructions, I entered upon the pursuit of these men; I found them, and we were saved ....[21]

It is amusing, even instructive, to contrast the narrative styles of these two eighteenth-century travellers. Gordon, who is terse, factual, and careful to conceal his emotions. Le Vaillant, who is gushing, ornamental and manifestly keen to display his feelings on all occasions. Both, however, belonged to The Enlightenment and both were ardent naturalists. Beyond this it is interesting to see how Le Vaillant portrayed Gordon. He shows us a different Gordon, romanticized, dramatized. Le Vaillant was not the only traveller to see Gordon so, but he projected this image better and more coherently than most, and the image he projected had more effect than most, since his *Travels* and *New Travels* (published 1790-1795) sold widely, and continued to sell, well into the nineteenth century. Undoubtedly Le Vaillant's view of Africa had a strong influence on his contemporaries as well as on later generations. His first work, *Travels*, was translated from the original French into English, Dutch, German, Italian, Swedish and Russian.

What was Gordon's opinion of the Frenchman? Apart from what Le Vaillant himself has told us, there is nothing in Gordon's papers about him bar, of course, the furious outburst concerning the giraffe, mentioned earlier.

We do know, however, that when Le Vaillant returned to Europe in July 1784, he was entrusted with a letter to Professor Allamand from Gordon, as well as with the skins of several animals: a leopard, a jackal and a stone-marten. Entrusting these items to Le Vaillant would argue, at least, that the men were on cordial terms when they parted company.[22]

It was later alleged that Gordon did not like the French, but there is ample proof that he was on good terms with individual Frenchmen and he conducted much of his correspondence in the French language. What is certain is that he 'abhorred French principles', meaning the ideas that brought about the French Revolution. Quite naturally, however, given his early service in the Scots Brigade, he was particularly friendly towards the British visitors to the Cape. Two different encounters at this time demonstrate this compellingly.

A certain Colonel William Dalrymple came to the Cape in January of 1784 and again in June 1785, travelling on this second occasion from St Francis Bay, where his ship – an English East Indiaman – had put in for repairs and revictualling. This journey across country did not go unnoticed by the authorities, and it was alleged – correctly – that he had made copious notes on the Colony, showing its military weaknesses. It was later revealed that he had also outlined a strategy for the invasion of the Cape. Of his meeting with Gordon, he had this to say: 'The colonel commands all the troops and has an English heart tho' born in Holland and is strong in the Prince of Orange's service.'[23] Dalrymple's plans were undoubtedly used when the British did invade the Colony ten years later, and his estimate of Gordon's loyalty to his Prince was to prove only too accurate.

Another visitor to the Cape at this time (1785) was Lord Macartney (later to become governor of the Cape under the first British occupation). He recorded his encounter with Gordon in his diary: 'Lt Colonel Gordon, Commander of the Troops, a very well informed and ingenious man, married to a lady from the Pays de Vaux (Nicolet was her name). He has been 26 degrees of S. Latitude in the country – saw his map – It is very curious and his travels must be more so when published.'[24]

The word 'curious' had at that time the meaning of accurate or skilful and therefore Macartney was commending the map, which almost certainly is Map 3 in the Gordon Atlas, now held at the Rijks Museum. This was Gordon's 'great map' of Southern Africa, and in the opinion of Professor Forbes was 'as well or better' done than the one that Barrow was later to make for this same Macartney. Professor Forbes remarks that it 'represents the culmination of Dutch cartography at the Cape. . . . The map bears everywhere the stamp of authenticity combined with the greatest accuracy obtainable under the circumstances in which it was drawn.'[25] The map is today in two sections; joined together it measures 179,3 cm north to south and 196,2 cm east to west. In other words, it is the size of a small dining room table. As we know from the journals and from certain collections of map-readings in his papers, Gordon was a diligent cartographer and there are several more maps extant and signed by him. Two of these – of Saldanha Bay and False Bay – are also in the Gordon Atlas. Furthermore, Gordon had a great collection of maps when he died. In the boxes that held his papers there were ninety-five maps, according to Captain Philip Gidley King, who is quoted in an earlier section of this work.[26] Today there are only fifteen – all of southern Africa and mostly made by such contemporaries as J.C. Frederici and C.H. Leiste.

Before turning to an examination of Gordon's fifth and last recorded journey, it would be well to have a brief idea of what had been happening in the Colony in these last few years.[27]

Unrest among the burghers was mounting. Under Governor Van Plettenberg, corruption among the Company's servants increased manifestly. Complaints about this and various Company rules quickened the burghers into action. There were deputations to Holland and constant petitions. In one case, the Fiscal Boers was forced to leave the country since accusations against him of corruption and high-handed behaviour were proved justified. Van Plettenberg too was forced to resign and return to the Netherlands.

On 14 February 1785, the new governor, Jacob van de Graaf, took office, though he was to do little to improve matters. Nevertheless, certain changes were introduced by the Here XVII. Burghers were to be invited to join the High Court of Justice as well as a board which was to be established to determine the yearly prices of the Colony's produce. This same board would advise on the methods of taxation, the possibility of coastal trade and also have the charge of looking after the roads and works of the Colony. Finally, a new district was to be created on the frontier, with its own landdrost and clergyman. (It was officially established in July 1786 and was called Graaff-Reinet, after the names of the governor and his wife.)

65. *Gordon's 'Caapse Baviaan' is the chacma baboon, or* Papio ursina, *encountered frequently on his travels.*

CHAPTER NINE

THE FIFTH JOURNEY: FAMILIAR PLACES AND FORGOTTEN MONUMENTS
(NOVEMBER 1785 – APRIL 1786)

Motives for the fifth journey; Roodezand and the Piketberg; the west coast; across the Roggeveld and Karoo; the Eastern Cape; the Dias Padrão; the Southern Cape

n 17 November 1785 Gordon attended a meeting of the Council of Policy. Two days later, on the 19th, he set forth on his fifth journey – so far as we know, the last that he was to record.

As on all previous occasions, Gordon does not specifically reveal the purpose of this journey in his journal, although from the copious notes of compass bearings and frequent altitude records, it would seem that one of the motives for this expedition was to gain further material for his mapping activities. But that is all there is to go on in the journal itself.

There is, however, another source that can be drawn on for some background to this journey: in a draft letter to the French scientist and '*philosophe*' Jean-Sylvain Bailly (1736-1793),[1] written shortly after his return from these travels – probably in the early part of April 1786 – Gordon sets out his reasons clearly, though *why* he is writing the letter is not easy to ascertain. In it he states that he had had an 'astronomical quadrant' made for himself in England by 'Ramsden'. After waiting five years he had finally received this 'perfect instrument'. It apparently gave him observations accurate to one second, and this had determined his decision to make the journey. So one can accept that one of the main reasons for the fifth expedition was to get fuller and more accurate records for his maps.[2]

However, the letter also suggests that Gordon had other less mundane reasons for this journey. He mentions that by 'following the unequivocal directions of Perestrelo... I found the remains of the hermitage of which he speaks'. Then, on a following page, he refers to another place where, 'On a hill jutting out into the sea...[I saw] a ruined monument. From it I carried away three stones which are covered with inscriptions. On one side there are Roman letters, like those on our old tombs, and on the other side there are Arabic ones. These stones which I took with me on my wagon to the Cape have the appearance of being terribly old....'[3]

On reading the journal there is no mention of the first event, but we do find a reference to the latter event. On 13 February 1786 Gordon records that between the 'Bokna' and 'Bosjemans' river mouths he 'found an old, shattered monument'. He gathered certain pieces together, he says, and ordered the wagon to collect them. They were already loaded by 16 February and travelling back to the Cape. What he had found was the Dias Cross at Kwaaihoek. Since the most easterly point in this journey was the Bushmans River mouth, it seems highly probable that Gordon was making deliberately for the Dias Padrão or Cross. However, nowhere in the journal is this intent recorded.

But there is further evidence that Gordon planned this expedition carefully and that he had the Padrão in mind when he did so. The name of Perestrelo was mentioned earlier. Who was this man and why did Gordon follow his 'unequivocal directions'?

Manuel de Mesquita Perestrelo was a Portuguese mariner and map-maker whose 'Roteiro' (or 'Rutter' in the anglicized form) was published around 1576.[4] It was a volume of charts, views and descriptions of the south-east coast of Africa. Later, parts of it were bound into another similar volume by the French mariner d'Après de Mannevillette and called *Le Neptune Oriental*. This edition appeared in 1775 and, since both mariners are mentioned in the letters to Bailly, it is highly likely that Gordon had this volume with him when he was planning his fifth journey. This probability is more than strengthened by the fact that among the Gordon papers there are four sheets in Gordon's hand discussing both Perestrelo's and d'Après de Mannevillette's work.[5]

These pages are obviously rough notes which Gordon took while paging through the volume, paraphrasing it in order to compare the earlier mariner's account with the contemporary state of navigational knowledge. But more to the point here are the references to a 'Hermitage', which he decides must be at Mossel Bay, and to a 'Pillar' near the Bushmans River mouth which is, of course, the Padrão. In both cases, detailed directions are given as to how to find these places.

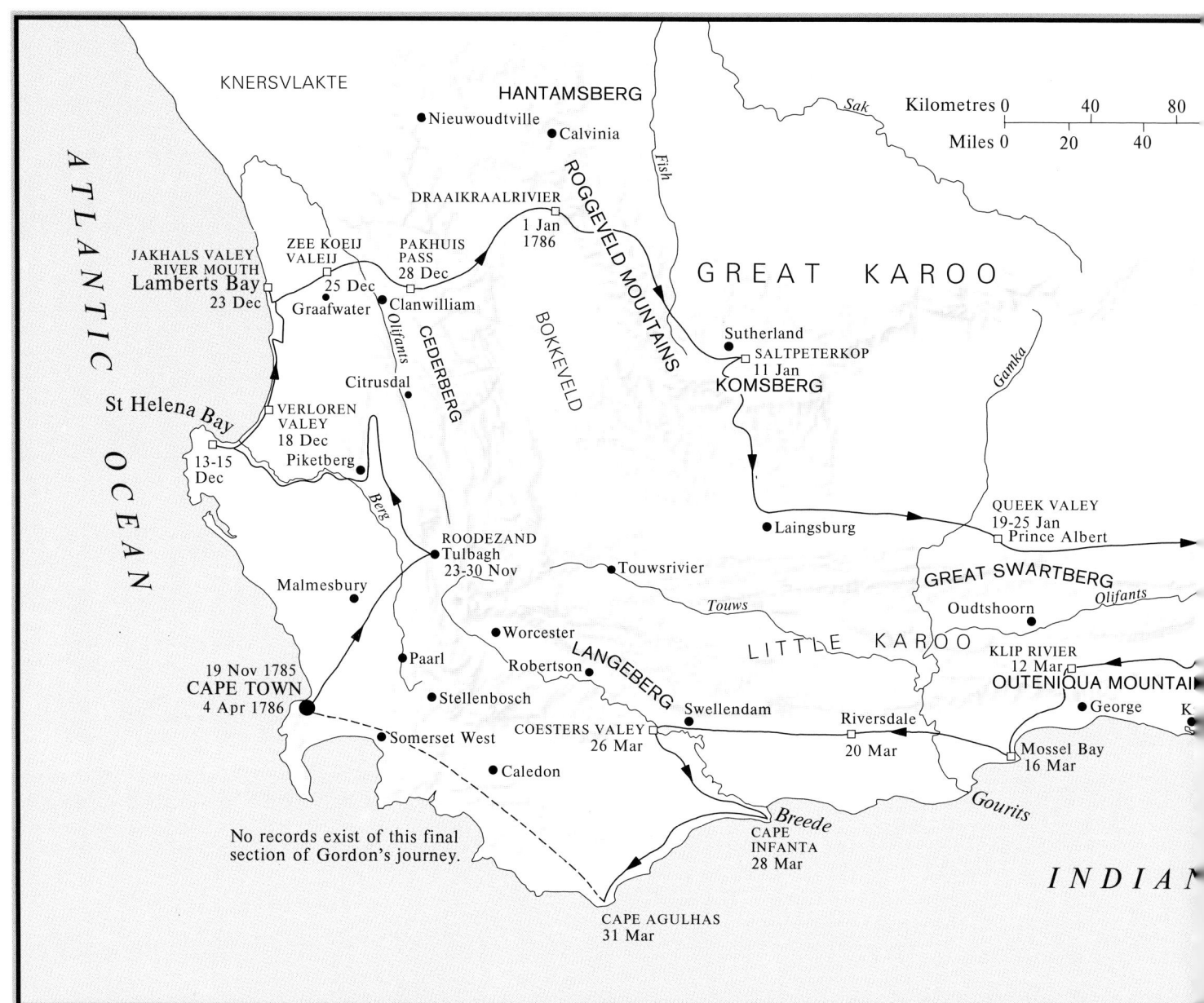

Map 8. *Gordon's fifth journey: up the west coast and then to the Bushman's River in the east.*

We can assume without much difficulty, therefore, that these notes were made preparatory to the fifth journey. They were an *aide-mémoire* to guide him not only in his map-making but in his search for the 'Hermitage' and the 'Pillar'.

No mention of finding the 'Hermitage' – a chapel built by the Portuguese 'at the time of the discovery of the sea route to India' – occurs in the journal, although we know from the letter to Bailly that Gordon did find it at Mossel Bay. It is not in the journal because, for some reason, Gordon stopped writing it before he reached Mossel Bay. However, from another page contained in his papers we learn that he was at this locality on 16 March 1786, four days after the journal ceased – a matter that is discussed later.[6] It appears that the chapel is now covered by the sheds of an agriculture co-operative.[7]

As we have noted above, Gordon seems to have found the Padrão or 'monument' without much trouble. On the face of it Perestrelo's instructions appear to be very detailed. Not only are there written directions but an illustration as well. But it is puzzling that later seekers after the Padrão, using many more sources than Perestrelo, had great difficulty in finding the site. The probable answer as to how Gordon found it so easily lies in a further passage from the letter to Bailly. After recording that he had loaded the stones on to his wagon he says: 'Some Hottentots have told me that the Caffers who lived in these parts a while ago, but who are now living more to the east, believed that this monument served to make women fertile when they rubbed themselves against it.' Ignoring the ironic, even mythopoeic, implications of this passage, we can clearly see that the site of the Padrão was well known to the local inhabitants and therefore they would have led Gordon straight to the 'monument'.

There is one more reason why Gordon could have

Familiar Places and Forgotten Monuments

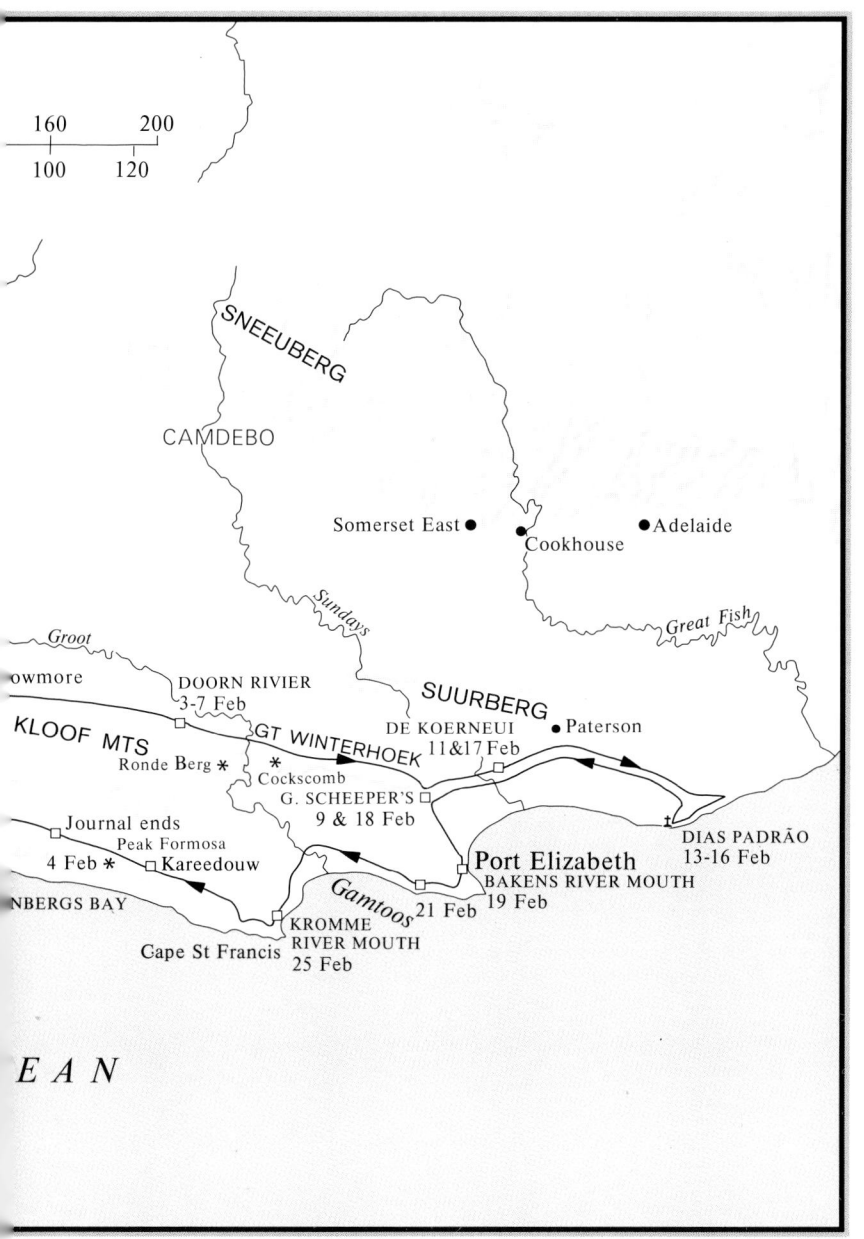

undertaken this expedition. We have seen earlier how a Colonel Dalrymple met Gordon at the Cape in 1784 and then later in June 1785. This latter meeting sprang from the fact that Dalrymple was on board the English Indiaman, *Pigot*, which had put into St Francis Bay on 7 May 1785. There were many sick people on board and they needed victuals and provisions. These were readily supplied by the farmers in the area. In the meantime, Dalrymple had decided to take this opportunity to travel to the Cape, and there is ample evidence that he used the journey to take notes on the opportunities for a military invasion of the country. Well aware of these observations and with some alarm, the Council of Policy decided to commandeer a hundred soldiers from the first ships arriving with troops on board and to send out detachments to Mossel Bay, Plettenberg Bay, St Francis Bay and Algoa Bay.

Ultimately this plan proved impracticable and it was decided to set up beacons with the arms of the Netherlands and the monogram of the Company at strategic points to demonstrate that the land was in the possession of the Dutch East India Company.[8] Whether this project was entrusted to Gordon is not recorded and he does not mention it in his journal. But he undoubtedly did visit all the important landing points across this section of the eastern coast, commenting on them in some detail.

To sum up then, it would seem that there were three main motives for this journey: to collect more data for his maps; to see if he could locate the 'hermitage' and the 'monument'; and finally, to observe how vulnerable the country would be to a sea-borne invasion along its southeastern coast.

Where Gordon went on his fifth journey is best summarized using modern names. In a more detailed look at the journal, the older names will be discussed as they occur.[9]

Gordon and his party set out on 19 November 1785. He arrived at Tulbagh after three days' travel, staying there until the 30th of that month. He then left for the Piketberg, exploring that region and subsequently going on to the mouth of the Berg River, St Helena Bay, where he stayed until 15 December. His next move was northward to Lambert's Bay and then south and east via Leipoldtville to the Pakhuis Pass beyond Clanwilliam.

On New Year's Day 1786 he trekked across to the Roggeveld, turning south past Sutherland down to Prince Albert in the Karoo, where he rested for six days until 24 January. Continuing east beside the Groot Swartberge and Baviaansgebergte, he came to the Groot Winterhoekberge. After a short stay there he resumed his course, moving in the direction of Uitenhage and then on to Coerney. The next stage of the journey brought him to the mouth of the Boknes River, which he reached on 13 February, staying there for three days.

His homeward journey now began. He first returned to Coerney and then struck south-west to the Bakens River mouth, Port Elizabeth. Continuing west along the coast he reached Cape St Francis on 25 February. Next, he took his party north-west along the Langkloof till they reached Avontuur, which bore the same name then. The following four days were spent by Gordon at and around Plettenberg Bay. Returning to Avontuur, he kept on his course through the Langkloof until, on 12 March 1786, he reached 'Klip River, the end of the Lange Kloof'.

Here Gordon's journal ends. However, it is not too difficult to follow roughly where he went — at least until 30 March of that year. This can be done by following the names placed on his map, going westward after Klip River. Until 'Hagel Kraal' (now Haelkraal) the actual route is also marked, so we can be virtually sure that he went down a pass, now no longer in use, through the Attakwasberge. This road was known as the Attaquas Kloof and had been followed by many travellers before Gordon. (It is six kilometres to the west of present-day Robinson Pass.)

At this point we must turn to some sheets of paper contained in the Gordon Collection at the Cape Archives and bound into the volume known as VC 596. Among other jottings there are several compass bearings noted, and among these is a list of places and dates which undoubt-

66. Roodezand, or Tulbagh as it is known today. Behind lies the Groot Winterhoek range, and the church, which is still standing, can be seen on the extreme right.

edly refer to this journey.[10] From these notes we can see that he had reached Mossel Bay by 16 March (presumably locating the site of the 'Hermitage' while there), that he had reached 'Cruis rivier' (near or at Riversdale) by the 20th, and that by the 26th he was at Coester's Valley – the farm of Jacob van Reenen, with whom he had stayed at the outset of his second journey. (This farm – called Lismore today – is approximately 22 kilometres west of Swellendam, at the foot of the Tradouw's Pass.)

The next date we have is 28 March when Gordon was at Cape Infanta, and the final date listed is 31 March, on which day (we deduce from his various notes and observations) he was at Cape Agulhas, the southernmost point of the continent. That he had arrived in Cape Town by 4 April is evident from the fact that he was present at a meeting of the Council of Policy on that day. We know too that on 9 April his third son, Alexander, was baptized.[11]

In composing the journal of these travels, Gordon used a double column format. Generally speaking the left-hand column consists of the narrative itself, the events of the day's travel, the distances covered (always in terms of time lapsed), and the names of the places which the party passed and also where it camped. The right-hand column was reserved, in the main, for compass bearings, temperature and meteorological observations. But the functions of these columns were by no means rigidly adhered to or used exclusively for these items. Notes on game seen, as well as geological comments, are to be found in either column from time to time.

This journal is also the shortest. It is Gordon at his most terse and reticent. Very few entries are longer than a page and there are no vivid passages, such as those describing his encounters with Xhosa tribesmen that so enlivened the pages of his second journey, when he passed through the same areas of the Eastern Cape. It therefore affords precious little additional insight into Gordon the man, although it is still of considerable interest to the historian.

But why did Gordon elect to change his style of record-keeping at this time? The reason was probably threefold. Firstly, Gordon had travelled much of this route before and had described many of the main features in detail. There was therefore no need to repeat previous observations and he was certainly not one to pad his account with verbal frills.

Secondly, since a major reason for this journey was cartographical, the journal became simply a record of each day – a diary, in other words, that was little more than an extension of rough notes. Indeed, even Gordon's compass bearings, the basis of his mapping activities, were kept on separate sheets of paper (now in volumes VC 596 and 597 in the Cape Archives).[12]

But perhaps, in the end, something deeper and more subtle was at play here. When Gordon set out on these travels he was still uncertain as to his military status and duties, confirmation and clarification of which were only received in February 1786, while he was still on this expedition. As we have come to know Gordon so far, it was not in his character to give vent to his frustrations in his journals, but the laconic military style, the 'scientific' objectivity, may well be seen as a kind of defence mechanism thrown up to mask his deeper emotions. Almost certainly, however, the process was unconscious.

To give some idea of the journal's new format the first few paragraphs are set out below as Gordon arranged them (see also page 145):

[COLUMN 1]
19th November 1785. Saturday.
I sent my wagon ahead to Schabord's in the Tiger Bergen yesterday evening so that it could travel in coolness and by moonlight. It had a team of 12 oxen and was accompanied by my orderly Jansen and the painter Schoemaker. In addition there was my Hottentot Hoedies as wagon rider* and Coerikei who led the oxen. Cabas and my Mozambique slave Castor went as helpers. And so at half past six this morning I set off alone on horseback to the Tiger Bergen and had reached Mr. H.O. Eksteen's by a quarter to nine.[13] At half past nine rode on to Schabord's where, at half past ten, I found the wagon which had arrived in the night.

When I had enjoyed a friendly meal with Schabord and family I ordered the wagon to break camp towards half past three and to travel to the southern corner of the Groote Paarde Berg. Jansen went ahead with me on horseback. Near Pompoene Craal** came upon my slave Jak who had brought my new dog Wolf*** and a letter from my beloved wife.

*His old father Matroos or Iteki is not able to accompany me any more, owing to illness and old age. This has upset him very badly.
**The usual camping place here is at an excellent spring of water which wells up through white sand, while that of the Tiger Bergen is very brack.
***It had been left behind.

[COLUMN 2]
Weather and Wind
Very hot towards noon and throughout the day. Thermometer in the shade.

6 am.	Noon.	At its hottest.	6 pm.
76	86	86	80

A S.E. wind in the morning at the Cape which blew fiercely yesterday. Slightly cloudy all day. Foggy, moist air as with a change in the weather. The wind blew S.W. in the direction of the Paarde Berg. (It generally turns to the S.E. in the mountains). Observed that in the Bottelary Berg just as in the Wynberg these ranges have foothills as outposts and that these run into one another.

The slow and regular rise of the ridges and the way they come together gives one to reflect much upon Buffon's theory, now accepted, in which such ridges may run in all directions and yet lie close to one another.

From the outset Gordon is careful to say who accompanied him on this journey. This time, besides the artist Schoemaker, he had an orderly to accompany him – as befitted his rank of commander of the garrison. Three servants and one slave formed the rest of the party. Of these, Coerikei (or Koerikei) and Cabas are already familiar to us. Hoedies, we learn, is the son of Gordon's old retainer, Iteki, who, it will be recalled, was greatly valued by Gordon. When Gordon sent his wagon north to the Orange from Ellenboogfontein in July 1779, it was 'under the supervision of my trusty Hottentot Iteki'. It comes as no surprise that the son follows the service of his father, for Gordon was undoubtedly a sympathetic and affectionate master. Not only did he engage the trust of his servants but, according to one observer, he was 'almost adored' by these people.[14]

In his journal of the fourth journey Gordon recorded unequivocally that he would send the 'Bushman' boy Cabas home once he had seen the Cape. That Cabas did not go is not hard to understand. The boy obviously enjoyed the security of Gordon's service and preferred this relative comfort to the rigours and near starvation of his own family. The journal also records how Cabas had attached himself to Gordon. Like his fellow countrymen, he, no doubt, also idolized this leader of expeditions.

Two slaves are mentioned in this first entry: Castor, who is with the party from the beginning, and Jak, who catches up with the party in order to bring Gordon a letter, as well as a 'new dog'. (Some insight into Gordon's views on slavery are provided in a remark which he wrote a few years later – in English – concerning Sparrman's *Travels*: '. . . thoug [sic] I don't approve of slavery, yet I find the slaves at the cape (in general) not ill-treated'. We can be sure here that Gordon is at least speaking for himself.[15])

The letter brought to him by Jak is, he tells us, from his 'beloved wife'. In the case of most writers one could take this conventional phrase of endearment for granted. However, with Gordon, and in the context of this journal, the words have an unexpected poignancy and depth of emotion. Nowhere else in his journals or papers does he ever say anything as 'sentimental' as this about his wife. In fact no mention of her is made again in this journal. If he missed her or his young family on this journey it is not recorded. But the weather, the temperature throughout the day, as well as the direction of the wind are all meticulously observed and noted in the right-hand column, as is the disposition of the mountains and hills. Thus Gordon starts his journey.

Leaving Cape Town, the party headed north-east, and travelling just south of the Perdeberg, it reached Tulbagh (then known as Roodezand) in three days. Many of the farms and places that Gordon mentions on this journey are still called by the same names, though the Dutch forms have given way to Afrikaans. Using the latest official topographical sheets (1:250 000), it has been possible to plot Gordon's course over the whole journey with a reasonable degree of accuracy. For the previous expeditions it was sensible to rely strongly on Professor Forbes's scrupulous mapping, but this was not possible for this last recorded journey since, without knowledge of the journals, it was impossible for him to infer where Gordon had gone.

The first three days of travel passed calmly, but it is worth noting that Gordon records that he was 'somewhat tired . . . exhausted' on the first day out and grateful that he could sleep 'in a clean room with a plank floor'. In the previous journals such admissions of fatigue are rare.

On the second day out, 20 November 1785, he recorded that he had his 'new English quadrant (astronomical)' with him. This is undoubtedly the 'Ramsden' – the 'perfect instrument' mentioned in his letter to J.S. Bailly. It was, he wrote, 'packed in a case, lying on straps, and this sits in another case'. His barometers too were carefully wrapped in his night shirt. He was thus equipped to take latitude and to estimate altitude.

At Roodezand Gordon stayed at the parsonage of the Reverend Kuis (or Kuys as it is usually spelled)[16] – a building which stands today virtually as it stood in 1785. A drawing was also made at this time showing the original church with the sexton's and reader's houses, gardens leading up from the river, and the Groot Winterhoek range lying beyond.[17] It was this range that Gordon now decided to climb and to explore. He was to spend the next five days clambering about, taking bearings and generally observing all he could in that august, precipitous landscape.

Before setting out for the mountains, it appears that Gordon made contact, here at Roodezand, with his old travelling companion Pieter Pienaar (or Pinar as he called him). It cannot be stated categorically that this was the same person but it seems very likely because, when meeting entirely unknown farmers or whites, Gordon usually prefaced their names with the words 'a certain'. Indeed, soon after his mention of 'Pinar' he talks about 'a certain Abram Meyer who had offered to accompany me'. But the most compelling argument for this being the same Pienaar – stock farmer and hunter – lies in the journal of the fourth journey. On 8 July 1779 Gordon wrote that at Van Zyl's on the Oliphants River 'I found my travelling companion Pinar, a burgher from Rodesand'.

It seems, however, that Pinar was not as tough or resourceful now as he had been five or so years back in the desert country surrounding the Orange River, and he soon abandoned the arduous climb towards De Hel – a part of the Winterhoek that still bears this name.

Though conditions and the weather were rough on the mountain, Gordon was certainly not deterred from doing his work. Neither does his scientific curiosity abate. His complicated descriptions of rock formations and other natural phenomena fill the pages of this part of the journal. They are witness to his continuing absorption in the pursuit of facts, and in the demonstration and explication of Nature.

Apart from taking bearings and altitude, and noting the temperature, Gordon had, as usual, an eye for the lie of the land even while he recorded the hardships he and the party were experiencing:

Found here many sweet-swelling herbs and shrubs, an abundance of grass and very good water. But being somewhat lower we are here 4020 English feet above the sea. Returned to our party in the evening. I had ordered them to look around for a hole in the rock because I had seen rainy weather coming up from the north. However they had not done this. Under a tree, between two rocks we made a shelter with bushes. But even before midnight we were all soaked through, making us very cold and the fire was more smoke than flame.

Wednesday 23rd November 1785.
With daylight we looked for a hole in the rocks and found one. We fashioned a fairly impervious hollow, though the wind blew into it and through it. We made fire and dried out bushes in order to lie on them. At about ten o'clock we had a heavy thunderstorm with much hail and sleet. Thunder clattered in the mountains as if it would crack them. This thundery weather lasted until the afternoon but was followed by wind and showers of rain.

On 25 November Gordon climbed one of the highest peaks in the range. Here he drank wine mixed with snow 'which was very refreshing', while continuing to observe the complicated geology of the mountains. The layers were a 'crystallized, quartzite, granular substance. We could find no mica in it and it was interspersed with varying sizes of quartzite pebbles, from a pea to a fowl's egg in size, and even larger'. On the following day he continued the same sort of activity: 'Climbed toward the S.W., to a mountain which I had first thought to be the highest of all. Here I did my work. For my starting point I had Table Mountain clear. Found that the highest of these peaks was 6500 feet above sea level.' This last summit could be the Grootwinterhoekpiek which is 2 078 metres above sea level – a little higher than Gordon's estimate.

He returned to Parson Kuis for the last few days of November and characteristically concerned himself with the ravages that 'a small red louse' was making on the orange trees of the Roodezand area.

29th November 1785. Tuesday.
Began to investigate what the scale, so-called, is. In this basin of the Rodesand and in many more places it has damaged, and still does damage, the finest orange trees. Thereafter rode back to Parson Kuis where I repeated my investigation, riding on to Pinar in the afternoon where I did likewise. I found that it was beyond doubt a small red louse which makes itself a very small abode upon the leaves and along the boughs. It may well be that it lays an egg which becomes its house. At the very least this

67. An example of the double column format used for the journal of the fifth journey.

burrowing creature sits beneath a small reddish-brown covering with russet stripes, like the top of a pie. Bitter things like aloe, gall, tobacco juice will drive it away, as well as keeping the plant clean by brushing.

The whole expedition was on trek again from 1 December. It travelled north-west to the Piketberg which it reached the next day. Gordon had time to record another of his believe-it-or-not anecdotes, which he had picked up along the way. This one was about turtles living for eight days after their heads had been cut off and the blood being used 'as an antidote'. He also noted that a 'Hottentot' had drowned himself out of jealousy, 'something Hottentots seldom do'. This was doubtless another fact to be considered when the time came to write an anthropological discourse.

On 3 December 1785 the party arrived at Groene Valey – or Groenvlei as it is now spelled. This farm is on the eastern flank of the Piketberg and it was from here that Gordon again began his mountain climbing. But before discussing this episode it is worth examining the entry in the right-hand column for this day. This is because it

68. *Female painted snipe*
(Rostratula benghalensis): *a shy waterfowl.*

poses the sort of question one must ask when trying to understand Gordon's mind and behaviour. The entry reads: 'A fair S.E. Breeze. Good weather. Thermometer: 75–88–80. Found the latitude of De Groene Valey to be: 32 deg. 43 min. 47 sec. We found a young slave hanging on an orange tree here. He hanged himself this morning. He was a Bengali.'

Totally consistent with his approach to journal-keeping for this journey, Gordon records first the facts about the wind, then the day's temperatures, and lastly the latitude of the place where they have stopped. It is only when these facts have been noted that the gruesome episode of the hanged slave is recounted. It is also totally in keeping with Gordon's attitude and training that he should observe that the tree used was an orange tree and that the slave was a Bengali.

Gordon was not a completely systematic, orderly person – he often shows in his writing that he had trouble in presenting a logical account – but he did *try* to be systematic and orderly, and this often creates an impression of coldness and indifference, as in the entry just quoted. It is perhaps also true that the death of a slave was a matter of slight importance in those times. Certainly any expressions of shock or dismay would have been absolutely out of keeping with the tone and tenor of this journal.

It is on this same day, 3 December 1785, that Gordon mentions meeting a party returning 'from the Warm Baths on the northern Olifants River'. Apparently leading the party was a 'Reverend Kolver'.[18] This was undoubtedly Andreas Lutgerus Kolver (1743-1797) who had been appointed the first Lutheran minister at the Cape in 1780. It can almost certainly be assumed that he was travelling towards the farm of Marthinus Melck, called Berg Rivier (still called by that name today).[19] The connection between these two families was close, for it was Melck's father, the prominent burgher Martin Melck, who had donated the building which became the first Lutheran church in the country and which still stands today in Strand Street, Cape Town.[20]

On 4 December Gordon met another old acquaintance. This was Gerrit Smit with whom Gordon had first stayed in January 1779 on his return to the Cape from his third journey, nearly six years earlier. He had again touched at Smit's farm, Droge Rijstkloof, in July of the same year at the commencement of his fourth journey. Now Gordon needed to climb the Piketberg for his observations, and Smit and his ten-year-old son joined the party.

The entries for 4 and 5 December follow:

[COLUMN 1]
4th December 1785. Sunday.
Departed west up the mountain with my Hottentots, two of Müller's slaves, Gerrit Smit and his young son who is just ten year's old. After riding for quarter of an hour we started climbing steeply on foot. Avoiding the steepest way (which we later found to be the best) we encountered cliffs and kloofs which made the ascent very difficult for us. Finally, with much labour

and after climbing for five hours we reached the first plateau. But, because I wanted to make my observations from the highest point, we had to go far around and across a plateau with many cliffs. We saw many fresh zebra tracks and dung. (This is the striped ass or wild horse as they call it here.) However we did not see any, only a few rhebok and a large troop of baboons. Gerrit Smit stayed behind from exhaustion but his small son, who had to carry his heavy gun himself for some time, held his own. The wind turning westerly and the sky becoming overcast, I left them there and clambered up over many cliffs before I reached the highest point. It is a deceptive mountain with several peaks. Found the highest point 4400 feet above sea level. It is all the same kind of rock but in this mountain, like all mountains close to the sea (so far as I have observed) the strata lie more horizontal. The sky became overcast with clouds in the west, betokening rain and making it very cold.

I had completed my work and we started off across steep cliffs, first in an easterly direction.

We climbed down along a difficult kloof so that eventually in the dark we found our way blocked by cliffs and found that we could neither go forward nor back. We suffered from thirst and after a faint flicker of lightning but without thunder it began to rain fairly hard. I laid myself down under a low rock where I was, to some extent, protected from the wind but still became wet and cold. So far as I could, I kept my people awake in order to keep them from catching cold, and with dismay, we longed for day. The rain stopped when the west wind turned S.E. and it cleared up completely. The wind is always cold when this happens.

5th December 1785.
Day came at last and we found ourselves on a steep cliff. It is probable that we would have had an accident had we tried to go further yesterday evening. After much searching about we climbed down the cliffs and after three hours reached Captain Müller's.

Gerrit Smit came all the way down at ten o'clock. He said he had to endure great cold on the top of the mountain, although he had made a fire there (which we were not able to do on account of the dark and lack of firewood.)

We still thought we could reach the bottom by late evening. While we were descending we heard a shot from Gerrit Smit who had climbed up by then. We only found water once and that but little. This mountain has scant water on account of its height and extent, and because of its steepness and hard rock.

[COLUMN 2]
Fine weather. Becoming cloudy. Wind S.W. Soft breeze.
Thermometer: 80–80–70 (on top)

The honey-bird, a sort of cuckoo, called chirr, chirr, loudly, but although we looked for honey we found none.[21]

N.B. I had to wear my repeater watch this night.
With a small bowl I caught about a wine glass of rainwater which refreshed me greatly.

S.E. Breeze. Hot during the day.
Thermometer (on top): 60–89–80.

Found much good-tasting water lying in the stones in the morning. It refreshed us greatly.

The Captain Müller cited here is very likely the 'Capitain Petrus Jesse Mulder' mentioned in a letter dated 29 March 1790 from Hendrik Cloete of Groot Constantia to Hendrik Swellengrebel.[22] If it was the same 'Capitain', then he seems to have been a man of some spirit. Cloete remarks that he gave Hendrik Oostwald Ecksteen 'a thrashing with his sword'[23] on account, it seems, of Ecksteen having accused Mulder in the Militia Council of 'neglect of duty'.

It is often difficult to know what to make of Gordon's attitude to the events he describes. What he felt about the Smits, father and son, is just such a case. How are we to understand the contrast between the ten-year-old son, who 'held his own' carrying a heavy gun, and the father 'who stayed behind from exhaustion'? Does Gordon find this episode sad, comical or insignificant?

At all events Gordon says he reached 'the highest point'. This was probably 'Die Toring' which is shown on the most recent topographical sheet as being 1 458 metres. This is somewhat higher than Gordon's height of 4 400 feet.

The following few days were spent travelling round the southern tip of the Piketberg, then along the Berg River to its mouth where it debouches into St Helena Bay. As he progressed down the river to the sea Gordon was hospitably entertained by the farmers along his route.

One of his hosts was Martinus Melck, mentioned previously. At this farm, Berg Rivier — but also known as Kersefontein[24] — Gordon records that he rested, went fishing and bathed in the river. He wanted, he wrote, 'to inform [himself] about the hippopotamus'. On the next day, 10 December, the party 'went hunting hippopotamus but saw nothing'.

Again on 12 December the party 'went hunting hippopotamus in a boat'. All to no avail. They could not even find the spoor of these animals. It would seem that Gordon was sceptical about their very existence and suspected that they had probably been shot out by the farmers. Earlier (8 December 1785), when told that hippopotamus sometimes came on to another farmer's land, he had scornfully remarked that they were 'River pigs rather, in my opinion'.

It will also be recalled that it was here on the Berg River that Gordon first observed hippopotamus in 1773. His words, then recorded by Professor Allamand, are pertinent:

The breed is not at present numerous in the environs of the Cape. The nearest place that one can find them now is the Berg River, which flows into St. Helena Bay.... One can hardly count a dozen, approximately, and this has obliged the Government of the Colony to forbid killing them without special permission, in order to preserve the species.[25]

Thus this earlier statement would appear to confirm Gordon's apparent suspicions now, in 1785.

On 13 December Gordon made camp with his wagon at the mouth of the Berg River. Here he also erected what he called his 'observatory'. Why he needed this structure — presumably some kind of tent — is not clear. After all, he had previously always been able to take the latitude with his quadrant without the fuss and paraphernalia of a special construction. At any rate, it must have made an unusual locale for farmers to eat a meal — an event which took place on the afternoon of 14 December when several of the local inhabitants came to dine at Gordon's invitation.[26]

But, as on all his expeditions, Gordon did not allow himself many leisurely interludes. The next day he was exploring and observing the peninsula west of the Berg River mouth. Having obtained the information he needed, he went off in a northerly direction up the coast the following day and reached the farm Duinfontein, which also belonged to Melck and which still bears the same name today.

Continuing to take his compass bearings and other observations, Gordon proceeded up the coast to present-day Verlorevlei. Here he again found Gerrit Smit, this time in more leisurely circumstances. Obviously the farmers moved around a great deal in these parts, hunting and fishing for the pot and for pleasure. At all events Gordon spent the next few days here enjoying the plentiful fish and wildfowl.

But Smit was not the only acquaintance Gordon met at 'Verloren Valey' (as he called it) on this eighteenth day of December 1785. The entry also mentions a certain 'Dirk Jacobus Coetse'. Now this Coetse was almost certainly the farmer, hunter and explorer who was the first white man to record that he had found and crossed the 'Great River'. This crossing of the Orange had taken place in July 1760 at Gudaos Drift, from where Coetse continued north up the Leeuwen or Houms River to Warmbad, just as Gordon was to do twenty years later. On his return, Coetse, who was illiterate, dictated his story to the secretary of the Council of Policy at the Cape.[27] It was his report that had led to Hendrik Hop's expedition of 1761 which reached what is now known as Keetmanshoop. Gordon was certainly familiar with Coetse's document, for he referred to it on his fourth journey in connection with the direction of flow in the Orange.[28] It is revealing too that in this passage Gordon calls Coetse 'Kobus', and not by his more formal first name, Jacobus, indicating that they were already on fairly familiar terms. (There is mention of Coetse's farm, Klipfontein, in the Piketberg, towards the end of the journal of the fourth journey when Gordon was recording a compass bearing.) The fact that Coetse obtained grazing rights to this farm in 1755 and to 'Verloore Valley in the direction of Lange Valley' in 1756 makes his identification very positive.[29] What fascinating comments Gordon might have made about this pioneer farmer-cum-explorer but, sadly, Gordon wrote nothing more about Coetse in this, his final journal.

Pursuing his course north, Gordon arrived on 22 December at the farm De Brand Wagt (called Brandwag today) near the outlet of the Langvlei River. The next day he made an excursion to where Lambert's Bay now stands — that is, 'at the mouth of the Jakhals Valey River', where, as usual, Gordon states that he 'took all [his] bearings'.

Yet another old friend makes his appearance here — Josias Engelbrecht, who had offered Gordon hospitality on both his previous visits to these parts, in January 1779 and 1780. His farm, Bergvallei, still lies just north of the Piketberg near Paleisheuwel, and it is also marked on Gordon's map. Here, on the way to 'Jakhals Valey', he was able to give Gordon some interesting information:

From Steenbokke Fontein the shore is very stony.[30]
Here we found the place where a large Shore-Bushman's kraal had stood. They also had the children's disease among them in 1713.[31]

Sandy shrub-country everywhere. In the past there was much game and elephant here but not any more.

Josias Engelbrecht showed me a shrub where the Bushmen of that time had placed a very old woman in a wooden kraal. (N.B. she had no friends or children.) They fenced it in and in order to get rid of her let her starve in this way, with an ostrich egg of water and some food. Josias who was passing by that way with one of these Hottentots (Shore-Bushmen) was shown this by him, a man called Courasi. He found the woman already dead. He had known her; she was called Kwabees and in his opinion she was over a hundred years old.

This custom of abandoning old people had earlier attracted Gordon's attention when he made rough notes to his fourth journey. He wrote then:

The casting out of their old people should be understood in the following way.
When a kraal moves from one place to another, and a very old person, be it man or woman, will not mount a pack-ox or allow himself to be lifted on to one in order to accompany the rest, then their closest friends make them a fence or little kraal and leave them there, with some provisions, to die. Some have been found who, on no account, will leave their old people. A slaughtering ceremony is associated with this. However, should some such cast out person wish to return he would be placed in some or other ant-eater hole and covered up with stones.[32]

But the practice had been noted from much earlier times — as early as 1668 — by a certain Gerrit Vermeulen who stopped at the Cape while travelling on the outward voyage to the Indies. He recounted: 'If any of their wives fall sick in their journeying they enclose her in a hedge of thorns so that she cannot come out nor can be devoured by the lions and tigers which are found there in great numbers, but shall die there.'[33] Indeed, this 'casting out' had also interested, and shocked, many better-known travellers and writers, such as Kolb and Sparrman.[34]

Resuming his journey on 24 December, Gordon and his party turned away from the coast and began to travel east into the interior. His Zee Koeij Valeij, where he spent Christmas Eve and Christmas Day 1785, must have been situated in the area of the Seekoevlei River, approximately ten kilometres to the north-west of Clanwilliam. Gordon held no holiday here. On Christmas Day he found the latitude as well as taking, predictably, 'all my bearings'.

It is clear that Gordon had little time to waste now. The next two days took him well north of present-day Clanwilliam, through the Nardouskloof, past Duikerfontein and Knolvlei to a place he called Betjesfontein. He associated this with the Brandewyns River on which the farm Elizabethsfontein now lies. Can the latter name be a corruption of the Dutch form — Betty/Elizabeth being inferred from Betje? Elizabethsfontein is exactly where he should have been if the present-day road is followed.

As far as can be determined from the text, Gordon sent his wagon on ahead, south-east to the farm De Biedouw, while he himself rode south-west to the Pakhuis Pass, to the source of the Brandewyns River, where the present homestead lies. The following entry for 28 December is interesting in more than one way. It immediately brings to mind Gordon's earlier comments about the farmers at the Groene River who 'mostly take a Hottentot woman or two which . . . they marry according to their custom':

[COLUMN 1]
28th December 1785.
In the morning left on horseback for a certain Mrs Coopman whom I discovered was a half-breed Hottentot woman who had been married to a white man called Coopman. Half-breeds, even if they are Christians may not perform any of the duties of a Burgher. The so-called cedar trees come to an end here, north in the mountains.[35] This was the reason I rode to this farm. By going an hour and a half with a turn through the W. and then to the S.W. I arrived on this farm and found the cedar trees to be Cypress trees. However they grow very tall here in the mountains and even stand up to 50 feet and higher and extend to the south for only a two days' journey. The same occurs with the Wolvegift shrub which only grows in the northern parts of the Biedouw and Maskamma.[36]

[COLUMN 2]
28th. Very hot. A thundery sky still in east. Thermometer: 80–94–86.
The wind again whirled with the course of the sun and blew freshly at noon.

N.B. But smaller cypress trees grow on many farms in this country.
The basin at J. Coopman's is low and deep and is called Het Pakhuis. Brandewyns River begins here. In a derisory way this place is called Little Cape Town by the neighbours on account of the many small and wretched huts.

The Mrs Coopman referred to here was almost certainly the widow of Cornelius or 'Kis' Coopman mentioned by Thunberg when he passed this way in October 1773. His farm was 'a loan place *over 't Olifantsrivier genaamt 't Pakhuis* . . . 22 km E.N.E. of Clanwilliam by the Brandewyn River'.[37]

But perhaps the most interesting thing about the above passage is the light it throws on Gordon's attitude to the various matters of this particular day, matters presented much as though they were part of a *catalogue raisonné*. In other words, a statement is made which is generally followed by some descriptive or explanatory qualification. This 'cataloguing' can be followed by analyzing the narrative as statement/qualification thus:

Mrs Coopman — half-breed
half-breeds — may not perform burgher duties
'so-called cedar trees' — actually cypress
to reach farm — ride west and then south west
height of trees — geographical distribution of trees (and wolvegift shrub)
weather very hot — thundery sky plus temperature to prove it
wind — follows course of sun
low basin — name of farm and of river
'derisory way this place is called Little Cape Town by the neighbours — on account of the many small and wretched huts'

The result of this account by Gordon is that we have a deal of information but very little idea of how to assess or interpret his own view of the matters he is recording. For example, it is not clear what Gordon himself thinks of the settlement called 'Little Cape Town' or the derision it arouses among the (presumably white) neighbours. Is it a joke, or rather, does Gordon see it as a joke? He does not pass any judgement, he recounts only what others have said — and that is an end to the matter. Anyway, it was, we may recall, the 'so-called cedar trees' he had come to see in the first place.

From the Pakhuis he rode due west to the Uitkyk Pass which has a high point of 753 metres according to the most recent topographical sheet. From here he turned south and rode to Biedouw farm where he spent two nights, using 29 December for taking observations and for gathering 'stones'. He also welcomed the return of his horses which had strayed somewhere near Seekoevlei. It was his orderly Jansen who had been sent to look for them. As might be expected, there is no hint whatsoever in this journal of this man's appearance, behaviour or character. Just as Schoemaker was his artist, so Jansen was his orderly.

The journey was resumed on 30 December, the party travelling down the Bidouw River towards the escarpment where the Bokkeveld overlooks the Karoo. They descended the hill at Sadelmakersbank (now known as Kleine Zadelmakers Bank) on New Year's Eve:

We broke camp at a quarter to four and after travelling for two and three quarter hours with the ox-wagon we reached the heights overlooking the Caro. This place was full of low mountains set against the ridge of this high plateau with the Caro and its vegetation on both sides.
The large subsidences in this country are immeasurably deep, like the moats of fortifications.[38]
By eight o'clock in the evening we had descended the large stony hill called Sadelmakersbank and after another two hours we had reached the now dry Wolwe river[39] and at midnight we had passed the place where the now dry Nonjes river runs into it. We passed many ridges of stones which seemed like lines of fortification. We passed beside and around one on the left-hand side of the Kleine Elandsbergen.[40] We celebrated New Year

Robert Jacob Gordon

while on the march with a glass of wine and a shot when it turned twelve o'clock, and we dealt out rations of the water we had brought with us. Here Willem van Wyk,[41] who had brought us to this point with his oxen, took leave of us. As day broke we rode around the top of Vogelfontein Bergje[42] and travelled on E.N.E. with the dry Nonjes River, alongside this mountain. The river here runs east and west beside the Grote Elands Berg and was full of thorn-trees on the right-hand side. A foothill of the high-lying land and parallel to the same high-lying land, has ravines in it, sometimes an hour's going and sometimes more. These end in the aforementioned deep, fortified moats through which small rivers flow away in the rainy season as through a gap in the hills.

Found this country frighteningly dry everywhere. For some years it has had little rain and presently hardly a drop for six months. We made camp at a quarter past ten in the forenoon in the basin where the Nonjes River has its source.

Sunday 1st January 1786.
We found scant but good water. We were all very weary; sleep overtook us so strongly that I fell asleep while on the march.

As far as can be ascertained, they camped that morning near the Draaikraalrivier which is approximately thirty-five kilometres south of Calvinia. Gordon identifies this as 'the basin where the Nonjes river has its source'. This may be the present Nooiensrivier but the precise location of where they reached the foothills of the Roggeveld is difficult to determine.

We can be more certain of his route thereafter when Gordon mentions Knegtsbank and Hartebeestfontein. Both these names can be found on the Williston topographical sheet dated 1983. However, many of the farm names that follow in the journal will be familiar to us, since they were mentioned in Gordon's journal of the third journey. As he reminds us himself on 2 January 1786: 'I was now on the road I had taken in 1778.'

Similarly, many of the farmers were also old acquaintances, but since, for the most part, he merely mentions their names, there is not much to interest the modern reader. Likewise, most of the journal entries for the next three weeks or so are very brief and mainly concern the weather, the course taken, latitudes and other matters of that nature. For this reason Gordon's progress across the Roggeveld during this period will be summarized only.

Despite having trouble with the wagon, he crossed the Aapberg (his Aape Berg) on 6 January 1786 and arrived at the farm Malan's Gat the same day. This is almost certainly the Malansgatrivier of today. On 7 January he climbed a mountain he called Sneeu Krantz – in all probability the 1 739-metre peak Sneeukrans which is a little more than ten kilometres to the south of Malansgatrivier, according to modern topographical maps. Here he took his observa-

69. *Queek Valey (present-day Prince Albert), where Gordon was hospitably received several times.*

tions and noted that his compass behaved eccentrically 'due to the iron or magnetic properties of the mountains'.

After further delays caused by mending the wagon, the party set out once more on 9 January 1786. During the next ten days they continued uneventfully in a south-easterly direction across the Roggeveld towards present-day Prince Albert in the Karoo, making a slight diversion on 11 January to examine the mount still known to this day as Saltpeterkop. As Gordon frequently reminds us, he was still on his 'previous road'. However, on 15 January he began to descend the Roggeveld plateau, and on 19 January 1786 he reached the farm known as Kweekvlei, or 'Queek Valey' in his spelling:

19th January 1786.
Made camp, exhausted, and found a pool of delicious water even though the river was dry. We saw fresh lion tracks here but observed nothing further except that the lions had drunk here recently and had rolled in the wagon-road like horses.

Rode ahead in the afternoon to Widow de Beer who is now married to Adam Raubenheimer. The farm is called Queek Valey and lies on the Swarte River which is half-way to The Gamka River. It was a pleasant sight for us who had now been travelling for a long time through dry, parched country. We found everything in abundance here with delicious fruit such as grapes, watermelons, peaches etc.

'Queek Valey' was, of course, well known to Gordon. He had visited it with Governor Van Plettenberg's party in 1778. Indeed, Gordon's words here largely echo the phrasing of the official chronicler, O.G. de Wet, who wrote then that the pleasure they experienced was the contrast between the verdant farm and the 'barren, dry and uninhabited countryside' that they had been travelling through.[43]

Speaking of Swellengrebel's visit here in September 1776, Professor Forbes writes: 'No Karroo farm of this period is better known than Kweekvlei, where Prince Albert is now situated, for not only did Gordon make a drawing of it,[44] but it was also visited and praised by Van Plettenberg, John Barrow, De Mist and Lichtenstein.' Forbes warns us, however, that 'Le Vaillant's claims to have been here are . . . open to considerable doubt'.[45]

After resting on 20 January, Gordon went off on a side expedition. As he says, this was 'in a southerly direction', which means the 'mountains' that he climbed would have been the Platberg. The fact that, in his words, the 'peak was very wide' tends to confirm the logic of this supposition. He may have gone as far into the range to the summit marked on today's maps as the Olievenberg, even if he did not climb it. He records its height as 5 700 feet and a neighbouring peak as being 6 000 feet. The Olievenberg is marked on a modern map as 1 857 metres which is 6 091 feet.

Returning from his southerly excursion, Gordon again rested for a day at Kweekvlei. On 25 January he resumed his travels. Again, for the most part, there is little cause for comment on the ensuing entries, as Gordon made his way eastward towards the Groot Winterhoek range. It is equally as interesting to follow his course on a modern map as on his original because so many of the names of the farms have remained the same, with only some slight alterations to conform to Afrikaans spelling. For example, Gordon's 'Sleutel fontein' is today Groot Sleutelfontein and his 'Soetendaals Valey', reached on 26 January, is now Soetendalsvlei.

At this point he turned south, travelling down the Toorwaterpoort and, at his encampment somewhere in the poort, he made this note: 'N.B. Most of the farmers have left here saying that this is because of the Bushmen: but they have gone over the Great Fish River into Cafferland.' What is implied here surely is that the farmers' actions have belied their words. They were going into 'Cafferland' because there was richer country and better grazing in that area. The 'Bushmen' presence had been used as an excuse. In addition, their move was, of course, quite against the dictate of the governor, Van Plettenberg, as laid down in 1778, and which Gordon reported in his third journey.[46]

Turning eastward once more, the party reached a farm called 'Struys font' on Gordon's map and Struisvogelfontein in the journal entry for 29 January. It is fascinating to see how names evolve and change. According to the map, and to some ingenious deductions by Professor Forbes, this would appear to be the farm known today as Skilpadbeen.[47] Gordon remarks in his journal that he had been here before. He was, in fact, on his 'previous road to Beere Valei'. This, of course, refers to the journey he made with Paterson to Beervlei in November 1777. At that time, in his journal entry for 5 November, Gordon had written that the farm was called 'Ámi Ćo or Struisvogel Been by the Hottentots when they lived here. But the inhabitants call it Struisfontein now.'[48] Paterson, on the other hand, has this to say about the same farm: 'We came to a place called *Simiko* in the Hottentot language which signifies Ostrich Leg.'[49] Thus, if we use the equivalent English words, the name has changed from 'Ostrich Leg' to 'Ostrich Spring' and then perhaps to 'Tortoise Leg'. To confuse matters more, the authoritative *Toponymica Hottentotica* defines the farm as present-day 'Vogelstruis Leegte', of which 'Ostrich Flats' is perhaps the English equivalent.[50]

Resuming their course on 31 January, they travelled south-west, then east along the Olifants River to Gannakloof and from there to Kenidouw (Dienie Douw) – both still so marked.

On 3 February 1786 they came to 'De Winter[hoek Mountain Range], to the farm of Stephanus Venter. This is called Doorn Rivier, and is behind the Ronde Berg, called thus by seamen'. 'De Winter' has the word 'hoek' added to it on Gordon's Map 3, and indeed a farm marked Doornrivier now lies approximately where Gordon placed it, a few kilometres to the west of the Groot Winterhoek range.[51] Immediately to the south of the present Doornrivier, less than five kilometres as the crow flies, is a summit with a height of 1 562 metres which would appear to be his 'Ronde Berg'.

This 'round mountain' is a conspicuous feature on Map 3, as is the Groot Winterhoek range to the east of it. The legend written above the latter translates thus: 'From far

70. *Rough going over rocks and mountains in the Southern Cape.*

off this is a very recognizable summit. Seamen call it Festooned Mountain (Gefestonneerde Berg) and it is called Craggy Mountain (sic) by the English. By the Hottentots it is called Hommoequa keimoe which means Blue Cloud.'[52] Quite obviously this refers to the conspicuous peaks of the Groot Winterhoek and in particular to the high point known as the Cockscomb, which is 1 758 metres high (5 766 feet) on the map. Gordon gives the height as 5 000 feet, a nice estimate; but he came even closer to the true height in his entry of 6 February when he made the 'highest point' 5 400 feet above sea level.

Whatever the accuracy of Gordon's measurements or estimates, it is worth examining this passage of 3 February 1786 for further clues to his mode of thinking and style of recording at the time. It is all too easy to be deceived by Gordon's objective, if not monotonous, way of expressing himself. One day begins to sound so much like another that one is deceived into believing that little of any great importance is taking place. Gordon tends to present his journey as a mostly routine, unexciting string of events. But this is often patently not so, as this particular day will demonstrate.

[COLUMN 1]
Departed at dawn around a high ridge and through a kloof. We then went, with some turns, over some steep places where we had to use the brakes. After four and a half hours of travelling we came to De Winter[hoek Mountain Range], to Stephanus Scheepers, Veld Wagtmeester.[53] This [farm] is called Doorn Rivier, and is behind the Ronde Berg, called thus by seamen.[54] Had the forked mountain to the east, 2 to 2½ miles from us.[55] Ronde Berg is to the south, three and a half hours on a difficult road.

Climbed Ronde Berg and took all my bearings and returned to the farm late in the evening.

[COLUMN 2]
Hot. Still thundery sky in the N.
Fresh S.E. wind.
Thermometer: 78–97–86.
N.B. Found all varieties of fruit ripe here.

Hurt my leg climbing down, fell down from a cliff and it could have cost me my life had I not held fast to a branch until I was hauled up. Was looking for herbs and because of the shrubs did not see the precipice. Fine weather but hazy. Wind veered with sun; was S.E. in the evening and calm.

Following the normal pattern of journal entries for the fifth journey, the left-hand column records details of the day's travel up to the arrival at Doorn Rivier, while the right-hand column provides the meteorological details. Especially of note, for it rates a paragraph of its own and is importantly marked 'N.B.', is the following solemn assertion: 'Found all varieties of fruit ripe here.' Then, in the concluding paragraph of the day, almost as an afterthought, Gordon informs us that he very nearly lost his life on the 'Ronde Berg . . . looking for herbs'. This last piece of information is of considerable interest since we know from outside sources that he became increasingly absorbed in botanizing as he grew older. But very little is said of this activity in the journal. There is not even a check list of plants that he saw or gathered. And yet he is quite prepared to risk his life hunting for specimens! Once again, how characteristic of Gordon (indeed, it is almost laughable) that, having described his close escape from death, he closes his account of the day with a few more remarks about the weather and the wind.

But he could not ignore the results of his fall. The bruising of his leg caused it to swell and he was forced to stay at Doorn Rivier for a further three days, only managing to mount his horse once more on 7 February, and that he found 'painful going'.

The following singular occurrence, which bears no date of entry in the journal, was presumably also recorded during Gordon's sojourn at Doorn Rivier. It is, as one has almost come to expect, sandwiched between a temperature reading and a geographical note.

Heavier thunder in the afternoon which lasted through the night, with rain.
Thermometer: 86–100–94.
At this place three years ago two Hottentots were struck dead by lightning, one in a house and one in the kraal. The one in the house was a woman who was sitting round the fire with several others. The lightning struck two holes in the chimney and came with such violence down the chimney that the others were tumbled over and pushed out of the door. The dead woman was unmarked and remained sitting in the same position. Lightning is attracted mainly to this Winter Hoeks Range which has its highest point in the Gefestonneerde Berg which is 5400 feet above sea level.[56]

Once more travelling east, the party made its way along the northern edge of the Groot Winterhoek range to a farm Gordon describes as a good hour's going beyond 'the large peak of the Gefestoneerde Berg'. Presumably this was somewhere in the vicinity of the present farm of 'Hillside'. On the way, Gordon noted that there had been 'Bushmen' incursions in the area of the Noaga River: 'This is the house,' he wrote, 'which, being remote, was defaced by Bushmen. Butter which was in the house was smeared on the walls. Doors had been pulled out and broken etc.' But not only were the 'Bushmen' giving trouble, so too were the Xhosa. On the farm where they spent the night Gordon wrote this brief and somewhat dismissive sentence: 'In the most recent so-called war the caffers came as far as this.' This is undoubtedly a reference to the First Frontier War of 1779-1781. What is important to note is that parties of the Xhosa reached as far west as this – a fact that two contemporary books dealing with this 'war' do not appear to recognize.[57]

The next day, 8 February 1786, travelling towards the Coegas River, Gordon decided to honour his eldest son by calling a 'fine, grassy valley with trees ... Robert Gordon's Valey'. It was this same child who also had an island in the Orange River named after him.[58]

On 9 February the party came to the farm of Gerrit Scheepers near present Sandfontein, five or so kilometres north of Uitenhage. Sparrman had visited this same farmer in 1776 and, in his book, *A Voyage to the Cape of Good Hope*, gave a revealing and amusing account of how this prototype of the 'slim boer' got his land:

Gert Skepper ... had long resided there, partly in conformity to some orders of government, and partly in direct opposition to them: for government, which, though it had long employed land surveyors, was yet left totally in the dark with respect to the geography of the country, had not permitted the colonists to

cultivate or dwell farther to the eastward than the *Cabeljaauw-rivier*, but had left them at liberty to inhabit what part they pleased to the south of the Camdebo; in consequence of which, this shrewd peasant had gone round about by way of the *Camdebo* from the Cape to this place, to take possession of it; and upon this pretence, had got a charter for the tenure of it; when on the contrary, he would have been severely punished, had he gone by the nearer and better road.[59]

'n Boer maak altyd 'n plan.

From this juncture it becomes progressively more and more difficult to plot Gordon's course with any accuracy the further east he proceeds. There are two reasons for this: firstly, the map begins to fade out at approximately this point; names and geographical features simply cease, with the Sundays River the last prominent river to be shown. Secondly, the names of the farms and towns become increasingly English from here on since so many of them changed their names after the advent of the British settlers in the 1820s. It is therefore the exception rather than the rule to find on a modern map a farm which was mentioned by Gordon in this part of the journal.

There is, however, no one convincing reason why Gordon failed to complete the map to the east of the Gamtoos River. Perhaps he felt that this region had been adequately covered by his contemporaries, or perhaps, due to his military duties, he just did not have the time once he had returned to the Cape. Maybe illness prevented him. What is certain is that he had all the necessary data, in the form of compass bearings and distance travelled, to finish off this section of the map had he the time, desire or opportunity to do so.[60]

The next entry, 10 February, reads:

We found that the axle of the wagon had broken but fortunately there was a wagon-maker at this place, since the wagon would not have gone another day.
Found the latitude of this farm: 33 deg. 39 min. 57 sec. Error: 26 deg. N.W.
Travelled with St. [Stephanus] Scheeper's wagon round to the mouth of the Bosjemans river in order to begin taking measurements on the shore with my new quadrant. This had been sealed up in the double-layered chest. It was perfectly in order notwithstanding the heavy jolting of the wagon. We rode to Holtshousen and the wagon went on to Sondags River.

Besides his evident pride and satisfaction that his instruments were in such good working order, these sentences confirm his intention to continue his mapping activities, and the evidence for these remains in volume VC 596 in the Cape Archives. For the rest, however, his words can be somewhat misleading. He writes: 'Travelled with St. Scheeper's wagon round to the mouth of the Bosjemans River.' It sounds as though he took the wagon to this destination the same day — a distance of 200-odd kilometres. However, although it is not entirely clear from this entry, what happened is that he left his own wagon to be repaired at Gerrit Scheeper's farm and took Stephanus Scheeper's wagon to travel to the Boknes and Bushman's river mouths, taking a week for this part of the journey. He returned to the farm on 18 February when, he says, he 'found the wagon repaired'.

Gordon's halt on the night of 11 February, at the farm he

71. *A view of 'Plettenbergs Bay or the Keurboom River mouth'.*

calls De Koerneui, is interesting for more than one reason. First, comparing his map with a modern one – in this case the topographical sheet 2234 Port Elizabeth – we can see that this farm can be identified with the modern farm and railway siding of Coerney, just outside the north-western boundary of the Addo Elephant Park. The first written mention of this place is in Beutler's journal of his 1752 expedition. He gave it the 'Hottentot' name of Kooernoe, saying it meant small or narrow wood. Other visitors were Sparrman, Swellengrebel and Paterson. Here Gordon records his own first visit to the place in January 1778 when he had written its name, as he recalls, as 'Aas Cou', meaning 'yellow-wood thorn-tree'.[61]

However, the main interest for this place in Gordon's journals must surely lie in the import of the sentence in the right-hand column for 11 February 1786. It reads: 'In my previous journal there were many Caffer kraals situated here but these have been driven beyond the mouth of the Great Fish River in the latest war.' The significance of 'the many Caffer kraals' is that in 1778 this area was populated, in his own words, by 'great bands' of tribesmen, 'my friendly caffers'.

It was near here that he had conferred with the 'Gounaqua' chief, Ruiter. In the intervening years, since Van Plettenberg's 'decree' that the Great Fish would be the boundary between the Colony and the Xhosa, a minor war and many further desultory skirmishes had temporarily pushed the tribesmen back across that river. Gordon's position here is strictly objective. He merely gives the facts. However, writing in 1786, he may have recalled with justified irony his parting words to these 'Gounaquas': 'Before I left I told these Caffers that our Great Chief wanted them to live on the other side of the Bosjemans River and us on this side. They were surprised at this and unsatisfied, asking what harm had they done?'[62] Of course the 'Gounaqua' had done no 'harm', and furthermore were not even to know then that their removal from these parts would take them to beyond the Fish, not just the Bushman's River.

Crossing, therefore, a relatively unpopulated landscape, Gordon and his party made their way down to the coast, passing farms where there had previously been kraals. His exact route is uncertain since he did not show it on his map, but his Kwaggas Valey seems to be in approximately the right place to correspond with a farm marked Kwaggavlakte today, about ten kilometres south of Paterson.

There was still plenty of game in this thickly wooded region lying towards the coast, as Gordon reports on 12 February.

12th. Good weather. Wind westerly, not much of it.
Thermometer: 67–80–70.
Saw numberless quantities of game; buffalo; kwagga, hartebeest, ostrich, springbok.

Grassy, lime-bearing ridges everywhere with thorn-bushes as well as other trees such as yellow-wood and stinkwood and other types. It appears that the game has come here to take refuge.

The 'refuge' Gordon refers to can only be from the encroaching colonists – superior in fire-power to the Xhosa and, by repute, deadly shots.

At last, on 13 February 1786, Gordon and his party came to the final, eastern reach of the journey, their turning point. Here is the day's entry in full:

[COLUMN 1]
For six hours we travelled with the ox-wagon around the high wooded ridge and came to the mouth of the Bokna or Vaders River on the shore.[63] It emerges from these high ridges here but has not flowed into the sea for a long time. It has formed, however, a fairly large marsh, fifty paces from the sea. We placed our observatory at this point.

I went E.N.E. along the shore, which is sandy here, up to a prominent green hill where I found an old, shattered monument. Gathered together the pieces in order to carry them on the wagon with us to the Cape. After I had taken bearings here, returned to the wagon.

14th February 1786.
Took my observations. Found latitude: 33 deg. 36 min. 13 sec. Error: 26-27 deg. N.W.

[COLUMN 2]
The same weather and a S.E. Breeze.
Thermometer: 70–86–72.

Two hours on foot W.S.W. from the Bosjemans River mouth. N.B. I went through the forest using elephant and buffalo paths. On a fresh elephant path we came directly upon a good fifty buffalo in a herd. I shot at a large bull and wounded it whereupon they all went much deeper into the forest, leaving the way open for us. We climbed over another wooded hill and came to the wagon.

The Vaders or, in Hottentot, the Bocnat River runs through this Kloof. Where it ends, an old cast-anchor was lying, half an hour from the shore. Six men were easily able to carry it. The Caffers had broken off the blades.[64] They found it in the forest not far from here. Fine weather. Westerly wind.
Thermometer: 65–84–77.

There is no hesitation or equivocation here and no hint of any searching for this 'monument'. As was discussed earlier, Gordon knew exactly where the Dias Padrão was, or rather someone accompanying him knew this, and led him to the spot. There can also be little doubt that he had planned this as the end point of his journey. He took both latitude and compass bearings here, evidence surely that he intended to plot this specific point on his map.

He spent three days exploring the vicinity: first riding westwards along the shore to a point where he could observe Bird Island, a matter of some thirty kilometres, and then going about eight kilometres eastward to the mouth of the Bushman's River.

His westward ride took him past the present settlement of Cannon Rocks and it was probably here that he saw the 'badly rusted' cannons from a wreck.[65] However, there is complete certainty that the 'low-lying island in the sea' was indeed Bird Island or what Gordon called 'Doddingtons Rock' in the journal entry for this day. The story of the *Doddington* shipwreck of 1755 is well documented and happened as Gordon relates.[66] One fact he does not note is that the place was called Bird Island by the survivors of the wreck — a name it has kept to this day.

[COLUMN 1]
15th February 1786.
Went W.S.W. along the shore. Half an hour from the observatory found a stony ledge where there were iron cannons, an 18 and a six or eight pounder. They were badly rusted so that it was impossible to make out any of the letters. After a three hours' brisk ride along the shore, which was mostly sand but with stony ledges in places, I saw a long but low-lying island in the sea. I estimated that it was 1 to 2 miles from the shore. There were yet more rocks above water surrounding it. I recognized this as being Doddington's Rock and that this was where the people from that ship built another boat and crossed to Moçambique etc. There were high, white sand-dunes at this place. It became very dark because of the smoke from a fire that our people had made close to the eland, setting alight the whole countryside. Returned in the evening.

[COLUMN 2]
N.B. Our people shot an eland (Canna) bull.
Fine weather. Fresh S.E. wind.
Thermometer: 60–80–70.
We saw very many hartebeest (Bubalis) today. Before we reached the shore we found a particularly sweet spring which came from high sand-dunes and which flowed into the sea among the rocks. Called it Pieter and Otto's Duinfontein after my two youngest sons.

As Gordon notes, the spring they found in the dunes was 'particularly sweet'. No one can accuse him of sentimentality, but it is at least touching to observe how he commemorates his two youngest sons here, having paid due tribute to his eldest boy a few days earlier. Pieter was baptized in November 1783 and Otto in January 1785.[67] Gordon's family was growing rapidly, a fourth son was baptized on 9 April 1786, a few days after he ended this journey.

On 16 February 1786 the expedition set forth along the road Gordon had used in 1778, when he had been surrounded by friendly black tribesmen. All he now records is that they found 'a certain Jansen living' there. This was the beginning of the return journey. The fragments of the Dias Cross had been duly loaded and the whole expedition was back at Coerney by evening the next day. Their host, Veld Commandant Khun,[68] had returned from the Cape with news of peace in Europe. It was probably too early for the announcement that Gordon's authority over all the Company's troops had been finally confirmed.

The next day, 18 February, he arrived back at Gerrit Scheeper's and found that his wagon had been repaired. Travelling hard, he arrived at the Bakens River mouth (the site of Port Elizabeth) by 19 February. The next day, at this same place, he once more set up his observatory and took the latitude. He also took his compass bearings from the 'furthest point'. Oddly, he bothered to record that he had eaten some 'very slimy' oysters.

From Gerrit Scheepers he had travelled due south to the Bakens River mouth. Now he began travelling west, for the most part continuing back on the road he had taken in 1778. But where the earlier journal described birds and wild animals in abundance there is now almost no mention of game, and he notes that 'the deep marsh' on Cornelis Cok's farm had entirely dried up. Whether the relative absence of wild life was due to the drought or to the increasing numbers of white farmers moving in, is not clear from Gordon's narrative.

Travelling familiar ground in these concluding stages of the journey, it is clear that Gordon's interest in his surroundings is less keen. On 21 February, however, he found it worth recording that there was a 'true caffer' working for a farmer called Vogel near the mouth of the Van Stadens River. Gordon calls him a soldier of 'Tsaka' — a petty chieftain whose name had been mentioned in the journal of his second journey of 1778.[69] It is surely a sign of the times, whether intended or not, that this erstwhile warrior can now be described as a 'game-keeper', occupied in cutting wood. It is also significant that, with his wife and children, he had already been living there for six or seven years. The final fact noted by Gordon — that he 'spoke a fairly understandable Dutch' — is a telling indication that times were changing and that new patterns and relationships were developing between the frontier colonists and the indigenous tribes.[70]

For the next few days Gordon and his party travelled along the coast, arriving at the Kromme River mouth on 25 February. Here he turned inland in a north-westerly direction towards the Langekloof, reaching the farm Jagersbos (still so-named) on 28 February. By 3 March he had reached the farm of Stephanus Ferreira which is close to the present-day settlement at Krakeelrivier. Here he climbed what he called the 'reële kenbare piek' which, it is evident from his map, must be Peak Formosa — a distinctive landmark of the region as the Dutch phrase implies. Clearly Gordon was determined to press on with his homeward course. His journal entries for each day dwindled to a few lines only. He even rode on to Avontuur on the same day on which he had climbed the mountain.

From Avontuur, where he again stayed with Mattys Sondag, who had been his host in February 1778, he once more made his way down to the coast at Plettenberg Bay. After taking the latitude and his usual observations along the shore, he returned to Avontuur on 9 March and was once more on his way west by the 10th. On 12 March 1786 the journal ends abruptly as he comes to the end of the Langkloof. As has been mentioned earlier in the chapter, we know from the Gordon Collection and from his map that he continued his course westward, passing by Mossel Bay, Cape Infanta and Cape Agulhas before reaching the Cape sometime before 4 April 1786.

This journal of his fifth journey is the last record that we have of Gordon's travels.

72. Gethyllis ciliaris.

CHAPTER TEN
THE TURBULENT YEARS
(1786-1794)

Botanists at the Cape; military duties; Otto Dirk Gordon; correspondents and visitors; Sparrman's Travels; illness; merino sheep; the 'Pepinierin' affair; more visitors; red hot cannon balls; the state of the garrison

lthough it appears that Gordon had achieved all the goals he had set himself for his fifth journey, it cannot be said that those goals were over-ambitious. The mapping, the appraisal of the Colony's defensibility and the recovery of parts of the Dias cross were modest achievements. (Gordon's recovery of the Dias cross inscription in fact only began to arouse interest from the early 1970s.[1] Certainly no contemporary account of this event has yet been discovered.) Nevertheless, the journey itself did advance Gordon's fame, and the years immediately following his return in April 1786 brought him increasing acclaim and reward.

Briefly stated, he had a happy marriage with a growing young family; in the February of 1786 confirmation of his full authority over all the troops at the Cape had at last been received from the Here XVII,[2] thus ending a long period of frustration and uncertainty; and finally, his reputation as a traveller and savant was spreading far and wide.

Gordon's growing fame can be seen not only in the remarks of foreign visitors to the Cape but in the words of his contemporaries and colleagues in the service of the Company. A curious but beguilingly exaggerated letter, written to the ex-governor, Van Plettenberg, by Olof Godlieb de Wet, provides evidence of this. It will be recalled that De Wet had been the official chronicler of the governor's visit to the Eastern Cape in 1778. At the time of writing this letter (20 February 1786) he was the landdrost at Stellenbosch.

> Once more colonel Gordon is travelling over the peaks of mountains and through awful kloofs and crevices, never visited before. He still remains capable of discovering and revealing wonderful rarities of this kind, never made known before. He has again been occupied doing this for just over three months so that he has not yet been able to enjoy the Triumphal Arch that stands waiting for him.[3]

Although the 'Triumphal Arch' cannot be considered anything more than a metaphor, it is nevertheless an indication of the esteem that was accorded Gordon at the time. It is not exactly clear from this extract which of Gordon's achievements was awaiting recognition in the form of this arch. Was it his explorations, his researches into fauna and flora, or the confirmation of his military authority that was to be celebrated? Possibly De Wet was pointing to all these activities, seeing them all worthy of a 'Triumph'.

Gordon's military duties were to keep him increasingly occupied after his return. However, he still found time to pursue his various scientific activities — botany in particular.

It will be remembered that during his first visit to the Cape in 1773 Gordon had made a short excursion around the peninsula with the botanist C.P. Thunberg, and that the English plant-collector, Francis Masson, had also been a member of the party. Sent once more by the great natural scientist, Sir Joseph Banks, Masson again visited the Cape in 1786, arriving in January while Gordon was still away on his fifth journey. He was to remain in the country until March 1795.

Then in June 1786, shortly after Gordon's return, two Austrians — Franz Boos and Georg Scholl — arrived with a letter of introduction to Gordon from Graf (or Count) Cobenzl. Cobenzl was a statesman in the service of the Austrian Emperor, Joseph II, whose gardens at Schönbrunn, outside Vienna, were justly famous for their beauty and for their rare and exotic plants.

Gordon was delighted with this influx of botanical collectors, as is evident in the whole tone of a draft letter, or rather of two draft letters, both, it seems, referring to a further draft letter in his papers. It would appear to be his reply to Cobenzl's letter of introduction and is dated 18 August 1786.[4]

Many matters of great interest are touched on as Gordon tries to formulate his reply in his fluent but somewhat eccentric French. The spelling, even given a certain eighteenth-century laxity in this regard, is bizarre and sometimes incomprehensible. However, most difficulties resolve themselves if the words are pronounced aloud so that one arrives at the sense aurally and not visually. It is as though Gordon spoke French readily and fluently but did not often write it. Though there is no evidence to back it, French may have been the language used in the Gordon household. Mrs Gordon came from a French-speaking canton of Switzerland and it would have been natural for her to use her native tongue at home, quite aside from the fact that it was, literally, the lingua franca of polite European society.[5]

In his drafts Gordon thanks 'Monsieur le Conte' (Count Cobenzl) for his letter which he has received from Boos. Indicating his awareness of the count's considerable knowledge of natural history, Gordon undertakes to do everything in his power to assist the success of the enterprise that the 'Great Joseph' (Emperor Joseph II of Austria) has planned.

From the two draft replies, it is clear that the 'enterprise' consisted of two parts: the first to capture wild animals alive and the second to collect plants. Both fauna and flora were, it would seem, destined for the Schönbrunn Gardens. Regarding the animals, Gordon cautions 'his excellency' not to nourish too high hopes of succeeding. Africa, he says, is too vast, too arid, and what rivers exist are useless for transport, being nothing more than 'torrents'. About the botanical aspect of the emperor's enterprise, however, he is altogether more sanguine, assuring the count that 'Messrs. Boos and Scholl [would] find much to occupy themselves most usefully', and stating that 'one could botanize for a lifetime without moving very far from the environs of the Cape [Cape Town]. There is always something fresh to be found because of the great number of plants flowering at different seasons ... and also because the plants occur at different heights and grow in varying aspects.'

Apart from these reasons, Gordon could assure the Count that his scheme would succeed because of the 'rare and unique plants' to be found at the Cape, and because the two botanists showed such 'indefatigable industry and knowledge'.

Gordon then goes on to mention a most interesting fact, a piece of information that does not appear anywhere in his journals. 'I also have Hottentots in several distant parts of the country who bring me bulbs and seeds from time to time. I shall not hesitate to share these with Boos. I have planted them in a garden at the foot of Table Mountain.'

Apparently (the draft is confusing at this point), the two Austrians had already planted some of their findings in this garden. 'I was enchanted,' Gordon continues, 'when I visited their garden yesterday: what they have already planted would astonish Your Excellency. How delighted I would be if all this was already, with the same perfection, in the garden at Schönbrunn.'

On a separate piece of paper, but apparently belonging to the same draft letter, is a further passage concerning the procuring of wild animals, but this time the subject is treated in more detail. Here Gordon expresses little hope of obtaining a giraffe or a rhinoceros since they are too far from the Cape. He is, however, more hopeful about obtaining a hippopotamus: 'There are still about a dozen in the Berg River ... protected by the Government.' After the October military exercises he proposes to 'entertain himself a little'. And even though the animals had become 'very cunning, being surrounded by Europeans' (farmers), nevertheless he flatters himself that he would be able to 'procure one of these singular animals for his majesty'. He would send the skeleton and the skin. (Presumably there was no hope of sending a live hippopotamus to Europe.)

In an interesting finale to this passage Gordon asks the Count to kindly enquire whether the Siberian fossil bones, now at St Petersburg and discussed by the traveller Gmelin, are not those of a hippopotamus? They are not those of an elephant or two-horned rhinoceros as Professor Camper has found, Gordon adds. That the solution to this question 'would make an interesting and curious addition to natural history' is his last reflection on the subject.

Naturally, Gordon's reply to the count raises several issues on which one would like to be better informed. There is no information that Gordon ever despatched a hippopotamus skeleton and skin to the emperor, though his despatch of giraffe remains to Willem V, a few years earlier is fully documented. However, we do know that when Boos returned to Europe in February 1788, he took with him: '10 chests of dried plants, seeds, bulbs, stuffed birds, skins of animals, two live zebra, 11 monkeys and 250 birds ....'[6] No wonder Gordon praised the diligence of the two collectors, for besides this material there was more that had to be left behind at the Cape for Scholl to forward as cargo space became available.

How, when and where these collections were made is very sketchily documented. We know from Masson's letters to Sir Joseph Banks and from correspondence between Boos and Count Cobenzl that in the next few years Gordon, Masson and Scholl made frequent 'short trips' and probably some much longer journeys, but details are few and vague. For instance, Count Cobenzl, writing to Boos in March 1787, somewhat drolly regrets that he cannot go strolling with him and Gordon in the region of the Four and Twenty Rivers.[7] So from this we can deduce that the botanists made an excursion to the Tulbagh area. Then from Gordon's own remarks, quoted above, we know that he *intended* entertaining himself with a trip to the Berg River mouth to shoot a hippopotamus – a feat, incidentally, he was unable to accomplish on his visit there in 1785.

Furthermore, from the collection of plants gathered by Scholl, there is evidence that some specimens came from as far east as the Grahamstown district and others from as far up the west coast as the region beyond the Kamiesberg. In a letter to Thunberg, Masson claimed that he had visited the Kamiesberg. Unfortunately, no dates are given for these plant-gathering expeditions, but both collectors remained in the Cape for some years – Masson until 1795, as has been noted, and Scholl until 1799, four years after the first British occupation had begun.[8]

There is no doubt then that expeditions were undertaken by these two botanists, and it is more than probable that Gordon accompanied, or rather led, them on several

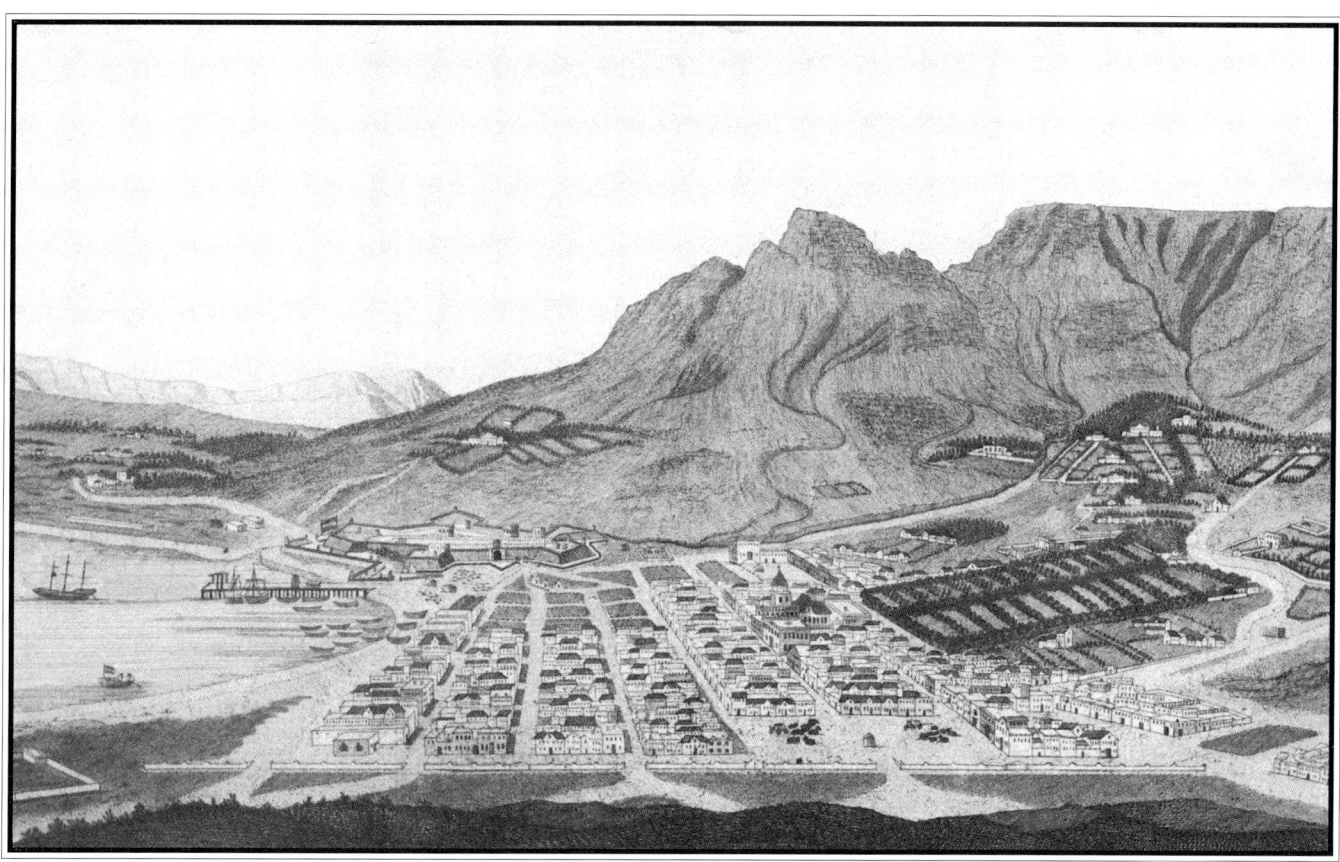

73. *A view of Cape Town from Signal Hill by Johannes Schoemaker.*

of these journeys and excursions. But for the present that is all we know.

Tantalizingly, in another letter to be discussed later, Gordon did talk of having made '*six* [translator's italics] journeys in different directions of which the least was about six months'.[9] Gordon wrote these words some time in 1789 but, given the facts of his life for the three years following his fifth journey, it seems unlikely, if not impossible, for him to have made a sixth journey lasting six months during this period. It is strange too that he should claim that all his journeys were in different directions, for as we have seen, this was manifestly not so, nor, strictly, did his fifth journey last for even six months. It is uncharacteristic of Gordon, as we have known him so far, to exaggerate his achievements — the reality was impressive enough. However, he wrote this in what was draft form and may have striven for greater accuracy in his final version.

But to return to the Gordon/Cobenzl correspondence: among Gordon's papers there is one more draft letter from him to the count which contains further revelations.[10] It must have been written about January 1788, since it discusses Boos's return from Mauritius with 'a most valuable collection'. (Boos left for the island a year earlier, in February 1787.) After acknowledging receipt of no less than four letters in succession from Cobenzl, the last dated 3 June 1787, Gordon praises Boos's tirelessness and zeal. He also hopes that the collection about to travel to Schönbrunn with Boos will give the emperor great pleasure. Then Gordon states: 'An illness last year, which laid me on the banks of the Styx, has hindered me from executing my designs on the hippopotamus.'

This statement is the first intimation that Gordon had been so gravely ill, close to dying, sometime in 1787. He gives no indication of the nature of his illness, but we know he was dogged by fevers and dysentery-like symptoms in his travels before 1785. Interestingly, there is no mention of illness in the journal of his fifth journey which ended in April of the previous year. But this is a subject to which we shall be returning with a great deal more attention later.

Furthermore, we now know that the expedition to the Berg River did not take place as had been planned, though this does not rule out the possibility of a later trip in that direction. But more revelations follow. Gordon now declares that he has good news about a rhinoceros, one of which, he says, he shot in the country of the Caffers during his last journey of 1785. He had buried the bones because it was impossible to bring them with him as he had been too occupied plotting the southern coast of Africa.

Now the interesting point here is that absolutely no mention of this rhinoceros occurs in the journal of the fifth journey — and surely such an event would have been chronicled in some detail, at least going by Gordon's previous journals. Yet the whole tone of this passage is one of total conviction. He has had a letter, he states, advising him that the skeleton is in good condition and he expects it to arrive at the Cape very soon, while Boos is still there. But if it has not arrived he will send it on another occasion, hoping to add the hippopotamus to it.

As far as he knows it will be the first complete rhinoceros skeleton in Europe. Again Gordon expresses the hope that it will be compared with the fossil bones found in Siberia and in Germany.

The draft becomes somewhat confused at this stage but it is apparent that Gordon was much preoccupied with current theories concerning the changing climate of the world: that there had been a shift in the poles and similar revolutions, producing a gradual cooling of the planet. The theories of Buffon regarding the 'epochs' of Nature are also touched upon. In particular, Gordon mentions Buffon's ideas regarding floods at an earlier period of the earth's formation, adding that he has seen unequivocal traces of these 'in this country'.

In what appears to be a continuation of this same draft on another sheet of paper, Gordon continues his theme of comparing or finding 'cameleopardalis' (giraffe) and hippopotamus fossils in Germany. He believes that these bones would prove to be the 'First', or primitive species, of the animals which he is hoping so desperately to procure for 'His Majesty, the Emperor'. He regrets that his post prevents him from travelling so far himself and that promises made by distant colonists evaporate when it comes to actually facing trouble and difficulty. But what now follows has an element of humorous indignation rarely found elsewhere in Gordon. Obviously referring to the giraffe skeleton sent to Europe after his fourth journey, he writes:

I wish with all my heart that His Majesty could have had the one in The Hague, for they tell me that it has been hidden in an attic. They never even informed me that it had arrived although I never had any other reason or interest in doing what I did but my own desire and enthusiasm for Natural History, and all at my own expense.

It is plain that the whole matter of the giraffe stirs him mightily, though quite who 'they' are is not very clearly specified. Gordon starts a new paragraph:

They have had only the stupidity to ask His Excellency, the governor, to ask me for a small giraffe, after having received one of the greatest in stature, so that they would be able to place it in an ordinary room in the Cabinet. Upon which, I replied that the Honourable Director could come here himself and choose one of a stature that he would judge correct and that I would show him with pleasure the country where they were to be found. All this for the most part springs from the jealousy that they have for my good friend, Professor Allamand, to whom from time to time I used to write about, as well as send, my discoveries of quadrupeds in this country. I infinitely regret his death, as of a true friend of excellent heart, a sagacious man, highly informed without preconceptions or prejudices and whom I had known for twenty-eight years.

The draft then proceeds with some advice from Gordon regarding the despatch of plants and animals from the Cape and the necessity of having trusted men to accompany them. The concluding paragraph talks of Scholl nearly dying but now being in better health and intending to accompany Gordon on his expedition to the Berg River for the hippopotamus. While there, Gordon adds, Scholl could collect seeds and bulbs.

In its way this letter reveals a great deal about Gordon that does not surface in his travel journals. In particular, his ability to express such scorn — although his indignation at the treatment meted out to his giraffe is absolutely understandable. His frustration at not being able to travel in search of giraffes for the emperor, whose interest in natural history appears to have been so much more zealous than that of Gordon's own sovereign, can also be sensed. Finally, we learn about Gordon's grave illness. Characteristically, Gordon's reference to it is brief, but the fact of that illness will have to be borne in mind when examining his actions and career from now on.

Gordon had many other matters to preoccupy him at this period of his life. Sometime before May 1788 he became the owner of a house in the suburb of Cape Town now known as Gardens.[11] Writing about it later one contemporary had this to say: 'His house, the constant resort of strangers, the seat of hospitality, at once exhibited the learning of the man, the dignity of the chief and the felicity of the husband and father.' Schoonder Sigt, as the house was called, was to become renowned for the Gordon family's hospitality. It also became well known for its garden, which is probably the one referred to in Gordon's first (1786) draft to Cobenzl. It was here that the specimens collected from his and other men's travels were assembled and planted. It was here too that the last moments of Gordon's life would be passed.

It would be easy to gain the impression that life for Gordon now was fairly leisurely: with time to write to European scientists and statesmen, time to botanize at will, and time to enjoy his growing family. But this was not the case. In fact he would have had to make time for these interests and pursuits as his military responsibilities were pressing.

It has been estimated that in the summer of 1787-8 Gordon had a force of 3 000 men under his command at the Castle.[12] This consisted of about 1 000 men in the permanent Cape garrison, of which approximately 400 consisted of sappers and artillerymen. But in addition to these he was also the overall commander of a German regiment, the Württemberg, which was made up of mercenaries in the pay of the Dutch East India Company.

The new governor, Van de Graaff, was a military engineer and when he took up his duties in February 1785 he at once set about extending the fortifications around the Cape Peninsula and strengthening the existing ones. After Gordon's authority over the Cape garrison had been confirmed in February 1786, he also played a significant part in preparing the Cape's defences. Most of his energies, however, appear to have been directed towards the improvement of the weaponry used by his troops.

Upon his appointment as commander in 1780 Gordon's first task had been to inspect the armoury, where he found the rifles to be in a poor state. He at once pressed

74. Rothmannia capensis: *a forest flower from the Eastern Cape.*

Van Plettenberg to obtain sufficient rifles from Holland, similar to those being used by the infantry there but with modifications to the firing chambers and the butts. It is clear that he wanted the rifles adapted specifically for the hot conditions at the Cape.

The rifles were ordered and made ready for despatch, as Van Plettenberg informed Gordon, but that was the last that was heard of them. They were never received – probably because of the war. In January 1787, however, Gordon again took up the issue, expressing his 'grievous anxiety' about the state of the Company's weapons. He urgently needed 6 000 'good' rifles, for the maintenance of the Cape's defence depended upon them.

Again he was very specific as to what was needed for the Cape conditions. He sent samples of the rifles stored in the armoury back to the Company governors, detailing their failings and capabilities. For instance a 'Zeeland' model of 1786 had too short a barrel and could be dangerous when a man in the rear rank fired, for he could wound a man in the rank in front of him. Another had a ramrod that was too thin which slipped past the cartridge and got stuck in the barrel.

But eventually Gordon did find a rifle that he wanted for his garrison. Recruits on the ship *Leviathan* were supplied with a rifle that he could use. Only minor adaptations were required: the butt was too light and an inch too short, and the barrel and the bayonet also needed to be an inch or two longer. Otherwise it was 'perfect'.

This was in May 1787, and this time the full Council of Policy backed Gordon's request that a sufficient supply of these rifles should be sent to the Cape, altered according to his specifications. There is no evidence that the rifles were ever received, and Gordon was obliged therefore to indent a supply of rifles from the outward-bound ship *Vrede*. They were far from 'perfect', but Gordon had to content himself with the thought that 'a bad gun was better than no gun' – hardly the most inspiring reflection for the commander of the Cape garrison, the man responsible for the defence of the Colony.

Gordon had every reason to be anxious about the state of readiness of his command. In Europe there was unrest and potential, if not actual, revolution. At the same time the Colony was experiencing trouble on its frontiers and dissatisfaction among the burghers.

To take events in the Netherlands first: the conduct of Willem V during the Anglo-Dutch war of 1780-1784 was considered pusillanimous and half-hearted by the faction known as the Patriots. This party, whose ideals were vaguely libertarian rather than revolutionary – at least to begin with – gradually increased their influence throughout the United Provinces, until by 1787 the country was divided into various spheres of influence that were loyal either to the Patriots or to the stadholder. By April 1787 Amsterdam was in the hands of the Patriots and Willem had been driven out. A few months later, after her arrest by the Patriots, Wilhelmina, Princess of Orange, appealed to her brother, the King of Prussia, to intervene. He invaded the Netherlands in September, dispersing the leading Patriots into exile – mainly to France, where the French Revolution was shortly to have its beginnings. Willem, Prince of Orange and stadholder, was once more in power. In April 1788 the Triple Alliance between the States General, Prussia and Great Britain was concluded. An uneasy state of peace prevailed for the time being.

There was no doubt where Gordon's loyalty lay in the conflict taking place in his fatherland. His prime allegiance had been, and would always be, to the House of Orange. But this was not the case with all his family. In the light of Gordon's unambivalent loyalty to the stadholder, it is worth touching on the remarkable story of his brother, Otto Dirk Gordon, a renowned supporter of the Patriots. Dutch loyalties in the 1780s were by no means straightforward or predictable.

Otto Dirk, it may be remembered from the opening pages of this study, was the brother immediately senior to Robert Jacob. One source claims that he also served under his father in the Scots Brigade and states that on leaving the regiment he identified with the Patriot Party, becoming 'colonel' of the Pro Patria Company of the Civic Guards of Utrecht, and lieutenant-colonel of the 'Hand & Foot Bowmen' in 1784. In March 1785

he entered the Stadthouse of Utrecht and obliged the magistrates to repeal an act they proposed the day before. He insists that the common people should have a part. His corps consists of about 700 effectives completely armed and even with canon. Almost all the inhabitants of Utrecht and a great number of ladys have subscribed to furnish him with powder for exercising his corps. Several of the English merchants at Amsterdam told me he was a most turbulent man and had done them great harm during the war.

With the return to power of the Prince and the Orange Party, Otto Dirk's property was 'forfeited, and such was the animosity against him, that while the stadholder was at Rhenen in 1787 the people burnt his effigy to show their devotion to the Prince. But Utrecht loved him, and for many a day remembered him in a street song beginning. "Mynheer Gordon is een brave kapiten".'[13]

All this concerning his brother would have little relevance to our study of 'Gordon the man' were it not for the fact that, despite a common upbringing as officers under their father in the Scots Brigade, the two brothers differed so greatly in their allegiances. It is recorded elsewhere that Otto Dirk had 'served in America' and this must undoubtedly have been on the side of the revolution. There is, it must be stressed, no mention of Otto Dirk in Robert Jacob's papers. We can only guess what opinion each brother had of the other.

Nevertheless, whatever the relationship between the two brothers might have been, events in Europe cannot but have influenced Gordon's view of his career and of his future. For one thing a Patriot Party, influenced by the Dutch model, had also been formed at the Cape; 'memorials' and delegations were constantly being sent to the States General to protest against what they saw as the arrogance, corruption and greed of the Dutch East India Company. Meanwhile, on the Eastern frontier there was an uneasy truce with the Xhosa, but the unending 'war' elsewhere with the so-called Hottentot-Bushmen continued.[14] To provide greater stability therefore to the frontier regions, a new district was formed during 1786 and named Graaff-Reinet in honour of the new governor and his lady.

Although events both in Europe and at the Cape were turbulent during the middle and late 1780s, and although Gordon had his hands full as commander of the garrison, he was, we know, able to conduct other correspondence besides that with Count Cobenzl. Earlier, the draft letter to M. Bailly, the French scientist and politician, was discussed in relation to Gordon finding the Dias Cross on his fifth journey. This was almost certainly written towards the end of 1786 or early in 1787. The supposition can be made since Gordon begins the letter by thanking the French savant for a valuable present which had been handed to him by the Chevalier d'Entrecasteaux. This can only have taken place on the Chevalier's visit to the Cape as he passed through on his way to Mauritius. (He was the administrator of 'Les Mascareignes' – as that island and its archipelago was then named – from 1787 to 1889.) That Bailly's emissary should have been this high-ranking officer demonstrates succinctly the level that Gordon's social and scientific life had reached.[15]

Besides discussing his travels, Gordon also promised to send plants and fruits to Bailly. In another draft letter, also alluded to earlier, Gordon promised to send stones. (This particular letter is the one where Gordon remarked that he had made six journeys.) Headed 'Cap de Bon Espérance le 8me Avril 1789', it was written to the celebrated Swiss scientist Horace Bénédict de Saussure, who was eminent in his day for his studies in meteorology, geology and botany.[16] The stones which Gordon sent were samples taken from the collection he had put together from his travels. There is a list of these stones in Gordon's papers dated 'Cabo 1789', specifying that they were sent to De Saussure.[17] The letter itself does not actually mention the Swiss scientist's name, starting 'Mon Cher Monsieur' and referring in the text only to 'mon cher professeur'.

An interesting facet of the draft is that in it Gordon acknowledges a previous letter from this correspondent, dated 5 February 1788. This is tantalizing, for it is not among Gordon's papers. However, Gordon warmly acknowledges his correspondent's 'excellent works' and 'renown', possibly seeing De Saussure as a substitute correspondent for the lately deceased Professor Allamand. It would appear then that De Saussure's letter of 1788 was the opening one in the correspondence – further proof, if that were needed, of Gordon's growing fame in Europe. By far the greater part of Gordon's five folio page reply is devoted to De Saussure's subject: the geographical formation of southern Africa as perceived by Gordon on his travels.

Sadly, there are no more draft letters in Gordon's papers, though there are other letters which have been published and which will be discussed later.

Gordon's reputation however did not depend on letters to and from Europe. It has already been seen how such diverse visitors as William Hickey and François le Vaillant were entertained, and during 1787 and 1788 many visits to Gordon are recorded, such as that of Captain Phillip on his way to New South Wales in October 1787:

As it was earnestly wished to introduce the fruits of the Cape into the new settlement, Captain Phillip was ably assisted in his endeavours to procure the rarest and the best of every species, both in plant and seed, by Mr Masson, the king's botanist, whom we were so fortunate as to meet with here as well as by Colonel Gordon, the commander in chief of the troops at this place; a gentleman whose thirst for natural knowledge amply qualified him to be of service to us, not only in procuring a great variety of the best seeds and plants, but to point out the culture, the soil and the proper time of introducing them into the ground.[18]

As we shall see, this was not the only way that Gordon would come to the aid of the infant British colony. Bligh of *The Bounty* also procured seed and plants at the Cape in 1788 and recorded that he was 'greatly assisted by colonel Gordon'.[19] But perhaps the most eloquent traveller to Australia was John White, the official physician for New South Wales, who also became a Gordon admirer during October 1787. In his journal he wrote:

Among the many [gardens] which afforded me delight, I must not forget that belonging to *Colonel Gordon, commander in chief* of the Dutch troops at the Cape; where not only the taste and ingenuity of the gardener, but the skill and knowledge of the botanist, are at once manifest. The colonel is a man of science of an active and well-cultivated genius, and who appropriates those hours that he can spare from his military duties (in which he is said to excel), to a perusal of the book of nature, and researches after useful knowledge. These pursuits tend not only to his amusement, but to his honour; and they will, doubtless, at some time or other, further conduce to the advancement of natural history, and to the honour of his country; as it is said that he intends to publish the observations and remarks which have been the result of his researches. Those he has made on the Hottentots, Caffres, and the countries they inhabit, will doubtlessly be valuable; he having made himself better acquainted with the subject, and penetrated further into the interior parts, than any traveller or naturalist that has hitherto visited the Cape. It is to be lamented that he has so long withheld from the world the gratification and improvement, which most assuredly must be derived from the observations of a person so well and so extensively informed. His polite attention and civility, during our stay at the Cape, claim our most grateful acknowledgements.[20]

There is unintended poignancy today in those words of White, lamenting that Gordon had 'so long withheld' publication of his 'observations'. In this he echoes the comments of Rear-Admiral Stavorinus written in 1778 and of others quoted earlier in this study. It is quite clear that Gordon gave these visitors the impression that one day he would indeed publish a work, or works, on his researches and travels.

Another caller at the Cape who greatly enjoyed the company of Gordon was Major-General Lachlan Macquarie who was later to be governor of New South Wales. In June 1788, however, he was on his way to India and had dropped anchor at Simon's Town. It was not just Gordon's learning and courtesy he admired, as the following extract from his journal demonstrates:

At the Cape of good Hope 1788 June 18 Colonel Gordon, Commandant of the Dutch Troops came on board the Dublin, with Mr Bligh, Mr van Carman and Mr Mason (botanist) . . . a merry day of it and a great deal of dancing with the Ladies in the Evening to fine Moon light on the Quarter Deck. Colonel Gordon is a very fine jovial Fellow, and a most agreeable Companion as can be; he has resided long in this Country, and has very much studied the manners and customs of most of the Savage Nations of Africa – especially of all these lying within the Distance of One Thousand Miles from the *Cape*; He has frequently travelled this distance into the interior Parts of the Country, and his Descriptions of the Savage and Wild Inhabitants of the different Nations he has visited are very entertaining – He sang a number of their Songs to us in their own real Manner and Language; – this Gentleman has so great a facility at learning Languages, that to my very great astonishment he entertained us with a *Gaelic song* altho not born in the Highlands or even in Scotland, being born in Holland but of Scotch Extraction; he is very communicative and extremely well informed – in short, as agreeable and facetious a Companion as I ever met with . . . in figure . . . Colonel Gordon is a tall stout Soldierlike Man; He spent the greatest Part of two Days with us, and we were not a little sorry when he went away from Simon's Bay.[21]

Macquarie's description is one of the sharpest and liveliest pictures we have of Gordon at this time. He comes across as being quite unpedantic, full of geniality and high spirits as he sings the songs of the indigenous peoples he has met, and gives that rendition of a Gaelic air – for which he almost certainly drew on his experience in the Scots Brigade. It was clearly a fine party – entertaining yet elegant – with Gordon at the centre of the festivities. But this bonhomie and congeniality is something very seldom conveyed by Gordon in his journals or in his odd writings. Perhaps only in his descriptions of happy encounters with the Xhosa and other indigenous tribesmen has this aspect of his nature shown itself, and then only fleetingly.

It is not entirely idle to speculate whether this more jocular element in Gordon's personality would have been present had he written a book on his southern Africa experience. What we have of his writing is mainly in journal form and, as we have seen, there is little that could be called jocular there. Likewise in the draft letters and other papers that have been preserved, a light or satirical mode appears meagrely, in tantalizingly brief passages. There is just one exception and that will be discussed a little later. But for some reason (because of his military upbringing perhaps?) the act of writing almost always evokes a heavy, official style in Gordon.

However, his thoughts could not have been far from the subject of publication at this time. In quick succession the books of contemporaries – his fellow naturalists and explorers – were now beginning to appear. Sparrman's *A Voyage to the Cape of Good Hope, 1772-1776* came out in 1785. The first volume of Thunberg's *Travels in Europe, Africa and Asia* was published in 1788. Both Paterson's and Le Vaillant's first accounts of their travels appeared in 1790. Even Francis Masson had fifty pages of print to his name in the *Philosophical Transactions of the Royal Society, 1776*.

It is virtually certain that Gordon read, or knew of, all these publications. In the case of Sparrman's book we are fortunate to have an amusing critical commentary in Gordon's hand. It demonstrates in an extended form (it is twelve folio pages long) that Gordon could bring a scathing, witty scorn to bear once his anger and contempt had been aroused.

To heighten the interest of this document is the fact that it is written in English, giving us some insight into his practice of a language he had been using from childhood.

In all fairness to Sparrman it should be recorded that Professor V.H. Forbes considers Gordon's criticisms unduly harsh, probably arising from 'his vastly greater travel achievements, as well as from his feeling of frustration because publication by him of a travel book could hardly have been undertaken by one in his official position'.[22] This may be the case as far as Gordon's travel achievements were concerned, but it should be noted that none of his contemporaries gave the slightest hint that his official position could prevent publication of a book.

But there is no mistaking Gordon's scorn for poor Sparrman's narrative and its pretensions. It is worth sampling some of Gordon's saltier remarks, using his orthography and punctuation to get the full flavour of his style.[23]

Early in the tale the young Swede recounts how a slave woman showed him the best way to cross a brook and

75. *Massonia depressa – found in the Karoo.*

archly hints that she 'seemed to lay her account in receiving some amorous kind of acknowledgement'. Gordon finds this altogether too much and comments: 'The amorous acknowledgement for showing him the path is drole. I think she would have preferred a sixpence.' Later Gordon has this to say about one of Sparrman's essays into zoology: '. . . this whole chapter of the hyena is the most stupid absurd learned stuff that could possible be wrote on the subject'. Further on Gordon fulminates: '. . . this is all nonsense and buff[24] some few things are true but ill-digested the rest are lies'.

The litany of scorn continues:

. . . lies and buff, these hottentot women here are no more true hottentots & all whores.
. . . so in two days Sparman learned the hottentot language.
. . . the black monkeys are a very pretty lye. They are reddish grey on the back.
. . . Sparman forgets the paches near the tits upon the belly and seems to have stole a good deal from the figure I send to Proff. Allamand.

... extraordinary lyes and nonsense about the bosjeman prince and princess.

Here is his opinion of the first volume of Sparrman's *A Voyage to the Cape of Good Hope*. Again the text is given verbatim:

This Volume is thus finished and it really is a shame that men how migth simply instruct the world and get credit eneog should out of vanity tell such a number of lies and make such a compound of all the stories they greedily catch at to make make [sic] a large book. Covering their ignorance and what they never saw with learned sistematical names.

Sparrman's second volume evokes equal, if not greater, scorn. Just a few quotations from Gordon's pithier comments will demonstrate this:

... the lion not stalking an animal is again nonsense, he does so every day for his food. he measuring the length of his leap and not pursuing and being ashamed is all buff. The lion being a coward is drole after all the buff of this lyon story, which is very disgusting.
... the story of the stones and monuments of old migthy nations is a damnd cunning lye, as likewise his praise of me whom he has never seen.
... if a lion had really roard near them I should not be wondered if they had dirtied their breeches, and fainted.
... thoug I dont approve of slavery, yet I find the slaves at the cape (in general) not ill treated. This whole story is misrepresented and very illnatured.
... finis fig for shame O great proffessor Sparman with your dwarf mouse.

What seems to have aroused Gordon's greatest ire in Sparrman's writings was his pretensions to being a naturalist — in other words, to have covered much of the ground Gordon himself had covered or was covering. Sparrman is obviously not anything like as expert or painstaking as Gordon in the fields of zoology, botany or ethnology, to name just some of the subjects in question. He is also given to whimsical anecdotes and fancies that manifestly repel the pragmatic Gordon. But for us today these savagely critical comments reveal an earthy, emotionally charged side to Gordon, rarely glimpsed elsewhere in his writing.

Great events beyond the quarrels of scientists such as Gordon and Sparrman were coming to a head at this time. Although the effects of the French Revolution took some years to reach and be felt by the rest of the world — and the Cape Colony in particular — nevertheless, 1789 was a year of great stress, turmoil and activity for Gordon personally.

To begin with he was once more very ill. In February 1789, writing to the governor and Council of Policy, excusing his absence from a meeting, he complains of a 'heavy cough, still mostly at night, accompanied by fevers'.[25] From two separate sources it is further recorded that Gordon gave up his command at this time. The burgher, Hendrik Cloete, writing to the younger Swellengrebel in March 1790, said: 'About a year ago Colonel Gordon laid down his command and has not yet entered on any other.'[26] Unfortunately nothing more is added to this rather terse announcement. However, the remark is confirmed by another letter, written in December 1789 to the stadholder, Willem V, by Governor Van de Graaff: '... because of the Military Chief's continual indisposition, the garrison has been commanded all this time by the honest and capable Baron Von Hugel'.[27]

Baron J. H. von Hugel was the chief of the German mercenary regiment known as the Württemberg. This unit replaced the Meuron Regiment, mentioned earlier, which was in transit to Ceylon. This German baron can hardly have been Gordon's choice as a replacement. But the matter of Gordon's illness and his relationship with the governor will be taken up later.

If Gordon was so ill that he had to relinquish his command, it is astonishing how much activity he was yet involved in during this period — including the breeding of sheep. During this year, 1789, Gordon imported four rams and six ewes from Holland.[28] They were merino sheep of Spanish origin and were provided by a benevolent group known as the 'Hollandsche Maatschappij tot Nut van het Algemeen'. They were specially imported to improve the blood line of the Colony's flocks and were intended, in the words of one authority, to be a source of 'survival and welfare for the people'.

It appears that Gordon had long planned this step. As far back as April 1778 he had written to his friend and patron, Hendrik Fagel, saying that nothing would give him greater pleasure than to receive the 'Spanish' sheep and that he would take every possible care of them.[29] Why the sending of the sheep was delayed for eleven years is not clear, but when they arrived Gordon sent them to the Company's farm, Groenekloof, which is near present-day Darling. Here the sheep were kept apart. They acclimatized very well and multiplied so that when the request came to return them to Holland, Gordon was able to comply, sending back the same number he had originally received, while keeping the surplus that he had bred.

In 1792 Gordon gave three rams to the Van Reenen brothers, who bred them with Cape ewes, systematically improving their flocks. Later with some Spanish ewes — a gift from Gordon — Sebastiaan van Reenen was able to build up another flock of pure-bred merinos, and this greatly assisted the distribution of fine animals in the Colony. When Commissioner Nederburg visited the Cape in 1792 he remarked that the wool of the merino sheep was six inches long while that of the hybrids reached four inches. The sheep flourished apace from then on and so it is that Gordon must be credited with the foundation of the South African wool industry.

Gordon's sheep also played a vital role in the inception of the Australian wool industry. At his death Mrs Gordon sold twenty-six of his flock of thirty-two merinos to two English sea captains who took them to New South Wales. Even though only a few survived the voyage, those that remained were eagerly accepted by at least half a dozen of the pioneer wool growers of that colony. Thus Gordon's flock, bred at Groenekloof, also played a valuable part in the establishment of the Australian wool industry.

In 1789, however, there were other matters of far less pleasant import occupying Gordon. From various documents and letters in the Cape Archives, it is clear that he was not on good terms with Governor Van de Graaff. Despite the fact that Gordon was seriously ill there was a major altercation raging between them.[30]

It is not necessary here to investigate all the tedious details of this row. In essence the dispute centred on the subject of the recruits, oddly called the Pepinieren – a name derived from the French word for a tree nursery. It seems that these recruits had given Gordon some cause for dissatisfaction as far back as 1787 when he had complained to a visiting commissioner that he had only eighty men in his 'pippiniere'. Of these, some were old and broken while others were diseased; at all events none was suitable for the Cape which needed strong, healthy men for its mountainous terrain.

A year later the Council of Policy decided to start a military training school for children at the Cape. But this came to nothing when the Here XVII broke off the whole project, indignantly protesting that their original plans had been exceeded and their wishes ignored. The governor and the Council of Policy (including Gordon) were made to pay the extra expenses out of their own pockets.

But the principal quarrel concerning Gordon and the recruits broke out in February 1789, just about the time that he fell so ill. The trouble stemmed from the fact that a French officer in the Meuron Regiment had been appointed, from Europe, over Gordon's head as commandant of the Pepinieren. This officer, a major, bore the resounding name of Simon, Chevalier de Sandolroy, though Gordon in his correspondence refers to him curtly and contemptuously as 'Sandol'.

The quarrel started when Sandolroy accused Gordon of withholding rations and so starving the Pepinieren. He then brought his accusation before a military commission that was visiting the Cape at the time. (It was there to see how the defences could be improved.) While this was being considered, Sandolroy went further: when paying the recruits he (Gordon) omitted to dock their wages with the cost of their shirts and boots as was customary.

Gordon fell ill at this point but still managed to send two reports on the matter to the Council of Policy during February 1789. It becomes clear that the whole affair brought about a clash between the governor and Gordon – the governor taking Sandolroy's side. This is documented in a series of letters written in 1790 and now housed in the Cape Archives.[31] Except for copies of letters purporting to be to and from the governor and the Council of Policy, this collection of letters is from Gordon. No indication of the person to whom the correspondence is addressed is given, but it seems likely that they were draft letters to one of the members of the military commission mentioned above.

The main letter in the collection shows Gordon in a

76. *Governor Cornelis Jacob van de Graaff – no friend to Gordon.*

highly indignant mood, stating that Sandolroy had waited until he had fallen ill to take matters into his own hands. The sequence of events is not very clear but it appears that Sandolroy was jailed at one stage and then released at the governor's command. ('The Governor supporting Captain Sandol, *haut à la main*', according to Gordon.) Despite Gordon's strongest protests that the good order and peace of the garrison was being disturbed, the governor took no notice 'saying that I was to obey, that he was the Governor and knew what he had to do, etc, etc'. To add to this high-handed behaviour, an increase in the recruits' wage allowance was given and two of their troublemakers were promoted to sergeant. In October 1789, to Gordon's fury, Sandolroy was promoted from captain to major.

Even though a commission of enquiry, set up by the governor and Council and reporting in January 1790, found that Sandolroy was guilty, it appears that he was left in command of his troops and undisturbed in his post. At any rate, this was the position at the end of April 1790 when Gordon wrote the letter from which the above quotations have been taken.

Before leaving this letter it is worth noting what Gordon has to say regarding his health, as he ends off his last paragraph. With no attempt at elegance of style in presenting his case – though perhaps it was not necessary in the circumstances, he states: 'I have been in this singular post for over ten years and in the most difficult of times I have never sought anything but the welfare of the Company and the Service, even to the neglect of my own fortune, and I have had almost nothing but unpleasantness, because of which my health has been badly damaged....'

A brief look at the character of Governor Van de Graaff would be instructive at this point, before continuing with the case of Sandolroy.

According to the historian Theal: 'He was arbitrary and headstrong in disposition, violent in temper and careless in business matters.'[32] Van de Graaff's behaviour in Council meetings was particularly odious: '. . . violent scenes often took place. On one occasion the governor in a passion drew his sword and would have wounded the dispenser Le Sueur, if the latter had not warded off the blow with his cane. The proceedings, as recorded, contain protests and counter-protests in great profusion.' As Theal puts it: 'Whole reams of paper are filled with records of petty quarrels of no interest to anyone now.'[33]

It can be seen therefore that Gordon was not recording something exceptional or out of character when he complained of the governor's action in supporting the French captain. Van de Graaff was behaving in his customary manner.

But the Sandolroy episode was not at an end. In June 1791 Governor Cornelis Jacob van de Graaff sailed to Europe, handing over the administration of the Colony to the secunde (or vice-governor) Rhenius. A year later, just before the arrival of the commissioners general, Nederburg and Frijkenius, Gordon had Sandolroy clapped in irons.

When the commissioners arrived in False Bay the first petition they received was from Sandolroy, asking to be released. The commissioners considered his plea immediately and informed the Council of Policy that he was to be freed. But hardly two days had gone by before Gordon came in person to the commissioners demanding that Sandolroy be re-arrested. They did not immediately accede to Gordon and he doggedly repeated his demand on 11 July, 21 September and 31 October 1792. On the final occasion a charge sheet containing forty-five accusations against Sandolroy was handed in accompanied by the signatures of twenty-six other persons.

At this the commissioners relented and Sandolroy was once more taken into custody. It was decided to send him to Batavia for legal proceedings. Sandolroy protested bitterly against arrest and again pleaded for release.

The commissioners were in somewhat of a quandary since, while admiring Gordon's abilities, they were unsure as to the impartiality of his accusations. Nevertheless they proceeded with their plans. The French officer was taken on board the ship *Regt door Zee* which was sailing to Batavia. However, they also sent secret instructions to the captain about Sandolroy. He was to be 'set free and handled with every respect once the *Regt door Zee* had left behind Table Bay and passed the Chavonnes Battery'. More telling was their message to Governor General Alting and Commissioner Stokkum concerning the Sandolroy affair. They requested that he should be the subject of an impartial legal investigation, alleging that 'his principal accuser Colonel Gordon, has demonstrated a personal animosity against this man that far exceeds the bounds of propriety'.

The end result of these communications and actions was that Sandolroy was discharged by the Council of Justice of Batavia in May 1793. It was not possible to judge him, it said, since there was insufficient information.

The story, however, does not end there. Gordon soon got to hear of the Batavian court's findings and again complained to Nederburg and Frijkenius, asking for the court's decision to be reviewed. They replied that they knew nothing about the proceedings in Batavia but that they would investigate the case on their return to the East. Once back in Batavia, however, the commissioners did absolutely nothing to investigate or re-open the case. As for Sandolroy, his career flourished: he was promoted once more to major and in 1794 he was made a lieutenant-colonel.

Gordon's role in this whole affair is a strange, almost pathetic, one. It is clear that the commissioners perceived his pursuit of Sandolroy as excessive and unbalanced, if not, indeed, as outright persecution. Even given Van de Graaff's rebarbative character, Gordon's pleadings first to the military commission and then to Nederburg and Frijkenius, lack total conviction, if not dignity.

What is not certain is how ill Gordon was, and how much his illness affected his behaviour during the whole Sandolroy affair. We know that his attendance at the Council of Policy was very irregular at this time, most of his communication with that body and the governor taking place by correspondence. Furthermore, if, as Hendrik Cloete reported, he laid down his command from about February or March 1789 and still had not resumed his post a year later, it argues that he was indeed gravely ill. Yet during 1789 Gordon was able to import and see to his merino sheep. He was capable enough to write a long and detailed letter, mentioned earlier, to Horace Bénédict de Saussure (without, incidentally, mentioning his illness). In addition, we know that he made an inspection of the defence works on 20 June 1789 in the company of the military commission alluded to above. It is baffling, for without further evidence no firm conclusion about Gordon's behaviour at this critical period of his life can be drawn. The fact that he started to keep a meteorological journal from his home in September 1789 could either mean he was so ill that that was all he could occupy himself with, or it could mean that he felt well enough to start a new daily scientific routine.[34]

A further puzzle is the duplicity of Nederburg and Frijkenius in the matter or Sandolroy. They were powerful men and did not need to hide their actions or bluff anyone. According to Dr Anna Boëseken, who has made a study of this affair, they would have been less tactful had they not admired Gordon so much. In their report of 13 May 1793 they speak of Gordon's 'exceptional zeal and exemplary lack of self-interest'. They made him a special award of 1 500 rix-dollars, an 'extra-ordinaire douceur' as they phrased it. Gordon expressed his gratitude for this but asked at the same time to be relieved of the debt imposed upon him for expenses incurred in connection with the military training school for children, referred to above. This was granted and in 1794 a remission of his debt was made. However, the cost of keeping his horses, reckoned at 600 rix-dollars per annum, was to be at his, and not the Company's, expense in future.

All this may demonstrate respect for Gordon by the commissioners, but in the old matter of the division of power between the governor and the military commander, they were less accommodating. The governor, they ruled, had the fullest right to act as head of the military (Hoof van Militêre Sake), only taking care that his orders were handed in person to the head of the militia (Hoof van Milisie) – in other words, to Gordon and not to subordinate officers.

Probably with the Sandolroy affair in mind, a further request for a separate military court was submitted by Gordon at this time (July 1793). This was refused by the commissioners, who ruled that all cases involving the military should be handled by the Council of Justice but that two officers from the garrison should be present at such times.

Interestingly enough, Gordon's status as a member of the Council of Policy was also changed at this same time. He was given permission not to attend the meetings of the Council unless military matters were to be discussed, or unless letters from the Here XVII or the Council of Batavia were tabled.

At this stage it is pertinent to ask: when did Gordon's health improve to the point that he was able to resume his command and normal activities?

In June 1791 a lady called Mary Anne Parker visited the Cape. She was accompanying her husband, a sea captain, on a voyage round the world. During her stay she had considerable contact with the Gordons. As the following extracts from her account of the visit demonstrate, there was nothing to show that Gordon was ill then. On the contrary, one can infer that he was in fine form. It is worth quoting fairly extensively from Mrs Parker since her descriptions of the Gordon family are vivid, sympathetic and enlightening.[35]

Our baggage arrived the next day, and we were busily employed, having engaged ourselves to dine with Colonel Gordon. The hour of dinner was two o'clock; the colonel obligingly sent his carriage for us, which was very acceptable, the weather being intensely hot, and the pavement intolerably bad. The Villa where the colonel resides is situated a few miles from the town, on the summit of a hill commanding a most pleasant and extensive view by sea and land. The good colonel is already well known for his Museum, and Manuscripts relative to Natural History, and his many enterprising journeys to the interior parts of that country; for which he was eminently qualified on account of his extensive knowledge of the language, manners, and customs of the Hottentots, by whom he is almost adored. The respect and regard which I bear to this family forbids my passing over in silence the polite and friendly attention I received from Mrs Gordon, who is a Swiss lady, and who most agreeably acquiesces in whatever may tend to render those comfortable who have the happiness of being ranked among her acquaintance. After what I have said, it will easily be supposed that their children are taught the same engaging attention to strangers....

We received another invitation from Mrs Gordon, and accordingly went in the afternoon to Green Point[36] to tea; after which we returned home to supper, and the evening concluded with dancing, which they are remarkably fond of at this town....

The next morning we again visited the hospitable villa, where we were regaled in a manner that bespoke the attention of the providers: during a desert [sic] that would have gained applause from the nicest Epicure, singing was introduced, in the course of which we were favoured with a Hottentot song from the Colonel: to describe any part of it would have been impossible; but, without a wish to offend, I must say that it appeared to me the very reverse of all that is musical or harmonious; and the Colonel, who gave us strict charge not to be frightened with what we were to hear, seemed to enjoy the laughter it occasioned. Different songs having gone round, the Colonel's son amused us with several pieces upon the organ; and shortly after we were agreeably surprised with the bands belonging to the regiments without: nor did this conclude the amusement; for, after drinking coffee, we danced until our return into town, when the same music accompanied us, to prevent, I suppose, our spirits from drooping at the thought of leaving such good company.

The last occasion on which the Parkers dined with the Gordons was as members of a 'select party' that included 'Mr. Pitt, a relation of Lord Chatham.... We were occupied in feasting and singing till the evening, when we returned home....'

Obviously Gordon had recovered from whatever illness had plagued him between 1789 and 1790. From Mrs Parker we have as genial a picture of the Gordon family as that in Macquarie's account of 1788. (Not mentioned by Mrs Parker is the fact that the previous month [May 1791] Mrs Gordon had given birth to a fourth son, James Charles Gerhard.[37]) Perhaps the whole atmosphere at the Cape had lightened with the departure of Governor Van de Graaff, an event which also took place during June 1791.

Another British visitor to the Cape at this time was a certain George Hamilton, a surgeon, who was travelling on HMS *Pandora*, the ship that had been despatched to arrest the mutineers of *The Bounty*. He has interesting things to say about Gordon's generosity with manuscripts and drawings: 'Here we met with many civilities from colonel Gordon; a gentleman no less eminent for his private virtues than his extraordinary military and literary accomplishments. From his labours all the host of voyagers and historians of that part of the globe will, at some future period, be favoured with his works unmutilated.'[38] Once again we have testimony to the belief, held by so many travellers, that Gordon would be bringing out his own book sometime in the future.

We have heard from various sources of Gordon's 'curiosities', or of his 'cabinet' at Schoonder Sigt. It was a veritable museum of natural history according to a German officer, C.C. Best, who wrote in May 1792:[39]

On a certain day I and my other fellow soldiers were introduced to the Commandant of the Garrison, the Commander in Chief, Gordon, a Scot by birth, a great Nature-studier who has completed various travels into the interior of Africa. He received us very courteously, told us of his journeys and showed us various

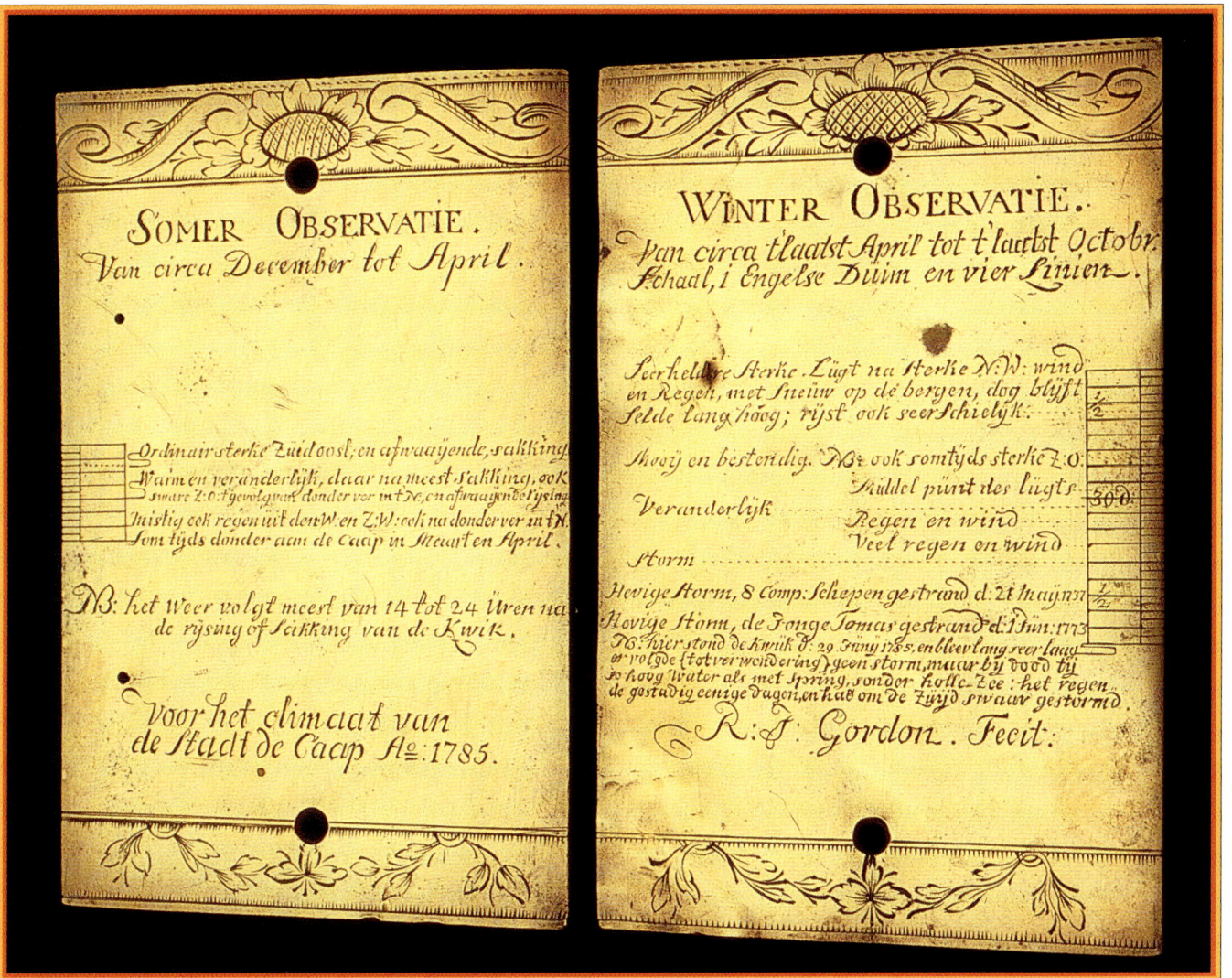

77. *The brass plates from Gordon's portable barometer.*

curiosities of the country; among others a stuffed 'Kameelpardel', a Giraffe, which was a female shot by himself. This singular animal is, from head to foot, fifteen or sixteen foot tall higher in front than behind and is the tallest of all four-footed animals known till now. Its hide is spotted like a tiger's; on its head are two small horns. It lives in deserts and forests, in herds. The commander owns a considerable Nature Cabinet of stuffed four-footed animals, birds, small reptiles and fishes which he let us see and describe more closely with the result that I spent a most agreeable morning with this eminent man.

Unfortunately the officer does not tell us where and when Gordon shot this giraffe and no one else had described this stuffed animal. It is just possible that it is the one mentioned in one of Gordon's papers. The description is on a full page written mostly in his eccentric English but with some Dutch phrases.[40] It starts thus: 'I have verified those dimensions on the skeleton and have found them exact. geschoten [i.e. shot] anno 1791. Skelet van het Cameelpard van Jan Visagie [i.e. skeleton of Jan Visagie's camelopard].' Gordon then goes on to give various dimensions of the animal and continues: '. . . thus should this cameleopard be 10 inches and taller than my second cameleopard and a foot taller than my first of which the dimensions are in my journal . . . N.B: this Cameleopard was shot on the 28 degree south latitude in the longitude of Capetown by Jan Visagie a lad thirteen years old. R.J. Gordon.' Nothing is said of the skin here so that we can do no more than speculate about this 'singular [stuffed] animal'. It is unlikely, however, if not nearly impossible, that Gordon himself shot the one standing in his 'cabinet'.

Gordon, it would seem from circumstantial evidence, had by now given up any idea of again travelling into the interior. It was almost certainly during the August of 1791 that he gave his portable barometer away to an English naval surgeon who had stopped at the Cape while travelling to the Hawaiian Islands. The surgeon's name was Archibald Menzies and he reported the matter thus:[41]

I brought with me a kind of portable barometer for which I was entirely indebted to the liberality of the late *Colonel Gordon*, at the Cape of good Hope. That gentleman, when he understood that we had no portable barometer on board for ascertaining the height of any mountain that might be ascended during the voyage, presented me, in the most generous manner, with his own, which he had long been in the habit of using in the interior parts of Africa, and which had accompanied him in his interesting journeys through that country for many hundred leagues.

Menzies then goes on to describe the instrument, praising its simplicity of operation and the ease with which it could be carried.

To cap this story, two plates which had been affixed to the barometer were recovered at Ceres in the Cape in 1925 and these are now in the South African Cultural History Museum in Cape Town. They are inscribed with a scale in fractions of an English inch together with information about the Cape weather. There is a winter plate which is dated 1785 and a summer plate which is inscribed 'R. J. Gordon Fecit'. They were probably removed by Gordon because the information would have been inappropriate for the regions to which Menzies was travelling.

Again there is a certain poignancy about this episode. Gordon must have realized then, in 1791, that he would not be travelling into the unknown and unmapped interior again. Was it his health, his taxing military duties, or the general state of the country that made him draw this conclusion?

There were indeed grave problems besetting the Cape Colony.[42] Van de Graaff's unsatisfactory and arbitrary rule had caused his recall. The Company itself was virtually insolvent. (In 1790 expenditure had already been drastically reduced.) The Württemberg Regiment was ordered to Java; all the work on fortifications was stopped and the military posts in the countryside were abandoned and sold. Even the governor's country retreat at Newlands was disposed of, and there was a wholesale reduction of Company slaves, animals and vehicles. Indeed, it was to investigate the sorry state of the Dutch East India Company that the commission, mentioned earlier in connection with the Sandolroy affair, was formed in August 1791. The two commissioners, Sebastiaan Cornelis Nederburg and Simon Frijkenius, were sent to the Cape and to Batavia to reorganize the entire structure of the Company. They arrived at the Cape in June 1792 – the one a senior legal man and the other a naval captain. In their words, the situation was 'appalling'; there was 'bitterness everywhere'.

Apart from their mandate to increase income and reduce expenses, the commission also saw fit to look at the defences of the Colony. Shortly after they had arrived they held a meeting, led by Gordon, to discuss the state of near war with the 'Bushmen' on the north-eastern frontier. As a result, the commandos were called out from Stellenbosch, Swellendam and Drakenstein and heavy losses were inflicted on the 'Bushmen' (over 500 were killed). The commandos returned home towards the end of 1792.

In 1793 there was trouble once more on the Eastern frontier when large numbers of Xhosa crossed the Fish River and devastated white farms. Again the commandos were called out, this time under the leadership of the new landdrost of Graaff-Reinet, Maynier. After some inconclusive engagements, an uneasy peace was made in November and the commandos were disbanded. Both these campaigns must have aroused somewhat ironic reflections in Gordon when he considered the time and effort he had spent in 1777 and 1778 trying to make peace with these frontier tribesmen.

In the meanwhile the commissioners had continued their reforms and restructuring of the Colony. Early in September 1793 they left for Batavia, having done what they could. As head of the Colony they appointed an official on the point of retirement, Abraham Josias Sluysken by name, who had been a director of trade for the Company in Surat. Since Van de Graaff was still nominally governor, Sluysken was given the title of commissioner-general.

It was in this same month of September that Gordon presented a report to Commissioner-General Sluysken in the Council of Policy. The report was on the subject of red-hot cannon balls and was of great importance to the defence of the Colony.[43] The matter was pressing, for in February 1793 France had declared war on the Netherlands and Great Britain.

The background to Gordon's studies and tests on this formidable weapon of war was the defeat by the British of a combined fleet of Spanish and French ships at Gibraltar in 1782. Victory was won when the British, by using red-hot cannon balls, set on fire and totally destroyed ten 'mobile fortresses' – massive ships armed with 212 cannons each. These ships had been deemed to be invulnerable to cannon fire.

The artillery of the Cape garrison had also begun to exercise with this newly discovered weapon. In 1789 an observer commented that he believed the Cape artillerymen were as proficient as any in the world in the use of these red-hot cannon balls.

Gordon, however, was not so impressed. He considered the technique used by the gunners to be inefficient. Not only did they take too long to load, but this was done in an unnecessarily cautious way. Believing that the glowing balls would explode the powder with disastrous consequences for the bystanders, they always fired the cannon too hastily. Accordingly, Gordon set his mind to this matter, and during September 1793 he performed a number of tests to prove that the prevalent fear of using red-hot balls was mistaken. As a result of these experiments he was able to develop a method of firing red-hot balls with almost the same ease as unheated ones. It was this method that he discussed in his report to Sluysken.

When he started his investigation he found the prevailing manner of working with the red-hot balls unsatisfactory. The guns would not have much success in action when enemy fire had to be faced 'without fuss or delay', Gordon told Sluysken. He was also anxious to determine how dangerous it really was to fire the balls red-hot. He wanted to see how long it took before the powder exploded and if this explosion would burst the barrel – a consequence, however, he strongly doubted. But these questions had to be answered in order to put the fears of the artillerymen at rest.

In his first trial, when Sluysken and others were present, Gordon showed very simply that red-hot cannon balls would not normally cause an explosion. He loaded an eighteen-pound cannon in the manner generally used for loading a heated ball. The cannon was not fired but Gordon and his party stood at a safe distance. They stood ready with a watch in order to determine how long it would take for the ball to burn through the elaborate wooden plug, which was between it and the powder, and then explode in the barrel. The ball merely cooled off and nothing happened.

As a further demonstration, Gordon proceeded to load a red-hot ball into the cannon, but this time against an ordinary rope plug, then in use only for cold cannon balls. At this point, to show the attendant artillerymen that there was nothing to be afraid of, Gordon sat on the cannon! After half an hour he had the rope plug pulled out. It had burned down by about an inch only and was still perfectly usable.

Further tests reinforced Gordon's demonstration that it was not necessary to use wooden plugs but that the ordinary rope plugs were perfectly usable with red-hot balls. His findings then were significant because they showed that the red-hot balls were just as easy to use and just as safe to handle as ordinary cannon balls. The cumbersome old manner of loading was therefore totally unnecessary and all the artillerymen's fears of the heated balls were completely unfounded.

Towards the end of his report Gordon said he was convinced that the Cape could not be conquered from the sea 'if everything were ready': an ironic comment in the light of the actual invasion. The Council of Policy showed 'great pleasure' at the report and at this demonstration of Gordon's 'zeal, management and skill'.

It is worth recording that during this same year of 1793 Gordon also had the time to keep up his correspondence with learned men in Europe. A letter to Professor Jan Hendrik van Swinden, 'a noted mathematician, physicist and an authority on magnetism', is preserved in the archives of the University of Leyden.[44] Gordon wrote to him on 4 February 1793, discussing the merits and demerits of various meteorological instruments and dealing in particular with measuring the humidity by means of a hygrometer. De Saussure's name is mentioned in this letter, but no reference is made as to whether Gordon was still in correspondence with the Swiss savant, though this may perhaps be inferred.

The letter to Professor Van Swinden appears to be the last one addressed by Gordon to his correspondents in Europe. No further letters have come to light and this should not surprise us. The Netherlands was now at war with France. Momentous events were taking place.

To start with, the Dutch East India Company was coming to the end of its life, and in February 1794 it declared itself unable to meet the interest on its loans. Then in July of the same year, Flanders fell to the French armies under General Pichegru. The outlook for the Orangists and Willem V, Prince of Orange, looked grim. In December the French armies crossed the frozen Waal and the Netherlands was defeated, though the French were welcomed by most of the Dutch populace. The Prince of Orange fled to England on 18 January 1795 and shortly afterwards the country declared itself 'the Republic of Batavia'.

Naturally these events had their effect on the Colony at the Cape. In October 1794, the chief advocate of the Company, P.J. Guepin, wrote a secret letter to Sluysken telling him of the French advances and warning him to be wary of European invaders of whichever nation they might be. Sluysken received the letter early in February 1795.[45]

The Colony itself was in turmoil. The burghers of Graaff-Reinet – a motley and disaffected collection of farmers – had many grievances, but were especially antagonistic to the landdrost Maynier, who, they claimed, did not act aggressively enough against the Xhosa or the 'Bushmen'. It was also alleged that he harboured runaway slaves and 'Hottentots'. In February 1794 these same burghers, calling themselves 'Nationals', ejected Maynier from office, forcing him to decamp to Cape Town. In response, Sluysken sent a commission to Graaff-Reinet, but after six weeks of parleying with the burghers, it too was expelled on 16 June 1795.[46]

The next day similar events took place in Swellendam where the landdrost was expelled and a 'republic', together with a 'national assembly', was declared by the burghers.

There was not much the commissioner-general or the commander of the garrison could do about these events. Fearing an invasion, all their energies were focused on the Cape fortifications. In March 1794 two forts were completed in Simon's Town, and later three forts (Sluysken, Gordon and Little Gibraltar) were built at Hout Bay. Installed at each gun emplacement was an oven to heat cannon balls.

The troops under Gordon's command were now sadly depleted since the departure of the Württemberg regiment. His infantry, known as the National Battalion, consisted of twenty-five officers and 546 soldiers, and his artillery of twenty-three officers and 403 rank and file. In addition to these units there was a corps of 'Pandours', made up of 210 'coloured' men and 'Hottentots'.[47]

Truly, it was not a great army – a fact recognized by a Dutch sea captain, Cornelis de Jong, who visited the fortifications with Gordon on 29 February 1795. His comments nevertheless had a surprisingly optimistic tone. The defences, he claimed, were in a 'formidable position', due to the efforts of Gordon. If only a further 2 500 soldiers were available, the country would then be well-nigh invincible to invasion by an enemy fleet. For instance, between Camps Bay and Fort Knokke there were nineteen ovens which together could heat up 450 cannon balls within fourteen minutes.[48]

The great fear was that an invading French fleet would use first-hand knowledge of the Colony's defences, gathered during the French regiments' presence at the Cape from 1781 to 1784. The great irony, however, was that the fleet that invaded the Colony just four months after De Jong's laudatory remarks was not French. It was British.

78. Hoodia gordonii. *'Stapelias' were of special botanical interest to Gordon.*

CHAPTER ELEVEN

BETRAYAL AND SUICIDE

(JUNE – OCTOBER 1795)

The British invasion; Patriots versus Orangists; dual loyalties; the Battle of Muizenberg; surrender of the Cape; Gordon's 'betrayal'; suicide; Gordon's achievements and character

On 11 June 1795 Commissioner Sluysken received a report from the resident officer at Simon's Town that a number of ships of unknown nationality had sailed into False Bay and were now lying at anchor there.[1] There was a Dutch frigate in the bay and the captain had sent a lieutenant to the ships to find out what country they represented. He was to wave a flag if the ships were friendly but this had not happened, and at the time of the report the lieutenant had not returned.

Sluysken immediately called an extraordinary meeting of the Council of Policy for about 10.30 pm in the Castle. Because the deliberations were clearly of a military nature, Gordon was also present. A unanimous decision was taken to raise the alarm and summon the burghers from the outlying districts to Cape Town. In addition, Lieutenant-Colonel De Lille was ordered to leave for Simon's Town immediately with 200 infantrymen and 100 bombardiers.

The Council adjourned shortly after midnight, but Gordon and his fellow members remained at the Castle. This was as well, for they were again summoned at half past two on the same morning, 12 June. The lieutenant had returned from the newly arrived ships with an 'officer' bearing letters for the authorities at the Cape. They were from the British admiral, Sir George Keith Elphinstone, and from Major-General James Henry Craig. This same 'officer' (who was Hercules Ross, Craig's secretary) had just arrived at the Castle on horseback.

The most important letter was for Sluysken and Gordon, and came from Admiral Elphinstone, inviting them to meet him on his flagship *The Monarch*. He had important information to convey as well as a letter from the Prince of Orange. In his letter Elphinstone stressed that he particularly wanted to see Gordon – alone, if possible.

Replying to these requests the Council of Policy said that Sluysken and Gordon's presence was required at Cape Town. However, they suggested that the information and the letter be sent to them by a trusted officer. In the meantime the Dutch lieutenant who had been aboard the flagship initially, now reported to the Council on the state of the British fleet. There were six heavy warships, together with a frigate and two sloops, and in addition there was an expeditionary force on board under the command of Major-General Craig.

The Council now found itself in a considerable predicament. So far as was known in the Cape, Great Britain was the ally of the Netherlands in the war against France. However, as mentioned in chapter ten, the Council had been warned in a letter from the Company's chief advocate, Guepin, that the Netherlands might suddenly change sides. Writing in October 1794, Guepin had pointed out that the country was in turmoil, and that the French army was advancing and had already overrun part of its territory. He therefore had advised the Cape Command to be on the alert and in the highest state of preparedness. This letter was received in February 1795 and was the most reliable information that the Council of Policy had at its disposal.

To add to this uncertainty, there were also divisions in the political loyalties of the garrison and burghers. The overwhelming majority of the burghers and a large proportion of the troops, including most of the artillery, were strongly committed to the Netherlands Patriot Party. Briefly speaking, this party wanted to abolish the stadholdership and form a republic in alliance with France. On the other hand, most of the company officials (including Sluysken) and most of the military officers (including Gordon) stood for the Orange Party, which was loyal to the stadholder and the House of Orange, and which wanted to maintain the status quo in the Netherlands.

That Gordon was an ardent supporter of the House of Orange has been demonstrated and affirmed more than once before in these pages. In the same way, Gordon's attachment to his former colleagues in the Scots Brigade and his warm pro-British feelings have been evident throughout his career. It will be remembered that in 1787, following his second 'visit' to the Cape, Colonel Dalrymple had written concerning Gordon: 'The colonel... has an English heart tho Born in Holland and is Strong in the Prince of Orange's Interest.' In the same letter to Henry Dundas — the future British minister of war — Dalrymple went on to say that, should the British attack the Cape, Gordon might take sides against the rule of the Company.

More than this, the British authorities firmly believed that Gordon would even welcome their attack on the Cape. The source of this belief had been the agent of the English East India Company in the Cape, John Pringle, who had visited the country early in 1795 and had reported that Gordon would be 'kicked out' should the Cape hear that France had overrun Holland. But if Gordon could be helped in time, then the Cape garrison could be persuaded to join Britain.

Certainly Elphinstone and Craig believed that Gordon would be willing to help them take the Cape, either in secret or openly. Presumably this was why they were so anxious to reach Gordon when they arrived in False Bay. Apart from Hercules Ross, they apparently sent another messenger — a certain Alexander Farquar — with letters for Sluysken and Gordon, the contents of which are unknown. Answers to these letters were received by Elphinstone on 12 and 14 June.

On 13 June the British commanders acceded to the Council's request and handed over the Prince of Orange's letter together with further 'valuable information'. Two officers, Lieutenant Colonel A. Mackenzie and Captain Hardy of the sloop *Echo*, were chosen to deliver these despatches.

The mission met Sluysken immediately on their arrival in Cape Town. Apart from the stadholder's letter, they delivered a report on the situation in the Netherlands drawn up by Elphinstone and Craig. The two officers next visited Gordon, apparently at his house. Hardy has given this account of the meeting:

... upon seeing us [Gordon] shewed us a Standard, saying there is the Orange Standard for you, and afterwards said if we were come to protect the Cape in favour of the Prince of Orange he was very glad to see us. And we should meet with his hearty support, but if we came to take possession of it for England he would fight against us till his last breath, this he said without any previous conversation.

This report succinctly captures the whole motive for Gordon's behaviour during the next few months. It is interesting that Gordon delivered his speech 'without any previous conversation'. It was as though he had thought his own position out very carefully and did not want any ambiguity about the priority of his loyalties. Nevertheless, it appears that the British officers were able to convince Gordon that the expeditionary force really had come to defend the interests of the House of Orange and not to take the Cape for Great Britain. Hardy writes: 'We parted perfect friends, upon assuring him of what he must have seen afterwards by the letter in Council.'

What took place in the meeting of the Council that same night is of great interest. First, the contents of the stadholder's letter were discussed. Briefly, it enjoined the Cape authorities to allow British troops into the Castle

79. *Admiral Sir George Keith Elphinstone at the Battle of Muizenberg.*

and elsewhere in the Colony; to allow British warships entrance to Cape harbours; and to regard these troops and ships as those of a friendly power, there to defend the Cape.

Elphinstone and Craig's report was intended to supply some background to the Prince's letter. It recounted the surrender of the Dutch armies to the French and the flight of the Prince of Orange to England. However, the report continues, Britain and her allies were amassing large armies and they were determined to drive the French from Holland.

But, as historians have pointed out, this information was deliberately incomplete and wrong. In the first place nothing was said about the fact that the Dutch Patriots had enthusiastically welcomed the French, or that the national government had changed and that the stadholdership had been abolished. The British version tried to give the impression that the Netherlands had been ruthlessly conquered. They certainly did not want the fact known that the Dutch government still stood and that the majority of the people saw the French as friends.

In the Council it appears that Gordon accepted the British commanders' interpretation without any more ado. He recommended that the British be accepted as allies, as the French had been between 1781 and 1783. Nevertheless, said Gordon, before they landed certain conditions should be set, namely: that the present Cape administration should not be changed; that the Cape should be held for its 'lawful sovereign' (that is, for the 'States General of the United Netherlands and the hereditary Stadholdership of the Prince of Orange'); and that the British troops should fall under the command of the commissioner-general.

However, although the other members of the Council were also strongly pro-Orange, they were not prepared to allow the British troops to land. It seemed wise to play for time. Accordingly, in the early hours of the morning of 14 June, the Council replied to Elphinstone and Craig: the fleet could take in provisions, but only small parties of unarmed men could be landed. The Council also expressed its gratitude to the British government for its interest in the 'protection' of the Cape. In case of a French attack the Council would be glad to make use of British troops, though the Colony was, it said – not without a hint of irony – in the happy position of being able to defend itself against an enemy power.

Since the arrival of the British in False Bay, Gordon had been observed with great suspicion by both soldiers and burghers at the Cape. One observer, writing a year later, had this to say about Gordon's attitude in the Council of Policy: 'It is said that Gordon at once advised the acceptance of the protection of the British. That he declared "that the English were nevertheless our friends that under any circumstances we had to fear nothing, that the French were atheists, regicides, robbers, etc."'[2]

Unquestionably Gordon was a faithful adherent of the House of Orange as well as being pro-British. He himself made this abundantly clear, as can be seen in the following two documents.[3] The first letter, written to Admiral Elphinstone on 14 June, must have been composed shortly after the Council meeting. It is given here without changing Gordon's syntax or spelling:

Honourable Sir ... I lament in the highest degree the unhappy turn of affairs in holland and wish you heartily welcome in this Colonie having read with the greatest satisfaction out of your official papers that the basis is, unanimously to repulse an Enemy that wants to wrest it from its lawfull Sovereign, the Republic of the seven United Provinces with their Hereditary Stadtholder the Prince of Orange, according to our ancient constitution (which I have sworn to) and Guard it together for them, and be assured that I shall use my utmost exertions in fulfilling this my duty. I am further sorry that impardonable neglectfullness of the Officer of our Frigate has been the cause of an allarm that has set the whole country in an uproar [Here Gordon was referring to the lieutenant who first went aboard Elphinstone's flagship and neglected to wave the flag, thus implying that the English were not 'friendly'.] which I must add is much augmented by bad designing people how [sic.] think to find their ruined finances reestablished by French principles and anarchy, and others how [sic.] are the endoctrinated dupes, however this is the case; and in this moment prudence is necessary to bring things to a proper end.

I am extremely sorry that I could not hitherto come aboard to pay my respects to you, being a Subordinate, however Sir George, be assured that I shall serve the Common cause with all my Exertions, that I abhor French principles, and that if our unhappy republic, where I am born in and served these 42 years, should surrender (which God forbids) that then I am a Greatbritainer.

I have the Honor to enclose a letter from Mr Pringle who I am very sorry is not here as he might be very useful – and remain with the greatest regard &c. (Signed) R.J. Gordon.

The second document is the letter from 'Mr Pringle' that Gordon mentions. It will be recalled that he was the agent for the English East India Company who had been at the Cape in the early part of 1795.

Cape of G.H., 18th March 1795.
Circumstances having rendered it necessary that I should leave this place, I think it advisable hereby to certify to the Commander-in-Chief of any British Force which may arrive here, that I solemnly believe the most perfect Confidence may be placed in the honor, Loyalty and Principles of Col. Gordon and that he may on all occasions be treated with accordingly. (signed) John Pringle, Agent for the Honble. English East India Comp.

The Commander-in-Chief of any British Force that may arrive at the Cape.

Both these documents deserve careful appreciation since they give an unequivocal expression of Gordon's loyalties at this time. To a large measure they can help us comprehend his subsequent behaviour.

From the first sentence of the letter to Elphinstone it is plain that Gordon welcomed the British presence precisely because he believed that it was there to 'repulse' an invasion by the French and in so doing to 'Guard' the interests of the House of Orange. The British presence, therefore, was eminently compatible with Gordon's own beliefs and loyalties. His reference to 'bad designing people' in the next sentence refers, quite clearly, to Patriot Party sympathizers in the army and among the burghers. Both are, he implies, 'endoctrinated dupes'. However, Gordon was not unrealistic about the situation: 'prudence is necessary to bring things to a proper end,' he wisely adds.

The next paragraph reveals that, to a certain extent, Gordon already saw himself in common service with the British when he defers, as a 'Subordinate', to the admiral. This is further emphasized when Gordon talks of their 'Common cause' which he promises to further by his 'Exertions'. There can be no doubt of Gordon's loathing for 'French principles', by which he meant to include all revolutionary or Patriot Party ideas. What, however, did he mean when he hinted at the possibility that 'our unhappy republic ... should surrender'? He knew that the United Provinces had fallen to the French since this was precisely the information that Elphinstone and Craig had given to the Council of Policy the previous evening. Probably he was referring to the cause of the Prince of Orange, seeing it as symbolic of his country, for, as he says, let that fail and he would become 'a Greatbritainer'. It is an astonishing avowal by any criterion.

In a sense this letter represents the culmination of a life-

80. *The south-western Cape: a detail from Gordon's 'great map'.*

time's beliefs and loyalties. It will be recalled how the allegiance of the officers of the Scots Brigade was simultaneously coupled to the House of Orange and the King of Great Britain.[4] Gordon's loyalties in this letter are totally consistent and, as he himself said, he had 'sworn to' them.

The open letter from Pringle is also worth examining, mainly because it presumes that there will be a British invasion. It also presumes, even before the news of the Prince's flight, that the 'honor, Loyalty and Principles' of both Gordon and the British will coincide. At all events it is a curious document, a kind of testimonial reflecting some kind of premonition on Gordon's part. It means that long before the arrival of the British force he had made up his mind that there should be no doubt whatsoever as to where his loyalties lay.

But the British commanders did not have to deal only with Gordon. They had to convince the whole Council of Policy that the Cape should be handed over to them or, as they put it, be taken into their 'protection'. On 19 June Major-General Craig explained this to the Council. In addition, he expected the Company's troops to take an oath of loyalty to the British Crown. They would also be paid by the British, Craig said. Not surprisingly these proposals were rejected out of hand.

The next step taken by Elphinstone and Craig was to issue a proclamation. Put out on 22 June, it again offered British 'protection' on Craig's conditions. It also invited the people of the Cape to send a committee to confer with the British commanders.

On the same morning Admiral Elphinstone sent a copy of this proclamation to Gordon, asking him to inform his troops of the contents. This Gordon unhesitatingly refused to do and was praised by the members of the Council for his attitude. He was also enjoined to see that the substance of the British proclamation did not reach the troops and so affect their morale. But despite this resistance on Gordon's part to the most blatant of the British propaganda, the two commanders still believed firmly that Gordon would not influence his troops against them. Writing to Henry Dundas, the British minister of war in London, Elphinstone and Craig had this to say: 'We have every reason to expect that Coll. Gordon's corps is well inclined to us, indeed we have grounds for hoping that they would join us as soon as we land.'

The Council of Policy, however, was beginning to lose patience. As a result of the proclamation they decided to break off all negotiations with the British and to cease all supplies to the fleet. This was done against Gordon's advice. He felt that since the supplies had been promised they should be given, but only on the condition that the British issued no more documents.

So matters rested until 28 June when an American ship, the *Columbia*, carrying official despatches from Holland to the Cape and Batavia, arrived at Simon's Bay. Elphinstone immediately seized the mail and orders were given that no newspapers were to reach land. Despite these measures, however, one did elude the vigilance of the guards and came into the hands of a burgher ashore. It contained a notice of the States General, dated 4 March 1795, whereby all Netherlanders at home or in the colonies were freed of their oath of allegiance to the Prince of Orange. Other letters received by the inhabitants of the Cape at the time made it clear that France considered Holland an independent republic, that the stadholdership had been abolished and that the Dutch regarded the French as their allies.

It can be argued that the duty of the Commissioner-General Sluysken and his Council of Policy was now clear: the Cape should be defended by a determined opposition to the British. But, as we have seen, this was not how Gordon and his fellow Orangists (who, for the most part, were the officers responsible for the Colony's defence) viewed the position.

Not only were they totally antipathetic to 'French principles', but their loyalty was to the Prince of Orange, to whom they had sworn allegiance. The issue at the Cape, therefore, was simply how best to serve the cause of the exiled prince.

On the surface, the easiest and most obvious course of action to have followed – assuming that the British indeed represented the House of Orange – would have been to accept the 'protection' offerred by the British and simply handed the Cape over. However, the fact of the matter was that most of the burghers and most of the garrison were so avidly pro-Patriot that they would never have allowed such a move. The handing over of the Cape would therefore have to be done in a more subtle way. That is why Gordon wrote in his letter to Elphinstone: '... in this moment prudence is necessary to bring things to a proper end'.

The great problem now was the extent to which 'prudence' had to be employed. In fact – and in effect – it demanded not just reticence about his true opinions but a considerable measure of inanition, cunning and dissembling, as will be seen.

It is evident that from the start Gordon took very little part in the actual details of defending the Cape. One critic, virulently anti-Gordon, draws the reader's attention to the fact that in his account of the defence of the Cape he rarely mentions Gordon's name. This is, he declares, because Gordon contributed nothing to the defence.[5] Clearly this is an exaggeration, but to some degree it can be sustained. Gordon did very little to actively lead or motivate his men.

On 29 June, Sluysken, in consultation with Gordon, ordered the troops to be withdrawn from Simon's Town. Two weeks later the British landed 450 troops, to be followed next by 400 marines. In the meantime, the Cape troops took up their position at Muizenberg. One of the artillerymen stationed there was a Lieutenant Marnitz, an avowed Patriot, who was later to write a bitterly derisive account of the eventual surrender of the Cape.[6] The position at Muizenberg was strategically an excellent place to defend. But, as Marnitz observed, 'nature had to be helped'. According to the officers present, it was necessary to place batteries and breastworks on the seaward side. There is not the slightest indication, though, that Gordon was in any way inclined to 'help' nature. Together with Sluysken he visited Muizenberg many times but declared that the position could not be improved upon.

Nevertheless, the officers insisted that more help be obtained. In response to this demand the French engineer, Louis Michel Thibault, was despatched to the camp at Muizenberg. Thibault, who was strongly anti-Orange, records the incident himself thus: 'I went to colonel Gordon to inform him why I would be absent from the Garrison. Gordon answered: "Ah, by Jove! Give them entrenchments up to the chin, since they want them, but the English are too much our friends to cause us the least fears." Then, sarcastically, he burst out laughing.'[7]

This was not the only incident to elicit comment from the men Gordon commanded. Both he and Sluysken were fully aware that their delaying tactics were causing dissatisfaction among the burghers as well as the troops. Some 'prudence' was called for; and so, towards the end of July, both Sluysken and Gordon removed their Orange cockades, causing the rest of the Company's officers and officials to follow their example.

The position at Muizenberg was under the command of Lieutenant-Colonel De Lille, Gordon's second in command. Serving under him he had 200 men of the National Battalion, 120 artillerymen, 300 burgher cavalry and 150 pandours. On 7 August the British decided to mount their attack. Major-General Craig formed a column of 1 600 soldiers, marines and sailors and, during the early afternoon, this force, marching from Simon's Town, fell on the Dutch position, while four ships bombarded it from the sea.

Hardly had the first shot been fired when De Lille ordered the retreat, fleeing with his infantry in the greatest confusion. They stopped only when they had reached Lochner's farm, near present-day Diep River. Only Lieutenant Marnitz and a few others stayed behind to conduct some kind of defence at Muizenberg, firing at the British with two twenty-four-pound cannons, even though the guns, not properly mounted, embedded themselves in the sand after every salvo. But soon he and his fellow-artillerymen were forced to abandon the camp as well.

It may well be asked where Gordon was during this miserable action. He was certainly not at the front. It was only on that evening of 7 August that he and Sluysken appeared at Lochner's farm. They arrived to find that there was great discontent among the burghers at De

81. *A view of Table Bay: one of several illustrations that embellish the 'great map'.*

Lille's headlong retreat. The two commanders did their best to calm the men and De Lille was ordered back in the direction of Muizenberg. The next morning he returned to the head of the marsh known as Sandvlei. However, as soon as he saw a detachment of British marines and sailors approaching, in some places up to their arms in water, De Lille promptly took to his heels, without firing a shot.

De Lille later alleged that he 'withdrew' because a rumour had spread among the troops that the attacking army had great advantage in numbers, as well as having two cannons. In fact, it is highly probable that he himself had a hand in spreading these rumours. At all events they caused much uncertainty and confusion among the troops and they fled in disorder – this time as far as Wynberg.

It appears that Gordon too contributed to this 'withdrawal'. On that same morning of 8 August he was near the front line, watching the movement of the British troops through his spyglass. He must, therefore, have been aware that the rumours were unfounded. However, there is no evidence that he made any attempt to calm his troops or to stop the retreat. It appears that he even confirmed the rumour, reporting to Sluysken that there were '1500 Englishmen in three columns with two pieces of ordinance marching up'. In addition, Gordon clearly approved the retreat to Wynberg, even though he knew it could not be justified. From Wynberg, Thibault records, Gordon 'returned to Cape Town, laughing like a madman and played all the way back with two big dogs that served as his escorts'.[8]

From all this it must be quite clear that Sluysken, Gordon and De Lille, as well as other sympathizers among the higher ranks of the Company, were most successfully sabotaging the defence of the Cape. As the historian Theal said of De Lille: '. . . his conduct cannot be attributed to either imbecility or cowardice. He was a devoted adherent of the Orange Party, and regarded the English as supporters of the Orange cause, so would not fight against them. Successful resistance, in his opinion, would have been equivalent to giving up the country to the Nationals whom he hated.'[9]

In fact, at the insistence of the burghers, De Lille was arrested on a charge of treason on 10 August. He was taken to the Castle, examined by the fiscal, and then acquitted of the charge. However, he was kept in custody as there were fears for his safety. Captain Van Baalen, another Orangist, took De Lille's place at the Wynberg camp.

Gordon did not return to Wynberg at all during the following month, let alone take over the command there – an obvious action, if not an imperative need. Yet Gordon must have known that the British would attack this point. But as was the case at Muizenberg, there is no evidence that he made even the slightest attempt to strengthen the fortifications of the camp. He was busy elsewhere.

From about the middle of July 1795, when the British first began landing their troops at Simon's Town, Gordon was expending a great deal of energy and activity in all the batteries around Cape Town. One of his projects

was to heighten the breastworks of the large and small Mouille batteries. To this end he employed the somewhat eccentric means of filling cattle-hide sacks with the hair of Cape sheep. In addition, he had Sluysken's permission to install a new battery, Kijk in de Pot, on Gallows Hill. He insisted that this new battery was there to protect the large Mouille battery in case of an enemy landing at Mouille Point.

According to Marnitz, writing about these events a year later, the main reason for all this activity by Gordon was to keep the engineers and fortification workers occupied in Cape Town when they should have been used at Muizenberg and Wynberg. No gunnery expert before had seen fit to erect a battery on Gallows Hill. The cannon were so far from the shore that enemy ships would be well out of their range. In addition to this, the shore at the point was so rocky that even a fishing boat could not approach. Besides, it was already covered by a strong battery, so what enemy would be foolish enough to try and land there? Marnitz asked:

Is it not extremely suspicious that Sluysken and Gordon, whilst the enemy were expected every moment from the South East, did everything in their power to drive them away at the North West? That instead of satisfactorily fortifying Muizenberg and after that Wynberg, they for no purpose whatsoever wasted

82. *The Battle of Muizenberg.*

time, men and money? To whom must these wrong doings, these clear proofs of treachery not be evident? Forsooth the gallows ought to have remained on this hill forever in memory of the erectors there.'[10]

Marnitz is equally scathing about the repairs done to the batteries, finding them expensive and useless. The droll 'invention' of cattle hides stuffed with sheep hair drove the Patriot lieutenant into paroxysms of ponderous sarcasm: 'merely the stench of the skins would have driven the enemy back'. It is a pity, however, that 'the dogs took a liking to them, so that these costly repairs . . . served merely as a feast for these animals. This certainly no one could have foreseen, for who could have believed that dogs could be so bold as to attack batteries.'[11]

The Patriot-minded Thibault also has some anecdotes about Gordon's eccentric attempts at fortification at this time: 'He [Gordon] had the idea of placing a battery on a sandbank, diametrically opposite the side where the enemy could gain access to Cape Town. I strenuously opposed this useless innovation because when they were fired, the cannons would sink into the sand. He flared up, in the presence of Governor Sluysken, and promptly put me under arrest.' Thibault was later released but still had to erect Gordon's battery, which the Frenchman called an 'extravagance'. Thibault continued his story with a telling anecdote about the commander of the garrison: 'I remember that the Colonel visited his creation daily, amusing himself with a rifle, shooting from this battery towards the ocean, instead of employing his powder and his time to serve his country and to defend it.'[12]

While Gordon and Sluysken were occupied with the fortifications at Cape Town, the burghers and artillery officers at Wynberg were trying to convince their commanders that an attack should be mounted on Muizenberg, where the British had dug in.

The burghers' discontent had increased to such an extent by the end of August that Sluysken was finally forced to order Gordon and his chief of artillery to draw up a plan for an attack on the British positions. Taking their time, the two officers began to employ themselves in this task. Everyone, however, knew of the plans, and they were extensively discussed. It appears that the British were also fully aware of what to expect.

At the beginning of September 1795, four British warships took up their positions in front of Muizenberg, ready, from the sea, to bombard any attackers. This circumstance alone might have been enough for the commanders of the Dutch forces to call off their plans. But even this pretext was not necessary. On 4 September a British convoy of fourteen ships sailed into False Bay. Sluysken immediately ordered cannon, which had been moved to Wynberg, back to Cape Town and there was no further talk of an attack on Muizenberg.

The British now made ready for a decisive attack on Cape Town. Under the command of Major-General Alured Clarke 3 000 troops were landed, including strong detachments of sappers and artillerymen. At nine o'clock on the morning of 14 September 1795 the order to march was given. Clarke's force, which consisted of over 4 000 men, advanced in two columns.

At Wynberg, Major Van Baalen, the officer in command, made ready to meet the onslaught of the British. As Theal puts it: '. . . [he] arranged to meet the shock of battle by drawing up his forces in a faulty manner and placing his cannon in such a position that they were practically useless'. From this it can be readily inferred where this officer's loyalties lay. The burghers and some of the artillery officers objected strongly, but to no avail. Anyway, the British had hardly come within range when Van Baalen and most of his infantry took to their heels, fleeing in the direction of Cape Town. The burghers exclaimed furiously that they were betrayed. In the confusion a detachment of foot soldiers and artillerymen tried to stand fast but were soon thrown back by the strength of the British attack.

At this point, the 900-odd burgher horsemen from the outlying districts also gave up the struggle. They firmly believed that they had been betrayed by Sluysken and Gordon and the other officers of the National Battalion. They refused to retire and man the so-called 'French Lines' (the area between Fort Knokke and Devil's Peak, which was the last defensive position before Cape Town). It was very possible, they believed, that they would be trapped by this manoeuvre and land up as prisoners of war. In their opinion they did the only logical thing: they went home.

Indeed, there can be no question that Gordon should have been at Wynberg to lead his troops against the British assault, given the premise that he wanted to resist such an attack. However, there need be no pretence about his attitude to the British advance. He, like Sluysken and the other loyal Orangist officers, invited and welcomed the British offensive. To label this treason and treachery, as many commentators have done, is to be blind to the true nature of these officers' principles and loyalty.

On the same evening as the retreat from Wynberg, the Council of Policy met at half past six. The situation for the defence of the town was hopeless. A strong, well-disciplined British force of over 4 000 men had advanced to Newlands where they had made camp. On the other hand, one half of the 1 700 Dutch troops had arrived demoralized at Drie Kopjes (present-day Mowbray) after the retreat, and the rest were manning various fortifications at Hout Bay, Camps Bay and Cape Town.

At the meeting Gordon and Sluysken pressed for an end to hostilities. It was no longer possible to defend the Cape against an army such as the British had, Sluysken claimed, especially since he could no longer rely on the burghers – a fine irony. In this opinion, he was fully supported by Gordon, who felt that any further resistance would be in vain. Accordingly, it was decided to sue for a forty-eight-hour truce from the British authorities in order to discuss a capitulation. For this purpose, the commissioner-general's aide-de-camp, Captain Zorn, was chosen and sent off to Newlands.

After the meeting, Sluysken, Gordon and other officers made a tour of inspection of the outer positions of the Castle. One indignant witness claims they were encouraged that night to fight on, even though the Council had already decided to surrender.

It was a busy night for Gordon. According to Marnitz he paid a visit to the British camp as well. It is not clear exactly what his mission was, but at about midnight General Clarke granted a twenty-four-hour truce. Towards three o'clock the following morning, 15 September, Gordon broke the news of the truce to the troops. At the same time he gave orders that the different units should stand down and return to their quarters, leaving only a few men on guard.

The whole of 15 September was spent in negotiations between the Council of Policy and the British. Despite some excitement caused by the artillery firing on British ships which had sailed a little too close to the shore batteries, thus breaking the truce, conditions for the surrender of the Cape were signed that evening. For the time being it seemed politic to the commanders to keep news of the capitulation secret – at least until the morning of 16 September. But the word somehow leaked out and many of the burghers and the military were furious. It is reported that they openly accused Gordon and Sluysken of treason and behaved towards them with the greatest disrespect.

The troops in particular felt great bitterness about having to lay down their arms and having to become prisoners of war without having had a chance to show their 'courage and zeal'. They blamed Gordon especially for this humiliation. In the barracks the artillerymen broke all the windows, while the infantrymen jeered and swore at Gordon. The situation was clearly out of hand and the commanders urged the British to come to their aid as soon as possible.

At two o'clock in the afternoon of Wednesday 16 September 1795, the British arrived – 1 400 men marching to the front of the Castle, where they were then drawn up in line. Meanwhile other units had occupied the batteries of the 'French Lines' and hoisted the British flag there. Another detachment went to the so-called 'Sea Lines' and at the same time the British ships in Table Bay fired salvos of salutes.

For the first time since the arrival of the British fleet, three months before, Gordon appeared at the head of his men. With standards waving and drums beating, the garrison marched towards the British columns in order to lay down their arms.

83. *Willem V, Prince of Orange (1748-1806).*

What happened next was an utter humiliation for Gordon. According to Lieutenant Marnitz and other eyewitnesses, the soldiers swore at him, upbraided him and jeered at him. Somehow he brought them to the halt and formed his lines. Then, it is said, for the first and last time since the British arrival, he drew his sabre. Sword in hand, he ordered the troops to present arms and to lay down their weapons. His order was greeted by jeers and insulting shouts. All formality was abandoned. Scornfully, the men threw their weapons to the ground. Cries rang out, such as 'Traitors! All our officers are traitors and rogues!'

In the midst of all this, one infuriated soldier leapt forward and grabbed hold of Gordon by the chest. 'You traitor,' he screamed, 'you are the sole cause of our misery!' Gordon would have shot him forthwith had not his officers rushed forward and pulled the man away. This whole miserable episode took place in full view of General Craig, his officers and his troops, all of whom acted as though they had neither seen nor heard a thing.

Thibault's vivid description of the surrender scene and a further incident is even more sensational:

> ... the soldiers, incensed with rage, wanted to kill him [Gordon] on the spot. One of them tried to snatch his sabre and pierce him with it, whereupon the Colonel demanded that the British lay hold of this soldier. But they merely looked with contempt. A few days later he was again shamefully ill-treated by other soldiers who thrashed him with their batons and, throwing him to the ground, jumped on his belly.[13]

Even if this report is an exaggeration it still demonstrates how bitterly Gordon was abused and hated by his own men. Nevertheless, it is indisputable that Gordon and Sluysken, together with other senior officials and officers of the Company, made sure that the Cape fell to the British. (It is recorded that, in a moment of candour, Gordon declared outright to one of his officers: 'They can do what they will but the British shall have the Cape.') To call this treason, though, as many contemporary and some modern commentators have done, is to ignore the complexity of the issue. To Gordon, and to his fellow officers and colleagues, their first loyalty was to the Prince of Orange. Therefore, once Gordon had decided that the British represented the Prince, it was his clear *duty* to hand over the Cape to them and work with them until such time as it could be returned to its rightful sovereign.

Prior to that decision, however, when Elphinstone's two emissaries had visited him on 13 June 1795, Gordon had been most emphatic about fighting the British to 'his last breath' should they mean to take the Cape for themselves and not for the Prince of Orange. The British themselves had been emphatic on this point too. Major-General Craig noted just this in a letter to Dundas, dated 16 June 1795: 'Col. Gordon by all accounts acts the most manly and open part. He declares himself most decidedly for receiving us as friends but with equal resolution to oppose us to the last drop of his blood if we mean to take the Colony for ourselves.'[14]

It is quite clear that the British were able to assure Gordon that they had come to take the Cape in the name of the Prince of Orange and that the Colony would be returned to its rightful sovereign once the stadholdership had been restored. That is why Gordon decided to support them.

It is also relevant that perhaps Gordon did not view a British presence to be as potentially threatening as that of some other foreign power, since from boyhood he had been inculcated with a loyalty to the British as well as the Dutch royal houses — in fact, from the time when he was an ensign in the Scots Brigade. In upbringing he had always been 'a Greatbritainer', to use his own words.

Further justification for Gordon's stance was his abhorrence of 'French principles and anarchy', as well as those who supported these principles — 'the endochtrinated dupes' he called them, indubitably referring here to the Patriots (or Nationals). Yet another reason for Gordon to detest the French Revolution and its followers was his almost certain knowledge of the death by guillotine in 1793 of his former correspondent, Jean Sylvain Bailly.[15] In short, given these facts and this background, Gordon could not have acted otherwise.

But even though we may accept that Gordon acted honourably in the 'betrayal' of the Cape, this does not mean that his experience was anything but distasteful. In the first place there was the fine line between what he called 'prudence' and the real fact of outright deception. To discharge his duty to the stadholdership he had to pretend to resist the British. It is clear he did not do this very well, making it patent to the Patriot junior officers and to the burghers that his defence was, to put it gently, half-hearted and ineffective. Nevertheless, the pretence was made and this undoubtedly involved a measure of outright duplicity, such as the removing of the Orange cockades in July 1795. All in all, this and similar acts of deception can only have constituted an appalling experience for a man of Gordon's character and principles.

As if that was not painful enough, suddenly he was being insulted by his own soldiers and was forced to remain secluded at home for his own safety — he who for many years had enjoyed the highest military rank in the Colony and who had won the esteem of not only the local inhabitants but of a host of foreign visitors (many of whom, ironically, had been British). Marnitz, who although a staunch pro-Patriot, and therefore decidedly hostile to Gordon, at least recognized the racking situation Gordon now found himself in.

> By the surrender of the Cape he had certainly gained his object and greatly seen his wishes realised; but on the other hand he found himself in the most horrible circumstances in which a man can find himself, who is still animated with feelings of honour and virtue. The conviction that he had not done his duty; that he had betrayed and deceived the military who had confided in him; by those means been reduced to misery; who had for that reason to bear the greatest insults from the rabble; been exposed to the most humiliating abuses from that quarter; that he was despised and detested by the people; that he was contemned by the English and disappointed in his expectations.[16]

Perhaps the cruellest humiliation suffered by Gordon came from the British. All the contemporary reports claim that he was despised by the British for his role in the surrender. Again, there is no confirmation of this from neutral sources, but there does appear to be some truth in the allegation if we accept the eyewitness reports of the surrender by Thibault, Marnitz and others. The British unequivocally allowed Gordon's soldiers to insult him. This lack of action was disgraceful enough, but worse was to come.

On the day of surrender it was the British flag that was raised — the Orange standard was not to be seen. Likewise, in the official surrender documents there was no mention made of the Prince of Orange. Furthermore, all Company officials and army officers were told that if they wished to keep their positions they would have to swear allegiance to the British crown. In other words, the British had betrayed their solemn assurances to Gordon that they would take over the Cape in the name of the Prince of Orange. It must have been quite clear to Gordon that he had been manipulated and thoroughly duped, that his surrender of the Cape had been in vain and that he was the victim of a humiliating confidence trick. It was no wonder that he remained at his house in a deep depression, brooding. He had been, as General Clarke put it, 'in a very low and desponding State of mind ever since its [the Colony's] surrender'.[17] It is noteworthy that General Clarke seems to have done nothing to reassure Gordon at this time.

There can be no doubt how completely the British had deceived Gordon. The French catch-phrase *'La perfide Albion'* — made current by the revolutionary poet Augustin, Marquis de Ximénès (1726-1817) — seems sickeningly appropriate here.

In a scurrilous pamphlet published in 1796 it was also alleged that even Mrs Gordon had now turned on her husband and insulted him.[18] It is almost certainly untrue, but one may gauge the degree of hatred for him merely by noting the allegation.

Gordon was in an intolerable position. He had been deeply insulted and grossly betrayed. Furthermore, there were no means by which he could get redress or justice. As an honourable man there was only one way he could resolve the appalling dilemma facing him.

On the morning of 25 October 1795 Gordon's family heard a shot ring out somewhere outside their house. They found Gordon's body in the garden, where the plants that he had so diligently collected from all over the country — the result of so many years of botanizing — now grew. There was a bullet wound in the head. Evidently he had died immediately. .

The official enquiry showed that Gordon had been killed by a pistol shot. According to Lieutenant Marnitz 'the bullet had entered the right side of the head, glancing upward and passing out at the left side'. It is worth quoting Marnitz here, as he declares that 'the fiscal gave a verdict (in substance) that he might possibly have been killed by somebody'. A footnote explains that 'The English Commanders suggested this declaration in order to save his family from disgrace, for according to the direction of the bullet such an explanation was untenable'.[19]

Gordon was buried the same evening. To quote the lieutenant again: 'He was buried quietly at night in the graveyard and the English officers sent their carriages to follow the corpse.' Marnitz continues with more bizarre and gruesome details:

Some days afterwards the Executioner hanged himself. This event gave the public cause for all kinds of satire and ridicule. It was said that the Devil would not receive Colonel Gordon without having an 'orderly' with him. However insipid and coarse these jokes may be they show unmistakably the hatred and contempt which the public cherished toward Col: Gordon and which followed him to the grave.[20]

There can be no doubt that Gordon's actions during the defence of the Cape, together with the humiliating consequences that followed, led directly to his death. Certainly some of the British considered this to be so. Here is how one of the officers who took part in the invasion saw Gordon's case:

Colonel Gordon was a man remarkable for his humanity and philanthropy. He was a traveller, an antiquarian, and a natural Philosopher. Botany was latterly his favourite study. He travelled farther inland from the Cape than any European had ever done. As he committed his observations on every subject to paper his MSS, which are in his widow's possession are probably valuable. His wavering conduct at a period when, whatever party he had chosen, he ought to have acted with resolution, may be deemed the original cause of his unfortunate end. He had long deservedly held the first most respected rank in the society in which he lived. He thought he was degraded and could not support the reflection. I have also heard that the stream of his Domestic Joys was poisoned. If so, it is not to be wondered at that a mind, whose powers were weakened by illness, should fall under such accumulated misfortunes. He was buried quietly and privately, but his corpse was attended to the grave by nearly forty English officers.[21]

Two important points are made in this account that go beyond the question of Gordon's 'wavering conduct', or the fact that he had been 'degraded'. Firstly, we have the hearsay statement that 'the stream of his Domestic Joys was poisoned'. The only other reference to this possibility is in the offensive pamphlet, mentioned earlier, where Mrs Gordon is meant to have insulted him after the surrender. There is no other reference to any unhappiness between Gordon and his wife, either at this time or later when, as his widow, she disposed of their belongings at the Cape, or when she passed through England on her way to Switzerland. On the contrary, all the accounts up till now emphasized how agreeable Mrs Gordon was and, by implication, how well suited the couple were. On the other hand, were there some truth in these allegations, then Gordon could well have been even more desperately depressed after the surrender.

The other reference in this account is to Gordon's mind 'weakened by illness'. We have seen how, in 1789 and 1790, Gordon's health was so poor that he had effectively laid down his command. His illness was, as he said, some form of a chest complaint, and it would seem that he continued to suffer from the same illness in the years following. He was hardly ever present at the Council of Policy during the years leading up to the surrender, but whether this was due to illness cannot, with any certainty, be ascertained.

In the pamphlet, mentioned earlier in connection with Mrs Gordon, there is a description of Gordon which portrays him as being 'as thin as a skeleton'.[22] The pamphlet is grotesque in its parody of him, but this observation is given in a footnote which serves to make it more factual. It was probably so. But did Gordon's illness affect his state of mind, as claimed by the English officer quoted above?

If we look at Gordon's actions at this last stage of his life, they seem to be very much at variance with his earlier more stolid behaviour, such as that described in his travel journals. There seems to have been something frenetic about his activities with the fortifications after the arrival of the British. The cattle-hide/sheep-hair bags have a bizarrely comic aspect which is hard to reconcile with, say, the sober and scientific experiments with red-hot cannon balls.

The Gordon that Thibault describes was also strangely quirky, even allowing for the fact that Gordon was no friend of his. The detail of the commander of the forces at Wynberg 'laughing like a madman' and playing with his big dogs is too closely observed to be dismissed as a totally hostile fabrication. In effect, it is possible that, at least, Gordon's judgement was unsound at this time, but there is no way we can be sure that this was due to illness.

Marnitz, who wrote a bitter denunciation of the commanders of the Cape and their role in the surrender, is strangely ambiguous about Gordon. It is worth quoting his assessment of his commanding officer, for again, it describes a much more mercurial personality than we have been accustomed to knowing:

He was eccentric in many matters. What he had once taken into his head or resolved upon, he was not easily dissuaded from. He cared very little for public opinion, whether or not it considered his conduct foolish or mad. [Here a footnote adds: 'For that reason some have called him Don Quixote the 2nd.'] He was in the highest degree headstrong, and thought a great deal of his intellect and knowledge, so that he imagined that it was impossible for him to make a mistake, that he was lifted above all other men in understanding. He had accustomed his body to bear all kinds of fatigue and, so successfully, that on the march, or in climbing mountains, another could with difficulty keep up with him. He loved no luxury either in clothes or equipage, in food or drink, but lived very soberly and abstemiously. But for all that he was personally neither avaricious, selfish nor grasping. For the slightest reason he became vindictive and revengeful in the highest degree. In general he was more upright than false, but jealously disposed towards and envious of those who were almost his equals in rank and always endeavoured to keep them under his thumb. For the rest we do not in the least doubt, that in other circumstances, he would have been an honest man and a brave commander.[23]

There are several interesting points about this assessment of Gordon, made, after all, by a man who was an avowed enemy of his. Firstly, it is astonishing how much praise is allowed, given the antagonistic intention of the writer. It is also very interesting that Gordon is described as having had a much more volatile character than we might have expected. He is said to have been 'eccentric', exhibiting conduct that could be construed as 'foolish or mad'; he

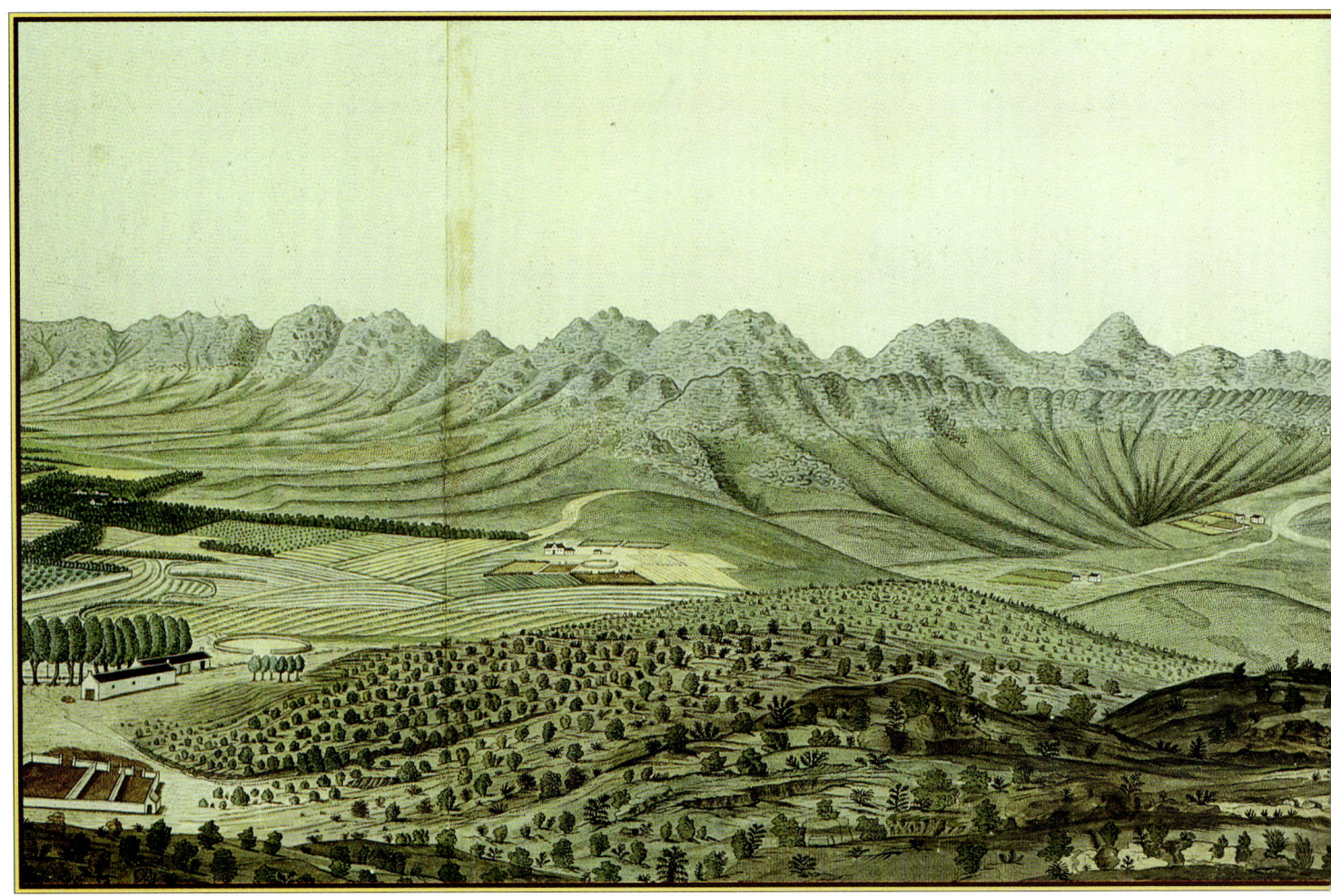

was called 'Don Quixote the 2nd'. Clearly this is how he appeared to both these junior officers, Thibault and Marnitz. We must accept to a certain extent that this eccentricity or quirkiness had become a characteristic of Gordon. It does not mean, however, that his mind was unsound, neither does Marnitz suggest this, but it does mean that our conception of Gordon at the end of his life must be tempered by this knowledge.

Another interesting observation made by Marnitz is that he 'was neither avaricious, selfish nor grasping'. Also pertinent is the fact that he was said to be 'more upright than false'.

These last observations are relevant because Gordon was accused by yet another hostile pamphleteer of owing the Company 10 907 guilders. This, allegedly, was the value of a consignment of clothing material received by Gordon for the garrison just before the arrival of the British. The material never reached the troops, it was said, and the amount remained unpaid in the trading book. The pamphleteer states that Gordon sold the material in Cape Town through 'a certain Michiel Haan and others', the transaction taking place with the full permission of Commissioner-General Sluysken, who also had a share in the transaction. However, the story continues, when inventories were made after the surrender, Sluysken revealed that the material had been received by Gordon; whereupon the above amount was debited to his name by the British who demanded that the material be delivered to them. The pamphlet concludes that Gordon, unable to deliver, betrayed by the commissioner-general in this and other matters, and hated by the burghers and the soldiers, then put an end to his life.[24]

This whole allegation is highly improbable. Firstly, it is certain that Marnitz and others like Thibault would also have included this story in their denunciation of Gordon, had it been common knowledge. Secondly, as we have seen, even Gordon's enemies, such as Marnitz, did not doubt his probity. Not a whisper against Gordon's honesty has been heard from any other source. Indeed, the following passage, taken from an obituary on Gordon in a contemporary English publication called *The Gentleman's Magazine*, affirms the common estimate of his integrity:

Although his time was much taken up in his official duties, and in the study of the most abstruse parts of science, he was, nevertheless of a cheerful and social disposition; open, candid and sincere; and of strict integrity, punctilious honour, and unshaken principles; but of too little subtlety, and of too impatient a mind, to treat with sufficient indifference the continual vexations he met with in a colony where despotism and pecula-

84. *A view of the Hottentots Holland Mountains, showing today's Sir Lowry's Pass and, on the extreme right, a part of the coast now known as Gordon's Bay.*

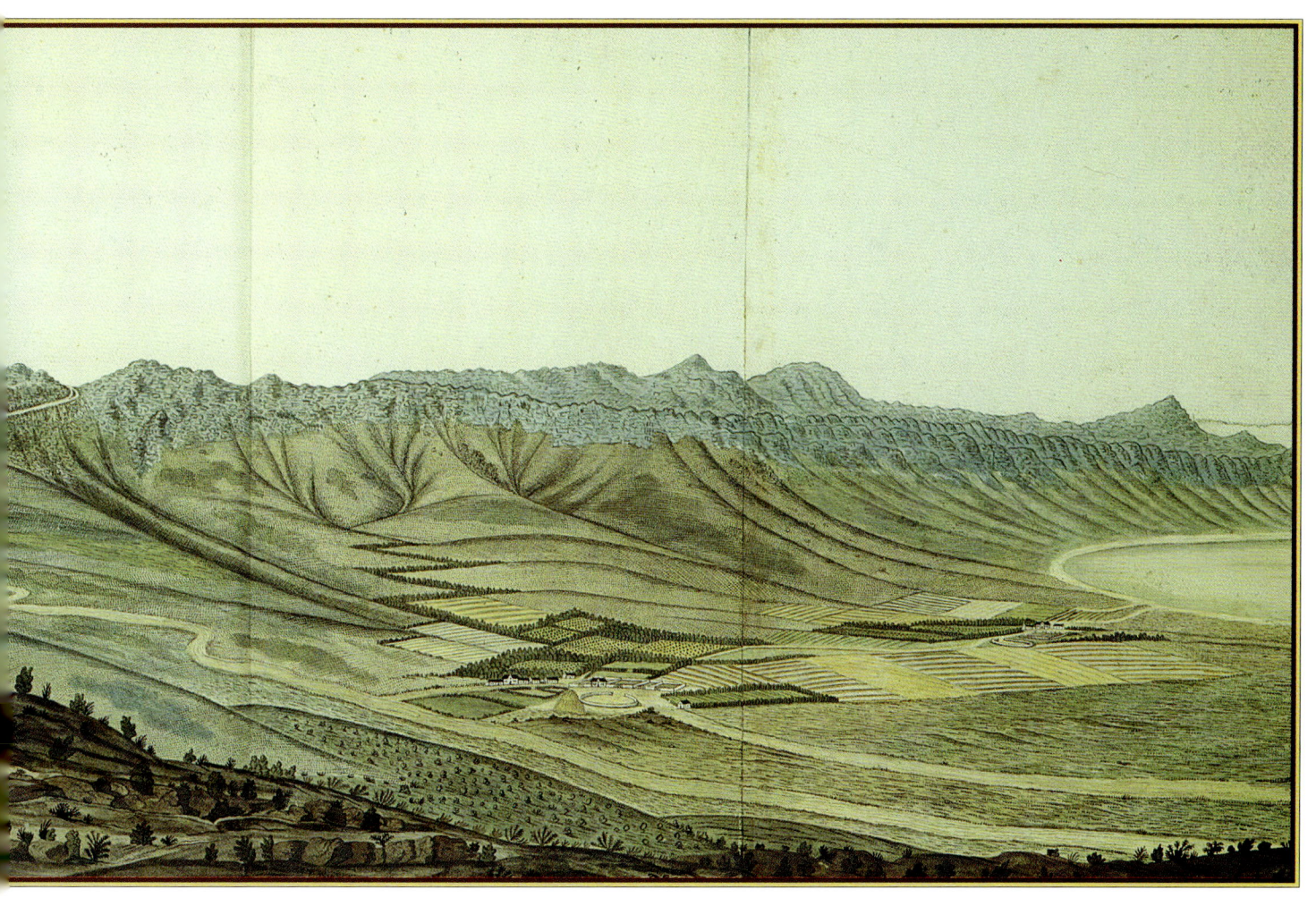

tion were uncontrollable, and where self-interest was universally prevalent.[25]

It is certain that had the British any case against Gordon it would have been generally known and an obituary of this nature would have been constrained to make it known.

It is interesting that this same obituary confirms the observations made by Marnitz but in an entirely positive way: 'He was handsome in his person, elegant in his manners, upwards of six feet high, thin, but muscular, strong, active, and capable of enduring great fatigue; of a dark complexion; and died at the age of 54.'[26]

Gordon's life ended in tragedy. His suicide was honourable, but the events leading to it and the circumstances surrounding it were morally squalid. This grim ending, however, should not allow us to forget the extent of his achievements or the reality of his successes.

Above all, Gordon considered himself a man of science and it is in this field, or fields, that we must initially attempt to assess him.

The first works by Gordon to gain notice were the studies he made in zoology. In this field Gordon was a true pioneer, adding to the eighteenth century's store of knowledge by contributing original, hitherto unknown material. His sketches and carefully recorded details of the animals he obtained in the wild interior – as well as many skins and skeletons – were regularly transmitted to his close friend in Holland, Professor Allamand, who in turn transformed the information into the widely praised articles that he published in Buffon's great encyclopaedia, *Histoire Naturelle*.

Gordon's contribution to science as a botanist is more difficult to assess. As we have seen, it was more as background helper and facilitator that his contribution was made.

The range of travellers who drew on his experience and aid is impressive. Many owe the recognition they eventually received in large measure to the help they got from Gordon. Masson, Paterson, Boos and Scholl, Le Vaillant, the first colonizers of New South Wales are all part of the list of men who recorded their debt to Gordon. Furthermore, much of his material, subsequently published by others, was not attributed to him.

Gordon's interest in geology was considerable and is the subject of a large part of his correspondence with learned men such as De Saussure. His observations must have been valuable to such people, based as they were on first-hand observation of a country that had never before been studied in this way by someone who had both a knowledge of contemporary theory and a keen eye for topography.

Gordon was, as his journals testify, fascinated by meteorology, and he went so far as to draw up a treatise on the Cape weather that today is in the Cape Archives. It was never published but will doubtless prove of great interest to experts in this field.

The foundation of wool farming in both South Africa and Australia owes a great deal to Gordon, as we have seen. It is indicative of his talents that this fact alone would assure him a place in history, whereas in reality it is only a minor facet of his life.

Whatever Gordon's achievements in other fields, it is important to remember that his profession was that of a soldier. Setting aside the disastrous events of the capitulation, it is patently clear that he was a distinguished commandant of the Castle garrison. His zeal and efficiency were singled out by several objective observers, among whom were the commissioners specially appointed to examine the state of the Cape's defences. Under trying circumstances, with great uncertainty as to his proper status and duties, Gordon fashioned a fine command at the Castle, improving both the weaponry and general state of the defences.

Ultimately, however, Gordon's main claim to greatness must lie in his travels and the records that he made of them. Even before the rediscovery of the travel journals Professor Forbes could write:

Gordon's journeys were the crowning accomplishment of 18th century travel in South Africa, not only in respect of sheer distance penetrated into the unmapped interior, but also in their rich cartographic and pictorial record. His most outstanding service to geography was that he drew up, or caused to be drawn up, chiefly from his personal observations on his extensive travels, by far the most accurate and detailed map (No. 3) then available of the very extensive areas of Southern Africa which it represents. Exhibiting a mass of remarkably accurate cartographic detail, supplemented by abundant vividly faithful pictorial material, and enriched by copious carefully written descriptions, this document sums up more geographic knowledge of South Africa in a single sheet than any other work of similar compass available up to the end of that century . . . . These essentially geographical documents were supplemented by a remarkable array of drawings some 400 in number, showing not only South African scenery, but its native inhabitants, fauna and flora. These constitute an unrivalled treasury of pictorial information of the highest value not only to geographers, but also to historians, ethnologists, zoologists and botanists.[27]

Now, with the contribution of the journals, it is possible to amplify and deepen our knowledge of this remarkable man. We can assess Gordon's accomplishment in finer detail. The journals confirm Professor Forbes's appraisal of the journeys and the value of their pictorial and cartographic records. With all their necessary imperfections – they are day-to-day records, not finished books – the journals stand as an impressive achievement by any standard. Written in the field, under exacting conditions, they are a monument to one man's unceasing energy, scientific curiosity and patient courage.

The magnitude of Gordon's achievements is slowly gaining recognition. Gordon the man, however, remains something of an enigma. His character is not easily defined or explained. The journals, for instance, bear witness to a methodical, even obsessional cast of mind as we read, day after day, his writing down of the weather and changes of temperature. It could be deduced that he had a fixation about this daily recording, this unrelenting habit. Yet there is evidence from the body of his journals that his mind was not that logical, that he allowed one thing to follow on another without much regard for an overall shape. He seems to have recognized this himself. Writing to De Saussure he could say: 'Initially it is necessary that I tell you that I am not at all systematic....'[28] His attitude to order was soldier-like and repetitive rather than rational. When his first giraffe was shot his response was to take a mass of measurements which were broken up and studded with comments on the general habits of the animal and various anecdotes. There is no apparent order or attempt to impose a structure.

In the journals the man displayed is vigorous and full of energy; only when he was ill did his activity flag. He was able to live off the land and maintain his pace even when his native-born companions faltered and complained of thirst and hunger. As Marnitz was later to remark, he had schooled himself to be hardy, accustoming his body 'to bear all kinds of fatigue' and, it will be recalled, from this same writer we have the comment that 'He loved no luxury either in clothes or equipage, in food or drink, but lived very soberly and abstemiously'. These observations — from a hostile pen, remember — merely confirm the evidence of the journals. For Gordon, drinking cool water or eating a meal of ostrich egg were about as sybaritic as he ever allowed himself to become. On his second journey he tells us that he only had one shirt. However, we do not need to have any other evidence than the sum total of the journals themselves to demonstrate how severe and hard a life this man was accustomed to lead.

Against this austere figure we must counterpose the genial and urbane personality encountered by so many of his visitors. There is, of course, no hint of overindulgence in any of their accounts, but it does come through strongly that Gordon and his family greatly enjoyed entertaining. Lachlan Macquarie and Mary Ann Parker, to name only two, both testify that the Gordons loved music and singing and dancing. Even before he was married Gordon was able to give his visitors original and charming diversions. One need only cite William Hickey's account of going up Table Mountain. But it is perhaps also characteristic of the energetic Gordon that this entertainment was part of a vigorous climb that put his visitor out of action for the next five days!

A more negative facet of Gordon's character that needs some consideration can be summed up by Marnitz's accusation that Gordon was 'in the highest degree headstrong' and that 'For the slightest reason he became vindicative and revengeful'. The most obvious incident to bear in mind here is the episode involving Sandolroy. There is no doubt that the commissioners, Nederburg and Frijkenius, were embarrassed by Gordon's animus towards the French officer and that they rushed Sandolroy off to Batavia and freedom as soon as they could. It would seem that there were good grounds for calling Gordon 'headstrong . . . vindicative and revengeful' in this affair. But it is difficult to draw the line between the demands of military discipline and excessively punitive action. Perhaps bitterness derived from the in-fighting with Van de Graaff and the fact that Gordon was ill can explain this sorry affair. There do not appear to be any other incidents such as this in Gordon's life

It is just the contrary when one comes to look at Gordon's relationship with his servants and with the indigenous peoples he met on his travels. His attitude to young Cabas when he ran away was anything but 'revengeful' and 'vindicative'. After the boy had been beaten by the servant Klaas, Gordon was quick to comfort and reassure him. But indeed one of the most remarkable things about Gordon was his facility for making friends with the tribespeople he found on his travels. As Mrs Parker remarked, he was 'almost adored' by the Hottentots, meaning that he was almost worshipped by them. How well Gordon got on with the Xhosa tribesmen was recorded by O.G. de Wet on Van Plettenberg's journey, but that happy relationship is manifest in all that Gordon himself wrote about those encounters. In all Gordon's writings there is not one contemptuous word about the tribespeople he met. He can laugh at them, or rather at their superstitions, but he never patronizes them.

If Gordon's character is enigmatic, even paradoxical, there is, nevertheless, one quality that seems to remain unchanging and unchanged from the first — his loyalty. From his days as a ten-year-old ensign in the Scots Brigade he was expected to give his fealty to his Prince and his allegiance to his brother officers in the regiment. It is clear that he accepted this principle of loyalty freely and with conviction all his life. He was, perhaps, too committed to those to whom he had sworn his allegiance. It is ironic that this fine quality proved to be a flaw, that it was precisely this loyalty that produced the grim farce that he had to play out during the last months of his life. He was too loyal. That is what killed him; and that is where the tragedy of Gordon lies.

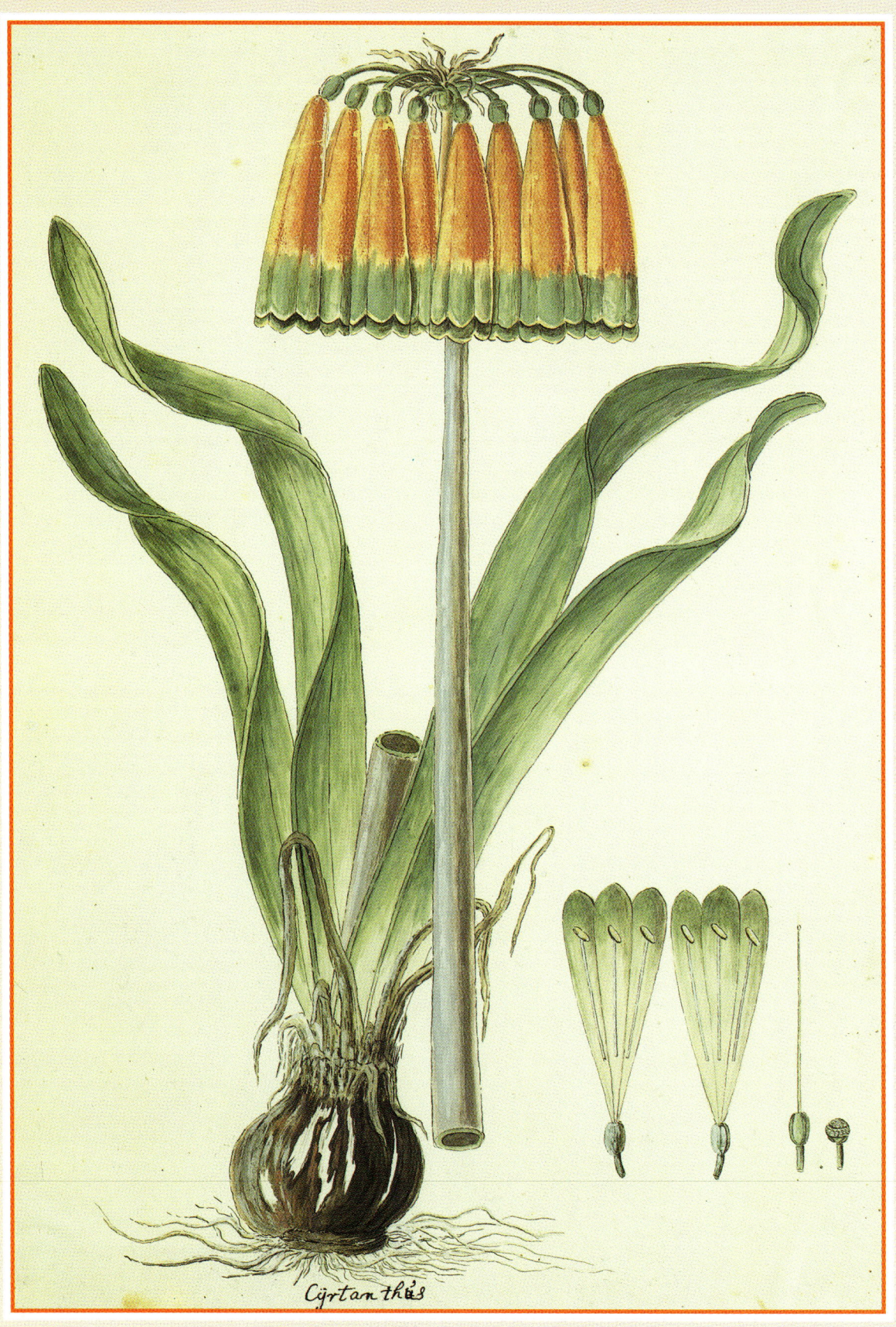

85. Cyrtanthus obliquus: *a rare amaryllid.*

EPILOGUE

GORDON'S DESCENDANTS

Gordon was survived by his wife and four sons. On 8 March 1797 Mrs Gordon sold their house, Schoonder Sigt, and shortly afterwards left the country, accompanied by her children. The family first travelled to England where Mrs Gordon endeavoured to sell her husband's papers, as has been related in the opening pages of this study. Towards the end of 1797 she moved to Lausanne, and from information obtained in the Cantonal Archives of that town, we know that she continued to live there, or in the vicinity, until her death. It is also recorded that she lent money to various individuals from time to time. She died in 1831, at the age of eighty-two.[1]

As noted earlier, Robert, the eldest son, joined the Cape garrison force as a cadet, eventually becoming an ensign. He was in his sixteenth year when he left the Cape in 1797. Once in Europe, it seems, he joined the French army, in whose service he attained the rank of colonel. Before the Battle of Waterloo he was appointed chief of staff to a French army division; however, for some unknown reason, he decided to turn traitor, revealing the numbers and positions of the French to the enemy. His treachery was discovered and he was shot in cold blood by the soldiers of the Governor of Condé on 7 July 1815.

It appears that Gordon's second son, Pieter, also joined the French army, rising to the rank of lieutenant. He is thought to have died in the Serbo-Turkish War.

Alexander, the third son, joined the French navy and was a nineteen-year-old sailor at the Battle of Trafalgar in 1805. He married a Dutch wife in Amsterdam in 1820, but after this nothing further is known of his life.

James Charles Gerhard, the youngest son, born in 1791, joined the Swiss Guards in France and was later married in Switzerland. It was said that he was struck by one disaster after another and finally went mad, dying some time between 1839 and 1861.

Gordon's only known grandchildren sprang from this same James Gordon. Two of these lived and died in Switzerland, but the second child, a son, settled in New York and was still alive in 1862. He, in turn, had four children, all born in New York. There is also a record of two other great-grandchildren being born in Switzerland, but apart from this, nothing more about Gordon's descendants has been brought to light.

86. *A decorative motif from Gordon's 'great map'*

Notes to the Text

Preface

1. The history of Gordon's manuscripts and 'Atlas' are discussed in the next section.

The Gordon Manuscripts and Atlas

1. L. C. Rookmaaker, *The Zoological Exploration of Southern Africa*, pp. 65-7. I am greatly indebted to Dr Rookmaaker for drawing my attention to the Pinkerton correspondence.
2. *Ibid.*, p. 65: 'Philip Gidley King (1757-1801) . . . became governor of New South Wales in 1800.'
3. *Ibid.*, p. 66. Edward Riou (1762-1801) ship's captain, commanded the *Guardian* en route to Australia. It struck an iceberg about 1 900 km from the Cape. Most men were lost, but Riou managed to bring the ship back to Cape Town where he met Gordon and Francis Masson. (Following Dr Rookmaaker, I have taken most of this information from M. Gunn and L. E. Codd [eds.], *Botanical Exploration of Southern Africa*, p. 297.) However, a fuller account of Riou's life, his stay at the Cape and his meetings with Gordon can be found in Nash, M. D. (ed.) *The Last Voyage of the Guardian, Lieutenant Riou, commander, 1789-1791* Second Series no 20, 1990 for 1989.
4. All these facts are communicated in the preface to *The Literary Correspondence of John Pinkerton Esq.* edited by Dawson Turner, a friend and contemporary of Pinkerton's, as well as a noted botanist and antiquary. (*Dictionary of National Biography*, vol. 57, pp. 334-5.)
5. Pinkerton, pp. 268-70.
6. *Ibid.*, p. 307.
7. *Ibid.*, p. 308.
8. *Ibid.*, pp. 309-14.
9. *Encyclopaedia Brittanica*, vol. 19, pp. 1163-4.
10. Pinkerton, p. 307.
11. V. S. Forbes, 'Col. R. J. Gordon's family', *Africana Notes and News*, vol. 11, p. 133. This passage is translated from the French.
12. Pinkerton, p. 307.
13. *Dictionary of South African Biography*, vol. 4, p. 789. This is, of course, the same Windham who was an early admirer of Lady Anne Barnard. He was called 'Weathercock' because his conduct was so vacillating and inconsistent.
14. G. McC. Theal, *Records of the Cape Colony 1793-1796*, pp. 420-21. The original is in the Public Record Office, London.
15. Pinkerton, p. 391. Since this is the last mention of Pinkerton it may be appropriate to record this description of his appearance from Turner's preface: '. . . it was that of a very little and very thin old man, with a very small, sharp, yellow face, thickly pitted with the small pox, and decked with a pair of green spectacles'.
16. *Dict. Nat. Biog.*, vol. 33, pp. 146-8, under 'Leveson-Gower, George Granville'.
17. Rookmaaker, *Zoological Exploration*, p. 67.
18. *Ibid.*
19. *Ibid.*
20. A. J. Clement, 'The journals of Robert Gordon', *Personality*, Bloemfontein, (8 July 1965), p. 46.

The Translation of Gordon's Papers

1. VC 595 in the Cape Archives, p. 123.
2. M. L. Wilson, '"By any other name": The nomenclature of the Khoisan', mimeo, n.d., a paper read at the biennial conference of the Southern African Association of Archaeologists, Grahamstown. It refers to a wide variety of views on the subject by most of the scholars, past and present, active in the field. I am also indebted to Dr Cyril Hromnic for his advice on this matter.
3. J. S. Stavorinus, *Voyages to the East Indies*, vol. 3, p. 456.

Chapter One

1. The history of the Gordon family in Holland can be found in J. M. Bulloch's *The House of Gordon* and *The Gay Gordons*. However, much of the information used here was drawn from letters and other papers lent to the writer by Miss Mary Gunn of Pretoria.
2. The history and background of the Scots Brigade and matters pertaining to Jacob Gordon can be found in J. Ferguson's *Papers Illustrating the History of the Scots Brigade in the Service of the United Netherlands 1572-1782*.
3. *Ibid.*, vol. 2, p. 394.
4. The journal *Nederlandsche Leeuw* (1911), provides much of the information about the Gordon family, but again, Miss Mary Gunn has been of great help to the writer and to C. J. Barnard, as he acknowledges in 'Robert Jacob Gordon se loopbaan aan die Kaap', *Archives Yearbook for South African History*, vol. 13, part 1 (1950), p. 326.
5. *Nederlandsche Leeuw*: (1911), pp. 239-40.
6. R. M. S. Pasley, *Private Sea Journals 1778-1782*, p. 85.
7. S. Urban, 'Col. Robert Gordon' (obituary), *The Gentleman's Magazine*. This obituary is one of the main sources for Gordon's early life.
8. VC 595, p. 148.
9. *The Gentleman's Magazine* is again a useful source for this period of Gordon's life. There are also further references in W. Paterson, *Narrative of Four Journeys into the Country of the Hottentots and Caffraria . . .*, V. S. Forbes and J. Rourke, *Paterson's Cape Travels, 1777-1779*, and W. Hickey, *Memoirs of William Hickey*.
10. C. P. Thunberg, *Travels in Europe, Africa and Asia . . .*, pp. 265-70. Also Forbes, *C. P. Thunberg: Travels at the Cape of Good Hope 1772-1775*, pp. 144-9.
11. Rookmaaker, *Zoological Exploration*, describes in detail Gordon's contact with Allamand and other learned men in Europe. Allamand himself refers to Gordon several times in his articles for *Histoire Naturelle*.
12. Forbes, 'Gordon's family', vol 11, p. 135.
13. A. M. Wilson, *Diderot*, pp. 646-50.
14. Elizabeth de Fontenay, *Diderot, Reason and Resonance*, pp. 91-6. This account of Gordon's meeting with Diderot has not been noted or discussed in any other publication known to me.
15. Diderot, *Oeuvres Complètes*, vol. 17, pp. 445-6.
16. Translation from the French of Diderot is by myself, except for the first paragraph which is mainly taken from De Fontenay.
17. Curiosity about the 'Hottentot apron' has always been intense, even hectic at times. It started with the first travellers to the Cape and continued until recent times. See R. Raven-Hart, *Cape of Good Hope*, vol. 2, p. 494, (index: 'Apron'); also P. V. Tobias, *The Bushmen: San Hunters and Herders of Southern Africa*, pp. 124-5, for a more modern explanation. Gordon himself records that he twice examined an 'apron' on his second journey. See chapt. 2, pp. 31, 35.
18. Abbé N. L. de la Caille was the French astronomer who visited the Cape from April 1751-March 1753. His *Journal Historique du Voyage au Cap de Bon Espérance* was published in 1762. According to Theal 'its chief worth, historically considered, is the exposure given to some of Kolbe's errors'.
19. Quoted in De Fontenay, p. 94.

20. Diderot, vol. 2, *Supplément au Voyage de Bougainville*, pp. 195-250.
21. Abbé G.T. Raynal, *A Philosophical and Political History of the Settlements and Trade of the Europeans in the East and West Indies*, vol. 2, pp. 306-21.
22. *Encyclopaedia Brittanica*, vol. 18, p. 1195, 'Raynal, Guillaume Thomas'.
23. Wilson (A.M.), p. 682.
24. Raynal, Book 2, p. 307.
25. De Fontenay unequivocally takes it for granted that Diderot is the author.
26. Barnard, p. 329 quotes from the Dutch East India Company's *Inkomende Brieven*, as well as from Hickey and Paterson.
27. Buffon and Daubenton, vol. 26, p. 142.
28. Hickey, vol. 2, pp. 107-11.

CHAPTER TWO

1. VC 595, p. 146.
2. The translation is made from VC 592, pp. 1-154. The plotting of this journey has followed V.S. Forbes, *Pioneer Travellers in South Africa*, pp. 83-4, 94-9 very closely. Forbes's study was made before the rediscovery of the Gordon journals, yet in almost every respect the written record confirms his deductions.
3. Forbes and Rourke, p. 76 and n. 147.
4. *Narrative of Four Journeys into the Country of the Hottentots and Caffraria* . . . .
5. All the Gordon quotations in English are taken from my translation of the original Dutch text (VC 592-8). Since my translation of the journals has not yet been published, the passages quoted will be identified by the date only.
6. Pieter Michiel Eksteen acquired Bergvliet in 1796 and built the first house there (H. Fransen and M.A. Cook, *The Old Buildings of the Cape*, pp. 122, 127). Unlike Gordon, Paterson was somewhat more forthcoming about his stay there: 'This night we rested at a place called Berg Fleet, the property of a rich farmer of the name of Ekstin. It is unnecessary to enlarge upon the hospitality of these people since that circumstance has been remarked upon by all who have travelled through the country.' (Paterson, quoted by P. Dane and S.A. Wallace, *The Great Houses of Constantia*, p. 61.)
7. VC 595, pp. 105-32. See S. Schama, *Patriots and Liberators*, p. 50: 'The Fagel family [held] the office of Greffier to the States General (a post whose pivotal diplomatic importance was belied by the humdrum title of, literally, "clerk").'
8. Forbes and Rourke, p. 70, n. 90.
9. VC 595, p. 54. See also chapt. 1, p. 23, n. 17.
10. No 55 in the Gordon Atlas.
11. Forbes, *Pioneer Travellers*, pp. 115, 116; A. Hallema, *Die Kaap in 1776-1777*, pp. 5-21; *Dict. S.A. Biog*, vol. 4, p. 549 (entry by V.S. Forbes); A.R. Willcox, *Great River: The Story of the Orange River*, pp. 32, 33.
12. Forbes and Rourke, p. 76.
13. It is clear that the animal was some sort of hyena.
14. Gordon Atlas, no. 63. See also Forbes, *Pioneer Travellers*, p. 65.
15. See chapt. 1, p. 21.
16. Evidently *Xerus inauris*. Rookmaaker, *Zoological Exploration*, p. 98, lists this animal among the drawings in the Gordon Atlas. See also Forbes, *Thunberg*, p. 305, n. 188.
17. J.J. de Beer was the owner of Vrede. See G.J. Schutte (ed.), *Briefwisseling van Hendrik Swellengrebel JR oor Kaapse Sake 1778-1792*, p. 51, n. 42. Also Forbes, *Anders Sparrman: Travels in the Cape 1772-1776*, p. 30, n. 65.
18. Forbes, *Pioneer Travellers*, p. 51. Tobias, pp. 9, 119.
19. See chapt. 1, p. 23, n. 17.
20. Tobias pp. 79-80. The chapter by A.R. Willcox ('The Bushman in history') provides a revealing background to these 'battles' between the 'Bushmen' and their enemies from 1655 to 1809.
21. L.C. Rookmaaker, 'De Bijdrage van Robert Jacob Gordon, (1743-1795) tot Kennis van de Kaapse Fauna', p. 11 and n. 58.
22. Forbes, *Pioneer Travellers*, pp. 84, 111.
23. *Ibid.*, fig. 28 (Gordon Atlas, no. 34).
24. Forbes, *Pioneer Travellers*, p. 70.
25. Peires offers detailed discussion of these tribes. For this period in particular and for their contact with Gordon see J.B. Peires, *The House of Phalo: A History of the Xhosa People in the Days of their Independence*, pp. 53-6.
26. *Ibid.*, p. 53.
27. Forbes, *Pioneer Travellers*, p. 46: '. . . the farthest point reached by Sparrman and his companion was the Great Fish River in the vicinity of Cookhouse'. This was on 6 February 1776. See also Forbes, *Sparrman*, vol. 2, p. 227.
28. Drawings 69-77 in the Gordon Atlas almost certainly appertain to the meetings with the Xhosa at this time.
29. Forbes, *Pioneer Travellers*, map 13.
30. Possibly Rharabe. See Peires, pp. 48-50.
31. Gordon's route can be followed in Forbes, *Pioneer Travellers*, maps 15 and 16.
32. The entry for 17 December 1777 records that an oribi was shot. On 18 December Gordon comments: 'At sunset came to the wagon where we had a good oribi soup. For this reason I gave this river the name of Oribi River.'
33. Forbes, *Pioneer Travellers*, p. 97: 'Ambassador Joseph Yorke was English ambassador at The Hague until 1780. (DNB)'.
34. On this same day, 23 December 1777, Gordon had commented: 'We shot a rietbok (A kei in Hottentot) which I drew and measured. Called this spring Riet Reebokke Fontein: it had very good-tasting and abundant water.'

CHAPTER THREE

1. For a full discussion of this episode and the resultant drawings see Forbes, *Pioneer Travellers* pp. 97-9.
2. *Ibid.*, p. 98.
3. Gordon Atlas, Map 3. Parts of the map are reproduced in Forbes, *Pioneer Travellers*, maps 15 and 21.
4. *Ibid.*, p. 72 and map 13. These references deal with Swellengrebel's route, which Gordon was apparently following at this point.
5. Peires, pp. 45-53. Also Forbes, *Sparrman*, vol. 1, p. 204, nn. 84-7.
6. Peires, pp. 23 and 47 in particular.
7. 'Thaka' is perhaps 'Tsaka' referred to below (same page), and is almost certainly the Tshaka in Peires, pp. 50, 51, 56, 138, 140. See also n. 2 above and Forbes, *Sparrman*, vol. 1, p. 204, nn. 84-87.
8. See nn. 5 and 7 above.
9. This name is not mentioned in Peires.
10. Almost certainly named after an officer in the Scots Brigade who had given his name to one of the regiments in that body.
11. Also not mentioned in Peires.
12. J. Barrow, *An Account of Travels into the Interior of Southern Africa in the years 1797 and 1798*, pp. 143-163.
13. Schutte, pp. 33, 34.
14. An intriguing, modern account of this shipwreck can be found in the *The Guns of Sacramento* by Geoffrey and David Allen. Using Gordon's 'map' (more properly a view or prospect) of the site of the wreck, these researchers and divers were able to place the last resting place of this Goa-built Portuguese gallion 'at a point . . . south west of Port Elizabeth, and nine miles east of the lighthouse at Cape Recife. It was on an uninviting stretch of coast between Sardinia Bay to the east and the village of Schoenmakerskop . . . to the west.'

The *Sacramento* ran aground and foundered in 1647, and some of the survivors made an 'incredible trek north' to Mozambique. Gordon, of course, did not know this, but he was right in assuming, on his second guess, that the wreck was Portuguese.

It may seem incredible that Gordon could still find skulls and other remains 130 years after the wreck, but in 1977 the

modern researchers rediscovered parts of the ebony that Gordon talks of seeing, i.e. well over 300 years after the ship ran aground. The Allens record that the bulk of the ship's cargo of bronze and iron cannon were found on the floor of the ocean 'stacked . . . exactly as they had been in the ship's hold'.
15. Forbes and Rourke, p. 124.
16. Buffon and Daubenton, 'Addition aux articles de l'Hippopotame', *Histoire Naturelle*, vol. 27, pp. 1-8.
17. Forbes, *Pioneer Travellers*, p. 75.
18. Gordon does not say who these four are.
19. Forbes, *Pioneer Travellers*, p. 76.

CHAPTER FOUR

1. Stavorinus, vol. 3, pp. 444-56.
2. The full text of the passage reads: 'Went to sleep at four o'clock. Coerikei, my young Hottentot, tried to wake me at five but could not rouse me. So at one o'clock was woken by the noise of the oxen. This was occasioned by a hyena.' Gordon then starts the entry of 18 September 1788 with the statement: 'Left at seven o'clock . . . .' It is not at all clear whether this entry relates to 28 August 1778 (Vergelegen) or to 18 September 1778 (Traka River). I believe that it belongs more logically to the former date and place. After all, why would Gordon say that he left at seven o'clock in the morning of 18 September when he states that he only woke at one o'clock (clearly afternoon) in the previous entry? It is another (small) Gordon puzzle.
3. The official account can be found in E.C. Godée Molsbergen, *Reizen in Zuid-Afrika in di Hollandse Tijd*, vol. 2, pp. 61-78, as well as in G.McC. Theal, *Belangrijke Historische Dokumenten over Zuid Afrika*, vol. 3, pp. 1-35.

My translation was made from VC 593, pp. 144-76. Forbes's *Pioneer Travellers* was used for tracking Gordon's journey.
4. Rookmaaker, *Zoological Exploration*, p. 98, records that there is a drawing of this animal in the Atlas. He identifies it as *Phacochoerus aethiopicus* (no. 214 in the Gordon Atlas). It is interesting that Gordon also gives the French appellation here, taking this from Buffon.
5. Bubalis are haartebeest: *ibid.*, pp. 84, 85 and fig. 34, p. 85 (*Alcelaphus buselaphus*).
6. The gnu is, of course, a wildebeest. It is not generally known that the name gnu (or *gnou* in French) was introduced by Gordon as being the 'Hottentot' name. This is acknowledged by Prof. Allamand in his article on the animal in *Histoire Naturelle*. Besides paying handsome tribute to Gordon in this piece, the professor states that the initial 'gn' was an attempt to represent a 'Hottentot' click. The word itself was meant to resemble the lowing sound that the wildebeest makes. See Buffon and Daubenton, *Histoire Naturelle*, vol. 15, p. 113; also Rookmaaker, *Zoological Exploration*, p. 93 and fig. 39, p. 89 (*Connochaetes gnou*).
7. Gordon Atlas, Map 3; also Forbes, *Pioneer Travellers*, map 15.
8. *Ibid.*, p. 102.
9. VC 595, pp. 105-132.
10. According to Theal in *History of South Africa*, p. 152, this Jacob Joubert, while taking official gifts to the Xhosa chief Rarabe, detected some hostility from the tribesmen and 'returned by night on foot to the camp at Prinsloo's farm'. The Xhosa chiefs here are also discussed on pp. 152 and 153 of the same work.
11. Chapt. 6, pp. 148-9.
12. Buffon and Daubenton, vol. 15, pp. 9-13.
13. Schutte, p. 304. The translation is taken from the English summary by Dr A. Boëseken, assisted by Prof. H.M. Robinson.
14. Forbes, *Pioneer Travellers*, p. 103.
15. *Ibid.*, fig. 35. 'Original in British Museum, Add. MSS 23, 920, fo. 23.'
16. *Ibid.*, fig. 34.
17. Lewis Williams, *Images of Power*, and Tobias ('Religion and folklore' by Megan Biesle), pp. 162-72.
18. Forbes and Rourke, p. 115, n. 175.
19. P.R. Kirby, 'Heerenlogement and its visitors' and 'A further note on the Heerenlogement', *S.A. Journal of Science*, vol. 38, p. 352 and vol. 40, p. 334, give a full account of the cave and its various visitors.

CHAPTER FIVE

1. VC 595, pp. 105-132. This is the draft of the letter, written in copperplate writing. According to Rookmaaker, 'Gordon en zijn bijdrage tot de zoölogie', p. 75, a copy of this letter is in the 'Fagel Archief . . . Algemeen Rijks Archief, Den Haag'.
2. One should not, however, overlook the written contributions to the early history of the Orange made by Wikar and Coetsé (E.E. Mossop, *Journals of Wikar, Coetsé and Van Reenen*), Brink and Rhenius (E.E. Mossop, *Journals of Brink and Rehenius*), and Paterson (*Four Journeys*, as well as Forbes and Rourke, *Paterson*).
3. Again the tracing of Gordon's journey closely follows Forbes's *Pioneer Travellers*. The translation is taken from the manuscript text contained in VC 592, pp. 155-80, and VC 593, pp. 1-103.
4. Forbes and Rourke, p. 139.
5. Buffon and Daubenton, vol. 1, pp. 23-222. See *Dict. Sci. Biog.*, vol. 2, pp. 578-9 for a summary of Buffon's theories about the earth.
6. 'Dasje' means a little badger in Nederlands.
7. This French phrase refers to menstruation.
8. 'Cos' is the *cos quadrum* of Linnaeus. 'This is defined as a hard sandstone that will break into rectangular blocks and hence it is good for building' (Forbes, *Pioneer Travellers*, p. 44).
9. The journal of this journey, which took place between 25 August 1685 and 26 January 1686, has recently been republished (see Waterhouse, *Simon van der Stel's Journey to Namaqualand*). It was first incorporated into François Valentijn's *Oud en Nieuw Oost-Indien*, vol. 5 (1726).
10. Forbes describes this episode in *Pioneer Travellers* p. 122 and also discusses it in a essay for the book *François le Vaillant, Traveller in South Africa*. See Quinton and Robinson, vol. 1, pp. 78-80.
11. Urinating at 'boys' puberty ceremonies' is also mentioned in Wikar's journal (Mossop, *Journals of Wikar . . .*, pp. 92-3). Raven-Hart, too, gives extensive references in *Cape Good Hope*, vol. 2 (see index under 'Urine', p. 511).
12. Forbes and Rourke, pp. 142-4.
13. *Ibid.*, p. 145.
14. See chapt. 6, pp. 93 and 96 for a discussion of the farmers of the Groene River and their 'wives'.
15. See Mossop, *Journals of Wikar . . .*, pp. 7-8 for an account of the various versions.
16. *Ibid.*, p. 2.
17. *Ibid.*, p. 199.
18. Tobias, chapt. 12 ('Religion and folklore' by Megan Biesele), pp. 170-1.
19. Raven-Hart, vol. 2, see index under 'Finger-mutilation', p. 507, for many historical references to this practice.
20. *Ibid.*, p. 524: 'Testicles'.
21. *Ibid.*, p. 510: 'Music' (gora). Also see Forbes, *Thunberg* (p. xxxi and pl. 4) and Sparrman (vol. 1, p. 220 and n. 147).

In Quinton and Robinson's *François le Vaillant* there is an essay by P.R. Kirby (vol. 1, pp. 155-64) devoted to the French traveller's musical references. The *gora* is discussed in detail and illustrated (p. 158).
22. Forbes and Rourke, p. 142.
23. According to Rookmaaker, *Zoological Exploration*, p. 99, there are two drawings of 'oliphantsmuis' in the Gordon Atlas,

namely nos. 230, 231. Rookmaaker identifies the animal as *Macroscelides proboscideus*.
24. In *The Bushmen*, p. 3, Tobias defines strandlopers as 'beachcombers' and goes on to say: 'For a long time they were regarded as a third group of indigenous people, distinguished from their landward cousins, the Bushmen and the Hottentots, by their beach-ranging life. Today the strandlopers are no longer considered to have been a separate population group. The term refers rather to a coastal way of life that was adopted by some San and also probably some Khoikhoi.' See also Wilson (M.L.), 'Shell middens and strandlopers', *Sagittarius*, (March 1989).
25. Forbes and Rourke, p. 150, n. 66.
26. *Ibid.*, p. 152, n. 71: 'Now Boegoeberg-Noord and Boegoeberg-Suid'.
27. *Ibid.*, p. 152, n. 72: 'Now Jam Pan'. See chapt. 3, p. 49 of this book for an identification of Count Bentinck.
28. Forbes and Rourke, p. 152.
29. *Ibid.*
30. Dutch: 'harders' and 'moggels'. According to the *Tweetalige Woordeboek* (ed. Bosman et al) the 'harder' is *Mugil spp. Liza ramado* or *Mugil cephalus*, a kind of mullet. The 'moggel' is also a kind of 'mud mullet' or barbel. Gordon's drawing (no. 112 in the Gordon Atlas) is identified by Rookmaaker as *Labeo umbratus*. See also Forbes and Rourke, pl. 54.
31. Map 3, Gordon Atlas. A good portion of the map is also illustrated in Forbes, *Pioneer Travellers*, maps 15 and 21.
32. Rookmaaker, *Zoological Exploration*, p. 79. There are two drawings in the Gordon Atlas: 106 '*Bitis cornuta* "other kind of hornslang"' and 107 '*Bitis caudalis* "*hoornsman* or *horenslang*"'.
33. Gordon scorned Kolb (or Kolbe), a German who lived at the Cape from 1705-1713. See chapt. 1, p. 23 together with n. 17.
34. Mossop, *Journals of Wikar* . . ., p. 5.
35. This is probably the African Pied Wagtail, *Motacilla aguimp* (*Roberts Birds of South Africa*, p. 481, pl. 59). A drawing of this bird is in the Gordon Atlas (no. 254).
36. According to descriptions found in Palmer and Pitman, the thorn-trees would appear to be either *Acacia giraffae*, Camelthorn (p. 153), or *Acacia karroo*, Sweet-thorn, (p. 157).

CHAPTER SIX

1. Forbes and Rourke, pl. 25: a drawing of a *Hydnora africana* from the Paterson collection. It is described as 'One of the most bizarre flowering plants . . . a root parasite on various species of *Euphorbia*'. Paterson also mistook it for a kind of mushroom, describing it as 'a curious species of the Fungus tribe'. See also the Gordon Collection at the Cape Archives, AG 7146, 197-9.
2. Either the Grey Penduline Tit, *Anthoscopus caroli*, or the Cape Penduline Tit, *Anthoscopus minutus* (*Roberts*, pp. 375-6, pls. 48, 530, 531). Both are still known today in Afrikaans as 'Kapokvoël'.
3. Gordon had made the same observation about the Kouwsie water on 3 August 1779 (see chapt. 5, p. 80).
4. Forbes and Rourke, p. 157.
5. Raven-Hart, see index, p. 509: 'Milk . . . Entries marked O mention blowing for'.
6. No. 89 in the Gordon Atlas.
7. According to Raven-Hart, p. 506, this word was already in use in 1661. Forbes and Rourke, p. 160, n. 117, refers to 'The Bathlaping or Thlaping, a people of mixed Tswana, (Bechuana) and Korana blood, the former predominating'. Several authorities for this identification are cited.
8. Mossop, *Journals of Wikar* . . ., p. 287.
9. Mossop, *Journals of Brink* . . .,   p. 9.
10. Forbes and Rourke, p. 160, n. 119.
11. Mossop, *Journals of Wikar* . . ., pp. 83-91.
12. See chapt. 5, n. 11.
13. Later generations were not so unprejudiced. While examining a transcription of the Gordon journals in the State Archives, Pretoria, I was puzzled at first to find that this whole passage was missing. Later, on reflection, my puzzlement disappeared.
14. See chapt. 5, n. 20.
15. Mossop, *Journals of Wikar* . . ., p. 14: The 'EYNICQUOAS or EYNIKKOA: The people of the River . . . were possibly descendants of the Koranas who settled along the Orange River during the years of the Korana migration'. On pp. 225 and 226 there is more discussion of these people by J. A. Engelbrecht. G. S. Nienaber, *Khoekhoense Stamname*, is, however, essential reading for all the tribes mentioned here. (For 'Einikwas' see pp. 320-8.)
Since writing chapts. 6 and 7 of this work I have been fortunate enough to have access to portions of a forthcoming Ph.D. thesis by Nigel Penn of the University of Cape Town. It is entitled 'The Northern Cape frontier zone 1700-1815' and discusses in detail all the tribes and clans referred to in these two chapters, as well as many of the individuals such as Klaas Baster, Barend Vrije and Pieter Pienaar. It is by far the most comprehensive work on this subject that I have yet seen.
16. See chapt. 5, n. 19.
17. Mossop, *Journals of Wikar* . . ., pp. 230-1: 'The identity of the Husingais or Spiderwebs, or, as Campbell called them, the Spinnekopsooger, about whom no Kora of the present day appears to have heard, will probably remain a mystery unless they are the same as Wangemann's Hu-ei eis . . . or Scorpion tribe . . . .'
18. These are the Korana.
19. Mossop, *Journals of Wikar* . . ., p. 25. Wikar wrote: 'On 4th September we set out for Claas Bastaards kraal called Kakais, where we remained for three days.' Le Vaillant also had Klaas Baster in his employ and drew a sketch of his 'place' (Quinton and Robinson, pl. 24). He was apparently the illegitimate son of the Cornelis van der Westhuizsen who later married Claudina Engelbrecht, the sister of Hermanus Engelbrecht. (See chapt. 5, n. 10.) Le Vaillant also wrote that he had a letter for Klaas from Gordon which, he believed, helped to save his life. (Le Vaillant, *New Travels*, p. 168.)
20. Mossop, *Journals of Wikar* . . ., p. 227: One of 'the tribes of which this people ie. the Eyniqua is composed . . . Tkouqua (i.e. !Aokwa) or Snyers'.
21. Forbes, *Pioneer Travellers*, p. 109: This 'is clearly the Kuruman, tributary of the Molopo which is a northern effluent of the Orange'.
22. *Ibid.*, pp. 105-6.
23. Graaf- or grafwater (both spellings occur in Gordon) is the original Dutch word which I have translated as 'underground water hole'. Literally the word means 'dig water' or perhaps 'spade water'. What I am attempting to convey here is that the water was under the surface of the soil and one had to dig down to get at it.
24. Mossop, *Journals of Wikar* . . ., p. 14: 'Namnykoa, the Karos-wearers (≠namma=Karos), living on Paarden Island and other islands East of Aughrabies Falls'. They were another one of the three tribes 'composing the Eynicquoas'. See n. 20 above.
25. This Model can only be the man described in Le Vaillant, *New Travels*, vol. 2, p. 252: 'His face proclaimed him fourscore; but his features were so strongly marked with villainy, that it was not necessary to know his name to conceive of him the opinion he deserved. It was Matthew Model, the intimate friend of Bernfry, and one of those fugitives proscribed by the colony and by the planters, for the atrocity of their conduct, and the blackness of their crimes.' ('Bernfry' is discussed in n. 35. below.)
26. A few days earlier, on 30 September 1779, Gordon had written: '. . . the kouw is a rojana, the same as those I found two years earlier on the Great Fish River. It

has the small red core inside the green capsule; the kernel tastes of almonds, and oil is made from it. They are very large here and the Bushmen get fat eating them.' The closest modern botanical name to 'rojana' is *Royena*, but this whole species is 'being sunk, and is now to be included in *Diospyros*', according to Palmer and Pitman, p. 88. The same authorities (pp. 135-6), write of the *Diospyros whytei* (*Royena lucida*): 'The berries are roundish in shape, contain from 2 to 4 yellow seeds, and when ripe turn a bright scarlet. The pulp round the seeds has a bitter-sweet taste. The whole berry is contained in a papery casket.'
27. Forbes and Rourke, p. 107, n. 143. Bushman grass: 'A generalized name applied to a number of Aristida species.'
28. Jeffreys, vol. for 1779, p. 409.
29. The *Aloe dichotoma*, or Quiver Tree. Noted extensively by the early travellers. 'Hottentots and Bushmen once used the hollowed-out branches of the kokerboom as quivers for their arrows' (Palmer and Pitman, p. 328, pls. 133, 149). See also Gordon Collection in the Cape Archives, AG 7146/173.
30. This was the rhinoceros bull shot near the source of the Gamka River on 2 November 1778. See chapt. 4, p. 64.
31. For a detailed zoological discussion on Gordon and giraffes see L. C. Rookmaaker, 'The observations of Robert Jacob Gordon (1743-1795) on giraffes . . .', *Journal S.W.A. Wissenschaftliche Gesellschaft*, from which much of this information has been taken.
32. Buffon and Daubenton, *Supplément aux Animaux Quadrupèdes*, vol. 27, p. 49.
33. *Ibid.*, pp. 57-8.
34. Le Vaillant, *New Travels*, vol. 2, p. 268.
35. Barend Vrije or Vry is undoubtedly 'Bernfry', the 'abominable wretch' of Le Vaillant's *New Travels*. Not only is he present at the shooting of the giraffe in this passage, but he is also present, as Bernfry, in Le Vaillant's account of the same episode. Gordon obviously had no doubt of the identification. This same 'Barend Freyn', (perhaps the true spelling of his name?) was also part of the two expeditions mounted by the Van Reenen brothers north of the Orange in 1792 and 1793. (See Professor Forbes's remarks in Quinton and Robinson, vol. 1, p. 85.) Besides its occurrence here, it should also be noted that there is mention of 'Barend Vry' elsewhere in this journal. On 26 November 1779 Gordon rather laconically records that both his old horse and Vry's horse had been eaten by lions at Soubesjes (present-day Klein Pella) while he was away on his journey up the Orange. This report, however, does not necessarily imply that Barend Vry was with Gordon's party.
36. See n. 34 above.
37. Le Vaillant, *Travels*, vol. 2, p. 397.
38. *Ibid.*, p. 401. This estimate, incidentally, is shared by Rookmaaker, 'Observations', pp. 9-10.
39. No. 64 in the Gordon Atlas.
40. No. 20 in the Gordon Atlas.
41. Toenema appears to be the 'Naugaap Toenemap' mentioned as being one of the Einiquas in the party on 3 October 1779, a passage not discussed here. He first makes his appearance in this section of the journal on p. 101.
42. Earlier in the entry for this day Toenema had identified these people as the 'Anoe Eis, the "Helders" (or "Bright") kraal who are Bushmen without cattle'. See p. 108 for the reason for this.
43. These people are possibly those mentioned in Mossop, *Journals of Wikar . . .*, p. 15: 'HUSINGAIS or Spinnekopdraad Kraal (Spiderwebkraal or People) in the approximate position of the present Koegas. The kraal is shown on the Gordon Atlas Map 3 as "Hoekingeis".' See also n. 17 above and nn. 24, 26, 28 in chapt. 7.
44. As it had on Gordon's second journey. See p. 52, 11 January 1778.
45. Presumably Gordon's *Kaw Heys, Kaw Eis* (Cutting Kraal) are the people referred to in Mossop, *Journals of Wikar . . .*, p. 14, as 'KAUKOA, the tailors or *Snijervolk* (Kora: !ao=to cut). These were living on Skanskop Island and other islands west of Keimoes.' It seems consistent that the 'cutting' refers to the semi-castration custom and has nothing to do with apparel! See also n. 17 above.

The '*Ogogua* or *Agokwa* (Narrow Cheeks) are Mossop's 'AUKOKOA, the Narrow Cheeks or Nouwange, living on Canon Island and other islands East of Keimoes. (Kora ≠ō=narrow)'.

Both these peoples, with the 'NAMNYKOA' (see n. 24 above) form part of the 'EYNIQUOAS'.
46. The Dutch phrase Gordon uses is 'polipentaten of camdebos hoenders'. 'Polipentaten' is derived from the French *Poule pintade*. 'Camdebos hoenders', however, appear to be some sort of jocular colonial coining. In the Gordon Atlas there is a drawing of a guinea fowl (no. 305), identified as *Numida meleagris* in Rookmaaker, *Zoological Exploration*, p. 108.

The francolin could be any one of about seven members of the Phasianidae family found in Southern Africa, with the right distribution for this area. There is, however, a drawing of the *Francolinus capensis* in the Gordon Atlas (no. 304), identified in Rookmaaker, *ibid.*, p. 108.

About four species of woodpeckers could have been see here, but there is a drawing of the *Dendropicus fuscescens* in the Atlas (no. 258), identified in Rookmaaker, *ibid.* p. 101.
47. 'A sort of guitar, strung with wire, and played with a plectum.' (*Shorter Oxford English Dictionary.*)

CHAPTER SEVEN

1. Forbes, *Pioneer Travellers*, p. 106. See also p. 113 regarding Gordon's predilection for 'later' naming.
2. *Ibid.*, p. 107 and map 21.
3. See chapt. 6, n. 45.
4. See chapt. 6, n. 42.
5. Mossop *Journals of Wikar . . .*, p. 15: 'GYZIQUOAS or Twin-kraal people. Hybrid Korana-BaTlaping living in 1779 along the Orange River near the present Upington.' See also Nienaber, p. 278.
6. Smallpox.
7. This river is shown on Map 3 of the Gordon Atlas (Forbes, *Pioneer Travellers*, map 21) as west of the Koeroemana River. It is not shown running into the sea, as claimed in the next paragraph of the journal. It is shown approximately where the Molopo River now lies. As an apparent afterthought, or emendation, Gordon adds that 'he has since learned that it . . . always contains water'. It is difficult, then, to know what to make of the inscription next to the Kaikaap River on the map, added, presumably, later than the journal, which reads: 'Kaaikaap means Great River in the Hottentot language. This misled . . . Lieutenant Brink . . . into the belief that the Great River or Garieb comes from the north. This Kaikaap River is usually dry and as shallow as the Lion [Houms River], running only after severe thunderstorms.'
8. I can find no other reference to these people.
9. Xhosa: *amanzi*, Tswana: *medzi*.
10. These could be the 'CHABOBE. //Habobe(n); (// Hawoben), or Veldskoendraers of Daberas-Hasuur, north of the Karas Mountains' (Mossop *Journals of Wikar . . .*, p. 13; also pp. 24, 25 and n. 10).
11. There is no Gharie River shown on Gordon's Map 3, but this is almost certainly a variant of Gariep or Garieb.
12. See n. 10 above.
13. These are probably the name of Batswana tribes. See Forbes, *Pioneer Travellers*, pp. 108-9.
14. Koang could possibly refer to the Okavango. See *ibid.*, p. 109.
15. It will be remembered that this river

was so named by Gordon and shown where it enters the Orange in his sketch of 23 December 1777. It is, of course, the present Caledon River. See Forbes, *ibid.*, p. 31.
16. Mossop, *Journals of Brink* . . ., p. 49 and n. 45.
17. Forbes, *Pioneer Travellers*, pp. 108-9.
18. *Ibid.*, p. 108.
19. *Ibid.*, p. 107.
20. Neither Forbes nor Mossop comment on this name. However, Map 3 in the Gordon Atlas (Forbes, *Pioneer Travellers*, map 21) does have an inscription just before the Draay Eilande (present-day Kheis) which reads: 'Sogenaamde wilde Bosjesmans Moncoboo geheeten – so called Wild Bushmen called Moncoboo.'
21. This hunt could refer to the poisoning method referred to on p. 121.
22. Buffon and Daubenton, vol. 14, pl. 1 (opp. p. 32).
23. Mossop, *Journals of Wikar* . . ., p. 15: 'KOURINGAIS or KLEYNE KORAKKOA (Kora Hottentot: !uri=proud, high) were later known as the Hoogstanders or Proud People. They were living near Kheis.'
24. Communication from Professor A.B. Smith to myself dated 13 June 1990. It is titled 'In the footsteps of Gordon' and is 'a first draft of a report on our work along the Orange last week'. Responding to some queries I had put to him regarding an article published in 1981 (Smith, 'Col. Robert Gordon on the Orange River', *Quarterly Bulletin of the South African Library*), Professor Smith took a small party to look for the 'Alabaster Klip' and for the place where Gordon decided to turn back. The group set out on 6 June from 'just north of the Boegoeberge on the east side of the river'. It was hard going since the Boegoeberg Dam had raised the level of the river since Gordon's day. In some areas members of the party had their movement reduced to 'finger tips and toe holds on the rock faces above the river'. Altogether this expedition achieved an exciting and commendable piece of detection and identification.
25. Mossop, *Journals of Wikar* . . ., p. 15. Where Gordon has marked 'Hoekingeis' Wikar's map has placed 'HUSINGAIS or Spinnekopdraad Kraal (Spiderwebkraal or People)'.
26. Probably the 'exorcism' referred to on 6 January 1779 near Loeriesfontein. See chapt. 3, p. 69, or perhaps the episode slightly earlier on p. 67.
27. See n. 25. However, n. 17 in chapt. 6 may provide the identification needed to reconcile the apparent contradiction here.
28. As mentioned, Raper and Boucher transcribe this word from Gordon's manuscript as 'Nokukeis'. Nienaber, pp. 749-50, has Noeukeis for the same word. A close examination of the photocopy in the Cape Archives has persuaded me that of the two transcriptions the latter is the more accurate. However, given the context of the word and other references to the same people by Gordon, I believe he could only be referring to the Noekeis here.
29. Forbes and Rourke, p. 135, n. 111: 'Xhosa-speaking AbaThembu who are not Xhosa proper'.
30. Forbes, *Pioneer Travellers*, p. 109: 'Furthest north of all, Gordon recorded, on Map 3 were the Schoenareba, Capii or Capeticoe from whom iron was obtained in bars. The first of these names suggests that they may have been the Shona who were the great blacksmiths of the interior and were neighbours of the Tswana until they were driven north by the Ndebele (Matebele).' It should be noted, however, that there is an apparent anomaly when Gordon states two paragraphs below that 'the Moetjoana' (as opposed to the Briqua?) 'get their iron and copper from the Europeans'.
31. The Barola must be the Barolong, the Shounarreba Capii, as seen above in n. 29, could be the Shona, while the Bapouru Boucana are the Phuduhutswana. See Forbes, *Pioneer Travellers*, p. 109.
32. Forbes, *Pioneer Travellers*, p. 108.
33. *Ibid.*, pp. 109-10.
34. The practice of removing a testicle. See entry for 16 October 1779, chapt. 6, p. 108.
35. See chapt. 1, p. 20.
36. Major P.H. Gielquin was head of the artillery at the Cape garrison. It is interesting, however, that Gordon's Map 3 contains no island called Gielquin. This was probably because, by the time the map was being drawn, Gordon had fallen out with the major. See chapt. 8, p. 133 for this assumption.
37. 'Veldschoenen' in the original Dutch. I have translated this as 'raw-hide shoes' since the term veldschoen was not current in eighteenth-century English.
38. It will be recalled that Gordon was met in the most friendly manner by Tamega on 18 October 1779, somewhere in the vicinity of Perde Eiland. See chapt. 6 p. 108 above.
39. Cabas's kraal must have been somewhere on the river near present-day Naries. See pp. 98 and 101 above.
40. The boat was left at Sandfontein on 28 September 1779. See chapt. 6, p. 98.
41. The place not the boy. It is still known as Kabas. See p. 98 above.
42. I owe this well founded contribution to the insight of my editor, Valerie Streak, whose interest in Gordon is as keen, at times, as my own.
43. On 26 November Gordon recorded that he rode, throughout the night, from a place marked Kaboes on the map, in a more or less direct line to Commas fontein (Pella today). He arrived at Sandfontein on 27 November. He also noted that two 'Bushmen' showed him the way.
44. See Le Vaillant, *New Travels*, pp. 161, 211, 212, 215-18 for references to this Schoenmaker. Also see Mossop, *Journals of Wikar* . . ., pp. 114-17.
45. Forbes, *Pioneer Travellers*, p. 124: 'Le Vaillant's Caminouquas are probably the people called Kamingou by Wikar, and now known as the Bondel-swarts of the Warmbad district.'
46. Present-day Warmbad, Namibia. Molsbergen, vol. 2, p. 51, is the reference here for 'the mountain called Comma'.
47. Ramansdrift today. See Forbes and Rourke, p. 105, n. 126.
48. Present-day Goodhouse. As Gordon says, the name means sheep path (or drift). The original name was 'Gudaos'. See Raper and Boucher, p. 126, and Nienaber and Raper p. 472. Homnaries could be Homgaris (*ibid.*, p. 565.)
49. Forbes and Rourke, p. 160, n. 124.
50. *Ibid.*, p. 103, n. 118.
51. Rookmaker, 'Gordon en zijn bijdrage tot de zoölogie', p. 75. The draft of the letter is in VC 595, pp. 105-32.
52. Forbes, 'Further notes on Colonel R.J. Gordon', *Africana Notes and News*, pp. 84, 85.

CHAPTER EIGHT

1. Cook and King, *Voyage to the Pacific Ocean*, p. 482.
2. Pasley, p. 85.
3. Sonnerat, *Voyage aux Indes Orientales et la Chine*, vol. 2, p. 93.
4. Barnard, p. 389, and Jeffreys, 1780, p. 25.
5. *Ibid.*
6. VC 595, p. 143.
7. Jeffreys, 1780, p. 409.
8. C.C. de Villiers and C. Pama, *Geslagsregisters van die Ou Kaapse Families*, p. 253.
9. For these details and discussion of Gordon's role as commander of the garrison, see Barnard (pp. 390-6), whom I have followed closely.
10. Rookmaaker, 'De bijdrage van R.J. Gordon', pp. 38, 39.
11. *Ibid.*, p. 39.
12. De Villiers and Pama, p. 253.
13. Le Vaillant, *Travels* and *New Travels*, *passim*.
14. Le Vaillant, *Travels*, p. 53.

15. *Ibid.*, p. 67.
16. Le Vaillant, *New Travels*, vol. 1, p. xvi.
17. *Ibid.*, p. xxiii.
18. *Ibid.*, p. 9.
19. *Ibid.*, p. 140.
20. *Ibid.*, p. 168.
21. *Ibid.*
22. A letter in the writer's possession confirms these details. It is addressed to 'Monsieur Allamand, proffesseur etc etc etc, A Leyden'. It is signed 'Le Vaillant, Amsterdam, le 27 Septembre 1784'.
23. Barnard (p. 408) quotes Paston and Marnitz. See also Forbes, *Pioneer Travellers*, pp. 86, 87.
24. *Ibid.*, p. 112.
25. *Ibid.*
26. The Gordon Manuscripts and Atlas, p. 11.
27. General historical background, here and elsewhere, is mainly taken from Theal (*History*), M.W. Spilhaus (*South Africa in the Making*), or Wilson and Thompson (*Oxford History of South Africa*).

CHAPTER NINE

1. VC 595, pp. 140-1.
2. In Forbes, *Pioneer Travellers*, p. 110, there is speculation that the 'unprecedented cartographic activity at the Cape in 1785-1786 may have arisen largely because the new governor, Van de Graaff, had been an engineer officer, but it is not unlikely that the English landing of the *Pigot* at St Francis Bay gave added incentive for the mapping of the south coast . . . Friderici and Jones may have begun their great map of the south coast in 1785 whilst in 1786 Duminy charted St Francis and Plettenberg bays. This cartography would have been of considerable interest to Gordon whose tastes lay in that direction, and it is conceivable that he may have accompanied the surveyors to initiate the works or that he may have paid them a supervisory visit.' There is, however, no record of such a visit.
3. VC 595, pp. 140-1. For a fuller discussion of this whole episode see P. Cullinan, 'Colonel R.J. Gordon: The Dias Padrão at Kwaaihoek, the Hermitage at Mossel Bay', *Quarterly Bulletin of the S.A. Library*, vol. 37, no. 2 (Dec. 1982), pp. 195-201 and pls. I, II and III.
4. A reproduction of this volume has been published under the title *Roteiro da Africa do Sul e Sueste . . .*, ed. A.F. da Costa, Lisbon, 1939.
5. VC 595, pp. 58-61.
6. VC 596, pp. 136, 137.
7. Cullinan, 'The Dias Padrão . . . the Hermitage', p. 199.

8. Theal, *History*, p. 215.
9. The tracking of Gordon's journey was undertaken by the writer using current 1/250,000 topo-cadastral sheets, printed by the Government Printer, Pvt Bag X85, Pretoria. The journal itself is contained in VC 593, pp. 104-43.
10. VC 596, pp. 136, 137.
11. Barnard, p. 383.
12. In a note to the journal entry for 22 November 1785, Gordon himself says that his bearings were 'recorded on loose sheets of paper – too long to insert here'. Examining the photocopies contained in vols. VC 596 and 597 one can see that the original pages were, in fact, individual sheets. Indeed, crease-marks show that many of the sheets had been folded so as to present two or four writing surfaces. There are also notes referring to other journeys, demonstrating that using 'loose sheets' was his normal practice.
13. In his correspondence with Swellengrebel, Hendrik Cloete mentions a Hendrik Oostwald Eksteen several times. The first time his name occurs the editor comments in a footnote that he was 'Born 1752, son of Petrus Michiel Eksteen and Sophia Cloete, a sister of Hendrik Cloete, living at *Bergvliet* in the Tygerberg'. (My translation.) But was the Petrus Michiel Eksteen he refers to, the owner of *another* Bergvliet – the elegant estate near Constantia where Gordon and Paterson stayed in October 1777 (see chapt. 2, p. 29)? And was it just coincidence that this Bergvliet was also inherited by a son named Hendrik Oostwald in 1783? (See Schutte, pp. 186, 198; also Dane and Wallace, p. 62.)
14. M.A. Parker, *Voyage Round the World in the Gorgon Man of War*, p. 49.
15. VC 595, p. 92.
16. *Dict. S.A. Biog.*, vol. 2, p. 376. Kuys, Johannes Abraham: He was born in the Netherlands in 1756 and 'was appointed the minister of Roodezand in the Land of Waveren (later Tulbagh) where he settled on 27.4.1777'. He returned to the Netherlands after ten years but was persuaded to return to Roodezand in 1789. He died in Cape Town in 1798.
17. No. 41 in the Gordon Atlas.
18. *Dict. S.A. Biog.*, vol. 3, pp. 476, 477.
19. Hendrik Cloete (see n. 13 above) also mentions Marthinus Melck. The English summary by Dr A.J. Boëseken follows: 'Marthinus Melk had second thoughts after becoming engaged to marry David Kriel's daughter. He became re-engaged and broke it off again. At last the marriage took place; yet as a married man he lives more dissolutely than ever.' Schutte, p. 245 (Dutch), p. 396 (English).
20. *Dict. S.A. Biog.*, pp. 596-8.

21. Rookmaaker, *Zoological Exploration*, p. 117: 'Indicator, indicator, "honingvogel"'
22. Schutte, p. 277 (Dutch), p. 410 (English).
23. See n. 13 above.
24. Information given to me by Mrs W. Melck. It is noteworthy that the same family still owns and lives on this farm, 200 years after Gordon's visit.
25. Buffon and Daubenton, vol. 15, p. 124. My translation.
26. 'What you don't put in, can't go wrong.' This aphorism of Henry Ford's was quoted by Professor V.S. Forbes when I discussed the question of Gordon's observatory with him. It is perhaps unwise of me, therefore, to indulge in speculation about this object, but it is my belief that in fact there exists a drawing of it. There is a map of Saldanha Bay described in Forbes, *Pioneer Travellers*, p. 113, 'without date or name of author'. Nevertheless, the handwriting is undoubtedly Gordon's. Professor Forbes's description continues: 'It depicts in enlarged elevation an impressive group of buildings at Hoetjes or Hoedjes Bay, including a strange pavilion-like structure, hexagonal in plan with domed roof and arched windows. Reproduced by Molsbergen 1916, I, p. 26.'

Of course, I have no proof that this 'strange pavilion-like structure' is Gordon's observatory. Certainly he says nothing of going to Saldanha Bay in this journal. However, there are many notes of bearings referring to Saldanha in VC 596, where notes of bearings on this journey are also contained.
27. 'The Narrative' is in Mossop, *Journals of Wikar . . .*, pp. 277-91.
28. 1st October 1779 (not quoted).
29. 22 November 1785 (not quoted).
30. Now called Steenboksfontein, it is about half-way between the mouth of the Langevlei River and Lambert's Bay.
31. According to Theal, *History*, vol. 1, pp. 426-8, smallpox made its first appearance in 1713 and almost destroyed the Hottentot nation: 'The very names of the best known tribes were blotted out by the disease.'
32. These notes were part of the photocopy for the journal of the fourth journey that I used.
33. Raven-Hart, vol. 1, p. 113.
34. *Ibid.*, vol. 2, index, p. 505: 'HOTTENTOTS, Abandonment of old'.
35. *Widdringtonia juniperoides*. Palmer and Pitman, pp. 127-8. As Gordon points out, these trees belong, correctly, to the Cypress family.
36. *Hyenanche globosa*: 'Commonly called the gifboom, this small tree rarely exceeds five metres and is more or less endemic to

the Gifberge behind the farm Wind Hoek.' This farm is five kilometres N.E. of Klawer. (Forbes and Rourke, p. 169, nn. 172 and 173.

37. Forbes, *Thunberg*, pp. 194, 195, as well as n. 125.
38. These are, no doubt, the deep ravines and high ridges of the 'Tanquas' Karoo.
39. Now Wolfrivier.
40. A part of the present-day Elandsberge.
41. Gordon and his party had stayed with Willem van Wyk on 30 December at his farm Mietjies Fontein in the Biedouberge.
42. Nearby present-day Voëlfontein River.
43. Molsbergen, vol. 2, p. 69: '. . . een dor, droog en onbewoond veld'.
44. No. 11 in the Gordon Atlas.
45. Forbes, *Pioneer Travellers*, p. 64, and map 11 will be found useful for this part of Gordon's journey.
46. See chapt. 3, p. 52, and chapt. 4, p. 62.
47. Forbes, *Pioneer Travellers*, p. 84 and maps 13 and 15.
48. Entry for 5 November 1777 (not quoted). The accents on Ámi Ćo represent clicks.
49. Forbes and Rourke, p. 74 and n. 139.
50. Nienaber and Raper, vol. 2, p. 1058.
51. See also Forbes, *Pioneer Travellers*, p. 149.
52. Nienaber and Raper, vol. 2, pp. 566, 567. See also Forbes, *Pioneer Travellers*, map 15, which is a careful, beautifully executed re-drawing from Gordon's Map 3.
53. I can find nothing more about Stephanus Scheepers than his baptismal date in De Villiers and Pama. There seems to be no mention of him elsewhere. For those interested, if this is the right Stephanus Scheepers he was baptized 3 April 1740.
54. The Rondeberg, evidently, is a peak in the Baviaanskloof Mountains to the south of Doorn Rivier.
55. This forked mountain is not shown on Gordon's Map 3, but it is probably the Cockscomb, the highest and most conspicuous peak in the Groot Winterhoek range. On Gordon's map the jagged nature of the peaks is emphasized; they are indeed 'forked'.
56. On Gordon's Map 3 a height of 5 600 feet is written over the top of the range, which means that these two altitudes differ by 200 feet. Port Elizabeth, topo-cadastral sheet 3324, gives the Cockscomb as 1 758 metres (5 757 feet).
57. Peires, pp. 50, 51; J.S. Bergh and J.C. Visagie, *The Eastern Cape Frontier Zone 1660-1980*, pp. 10-11.
58. Robert Gordon, born in September 1781, would have been nearly four-and-a-half years old at this time.
59. Forbes, *Sparrman*, vol. 2, pp. 232-33, as well as nn. 12 and 13.
60. VC 596. Bearings, etc. for this region can be found in this vol.
61. Nienaber and Raper, vol. 1, pp. 290-1.
62. See chapt. 3, p. 52.
63. Nienaber and Raper, vol. 1, pp. 264-5. Gordon's Vaders (or Father's) River is emphatically accepted. The meaning 'nes van bokke', or 'buck's nest', is rejected with some humour.
64. Presumably to use for weapons or implements.
65. V.S. Forbes, 'Colonel R.J. Gordon and the Diaz Cross, Kwaaihoek 1786', *Quarterly Bulletin of the South African Library*, vol. 27 (1972), p. 3: 'These are the two pieces of ordinance that gave rise to the name of the locality and to the new township of Cannon Rocks that is now established 4 km W.S.W. of Boknes River mouth.'
66. G. and D. Allen, *The Guns of Sacramento*, gives a vivid account of this incident. An 'official' as well as a 'secret' journal was kept by the first mate, Evan Jones. In these he describes the wreck of the East Indiaman *Doddington* on Bird Island and how the survivors eventually reached Moçambique.
67. Barnard, p. 383.
68. Forbes, 'Gordon and the Diaz Cross', pp. 2, 4 and n. 7. This quotes Kirby's *Jacob van Reenen and the* Grosvenor *Expedition*, identifying him as Daniel Willem Kuen.
69. Peires, pp. 50-1: 'Ndlambe's chief rivals were the Gqunukhwebe under Tshaka and his son Chungwa. Ndlambe killed Tshaka in battle around 1782.'
70. For interesting modern contributions on these changing relationships see N.G. Penn, 'The frontier of the Western Cape' – a paper presented at a workshop organized by the Spatial Archaeology Research Unit, UCT (Oct. 1984); 'Anarchy and authority in the Koue Bokkeveld, 1739-1779: the banishing of Carel Buijtendag', UCT (1984); 'Pastoralists and pastoralism in the northern Cape frontier zone during the eighteenth century', *SA Archaeological Society Goodwin Series* 5. Also see H.C. Bredenkamp and S. Newton-King, 'The subjugation of the Khoisan during the 17th and 18th centuries', Conference on Economic Development and Racial Discrimination, paper 1 (1984).

CHAPTER TEN

1. Forbes, 'Gordon and the Diaz Cross', pp. 1-4; also P. Cullinan, 'Colonel R.J. Gordon, the Dias Padrão at Kwaaihoek, the Hermitage at Mossel Bay', *Quarterly Bulletin of the South African Library*, vol. 37, no. 2 (Dec. 1982), pp. 195-201.
2. Barnard, p. 393.
3. Molsbergen, vol. 2, p. 64, n. 1.
4. VC 595, pp. 133-5.
5. In another draft letter referred to later (VC 595, p. 146) Gordon remarks: 'I do not reply that my French is good, not being the language in which I think; I hope, however, that you will understand me and that will suffice.'
6. Gunn & Codd, p. 100. Boos had just returned from Mauritius where he had been from February 1787 to January 1788.
7. Rookmaaker, 'Bijdrage tot de zoölogie', p. 41.
8. Gunn & Codd, p. 318.
9. VC 595, p. 146.
10. VC 595, pp. 136-9. See also Nash, p. 33, which has a letter from Lieut. Edward Riou to Sir Joseph Banks which seems to confirm that Gordon *intended* to make a further journey at this time. Headed 'Cape of Good Hope, 10 Decr. 1789, *Guardian*' the penultimate sentence reads: 'I mentioned to Col. Gordon, what you did me the Honour to write about Human Skulls, & the Col. who shortly means to make a journey far Northward told me he would endeavour to get some of the Hottentots and different Caffres!'
11. It is probable that parts of Schoonder Sigt still remain at 3 Flower Street, Gardens. Denis Verschoyle, a retired town-planner, who has extensive knowledge of the area, having once prepared a policy plan for Upper Table Valley, believes that the metre-thick walls incorporated into the house now standing there, are part of the original Schoonder Sigt. Gordon bought the property from the estate of a certain Jean de Bonnaire in May 1788, according to the deed of transfer still to be found in the Cape Town Deeds Office. The building cited by Barnard (pp. 383, 384, and illustrated by a photograph facing p. 384) has been demolished. It was part of the same property but was probably built later.
12. Almost all the information about Gordon's military responsibilities and activities comes from Barnard, pp. 389-400.
13. J.M. Bulloch, *The Gay Gordons*, pp. 157-8.
14. See Bredenkamp and Newton-King: in particular p. 21 for the Swellendam 'upheaval'.
15. VC 595, pp. 140, 141.
16. VC 595, pp. 143-7. But this letter, which is in Gordon's hand, is followed by a fair copy in copperplate hand: VC 595, pp. 148-52.
17. VC 598, pp. 44, 52.
18. D. Collins, *An Account of the English Colony*, p. 8.

19. W. Bligh, *A Voyage to the South Sea . . .*, p. 38.
20. J. White, *Journal of a Voyage to New South Wales*, pp. 90, 91. A further acknowledgement of Gordon's help comes at the beginning of the same letter quoted in n. 8 above (Nash, p. 31). Lieut. Riou writes to Sir Joseph Banks concerning plants loaded in the *Guardian* for New South Wales: 'To Col. Gordon and to Mr. Masson do we owe a great deal, and indeed the most part of the plants came from the Colonel's garden.'
21. Journal kept by Macquarie, governor of New South Wales. Copy of part of a typescript extract (1933) in the Gubbins Library, University of the Witwatersrand. Original MS. in the Mitchell Library, Sydney. See Forbes, *Pioneer Travellers*, p. 93.
22. Forbes, *Sparrman*, vol. 1, p. 12.
23. VC 595, pp. 80-92.
24. Forbes, *Sparrman*, vol. 1, p. 209: 'Buff . . . is of Scots origin and means nonsense or idle talk.'
25. Rookmaaker, 'Bijdrage tot de zoölogie', p. 41.
26. Schutte, p. 279 (Dutch), p. 411 (English).
27. Rookmaaker, 'Bijdrage tot de zoölogie', p. 42.
28. This account concerning the merino sheep is taken mainly from Barnard, chapt. VI. His chief sources are: Thom, *Die Geskiedenis van die Skaapboerdery in Suid Afrika*; Bouchenroeder, *Beknop Berigt nopens de Volkplanting de Kaap de Goede Hoop*; as well as Brown, *Sheep Breeding in Australia*.
29. Rookmaaker, 'Bijdrage tot de zoölogie', p. 42.
30. The whole controversy concerning the Pepinierin and the ensuing comments concerning Gordon's military career can be found in A.J. Boëseken, 'Die Nederlandse Kommissarisse en die 18de Euse Samelewing aan die Kaap', *Argiefjaarboek vir Suid Afrikaanse Geskiedenis* (1944).
31. VC 123.
32. Theal, *History*, p. 210.
33. *Ibid.*, p. 229.
34. VC 594, pp. 1-33.
35. Parker, pp. 49-57.
36. It seems that Mary Anne Parker mistook the location of the Gordon's home, since Green Point today is on the other side of Table Mountain from where Schoonder Sigt stood.
37. Barnard, p. 383.
38. E. Edwards and G. Hamilton, *The Voyage of H.M.S. Pandora*, p. 170.
39. C.C. Best, *Brieven Over Oostendien*. The translation is by the writer. There is another translation of this passage in *Africana Notes and News*, June 1970, p. 75, by Raven-Hart.
40. VC 594, p. 171.
41. Forbes, 'Further notes', pp. 85, 86.
42. In this section the sources for background material are again Theal (*History*); Spilhaus, and Wilson and Thompson.
43. This account of Gordon's experiments with the red hot cannon balls is taken almost entirely from Barnard pp. 400-405.
44. Forbes, 'Gordon's family', facing pp. 134, 135 and 135.
45. Theal, *History*, p. 288.
46. *Ibid.*, p. 283.
47. *Ibid.*, p. 286.
48. Barnard, p. 404.

CHAPTER ELEVEN

1. Once more the writer must acknowledge his great debt to C.J. Barnard's M.A. thesis, 'Robert Jacob Gordon se loopbaan aan die Kaap', for this section. On military events and background this work can hardly be faulted. Barnard in turn has relied greatly on Theal, though this source has been amplified by plentiful quotations from original sources such as Marnitz and Campagne.
2. Marnitz, VC 75, p. 499, n. 1. (N.B. I am using what seems to be a nineteenth-century English translation which has been appended to the Dutch copy in the Cape Archives.)
3. Theal, *Records of the Cape Colony 1793-1796*, pp. 45, 46.
4. See chapt. 1, p. 21.
5. Barnard, p. 416, who quotes Campagne, VC 76.
6. Marnitz, VC 75.
7. H.R. de Puyfontaine, *Louis Michel Thibault 1750-1815: His Official Life at the Cape of Good Hope*, p. 7.
8. *Ibid.*, p. 9.
9. Theal, *History*, p. 308.
10. Marnitz, VC 75, p. 355.
11. *Ibid.*, p. 359.
12. De Puyfontaine, p. 10.
13. *Ibid.*, p. 15.
14. Theal, *Records*, p. 230.
15. *DSB*, vol. 1, p. 401.
16. Marnitz, VC 75, p. 505.
17. Theal, *Records*, p. 230.
18. Anon., *Apologie de Robert de Gordon . . .*, p. 17.
19. Marnitz, VC 75, p. 250.
20. *Ibid.*
21. G. Paston, *Side-lights on the Georgian Period*, pp. 219-37.
22. Anon. p. 6, n. 1.
23. Marnitz, VC 75, pp. 513-514.
24. Barnard, pp. 434, 435, who quotes Campagne, VC 76.
25. Urban, p. 442-3.
26. *Ibid.*
27. Forbes, *Pioneer Travellers*, p. 116.
28. VC 595, p. 148. The passage reads: 'Il faut premierement que je vous dise que je ne suis nullement systematique, et que j'ai appris a ne pas facilement croire et que quoique j'admire l'ingenieux et sublime Buffon je n'ai jamais plus m'imaginer totales ces suites si regulierement calcules des evenements de la terre . . . .' It could thus be maintained that Gordon was not decrying so much his own lack of system but rather that he did not belong to a school of system-builders such as Buffon's.

EPILOGUE

1. Most of the information contained here can be found in Forbes, 'Gordon's family', and in Barnard, pp. 435, 436. The latter quotes material communicated to him by Miss Mary Gunn of Pretoria.

Bibliography

ALLEN, GEOFFREY and DAVID. *The Guns of Sacramento*, London, Robin Garton, 1978.

ANON. *Apologie de Robert de Gordon, ci-devant Commandant Générale des Troups du Cap de Bonne Espérance. Par un de ses amis.* Au Cap de Bonne Espérance: au puits de la verité, 1796.

AXELSON, ERIC. *South-East Africa 1488-1530*, New York, Kraus, 1969.
Congo to Cape: Early Portuguese Explorers, London, Faber & Faber, 1973.

BARNARD, C.J. 'Robert Jacob Gordon se loopbaan aan die Kaap', *Archives Yearbook for South African History*, vol. 13, part 1, Parow, Cape Times, 1950.

BARROW, J. *An Account of Travels into the Interior of Southern Africa in the Years 1797 & 1798*, 2 vols., London, Cadell & Davies, 1801.

BERGH, J.S. and VISAGIE, J.C. *The Eastern Cape Frontier Zone 1660-1980*, Durban, Butterworths, 1985.

BEST, C.C. *Brieven Over Oostendien*, Amsterdam, Johannes Allart, 1808.

BLIGH, W. Lieut. *A Voyage to the South Sea . . .*, London, George Nichol, 1792.

BOESEKEN, A.J. 'Die Nederlandse kommissarisse en die 18de euse samelewing aan die Kaap', *Argiefjaarboek vir Suid Afrikaanse Geskiedenis*, Cape Town, Cape Times for Government Printer, 1944.

BREDENKAMP, H.C. and NEWTON-KING, S. 'The subjugation of the Khoisan during the 17th and 18th centuries', Conference on Economic Development and Racial Domination, paper no. 1 (1984).

BUFFON and DAUBENTON. *Histoire Naturelle: Générale et Particulière*, Amsterdam, Chez J.H. Schneider, 1771.

BULLOCH, J.M. *The House of Gordon*, Aberdeen University Studies, 1903-1912.
The Gay Gordons, London, Chapman & Hall, 1908.

BURMAN, JOSE. *So High the Road*, Cape Town/Pretoria, Human & Rousseau, 1963.

BURMAN, JOSE and LEVIN, STEPHEN. *The Saldanha Story*, Cape Town/Pretoria, Human & Rousseau, 1974.

CAMPBELL, JOHN. *Travels in South Africa*, London, Black & Parry, 1815.

COLLINS, D. *An Account of the English Colony*, 2 vols., London, Cadell & Davies, 1798-1802.

COOK, J. Capt. and KING, J. Capt. *Voyage to the Pacific Ocean*, vol. 3, London, Nichol & Cadell, 1795.

CULLINAN, PATRICK. 'Colonel R.J. Gordon: The Dias Padrão at Kwaaihoek, the Hermitage at Mossel Bay', *Quarterly Bulletin of the South African Library*, vol. 37, no. 2 (Dec. 1982).
'Robert Jacob Gordon and Denis Diderot: The Hague, 1774', *Quarterly Bulletin of the South African Library*, vol. 43, no. 4 (June 1989).

DANE, P. and WALLACE, S.A. *The Great Houses of Constantia*, Cape Town, Don Nelson, 1981.

DE FONTENAY, ELIZABETH. *Diderot, Reason and Resonance*, New York, George Braziller, 1982.

DE PUYFONTAINE, H.R. *Louis Michel Thibault 1750-1815: His Official Life at the Cape of Good Hope*, Cape Town, Tafelberg, 1972.

DE VILLIERS, C.C. and PAMA, C. *Geslagsregisters van die Ou Kaapse Families*, Cape Town/Rotterdam, Balkema, 1987.

Dictionary of National Biography, 63 vols. London, Smith Elder, 1885-1900.

Dictionary of Scientific Biography, 14 vols. New York, Scribners, 1970-1976.

Dictionary of South African Biography, 5 vols., Pretoria, Human Sciences Research Council, 1987.

DIDEROT, *Oeuvres Complètes*, edited by J. Assezat & M. Tourneux, 20 vols. Paris, Garnier, 1875-1877.

DYER, R.A. 'Colonel R.J. Gordon's contribution to S.A. botany', *S.A. Biological Society*, pamphlet 14. (1948).

EDWARDS, E. Capt. and HAMILTON, G. Surgeon. *The Voyage of H.M.S. Pandora*, edited by B. Thomson, London, Francis Edwards, 1915.

ELPHICK, R. *Khoikhoi and the Founding of White South Africa*, Johannesburg, Ravan Press, 1985.

Encyclopaedia Brittanica, 24 vols., Chicago, etc., William Benton, 1970.

FERGUSON, J. *Papers Illustrating the History of the Scots Brigade in the Service of the United Netherlands 1572-1782*, 3 vols. Edinburgh, The Scottish History Society, 1899.

FORBES, V.S. 'Further notes on Colonel R.J. Gordon', *Africana Notes and News*, vol. 9 (1952).
'Colonel R.J. Gordon's family', *Africana Notes and News*, vol. 11 (1954).
Pioneer Travellers in South Africa, Cape Town, A.A. Balkema, 1965.
'Colonel R.J. Gordon and the Diaz Cross, Kwaaihoek, 1786', *Quarterly Bulletin of the South African Library*, vol. 27 (1972).
Anders Sparrman: Travels in the Cape 1772-1776, 2 vols., Cape Town, Van Riebeeck Society, 1975-1977.
(ed.) *C.P. Thunberg: Travels at the Cape of Good Hope, 1772-1775*, Cape Town, Van Riebeeck Society, 1986.

FORBES, V.S. and ROURKE, J. (eds.) *Paterson's Cape Travels, 1777-1779*, Johannesburg, The Brenthurst Press, 1980.

FRANSEN, H. and COOK, M.A. *The Old Buildings of the Cape*, Cape Town, A.A. Balkema, 1980.

GARSIDE, S. 'Baron Jacquin and the Schönbrunn Gardens', *Journal of South African Botany*. vol. 8 (1942).

GUNN, M.D. 'Colonel R.J. Gordon', *Africana Notes and News*. vol. 11 (1954).

GUNN, M. & CODD, L.E. (eds.) *Botanical Exploration of Southern Africa*, Cape Town, A.A. Balkema, 1981.

HAAGNER, A. *South African Mammals*, London/Cape Town, Witherby/Maskew Miller, 1920.

HALLEMA, A. *Die Kaap in 1776-1777*, Constantia/Johannesburg, A.A.M. Stols, 1951.

HICKEY, W. *Memoirs of William Hickey*, 3 vols., London, Hurst & Blackett, 1925.

JEFFREYS, K.M. *Kaapse Archiefstukken . . . 1779; 1780; 1781; 1782*, Cape Town, Cape Times, 1927-1931.

KIRBY, P.R. 'Heerenlogement and its visitors', *S.A. Journal of Science*, vol. 38 (1941), p. 352.
'A further note on the Heerenlogement', *S.A. Journal of Science*, vol. 40 (1943), p. 334.

KOEMAN, C. *Tabulae Geographicae . . . Eighteenth Century Cartography of Cape Colony*, Amsterdam/Cape Town, N.V. Hollandsch-Afrikaansche Uitgewers, 1952.

LE VAILLANT, F. *Travels into the Interior Parts of Africa . . .*, 2 vols., London, G.G. & J. Robinson, 1790.
New Travels into the Interior Parts of Africa . . ., 3 vols., London, G.G. & J. Robinson, 1796.

LEWIS WILLIAMS, DAVID and DOWSON, THOMAS. *Images of Power*, Johannesburg, Southern, 1989.

McLACHLAN, G.R. and LIVERSIDGE, R. (eds.) *Roberts Birds of South Africa*, Cape Town, the John Voelcker Bird Book Fund, 1978.

MENTZEL, O.F. *A Geographical-Topographical Description of the Cape of Good Hope*, 3 vols., edited by H.J. Mandelbrote, Cape Town, Van Riebeeck Society, 1921-1924.

MOLSBERGEN, E.C. GODEE. *Reizen in Zuid-Afrika in de Hollandse Tijd*, 4 vols., 's Gravenhage, Martinus Nijhoff, 1916-1932.

MOODIE, D. *The Record*, Amsterdam, A.A. Balkema, 1960.

MOSSOP, E.E. *Journals of Wikar, Coetse and Van Reenen*, Cape Town, Van Riebeeck Society, 1935.
Journals of Brink and Rhenius, Cape Town, Van Riebeeck Society, 1947.

NASH, M.D. (ed.) *The Last Voyage of the Guardian, Lieutenant Riou, Commander, 1789-1791*, Cape Town, Van Riebeeck Society, Second Series no. 20, 1990 for 1989

NIENABER, G.S. *Khoekhoense Stamname*, Pretoria/Cape Town, Academica, 1989.

NIENABER, G.S. and RAPER, P.E. *Toponymica Hottentotica*, 2 vols., Pretoria, S.A. Naamkundsesentrum, 1977.

PALMER, E. and PITMAN, N. *Trees of South Africa*, Amsterdam/Cape Town, A.A. Balkema, 1961.

PARKER, MARY ANNE. *Voyage Round the World in the 'Gordon' Man of War*, London, John Nichols, 1795.

PASLEY, R.M.S. *Private Sea Journals 1778-1782*, London/Toronto, Dent, 1931.

PASTON, G. *Side-Lights on the Georgian Period*, London, Methuen, 1901.

PATERSON, W. *Narrative of Four Journeys into the Country of the Hottentots and Caffraria . . .*, 2nd edition, London, J. Johnson, 1790.

PENN, N.G. 'The frontier in the Western Cape', a paper for the workshop organized by the Spatial Archaeology Research Unit, University of Cape Town (October 1984).
'Anarchy and authority in the Koue Bokkeveld, 1739-1779: The banishing of Carel Buijtendag', Cape Town, Department of History, University of Cape Town (1984).
'Pastoralists and pastoralism in the Northern Cape frontier zone during the eighteenth century', *South African Archaeological Society Goodwin Series 5*, (1986), pp. 62-8.
'Labour, land and livestock in the Western Cape during the eighteenth century', Cape Town, Centre for African Studies, University of Cape Town, (1986).

PEIRES, J.B. *The House of Phalo: A History of the Xhosa People in the Days of their Independence*, Johannesburg, Ravan Press, 1981.

PINKERTON, JOHN. *The Literary Correspondence of John Pinkerton, Esq.*, edited by Dawson Turner, London, Colman & Bentley, 1830.

QUINTON, J.C. and ROBINSON, A.M. (eds.) *François le Vaillant, Traveller in South Africa*, Cape Town, Library of Parliament, 1973.

RAPER, E. and BOUCHER, M. (eds. and trans.) *Robert Jacob Gordon, Cape Travels, 1777 to 1786*, 2 vols., Johannesburg, Brenthurst Press, 1988.

RAVEN-HART, R. *Cape Good Hope*, 2 vols., Cape Town, A.A. Balkema, 1971.

RAYNAL, ABBE G.T. *A Philosophical and Political History of the Settlements and Trade of the Europeans in the East and West Indies*, 8 vols., translated by J.O. Justamond, London, Strahan & Cadell, 1788.

ROOKMAAKER, L.C. 'Robert Jacob Gordon (1743-1795) en zijn bijdrage tot de zoölogie van de Kaap de Goede Hoop', doctoral thesis, Biohistorisch Instituut le Utrecht (unpubd.), 1979.
'De Bijdrage van Robert Jacob Gordon (1743-1795) tot Kennis van de Kaapse Fauna', Ommeren, Documentatieblad Werkgroep 18de Eeuw, no. 46 (1980)
'The observations of Robert Jacob Gordon (1743-1795) on giraffes (giraffa camelopardalis) found in Namaqualand', *Journal S.W.A. Wissenschaftliche Gesellschaft*, 36, 37 (1983), pp. 71-90.
The Zoological Exploration of South Africa, Rotterdam/ Brookfield, A.A. Balkema, 1989.

SCHAMA, S. *Patriots and Liberators: Revolution in the Netherlands 1780-1813*, London, Collins, 1977.

SCHAPERA, I. *The Khoisan Peoples of South Africa*, London, Routledge, 1930.

SMITH, A.B. 'Col. Robert Gordon on the Orange River', *Quarterly Bulletin of the South African Library*, vol. 36, no. 2 (December 1981).

SONNERAT, P. *Voyage aux Indes Orientales et La Chine*, 2 vols., Paris, Chez l'Auteur etc, 1782.

SPILHAUS, M.W. *South Africa in the Making*, Cape Town, Juta, 1966.

STAVORINUS, J.S. *Voyages to the East Indies . . . translated by S.H. Wilcocke*, London, Robinson, 1798.

SCHUTTE, G.J. (ed.) *Briefwisseling van Hendrik Swellengrebel Jr oor Kaapse Sake 1778-1792*, Cape Town, Van Riebeeck Society, 1982.

THEAL, G.McC. *History of South Africa, 1725-1795*, London, Sonnenschein, 1897.
Records of the Cape Colony 1793-1796, Cape Town, The Government of the Cape Colony, 1897.
Belangrijke Historische Dokumenten over Zuid Afrika, vol. 1, Cape Town, Van de Sandt de Villiers & Co., 1896.

THUNBERG, C.P. *Travels in Europe, Africa and Asia . . .*, 4 vols., London, W. Richardson & J. Egerton, 1793-1796.

TOBIAS, P.V. (ed.) *The Bushmen: San Hunters and Herders of Southern Africa*, Cape Town/ Pretoria, Human & Rousseau, 1978.

URBAN, S. 'Col. Robert Gordon' (obituary), *The Gentleman's Magazine*, London, John Nichols (May 1796).

WATERHOUSE, G. (ed.) *Simon van der Stel's Journey to Namaqualand in 1685*, Cape Town/Pretoria, Human & Rousseau, 1979.

WHISSON, M.G. 'Khoi and San: What's in a name?', Grahamstown, Anthropology Dept, Rhodes University, (1985).

WHITE, J. *Journal of a Voyage to New South Wales*, London, 1790.

WILLCOX, A.R. *Great River: The Story of the Orange River*, Winterton, Drakensberg Publications, 1986.

WILSON, A.M. *Diderot*, New York, Oxford University Press, 1972.

WILSON, M.L. '"By any other name": The nomenclature of the Khoisan', mimeo, n.d., a paper read at the biennial conference of the Southern African Association of Archaeologists, Grahamstown (1985).
'Notes on the nomenclature of the Khoisan', *Annals of the South African Museum*, vol. 97, part 8 (August 1986).
'Shell middens and strandlopers', *Sagittarius*, vol. 4, no. 1 (March 1989).

WILSON, M. and THOMPSON, L. *The Oxford History of South Africa, Volume I, South Africa to 1870*, London, Oxford University Press, 1969.

ARCHIVAL SOURCES

The Cape Archives

CAMPAGNE, H.D. 'Memoire en Byzonderheden wegens der Kaap de Goede Hoop . . .', (1795), VC 76.

GORDON, R.J. 'Robert Dagboek', vols. 1-7 (photocopies of originals in Stafford County Archives, England), VC 592-598. (Originals now in Brenthurst Library, Johannesburg.)

GORDON, R.J. 'R.J. Gordon over der Peppinierin', 1790, VC 123.
'Korte stellingen omtrent de Meteorologie in het generaal, beneffens eene schets van het weer aan de Caap de goede hoop in het bysonder', n.d., VC 170.

MARNITZ, P.W. 'Verhaal van de Overgaave van de Kaap de Goede Hoop aan de Engelschen door een vriend de waarheid aldaar. In 't tweede jaar der batavische Vryheid', n.d., VC 75.

SWELLENGREBEL, H. 'Copies of three journals of journies to Saldanha Bay & St Helena Bay; Heeren Logement & Elephant's River estuary; North-eastern Cape and South-east coast', ACC. 447.

INDEX

NOTE: The page numbers of illustrations are indicated in **bold** *type.*

A
Aape Berg 68, 151
aardvark **117**
Aberdeen 21, 27, 33, 64
Acacia karroo **46**
Addo Elephant Park 156
Adelaide 43
African Pied Wagtail 197 (Ch. 5, n. 35)
Agha Lè 43
Agter Bruintjieshoogte 40
Aiaas *see* Eyas
Akkerendam 68
Albaster Klip 115-16
Algoa Bay 53, 56-7, 141
Alicedale 27, 50
Allamand, Jean Nicolas Sebastien 25, 44, 162, 165
    animal studies 22, 29, 137, 166, 188: giraffe 101-4; hippopotamus **37**, 54, 56, 147; rhinoceros 64-5
Aloe dichotoma **18**
Aloe Ridge 56
Aloes Kloof 93
Alting, Willem Arnold 169
Amaquas *see* Namaquas
AmaXhosa *see* Xhosa
Ami Cò 152
Amsterdam 99, 164
Anthoscopus caroli 197 (Ch. 6, n. 2)
Anthoscopus minutus 197 (Ch. 6, n. 2)
Aree, Chief 44
artist *see* Schoemaker, Johannes
Asclepias fruticosa **127**
Ashton 66
Attaquas Kloof 141
Attaquasberge 141
Augrabies Falls 98, 100, 105, **106-7**
Augustin, Marquis de Ximénès 185
Australia 165, 167-8, 188 *see also* New South Wales
Austria, Emperor Joseph II 159-60
Avontuur 28, 56, 141, 157
Azia 22

B
baboons 57, 107, **138**, 147
Bailly, Jean-Sylvain 139-40, 144, 164, 184
Bakens River 141, 157
Bamboesberg 44
Banks, Sir Joseph 11, 48, 129, 159, 160
Bapouru Boucana 117, 199 (Ch. 7, n. 31)
Barberà, Chief 40, 43
Barend, Klaas 98, 100, 109
Barolo 117, 199 (Ch. 7, n. 31)
Barrow, John 12, 53, 137, 152
Basson (farmer) 33
Baster, Klaas 98, 104, 109, 136, 198 (Ch. 6, n. 19)
Baster, Piet 98, 109
Batavia 133, 169, 170, 172, 178, 189
    Republic of 173
Batlaping 113 *see also* Briquas
Batswana *see* Briquas
Baviaansgebergte 141
Beervlei 27, 32-3, 152
Beesbank 97
Bengali slave 146
Bentinck, Count Charles 49, 80
Bentincks Valey 91
Berg River 21, 141, 147, 160-2
Berg Rivier (farm) 146-7
Berg Valey 129
Bergen-op-Zoom, Siege of 20
Bergvallei 148
Bergvliet 29, 196 (Ch. 2, n. 6)
Best, C.C. 170-1
Bethulie
    2nd journey 27, 43, 45, 48
    4th journey 93, 97, 109, 118
Betjesfontein 149
Beutler, August Friedrich 156
Bidouw River 149
De Biedouw (farm) 149
Bird Island 156-7
Bitjoana *see* Briquas
Bitsiana *see* Briquas
Bligh, Capt. William 165
Blue crane 42
Bo-Naries 98, 101
Boegoeberg Dam 115
Boëseken, Dr Anna 169
Bokkeveld 68, 73, 149
Boknes River 141, 155
Bonne Espérance 68
bontebok 29, 60
Boos, Franz 159-61, 188
Borroeniana 113
Bosberg 40, 62
botany 19, 21, 33, 153-4, 159-60, 165, 188
    see also names of botanists eg F. Masson, W. Paterson, C.P. Thunberg
Botha, Teunis 40
The Bounty 165, 170
Bovenseekoebaart 115
Bradypodion pumilum **15**
Brak River 33
Brakfontein Berg 96
Brand Fortuin 68
Brand Valeij 68
Brandewyns River 149
Brandwag (farm) 148
Brenthurst Library 15, 16
Brina *see* Briquas
Brink, C.F. 93
Briquas 68, 93, 98, 111-13, **114**, 116-19 125
Britain *see* Great Britain
Broekspruit 44
Bronkhorst, Dolf 64
Bruintjieshoogte 40, 62-3
Brunswick, Duke of 20
bubalis see hartebeest
Buchanan, Major 20
buffalo 36, 52, 113, 120, 156
Buffels River 78, 93
Buffelskraal 65
Buffon, George-Louis Leclerc, Comte de
    Histoire Naturelle **21-2**, **22**, 29, 188: geology 30, 73, 78, 143, 162; giraffe 101-2, 105; hippopotamus **37**, 54, 56; Jocko chimpanzee 114, **116**; rhinoceros **64**
Buffon River 44
Buis, Pieter 53
Burgher Council of War 131
bush pigs 60
Bushman's candles **79**
Bushman's River 27, 50-2, 139, 155-6
Bushmen 16, **66-7**, 80, 101, 113, **118**, 120-21, **121**
    customs 69, 107
    language 35, 65
    paintings 35-36, **36**, 49, 69, 115
    relationship with Gordon 34-5, 44, 68-9, 104, 106-7, 111, 114
    warfare 27, 36-7, 49-50, 59, 61-2, 120-1, 152, 154, 172

C
Cabas
    character & appearance 101, 123-6
    relationship with R.J.G. 124-9, 143, 189
    travels with R.J.G. 109, 121, 129, 143
Cabas Riviertje *see* Kabas
Cabeticoe 113
Caboes Mountains 125
Cabouws *see* Koboop
Caledon 29-30
Caledon River **43**
Calvinia 68, 151
Camagaqua River 109, 122
Camagga *see* Camagaqua
Camasauws *see* Komasoas
Cambushi, Chief *see* Gagabe
Camdebo 33, 63, 115, 155
Camdebo chickens *see* guinea fowl
Camdebo Hottentots *see* Korana
Camdeni *see* Kamdanie
Caminoekwas tribe 127, 199 (Ch. 7, n. 45)
Campbell, Sir Archibald 44-5
Campbell, John 75
Camper, Peter 37, 160
Camps Bay 173, 182
Cango Caves 32
Canna *see* eland
Cannaland 31
cannon balls 172-3, 186

Cannon Rocks 156
Cape Agulhas 142, 157
Cape dwarf chameleons **15**
Cape Hangklip 27, 29
Cape Infanta 142, 157
Cape penduline tit 197 (Ch. 6, n. 2)
Cape Peninsula 21
    fortification of 134-5, 162-3, 173, 180-2, 186, 188
Cape St Francis 56, 141
Cape Town 64, 65, 67, 69, 71, 101, 125, **136**, **161**, 173
    description of 106, 134-6, 160-1
    fortification of 180-2
Cape wagtail **46**
Carpobrotus sauerae 78
cartography
    R.J.G.'s skill 19, 48, 71, 137, 188
    2nd journey 27, 29, 53
    3rd journey 59, 65-6
    Orange River 93, 97
    4th journey 125
    5th journey 139, 141-2, 155, 159
The Castle **132**, 175-6
    R.J.G.'s duties 25, 71
    garrison 162-3, 188: commander *frontis.* 57, 131-7, 167
Ceres 172
Ceylon 167
chameleons **15**
Chavonnes Battery 169
Chinese (Bushmen) 34-5, 44, 59, 65
Clanwilliam 141, 148-9
Clarke, Maj. Gen. Alured 182, 185
Cloete, Hendrik 65, 147, 167, 169
Coba, Chief **38-9**, 40-1, **42-3**, 50, 62-3
Cobenzl, Count 159-62, 164
Coboopfontein 93
Cockscomb 153, 201 (Ch. 9, n. 55-6)
Coenap River *see* Koonap River
Coegas River 53, 154
Coerney 141, 156, 157
Coerney River 53
Coester's Valley 142
Coetse, Dirk Jacobus 148
Coetsee, Jacob (Jansz) 93, 101
Cok, Cornelis 157
Colesberg 27, 36, 71
Columbia 178
De Combuis 29
Commas *see* Pella
Company Post *see* George
Companys Drift 89, 91, 128
    see also Ramans Drift
Concordia 93
Condé, Governor of 191
Conga, Chief 52
Conradie (farmer) 65
Cookhouse 27, 50
Coopman, Cornelis 'Kis' 149
Coopman, J. 149
Cora *see* Korana
Coraqua 98
Council of Justice 132, 170

Council of Policy 141, 148, 168-9
    negotiations with British 175-8, 182
    relationship with R.J.G. 131-3, 139, 142, 163, 167, 170, 172
Cradock 44, 50, 52
Craggy Mountain 153
Craig, Maj. Gen. James Henry 175-9, 184
cucumber, wild 96, **97**
Cupido, Chief 77
cypress trees 149, 200 (Ch. 9, n. 35)
Cyrtanthus obliquus 190

D
Dalrymple, Col William 137, 141, 175-6
D'Après de Mannevillette, Jean Baptiste Nicolas Denis 139
Darling 167
dassie 74
De Beer, J.J. (Hannes) 43, 44, 48, 61, 63-5, 115, 196 (Ch. 2, n. 17)
De Beer, Widow 152
De Jong, Cornelis 173
De la Caille, Abbé Nicholas L. 23, 195 (Ch. 1, n. 18)
De Lille, Lieut-Col 175, 179-80
De Mist, Jacob Abraham Uitenhage 152
De Saussure, Horace Bénédict 132, 164-5, 169, 173, 188-9
De Vos, Wouter 65
De Wet, Olof Godlieb 59, 63, 152, 159, 189
Deca, Chief 43
Dias Padrão 139-40, 156, 159, 164
Diderot, Denis 22-4, 31, 34, 69
Diep River 179
Diepe Kloof 80
Doddington (shipwreck) 157, 201 (Ch. 9, n. 66)
Doerop, Chief **66-7**, 68
Doesburg 20
Doorn Rivier 152-4
Douglas, Colonel 52
Douglas Valley 52
Downes 68
Draaikraalrivier 151
De Draay Eijlande 114
Drakenstein commando 172
Drie Kopjes 182
Droedap 129
Droge Rijstkloof 69, 146
Duikerfontein 149
Duinfontein 148
Duivenhoks River 57
Dundas, Henry, Lord Melville 176, 178, 184
Durand, A. 44
Durand, Jan 43, 62-3
Dutch Dragoon Guards 19
Dutch East India Company 24-5, 141, 162, 164, 172-3

E
Echo 176
Eerste Stap 48
The Egypt 57

Ein Eip 68
Eina 16
Einiquas 97-8, 100, 105-8, 117, 119
Eksteen, Hendrik Oostwald 143, 147
Eksteen, Pieter Michiel 29, 196 (Ch. 2, n. 6)
eland 36, 53, 83, 88, 113
elephant 52, 71, 81, 106, 113
    hunts 40, 78, 108
    R.J.G. encounters 88-9
elephant mouse 78
Elizabethsfontein 149
Ellenboogfontein 73, **75**, 76, 89, 91-3, 97, 101, 125, 129, 143
Elphinstone, Admiral Sir George Keith 175-9, 184
Engelbrecht, Hermanus 73, 75, 76, 92, 96
Engelbrecht, Josias 129, 148
English East India Company 176-7
Entrecasteaux, Chevalier Bruni d' 164
Erasmus, Jacob 50
Essenbos 57
Euphorbia virosa **122**, 121
euphorbias 80, 92
Eyas 98

F
Faber, Lucas Sigismundus 56
Fagel, Hendrik 16, 196 (Ch. 2, n. 7)
    patron of R.J.G. 30, 61, 71, 129, 134, 167
    place names 44, 48
False Bay 21, 137, 169
    British fleet in 175-7, 181-2
Farquar, Alexander 176
Ferreira, Stephanus 157
Festooned Mountain 152-4
fish & fishing **82**, 85, 107, 148
Fish River *see* Great Fish River; Little Fish River
flamingoes **55**, 81
Forbes, V.H. 144, 188
    places identified
    2nd journey 35, 44, 48, 50
    3rd journey 68
    4th journey 76, 93, 98, 106, 113, 118
    and R.J.G.'s cartography 137, 188
    and R.J.G. & Sparrman 166
    and J. Schoemaker 32
    and Swellengrebel's journey 152
    and v. Plettenberg's Beacon 61
Formosa Bay 56-7
Fort Knokke 173, 182
fortifications
    Cape Peninsula 135, 162-3, 173, 180-2, 186, 188
De Fortuin 68
De Fraaije Schoot 44
France
    army & navy 191
    Dutch allies 178
    troops at Cape 133-4, 173
    war with Netherlands & GB 172-3, 175-6
Franschhoek 28, 57
Frederici, J.C. 137

French Revolution 137, 164, 167
  R.J.G.'s views on 24, 177, 184
Frijkenius, Simon 169-70, 172, 189
Frontier wars 154, 156, 164

G

Gagabe, Chief 43, 50
Gallows Hill 180
Gam Ey *see* Gomnuip
Gamka River 64-5
Gamtoos River 54-5, 155
Gannakloof 152
Garie River *see* Orange River
Gariep River *see* Orange River
Garies 124, 129
Garies Poort *see* Bo-Naries
Gefestoneerde Berg 152-4
Geisiqua 111-13, 117, 120
geography *see* cartography
geology 19, 162, 164-5, 188
  2nd journey 30, 33
  4th journey 73, 78
  5th journey 143-5
George 57
geraniums 78, 81
Gethyllis ciliaris **158**
Gharie River *see* Orange River
Giant's Castle (Sneeuberg) 33
Giant's Causeway (Ireland) 21, 33
Gibbon, Edward 11
Gildenhuisen, Dirk 29
Gilquin, P. H. 120, 133-4, 199 (Ch. 7, n. 36)
Gilquin's Island 120
giraffe 71, **90**, 101, 113
  tracking 93, 98-9, 101
  hunting 101-5, **102-3**, 125, 127, 129, 189
  skeleton 104-5, **104**, 123, **128**, 160, 162, 171
Gmelin, Johann Georg 160
gnu 22, **35**, 36, 45, 60, 113, 196 (Ch. 4, n. 6)
Godissa, Chief 40-2, 50
Goewaap 81
Goldbach (Goldbag), Rev. 69, 73
Gomnuip 98
Gonaqua 27, 50-3
Goodhouse 125-6, **128**, 199 (Ch. 7, n. 48)
Gordon, Adam Bernard (brother) 20, 119-20
Gordon, Alexander (son) 45, 142, 191
Gordon, Jacob (father) 19-21, 24-5, 119
Gordon, James Charles Gerhard (son) 157, 170, 191
Gordon, Joan (Johan) (brother) 20
Gordon, Johanna (daughter) 111
Gordon, Menso (brother) 20
Gordon, Otto (son) 157
Gordon, Otto Dirk (brother) 20, 164
Gordon, Pieter (son) 134, 157, 191
Gordon, Robert (son) 113, 134, 154, 191
Gordon, Robert Jacob
  contemporary opinions of 25, 131, 134, 135-7, 159, 165-6, 170-1, 185-9
  education 21, 22 *see also* Scots Brigade
  health: during 2nd journey 56, 57; during 3rd journey 63-5, 71; during 4th journey 73, 76-7, 91-3; as garrison commander 161-2, 167-70, 185, 189
  papers 11-15
  portrait *frontis.*, 13
  relationship with colleagues etc.
    see under names of individuals eg W. Paterson etc
  relationship with indigenous peoples
    see under names eg Bushmen etc
  suicide 11, 19, 21, 185-8
Gordon, Susanna (wife) **130**, 160
  courtship & marriage 21, 25, 99, 131-3
  home life 143-4, 170, 185
  leaves Cape 11, 191
  and Gordon papers 11-14
Gordon family 19, 159, 170, 189, 191
Gordon's Bay 29, **186-7**
Gordon's Kop 33
Gordon's River 61
Gouritz River 32
Gower, Elizabeth Leveson, Marchioness of Stafford 14
Gqunukhwebe 40
Graaf Benting's Fontein 49
Graaff-Reinet 34, 59, 137, 164, 172
  Republic 173
Grahamstown 160
Great Britain
  R.J.G.'s loyalty to 21, 178
  invasion of Cape 173, 175-89
  war with Dutch 133-4, 164
  war with France 175-6
Great Fish River
  as boundary 63, 152, 156
  1st journey to 21
  2nd journey to 27, 40-2, 44, 50
  3rd journey to 63
Great River *see* Orange River
Greater flamingo 55
Green Point 170, 201 (Ch. 10, n. 36)
Greffier Fagel Fontein 48
grey penduline tit 197 (Ch. 6, n. 2)
Groblershoop 114
Groene River 93, 96, 129, 49
Groene Valey 145-6
Groenekloof 167-8
Groenvlei 145
Gronjam, Chief **66-7**, 68
Groot Sleutelfontein 152
Groot Swartberge 141
Groot Winterhoekberge 141, 144-5, 152-4
Groote Sand River (Kouwsie) 78, 80
Grootmis 78-9, 92
Grootvadersbos 31
Grote Elands Berg 151
Gudaos Drift 148
Guepin, P.J. 173, 175
guinea fowl 108
Gysmanshoekpas 31

H

Haan, Michiel 187
Haelkraal 141
Hamilton, George 170
Hantam 65, 67
Hantamsberg 68
Harderwijk University 21, 22
Hardy, Capt. 176
hares 40, 52, 78
Harmonie 65
hartebeest 53, 60, 99-100, **113**, 120, 156
  skins 112, 117
Hartebeest River 109
Hartebeestfontein 65, 151
Haussa eip 97
Heerenlogement **69**, 129
Heip *see* Naip
De Hel 144
Held Woltemade **133**
Hendrik de IV Berg 124
Here XVII 99, 137, 168, 170
  R.J.G.'s appointment & status 131, 133-4, 159
Hermitage 139-40, 142
Heron, Robert, *pseud.* 11
Hex River Valley 65
Hickey, William 25, 165, 189
Hillside 154
hippopotamus 85, 106, 160
  description of 21-2, 36-7, **37**, 48, 53, 71, 88, 147
  hunting of 47-8, 54-5, **61-2**, 109, 120, 147
Histoire Naturelle see Buffon, Comte de
Hoekingeis kraal 115-16, 119
Hoengiqua *see* Gonaqua
Hoensing eib 98
Holgat River 80
Holland 21
Hom River *see* Houms River
Hollandsche Maatschappij tot Nut van het Algemeen 167
Holtshousen 155
Homoglossum watsonium **14**
Homnaries 128
Honceib River 124
Hoodia gordonii **174**
Hop, Hendrik 93, 101, 125, 127, 148
Hosabees 121
Hottentot 'apron' 23, 24, **25**, 31, 35 (Ch. 1, n. 17) fig **78**
Hottentots 16, **25**, **26**, 51, 145
  body mutilation 23, 31, 35, 97-8, 119
  customs 23-4, 30, 63, 75, 77, 92
  dancing & music 33, 63, 77, 92-3, **94-5**, 113
  death & burial **99**, 108, 148
  R.J.G.'s relationship with 19, 30, 33-4, 96, 100-1, 107-8, 114-15, 189
  R.J.G.'s servants 27, 52, 63, 98, 109, 143, 189 *see also* Iteki, Koerikei etc.
  language 22-3, 25
  marriage 93, 96
  physique 23-4
  sorcery 66-7, 119-20
  weapons 84
Hottentots Holland Mountains **186-7**
Houms River 93, 125, 127, 148

Hout Bay 173, 182
Hugel, Baron J.H. von 167
Huib *see* Naip
Humansdorp 56
hunting
    elephant 40, 78, 88-9, 108
    giraffe 101-5, **102-3**, 125, 127, 129, 189
    hippos 47-8, 54-5, **61-2**, 109, 147
    hyenas 56
    lion 56
    rhinoceros 99-100
    zebra 82, 91
Hydenryk, Dame Johanna Mariah (mother) 20
Hydnora africana 197 (Ch. 6, n. 1)
hyena 52-3, 56, 80

I

Ireland 21
Iteki 63, 77, 97, 98, 143
ixia 80, 109

J

Jacobs, Widow 67
Jagersbos 157
Jakhals Valey River 148
Jansen (farmer) 157
Jansen (orderly) 143, 149
Java 172
Johnstone, Commodore George 133
Jonge Robert Gordons Eijland 113
Joseph II, Emperor of Austria, 11, 159-60
Joubert, Gideon 67
Joubert, Jacob 62-3, 197 (Ch. 4, n. 10)
Joubertina 56

K

Kabas (R.J.G.'s servant) *see* Cabas
Kabas (place) 98, 124
Kabeljous River 54
Kakamas 98, 111, 121
Kamdanie River 68
Kamfer, Roelof 32
Kamiesberge 65, 73, 75, 160
Kamieskroon 76, 93, 129
kaniep 92
Kanoneiland 113
kapok bird 92
Kareedouw Pass 56
Keetmanshoop 148
Keimoes 111
Keinkaap River 111
Kenidouw 152
Kersefontein 147
Keurbooms River 56-7, **154-5**
Kheis 114
Khoi *see* Hottentots
Khun, Veld Command. *see* Kuen, D.W.
Kieser, Dr A.J. 15
King, Capt James 131
King, Philip Gidley 11, 48, 137, 195 (Gord. MS n. 2)
Klawer 69
Klein Pella 98, 124

Klein Roggeveld 67
Kleine Elandsbergen 149
De Kleine Hoge Craal 57
Kleine Zadelmakers Bank 149
Kleinsee 79
Klip River 141
Klip Valey 129
Klipfontein 148
Klipvlei 75
Knolvlei 149
Knysna 28, 29, 56
Koboop 98
Koeang River 113
Koegas 88
Koegasbrug 109
Koekabassi 105
Koerikei (R.J.G.'s servant)
    accompanies R.J.G.: 4th journey 73, 82, 84, 98, 100-1, 109, 124; 5th journey 129, 143
    character & appearance 91, 92, 96, 101, 114
K̀oeriK̀ei, Chief 34-5
De Koerneui 156
Koeroemana River 98, 112-13
Kok, Jacob 56
kokerboom 78, 100
Kolb(e), Peter 23, 64, 88, 148, 197 (Ch. 5, n. 33)
Kolver, Rev Andreas Lutgerus 146
Komasoas 93, 97
Komsberg 68
De Koo 56, 69
Kooberg 65-6
Kooks Fontein 78
Koonap River 27, 43, 50
Korana 34, 44, 71, 98, 112-13, 116-18
Kouqua 98
Kouwsie River 78, 80, 88, 91, 92
Kraane Valey 35, 37, 59
Kraggas Kamma 53-4
Krakeelrivier 157
Kromme River 56, 157
Kruger, J. Jacob 64
kudu 106
Kuen, Daniel Willem 157, 201 (Ch. 9, n. 68)
Kuruman River 198 (Ch. 6, n. 21)
Kuys, Rev. Johannes Abraham 144, 145, 200 (Ch. 9, n. 16)
Kwaaihoek 139
kwagga 113, **119**, 156
Kwaggas Valey 156
Kwaggasvlakte 156
Kweekfontein 93
Kweekvlei *see* Queek Valey

L

Lacaille, Abbé N.L. *see* de la Caille, Abbé N.L.
Lachenalia bulbifera **58**
Lady Campbell's of Ramsay's Valey 44
Laingsburg 65
Lake Geneva 21, 132

Lambert's Bay 141, 148
Lambrechtsdrift 114
Langa, Chief 50
Langeberg 65
Langkloof 28, 56, 141, 157
Langvlei River 69, 148
Lausanne 21, 132, 191
Le Sueur, H. 169
Le Vaillant, François
    character 28, 69, 75, 126, 152
    illustrations **25**, **69**, **80**, **97**, **135**, **153**
    giraffe 104-5
    life at Cape 134-6
    relationship with R.J.G. 17, 134-7, 165, 188
    writings 28, 51, 76, 166
    Xhosa 51-2
Leeuwen River 64, 125, 127, 148
Leiden University 22, 101, 173
Leipoldtville 141
Leiste, C.H. 40, 137
Leveson-Gower, Elizabeth, Marchioness of Stafford 14
Leviathan 163
Lewis-Williams, Prof J.D. 69
Leyden *see* Leiden
Lignerolle (Switzerland) 132
Lind, James 129
Lindequast family 56
Linnaeus, Carolus 21
lion 32-3, 50, 53, 56, 62
    tracks 81, 88-9, 120, 152
Lions River *see* Leeuwen River
Lismore 142
Little Fish River 42, 50
Lochner's farm 179
locusts 123
Loeriesfontein 68
Lutheran Church, Cape Town 146
Luxemburg Regiment 133-4

M

Macartney, Lord George, 1st Earl Macartney 137
Mackenzie, Lieut. Col. A. 176
Macpherson, Sir John 111, 113
Macquarie, Maj. Gen. Lachlan 165, 170, 189
Macroscelides proboscideus 197 (Ch. 5, n. 23)
Mahoti, Chief 50
Malan's Gat 151
Malansgatrivier 151
Malmesbury 69, 73
Mannevillette, J.B d'Après de *see* D'Après de Mannevillette, J.B.
mapping *see* cartography
Marnitz, Lieut. Philip Wilhelm 179-82, 184-9
Maskamma 149
Massepa, Chief 117
Masson, Francis 56, 159, 160, 165-6, 188
Massonia depressa **166**
Matroosberg 65
Matsiboa, Chief 111
Mauritius 161, 164
Maynier, H.C.D. 172-3

Meerhof's Casteel **74**
Meintjies, Hannes 43, 44
Melck, Marthinus 146, 147, 148, 200 (Ch. 9, n. 19)
Melck, Martin 57, 146
Menzies, Archibald 171-2
Mentz, Joachim Friedrich 56
merino sheep 19, 167, 169
mesembryanthemums 78, 80
meteorology 19, 27, 48, 188
Meuron Regiment 132, 133-4, 167-8
Meyer, Abram 144
Middelberg 59
Mocodoe, Chief 111
Model, Matthew 98-100, 198 (Ch. 6, n. 25)
Moebees *see* Keimoes
Moetjoana 113, **114**, 117, 121, 125
moggel **82**
Molsbergen, Prof Godée 15
The Monarch 175
Moncoboo 114
Morroena 113
Mossel Bay
    2nd journey 28, 29, 57,
    5th journey 139-40, 141, 142, 157
Mossop, E. E. 77
Motacilla aguimp 197 (Ch. 5, n. 35)
Mouille Point 180
Mowbray 182
Mozambique 143, 157, 201 (Ch. 9, n. 66)
Mtamboenas 44
mud mullet **82**
Muizenberg, Battle of 179-82, **180-81**
Mulder, (Muller) Capt. Petrus Jesse 146-7
music
    R.J.G. and 25, 40, 109, 165-6
    Hottentots 33, 63, 77, 92-5, 113
    Namaquas 77, 92
    Xhosa 41, 50, 63

N
Naip 93
Naisees *see* Nanseep
Namaqua bull **115**
    partridge **126**
Namaqualand 48, 73, 84, 113, 125
Namaquas 65, 68, 75-7, **76**, 92, 98, 112-13, **123**
Namgas Riviertje 67
Namibia 93, 101, 102, 125
Namur 20
Nardouskloof 149
National Battalion 173
natural history
    R.J.G.'s interest in 21-2, 25, 29, 29, 36, 53, 104, 162 *see also* under names of animals: giraffe, hippopotamus etc
Nederburg, Sebastian Cornelis 167, 169-70, 172, 189
Neisenas *see* Knysna
Netherlands 173
New South Wales 11, 165, 167, 188
New York 191
Newlands 172, 182

Nicolet, Susanna *see* Gordon, Susanna
Nieuwoudtville 68
Niewenhuisen (farmer) 33
Noa Gore *see* Sneeuberg
Noekeis kraal 116, 119, 199 (Ch. 7, n. 28)
Nonjes River 149, 151
Nooiensrivier 151
Nou Eik 68
Nouka, Chief 53
Nouman's farm 53

O
Oerebies River 44
Oesjswana 34-5
Ogoqua 108, 111-12
Olievenberg 152
Oliphants River
    3rd journey 56, 67, 69
    4th journey 73, 75
    5th journey 144, 146, 149, 152
Onseepkans 93
Oorlogskloof River 68
Oppenheimer, H. F. 15
Orange, House of
    and Scots Brigade 20
    R.J.G.'s loyalty to 45, 61, 164 175-8, 182
Orange River 59, 61, 111, 148
    2nd journey to 27-9, 37, 40, **43-5, 47-50**
    4th journey to 93, 97-8, 112-13, **118**
    mouth (4th journey) 22, 31, 49, 64, 71, 81
Oranje Fontein 68
ostrich 53, **70**, 106, 156
    description of 81, 97
    eggs 81, 82-5, 88
Ouplaas 69
Outeniqua Mountains 56-7

P
Pakhuis Pass 141, 149
Paleisheuwel 69, 148
Palò (Parò), Paramount Chief 50
HMS *Pandora* 170
de Parel 132
Parker, Mary Anne 170, 189
Pasley, Sir Thomas 131
Paterson, William 16, **32**, 125, 166
    accompanies R.J.G. on 2nd journey 27, 29-33, 152
    describes R.J.G.'s 1st journey 22; 2nd journey 27, 59; 4th journey 93, 98
    meets R.J.G. on 4th journey 73, 76-85, 92, 101, 129, 136
    relationship with R.J.G. 25, 27, 31-3, 65, 77, 80, 188
    travels in E. Cape 51, 54, 56, 156
Paterson 156
Patriot Party 20, 164, 175-9, 184
Peak Formosa 157
Peires, J. B. 40
Pella 93, 98
Pepinieren 168 *see also* Sandolroy, S. Chevalier de
Percy, Bishop Thomas 11
Perde Eiland 107

Perdeberg 144
Perestrelo, Manuel de Mesquita 139-40
Phillip, Captain 165
Phoenicopterus ruber **55**
Pichegru, General Charles 173
Pienaar, Pieter 104
    accompanies R.J.G. on 4th journey 73-5, 78, 81-2, 91, 97, 101, 123, 125; 5th journey 144-5
    farm (Sandfontein) 93, 96-8, 124-5
    shoots elephant 88-9, 108-9
    shoots giraffe 101-2
Pienaar's island 114
Pienaarskloof River 67
Pigot 141
Piketberg 69, 141, 145-8
Pinkerton, John 11-14, 195 (Gord. MS, n. 15)
Pitt, William 170
Platberg 152
Plattekloof 27, 31, 57
Plettenberg Bay 21, 28, 56-7, 141, **154-5**
Plettenberg(s) River 36, 60-1
Pofadder 98
poison tree **122**
Pondicherry Regiment 134
porcupine 78
Port Elizabeth 28, 53, 141, 157
Port Nolloth 80
Potgieter, Jacobus 40, 42
Prehn, Hendrik 25, 32, 131, 132
Prieska 88, 109, 118
Prince Albert 59, 141, **150-1**, 152
Prince Alfreds Pass 56
Princes Wilhelmina River 45
Pringle, John 176-8
Prins Willem's de V Berg 45
Prins Willem's de V Rivier 45
Prinsloo, Jochem 40
Prinsloo, Willem 40, 42, 43, 62-3
Prussia, King of 164
Pterocles namaqua **126**

Q
quagga *see* kwagga
Qweek Valey **150-1**, 152
Qweekfontein 93
Queina 16
Quoi Queuna 16

R
racial prejudice 93, 96, 104
    see also R.J.G.'s relationship with indigenous peoples under Bushmen, Hottentots, Xhosa
Raman's Drift 89, 91, 93, 125, 128, 199 (Ch. 7, n. 47)
Raubenheimer, Adam 152
Rautenbachs Drift 51
Raynal, Abbé Guillaume Thomas 24, 195 (Ch. 1, n. 21-2)
Regt door Zee 169
Renoster Kop 78
Reuse Kasteel (Giant's Castle) 33

rhebok 147
Rhenius, Johan Isaac 169
rhinoceros **64**, 106, 113
    description 71
    hunt 99-100, 120, 161-2
Riet River 65
Rietfontein 32
Rietvaley 30-1
Riou, Capt. Edward 11, 195 (Gord. MS, n. 3)
Riversdale 142
Robertson, Alex 45
Robertson 65
Robertson Strowan Bergen 45
Robertsons Fontein 45
Robertsons Macleods Bergen 45
Robinson Pass 141
rock hyrax 74
rock paintings 35-6, **36**, 49, 69, 115
Rode Bergen 40
Rodesandland 73
Rodesands Mountains 33
Roggeveld 67-8, 92, 141, 151, 152
Ronde Berg 152-3
Roodezand **142-3**, 144-5
Rose, George 11
Ross, Hercules 175-6
Rostratula benghalensis **146**
Rothmannia capensis **163**
Ruiter, Chief 50-3, 68, 156
Ryk, Mrs 68, 69

S
Saana *see* San
Sabies 128
Sacramento 54, 196 (Ch. 3, n. 14)
Sadelmakersbank 149
Sak River 65
Saldanha Bay 133, 137
Saltpeterkop 152
Samoep 101, 124
Samoeprivier 98, 100
San 16, 27, 34-6, 115 *see also* Bushmen
Sandfontein (P. Pienaar's farm) 93, 96-8, 124-5
Sandfontein (Uitenhage dist.) 154-5
Sandolroy, Simon, Chevalier de 168-70, 172, 189
Sandvlei 180
Sarcocaulon l'heritieri **79**
Schabord, J. C. 143
Scheepers, Gerrit 154-5, 157
Scheepers, Stephanus 153, 155, 201 (Ch. 9, n. 53)
Schepmoedpoort 44
Schiedam 20
Schlegel, Friedrich von 13, 15
Schoemaker, Johannes (R.J.G.'s artist)
    drawings 48, 68, 88, 102-4, **161**
    relationship with R.J.G. 32, 56-7, 73, 104-5, 124, 149
    2nd journey 27, 29, 36, 44
    3rd journey 65
    4th journey 73, 98, 100, 109, 120, 125
    5th journey 143

Schoenmaker, Volkers 125, 128, 136
Scholl, Georg 159-60, 162, 188
Schönbrunn Gardens 159-61
Schoonder Sigt 160, 162, 165, 170, 185, 191, 201 (Ch. 10, n. 11)
Schumacher, Johannes *see* Schoemaker, Johannes
Scotland 11, 19-20, 165
Scots Brigade **21**
    R.J.G. joins 20-2, 24, 164
    influence on R.J.G. 45, 49, 111, 137, 165-6, 175, 184
    traditions of 19-21, 178, 189
Sedgefield 57
Seekoevlei River 148
Serambane, Chief 43
Serbo-Turkish War 191
sheep farming 19, 60, 167, 169
shells 78, 80, 92
shipwrecks 54, 157, 196 (Ch. 3, n. 14), 201 (Ch. 9, n. 66)
Shounarreba Capii 117, 199 (Ch. 7, n. 30-31)
Silver Fontein 129
Simon's Town 173, 175, 179-80
Sir Lowry's Pass **186-7**
Sitse Camma 53
Sjomossi, Chief 50, 52
Skilpadbeen 152
Skuitdrift 124
slavery 134-5
    R.J.G.'s views on 143-4, 146
Sleutel fontein 152
Sluysken, Abraham Josias 172-3, 175-6, 178-82, 184, 187
Smit, Gerrit 69, 146-7, 148
Smit, Stephanus 60
Smith, Prof. A. B. 115-16, 199 (Ch. 7, n. 24)
Smitswinkel 67
snakes 25, 32, 57, 85, 88, 197 (Ch. 5, n. 32)
Sneeu Krantz 151
Sneeuberg
    2nd journey 21, 27, 33-4, 44
    3rd journey 60, 62, 123
    4th journey 98
snipe, painted, female **146**
Soet Waterfontein 68
Soetendaals Valey 152
Soetendalsvlei 152
Somerset East 27, 40, 62
Somerset West 29
Sondag, Mattys 56, 157
Sondags Rivier *see* Sundays River
Sonnerat, Pierre 131
Soubiesjes *see* Klein Pella
South African Cultural History Museum 172
Sparrman, Anders
    description of Hottentots 31, 48
    travels in E. Cape 40, 42, 51, 56, 154-5, 156
    Voyage to Cape of Good Hope 166-7
spinosa 81
springbok 22, **23**, 33, 36, 45, 60, 81, 156

Springbok 93
squirrel, ground 33-4
St Francis Bay 137, 141
St Helena Bay 141, 147
St Petersburg 160
Standvastigheid 68
Stavorinus, Rear Admiral J. S. 17, 59, 165
steenbok 80
Stellenbosch 93, 172
Steynsburg 27, 44
Stokkum, Commissioner *see* van Stockum, H.
De Straat 67
Stafford Archives 11, 15
Strandlopers 73, 79, 82-8, **86-7**, **123**, 197 (Ch. 5, n. 24)
Struisfontein 152
Struisvogel Been 152
Struisvogelfontein 152
Struys font 152
Sully, Maréchal de 124
Sundays River 52, 68, 155
Susannadal 98-9, 132
Sutherland 141
Swartbaaskraal 69
Swartkops River 53, 54
Swartland 69
Swartvlei 57
Swellendam 27, 28, **30**, 57, 142, 172, 173
Swellengrebel, Hendrik 65, 147, 167
    accomp. by J. Schoemaker 27, 32
    journey to E. Cape 27, 32, 40, 43, 50-4, 56, 152, 156
Swellengrebelsfontein 68
Swiss Guards 191
Switzerland 11-12, 99, 132, 160, 191

T
Table Bay 169, **179**
Table Mountain 21, 25, 75, 145, 160, 189
Tachard, Father Guy 75-6
Takemas *see* Kakamas
Tarka River 27, 44, 50
Terblanche, Stefanus 57
Thaka, Chief 51 *see also* Tsaka
Theal, G. M. 169, 180
The Hague 22-3, 162
Thibault, Louis Michel 179, 181, 184, 186-7
Thompson, George 32
Thunberg, C. P. 21, 56, 149, 159, 160, 166
Tierberg 111
Titi, Chief 52
Toenema 100, 106-9
topography *see* cartography
Touws River 65, 67
Towerwaterpoort 32
Tradouw's Pass 142
Trafalgar, Battle of 191
Traka River 59
Triple Alliance 164
Troe Troe River 69
Tsaka, Chief 51, 157 *see also* Thaka, Chief
Tswana *see* Briqua

Tulbagh 141, **142-3**, 144, 160
Twee Gebroeders 80, 91

U
Uitenhage 141, 154
Uitkyk Pass 149
Umsella, Chief 51
Upington 88, 113, 125
Utrecht 164
Utrecht, Peace of 20

V
Vaders River 156
Van Baalen, Capt. 180, 182
Van Carman, Mr 165
Van de Copello, Mr 22
Van de Graaf, Cornelis Jacob 137, 162, **168**, 170, 172
    relationship with R.J.G. 167-9, 189
Van den Berg, Mr 49
Van der Hever, Jan 129
Van der Merwe, Carel 34-5
Van der Stel, Adriaan 74
Van der Stel, Simon 74, 75, 93
Van der Walt family 36, 65
Van der Westhuijsen, Cornelis 129, 198 (Ch. 6, n. 19)
Van der Westhuizen, Claudina 74-5, 129, 198 (Ch. 6, n. 19)
Van Heijden, Capt. Lieut. 60
Van Jaarsveld, Adriaan 37
Van Plettenberg, Governor Joachim 137, 152, 156, 159, 163, 189
    journey to E. Cape 56, 59-63, 65, 67
    negotiations with Xhosa 52, 63
    relationship with R.J.G. 133-4
Van Plettenberg's Beacon 36, 61
Van Reenen, Jacob 31, 54, 56, 81, 91-2, 142
Van Reenen, Sebastiaan 73, 101, 125, 167
Van Reenen family 65, 89, 167
Van Rhynsdorp 69
Van Ryneveld, Daniel 30
Van Stadens River 53, 157
Van Stockum, H. 169
Van Swinden, Prof Jan Hendrik 173
Van Wyk, Willem 151, 200 (Ch. 9, n. 41)
Van Zyl, Adriaan 68

Van Zyl, Pieter 69, 73, 144
Venter, Stephanus 152
Vergelegen 29, 59
Verkeerdevlei 67
Verlorevlei 148
Vermeulen, Gerrit 148
Vicar *see* Wikar, H.J.
Vienna 159
Viljoen, Mr 64
Viooslsdrif 97
Vis River 65
Visagie, Jan 171
Vlekpoort River 27, 44
Vogel, Mr 157
Vogelfontein Bergje 151
Vogelstruis Leegte 152
Von Schlegel, Friedrich 13, 15
Vosmaer, Aernout 22, 105
De Vrede
    2nd journey 34, 37
    3rd journey 59, 61, 63-5
    4th journey 115
Vrije, Barend 104, 198 (Ch. 6, n. 35)
Vyemonds se Berg 75

W
Wageningen 20
wagtail, African pied 197 (Ch. 5, n. 35)
wagtail, Cape **46**
Waldener Regiment 133
Walpole, Horace
Warmbad 101, 102, 125, 127-8, 148, 199 (Ch. 7, n. 46)
Warnek, Mr 74
Waterloo, Battle of 191
weaponry 162-3, 172-3, 186
White, John 165
Wikar, Hendrik Jacob 76-7, 93, 98, 101, 115-16, 118
    map 88, **89**
wildebeest *see* gnu
Wilderness 57
Wilhelmina, Princess of Orange 164
Wilhelmina's River **43**, 45, 113
Willcox, A. R. 32
Willem V, Prince of Orange, 22, 164, 167, 173, **183**

and British occupation 175-8, 185
giraffe skeleton 102, **104**, **128**, 160
naming of Orange River 45, 81
R.J.G.'s loyalty to 134, 137, 178, 184, 189
The Willows 35, 59
Wiltschut, Chief 75, **76**, 77
Windham, William 14
Witte Drift 56-7
Wolwe River 149
Wolwepoort 93
Woodcutters' Post *see* George
woodpecker 108
wool industry 167-8, 188-9
Worcester 65
Wurttemberg Regiment 162, 167, 172, 173
Wynberg 180-2, 186

X
Xerus inauris 34, 196, (Ch. 2, n. 16)
Xhosa 27
    customs 41, 43, 50-1, 63
    language 40-1
    relationship with colonists 52, 62-3, 154, 156-7, 164, 172
    relationship with R.J.G. 19, 40-3, 50-3, 69, 104, 189
    see also names of specific tribes and chiefs

Y
Yorke, Ambassador Joseph 196 (Ch. 2, n. 33)
Yorks Fontein 45
Ypres 20

Z
Zak River *see* Camagaqua River
zebra 81, 85, 106, 113
    hunt 82, 91
    equus (mountain) **83**
Zeekoei River 27, 36-7, 56, 61, 64
zoology 19, 71, 188
    see also under names of animals eg giraffe, hippopotamus etc.
Zorn, Capt. 182

List of Subscribers

Sponsors' Edition

G. K. H. Anderson
Mrs S. A. G. Anderson
Steve Bales
W. A. Barlow

Eberhard Bertelsmann
Jim Gerard Paul Broekhuysen
Silvano del Sette
Dr H. B. Dyer
Robert E. Levitt
Lorenzo & Stella Chiappini
    Charitable & Cultural Trust

Struik Winchester
The Brenthurst Library
G. A. Upfill-Brown
Vereeniging Z.A.S.M.

Collectors' Edition

Alex A. Barrell
Maj. John E. Bishop
Sarah, Caroline & Simon Borchert
Jehan Bouyal
B. Braude
Peter McKenzie Brown
A. J. Bryant
Mrs S. W. Caroline
Shirley Cloete
R. M. Crawford
Gilles Cristini
Patrick Cullinan
Leicester Dicey
Dr John Fannin
Peter Ford
Russel, Bonnie & Gabriella Friedman

Lily & Lionel Gill
Lydia Gorvy
Adin & Sharon Greaves
R. A. Harvey
John K. Hepburn
Basil Hersov
M. J. Hyde
Sam Jaff
J. D. Jeffery
Phyllis Jowell
Michael M. Katz
Jack Koen
Ernst Kohler
Deon Krige
I. Leitch
Jacques Pagot

Marc B. Player
J. A. Rochford
Dr L. C. Rookmaaker
Carl Schlettwein
Steffen G. Schneier
Rainer Scholz
Pieter Struik
Struik Winchester
The Stellenbosch University
    Library Service
Russell E. Train
Ian R. F. Trollip
Raymond Tucker
Pieter C. Wagener
Lyle Wood
Solm Yach

List of Subscribers

Standard Edition

A
Enid & Willem Aarts
Africana Book Collectors
Alexander L. D. Agenbacht
R. H. Aitchison
M. Alberts
Will Alexander
K. Lewer Allen
Henk Alosery
Nigel Peter Amschwand
Dr Ingram F. Anderson
Anita Arnott
Ashbey's Galleries
Eric Axelson

B
H. J. S. Banks
Mr & Mrs F. J. & Shara Barrell
Bartolomeu Dias Museum
A. A. J. Bastenie
Peter Bedborough
F. H. C. Beech
Hans Beetge – Mopane Safaris
Vernon & Jean Beeton
Clementine Beit
R. H. Benecke
Sybil Bennett
Heidi Bergh
David & Anne Marie Berry
John Bickford-Smith
Dr John Vivian Bickford-Smith
Dr Pierre Boisacq & Marie-Jeanne Generet
Michael Boltman
C. Boucher
E. P. Bowker
A. Bozars
Edna & Frank Bradlow
J. R. Bradshaw
Dr Michael Brittan
Naomi Bruwer
H. J. & M. A. Brynard
Dr K. F. R. Budack
J. H. Buhr
S. F. Burger
Frederick Guy Butler

C
David R. Calder
H. Cantor
Jane Carruthers
C. J. Chorlton
Dr H. J. H. Claassens
Clarke's Bookshop
Ted & Estelle Clayson
Philip Clinton
Tony & Jacqueline Cole
Joy Collier
D. E. Cooper
M. M. Corbett
B. K. Corder
J. D. Cowburn
Graham & Jillian Cox
Dan Craven
J. B. S. Crawford
Mark & Clare Cresswell
Caroline M. Cullinan
Diane Cullinan
Matthew Cullinan
Wendy Cullinan
Mary Ann Cullinan-Haysom

D
Mrs J. L. R. Dagut
Graham Darling
Julian David
R. & A. E. Dean
Richard & Maureen de Beer
Chris de Hart
Nick Francois de Jager
Mark de Kiewiet
C. J. & M. J. Dekker
Gerhard C. de Kock
J. C. de Korte
Charles Philip de la Harpe
D. de Milander
D. P. de Villiers
J. Louis de Villiers
W. N. de Vos
Dr Nic de Wet
Graham Dickason
Don Africana Library
Claude Donaldson
R. Donelly
Ted Dowling
I. M. McK. Drummond
J. C. M. D. du Plessis
Phil du Plessis
S. E. du Toit
Stephan du Toit
Dr H. B. Dyer

E
F. G. Eckl
Christopher R. Enslin
Don Essery
A. L. Evans

F
Gwen Fagan
I. G. Farlam
Pauline Farquhar
Michael J. Farrell
Pierre & Sheila Faure
T. Fawdry
Norman J. Feitelberg
Jan & Freya Fischer
Margaret M. Flint
Grahame Fogel
Vernon S. Forbes
Dorothy Foster
P. du T. Fourie
Nigel Fox
D. S. Franklin
J. E. Fraser Jones
Dr S. Freedberg
Ian Frielinghaus
K. A. Frizelle

G
Chris & Family Gaigher
Maureen Gaisford
Douglas Gardner
H. W. Gebers
Volker Gebhardt
Noël G. Geldenhuys
B. C. Gertzen
Rupert Gettliffe
David Gevisser
Antoinette Gibbons
D. D. V. Gibson
L. S. Glaser
Jon Glenton

Alice Goldin
M.G.N. Goodwin
Belinda Gordon
Neale Gordon
Dr G.J.M.R. Gorter
Murray Graham
Jerome A. Greenbaum
Ryno Greenwall
Ann Griffiths
Pauli Marie Grindrod
Charmaine Grobbelaar
Claude Groenewald
Siegfried J. Gross
Mauritz A.S. Grundlingh

H
Jean & Eric Hall
Wolf-George Harms
Derek Harraway
Elizabeth Harris
C.A.S. Hayne
Margaret Hemsted
C.V. Hen-Boisen
Dudley Henn
Miss N.G. Henshilwood
Glynn & Anne Herbert
Basil Hersov
Leslie J. Hill
David Hilton-Barber
Josephine & Brett Hilton-Barber
Prof. Dr M.O. Hinz
David G.M. Hofmeyr
Tineke Honig
T.J. Hops
George B. Horsley
C.R. Househam
Dr W. Hudson
C.E.B. Hughes
John Hughes
Eva Hunter
R.J. Hutchison

J
Brig. D.J.D. Jacobs
S.M. Junod

K
D. Keenan-Smith
Raymond E. Keeping
B.M.R. Kindler
Dudley King

Werner Kirchhoff
Abraham Klapwijk
Menno Klapwijk
Bruce H. Knoefel
J.E. Knoll
Knysna Museum
Deon Krige
A.W. Kuhn

L
Neil & Lesley La Croix
Joy Lagaay
Martin Langen
P.J. Latham
Johan Latsky
Roy & Patricia Leaver
Paul Lee
Jean-Marie & Astri Leroy
Michael Levi
Mary Lewis
André P. Liebenberg
E.R. Liefeldt
S.P. Liell-Cock
Rhona Lindhard
Bruce Little
R. Liversidge
Philip & Angela Lloyd
Robert Lochtenbergh
Merle & David Loewenthal
Johannes Loock
Eduard A. Loubser
J.E. Loubser
Albertus Louw
At & Julene Lubbe

M
Ian Mackenzie
Tim Maggs
V.C. Malherbe
Wilma Malherbe
Barry Manchip
M.W. Marais
Paul Marchand
Gerhard & Rykie Maritz
Guy Matthews
Nigel Matthews
M. Stuart Mattinson
D.B. McLennan
Julian Melck
Wenda Melck
Dr & Mrs K. Menck

John L. Merriman
N.G. Meyer
Friedhelm Meyer-Rust
Philip Middleton
Rita Miller
Samuel Miller
Moira Mills
J.R.L. Milton
P.D. Minnaar
David B. Mitchell
Richard Moffat
Douglas H.D. Moodie
Alan G. Morris
A. Mouton
J.D. Muller
D.M. Mullins
The Hon. Mr Justice G.G.A. Munnik
Keith & Jean Munro-Perry

N
Graham Neame
T.C. Nel
W.S. Nel
O.R. Newton
Prof. G.S. Nienaber
Oscar I. Norwich

O
S.C.V. O'Brien
Eileen O'Grady
E.G.H. Oliver
K.F. Owen

P
Owen & Di Parnell
Mary Whiting Paterson
Marie Peddle
Anthony Peepall
R.A. Penhallrick
Peter Pentz
D.J. Penwill
Jeffry Perlman
John C. Philip
Norah Massey Pitman
C. Plewman
Cornelis Plug
J.W. Pont
George & Penny Poole
Mr & Mrs L.E. Posniak
Sydney Press
S.L. Pretorius
Henriette Prince

R

Edith Raidt
Chris & Jill Rainier-Pope
A.G. Raphaely
Mr & Mrs Graham Rawdon
R.F. Raymond
W.A.C. Reniers
Sally Reunert
Dr F.D. Richardson
P.B. & J.A. Rissik
Sean Charles Roberts
Mags Robertson
Cedric Roché
Carol Roehm
David L. Rose
Frederik J.P. Roux
G.D. Roux
Jalmar & Ione Rudner
J.A. Rupert

S

Carl Schlettwein
J.B. Schmidt
Theo Scholtz
Dr Carmel Schrire
Robert & Diane Scott
R. Sealy
P.W. St L. Searle
Ron & Maureen Searle
Dr Johan A. Senekal
Eduard en Albri Sevenster
Maureen Shilling
H. Sibul
Phillida & Richard Simons
D.W. & H. Skawran
Thelma & Cecil Skotnes
Robert Slavin
John O. Slingsby
Ansie & Dennis Slotow
Leon & Rochie Slotow
Prof. & Mrs A.B. Smith
Gideon F. & El-Marié Smith
Keith & Dorothy Smith

L.G.A. Smits
Mr & Mrs P.L.T. Snyman
N.A. Squires
Wald & Lilla Stack
June Stannard
Barrie & Jeanette Stead
Dr J.W. Stephens
Michael Stevenson
S.J. Streicher
J.H. Stretton
S. Stretton
D.R. Susman
J.P. Sutten
Wessel Swanepoel
Prof. M.B.E. Sweet
Niels J.H. Swellengrebel

T

Carla Tanner
Colin & Ann Tedder
Dr Walther Thiede
W.G. Thring
Dr & Mrs P.D. Toens
J.R.H. Tooke
Théa Toussaint van Hove
Neil Trollope
Kate Turkington
Doug & Guntie Twine
Harvey Tyson
Prof. P.D. Tyson

U

Universiteit van Port Elizabeth Biblioteek
Prof. C.J. Uys

V

J.A. van de Kraats
Hettie van den Bergh
Arsene van den Driessche
J.H. van der Byl
H.J. van der Hoven
F.J. van der Merwe

Dr Gerdrie van der Merwe V.D.M.
B.J. (Ben) van Eck
B.P.S. (Stefan) van Eck
C.P. (Casper) van Eck
H.J. (Hendrik) van Eck
H.J. (Hennie) van Eck
J.M. (Johan) van Eck
Johannes van Heerden
P.L.J. van Rensburg
M. & M.A. van Rijswijck
C.W. van Wyk
Elkie & Tommie van Zyl
Paul Veit
Paul Venter
Dr William P. Venter
H.J. Viljoen
Yvonne Viljoen
Eugéne Volsteedt
E.J. von Maltitz
Dr & Mrs P. Vorster

W

Brian Warner
Barry Wasdell
A.F. & S.J. Watermeyer
Anne Watt
P. Whitlock
Cyril Wiggishoff
A.R. Willcox
A.J. Williams
Geraldine Williams
Nigel Willis
Kenneth J. Wilson
M.L. Wilson
Hilda & Jurgen Witt
B. Nigel Wolstenholme
Rob & Janet Wood
E.J. Woodcock
G.W. Woodland

Y

Solm Yach
York Timbers Limited
John Ysbrandy

STRUIK
WINCHESTER

An imprint of
The Struik Publishing Group (Pty) Ltd
Cornelis Struik House
80 McKenzie Street
Cape Town 8001

Reg. No. 71/09721/07

Text © Patrick Cullinan 1992
Illustrations © the respective institutions mentioned on pp. 6-7
Map nos 1, 2, 3, 4 and 8 © The Struik Publishing Group (Pty) Ltd 1992
Map no. 5 © The Van Riebeeck Society
Map nos 6 and 7 © Professor V.S. Forbes

All rights reserved. No part of this publication may be reproduced, stored
in a retrieval system, or transmitted, in any form or by any means, electronic,
mechanical, photocopying, recording, or otherwise, without the prior written
permission of the copyright owner.

First published in 1992

Editor Valerie Streak
Designer Abdul Amien
Cover designer Abdul Amien
Cartographer Angus Carr
Indexer Leonie Twentyman-Jones
Proof-reader Tessa Kennedy

Typesetting by Diatype Setting (Pty) Ltd, Cape Town
Typeset in Berkeley Old Style book
Reproduction by Unifoto (Pty) Ltd, Cape Town
Printed by Tien Wah Press (Pte) Ltd, Singapore
Sponsors' and Collectors' Editions bound by Peter Carstens, Johannesburg
Standard Edition bound by Tien Wah Press (Pte) Ltd, Singapore

The Sponsors' Edition is limited to 26 copies lettered from A to Z
The Collectors' Edition is limited to 150 copies numbered from 1 to 150
The Standard Edition comprises 2 500 unnumbered copies

ISBN 0 947430 35 0 (Sponsors' Edition)

ISBN 0 947430 34 2 (Collectors' Edition)

ISBN 0 947430 33 4 (Standard Edition)